Cleopatra

Cleopatra

A Sphinx Revisited

Edited by

Margaret M. Miles

UNIVERSITY OF CALIFORNIA PRESS

Berkeley   Los Angeles   London

University of California Press, one of the most distinguished university
presses in the United States, enriches lives around the world by
advancing scholarship in the humanities, social sciences, and natural
sciences. Its activities are supported by the UC Press Foundation and
by philanthropic contributions from individuals and institutions. For
more information, visit www.ucpress.edu.

University of California Press
Berkeley and Los Angeles, California

University of California Press, Ltd.
London, England

Library of Congress Cataloging-in-Publication Data

Cleopatra : a sphinx revisited / edited by Margaret M. Miles.
   p. cm.
  Includes bibliographical references and index.
  ISBN 978-0-520-24367-5
   1. Cleopatra, Queen of Egypt, d. 30 B.C. 2. Egypt—History—332–
30 B.C. 3. Rome—History—Republic, 265–30 B.C. 4. Queens—
Egypt—Biography. 5. Egypt—Kings and rulers—Biography. I. Miles,
Margaret Melanie.
  DT92.7.C54 2011
  932′.021092—dc22
  [B]   2011012446

Manufactured in the United States of America

20 19 18 17 16 15 14 13 12 11
10 9 8 7 6 5 4 3 2 1

In keeping with a commitment to support environmentally responsible
and sustainable printing practices, UC Press has printed this book on
50-pound Enterprise, a 30% post-consumer-waste, recycled, deinked
fiber that is processed chlorine-free. It is acid-free and meets all ANSI/
NISO (Z 39.48) requirements.

CONTENTS

ILLUSTRATIONS

Cleopatra VII, Queen of Egypt, still fascinates us. Her life, her reception in Rome, and the continuing interest she attracts, so many centuries after her lifetime, are subjects that have been taken up in a wide variety of fields. This book presents a set of papers that consider Cleopatra and her legacies from the points of view of scholars working in archaeology, art history, history, and literary and film studies. We considered questions about the combinations of Greek and Egyptian culture that proved so successful for the Ptolemies; their art and architecture, some of it newly recovered in underwater excavations at Alexandria; and Cleopatra's personal ingenuity as a woman in adapting to the requirements for ruling her country. Also significant is the Roman response to Egypt and to Cleopatra herself. This includes the literary evidence for Roman attitudes toward Egypt and Cleopatra, and the history of the Egyptian temples and monuments in Rome. The Egyptian monuments in Rome and the reading of Roman authors kept alive interest in Cleopatra, and, together with Napoleon's adventures in Egypt, were responsible for persistent modern curiosity about Egypt. They inspired various periods of "Egyptomania" in early modern Western art and eventually became the basis for Cleopatra's depiction in early film. So strong was her personality that Cleopatra came to represent Egypt itself. In these studies we can witness how Greece, Egypt, and Rome interacted with each other and continue to influence our cultural perceptions, and how this symbolism has been used and reused through the centuries.

These topics were addressed at a symposium on Cleopatra and Egyptomania held at the University of California, Irvine, in March, 1999. We wanted to enhance the experience of graduate students in Classics and Visual Studies at UC Irvine and to extend it further to the public, and now to an even wider reading public. The papers have been updated since the conference to include current scholarship. I warmly thank the Gerard Family Trust, whose generous subvention made the symposium possible and also supported many of the illustrations in this book. In one instance a paper was contributed after the symposium (by Sally-Ann Ashton), and two contributions (by Erich Gruen and Peter Green) have been published elsewhere in the meantime but are reprinted here with the permission of the authors and presses, because they are so germane to our subject.

I am grateful to the Departments of Art History, Classics, and Film Studies at the University of California, Irvine, both faculty and staff, for their continued interest and support of this book. The Thesaurus Linguae Graecae of the University of California, Irvine, and its director, Maria Pantelia, also gave unflagging support. I thank too members of the Archaeological Institute of America, Orange County Society, for their interest and participation in the symposium, and the Orange County Museum of Art. I add special thanks to Jewel Wilson, M. B. Richardson, and editors at the University of California Press Stephanie Fay and Eric Schmidt, for all their help and support in seeing this book to press.

Margaret M. Miles
July, 2010

Cleopatra in Egypt, Europe, and New York

An Introduction

Margaret M. Miles

In Cleopatra (69–30 B.C.E.) we see a heroic figure, an actual, historical woman who was extraordinarily brave and astute, and as queen protected her country, extended its boundaries, and held off the threat of Rome as long as she could. Charming and passionate, she had a personality so strong that she came to represent Egypt itself, symbolism that took on new meanings after she was conquered. The Roman view of Egypt and Cleopatra and the Egyptianizing monuments in Rome itself were used and reused through the centuries. This imagery continues to appear in film, television programs, and advertisement. To paraphrase Shakespeare, neither the life nor the personality of this primary actor in the most complex circumstances of the Hellenistic Mediterranean has withered or become stale.

A BRIEF BIOGRAPHY

Cleopatra's father was Ptolemy XII Auletes (d. 51 B.C.E.), and it is uncertain who was her mother, possibly a sister-wife of her father, Cleopatra Tryphene, or an Egyptian; Cleopatra VII might have been illegitimate. When Cleopatra first ruled after the death of her father, she did so jointly with her younger brothers, first Ptolemy XIII and, after his death, Ptolemy XIV. Her son by Julius Caesar, Ptolemy XV, also known as Ptolemy Caesarion, is mentioned in inscriptions as her co-ruler from 45 B.C.E. Marc Antony fathered her other three children, the twins Cleopatra Selene and Alexander Helios (born in 40 B.C.E.) and their brother Ptolemy Philadelphus (born in 36 B.C.E.). She died a suicide, by the bite of a poisonous asp.

Cleopatra VII (the Great) was the last of the Ptolemies to rule Egypt. She had the titles Philopator and Philopatris ("father-loving" and "loving her country"). A shrewd politician and diplomat, she managed to hold on to her independent authority in Egypt during tumultuously uncertain years in the late Roman Republic, and with the backing of her Roman partners she even expanded Egyptian territory to include Cyprus and parts of Syria and the Levant. She spoke many languages, including Egyptian, and supported traditional religion in Egypt by her patronage of temples. Fond of literature and learning, she was given the entire library of Pergamon as a gift from Marc Antony. Cleopatra appeared as Isis in important ceremonies and was worshipped as a manifestation of that goddess. Later authors attributed to her some treatises on hair care and cosmetics, including recipes for beauty products. The fullest (and most famous) description of Cleopatra's personality is Plutarch's, in his *Life of Antony*, 27.2–3:

> Her own beauty, so we are told, was not of that incomparable kind which instantly captivates the beholder. But the charm of her presence was irresistible, and there was an attraction in her person and her talk, together with a peculiar force of character which pervaded her every word and action, and laid all who associated with her under its spell. It was a delight merely to hear the sound of her voice, with which, like an instrument of many strings, she could pass from one language to another, so that in her interviews with barbarians she seldom required an interpreter, but conversed with them quite unaided, whether they were Ethiopians, Troglodytes, Hebrews, Arabians, Syrians, Medes or Parthians. In fact, she is said to have become familiar with the speech of many other peoples besides, although the rulers of Egypt before her had never even troubled to learn the Egyptian language, and some of them had even given up their native Macedonian dialect.[1]

Ancient authors discuss Cleopatra's life and character because of her interaction with important Roman generals: Pompey (Pompeius Magnus) had been involved indirectly with the political affairs of Cleopatra's father, whom he supported. Pompey came to Egypt after his defeat at Pharsalos by Julius Caesar, the final battle of his civil war with Julius Caesar, but was murdered as he landed, probably with the connivance of the courtiers of one of Cleopatra's younger brothers, on September 28, 48 B.C.E. Julius Caesar, arriving in Egypt in that same year in pursuit of Pompey, is said to have wept at the sight of Pompey's severed head, which was presented to him in the hope of a reward. After meeting with her, Caesar supported Cleopatra in preference to her brother Ptolemy XIII. Cleopatra and Caesar during their time together took a long journey up the Nile, when their son Ptolemy Caesarion was conceived. Cleopatra visited Caesar in Rome twice, in 46 and in 44. She sailed to Tarsus in 41 to meet Marc Antony and provided legendary hospitality for him and his officers aboard her ship the *ISIS*. Marc Antony came to Egypt afterward, in the course of hunting down the assassins of Julius Caesar. They became political and military allies, hoping to rule the whole eastern Mediterranean. Cleopatra supported Marc Antony with her royal Egyptian fleet at the battle of Actium in 31, where Octavian defeated their combined forces. Octavian (later named Augustus) pursued Marc Antony and Cleopatra to Egypt and met with Cleopatra before her death.

Cleopatra's actions and style of life were very much in the tradition of the Ptolemies. She is said by ancient authors to have followed patterns set by male and female Ptolemies and Macedonians: riding, hunting, going into battle personally, practicing serial monogamy and adultery, engaging in determined political intrigue and military rule, marrying brothers, eliminating siblings so as to rule alone, and making lavish use of perfumes and unguents. For her, the liaisons with Julius Caesar and Marc Antony were dynastic marriages. Octavian generated propaganda vilifying her as an "Eastern courtesan" as part of his defamation of Marc Antony, his chief opponent. Even after her death many Roman authors continued to present a hostile or, at best, ambivalent view of her. Their literary accounts, especially the biographies of Plutarch, captured the imagination of much later authors such as Chaucer, Boccacio, and Shakespeare, who wrote fresh portraits that reshaped Cleopatra's reputation.

EUROPEAN INTEREST IN EGYPT

The interest of outsiders in Egypt and Egyptian culture may be divided into four phases, each impelled by cultural currents and historical events, and fueled by classical texts. During the first phase in the early Archaic period, Greek commerce with Egypt led to Greek settlement in the Delta and the foundation of the Greek city Naukratis, with the permission of the pharaoh (probably Psammetichus I, by about 625 B.C.E). The impact of these intensified relations may be seen in the early beginnings of monumental stone sculpture and architecture in Greece, carved and constructed with techniques and motifs borrowed from the art and architecture of Egypt but duly fashioned to reflect Greek values and religious ritual. Greek mercenaries, hired in Egypt at least as early as the reign of the pharaoh Psammetichus II, ca. 591 B.C.E., scratched graffiti on the left leg of one of the colossal seated statues of Ramesses II on the south side of the entrance to the great temple at Abu Simbel.[2] From this beginning, contact and trade between the cities of Greece and Egypt increased, and after the rise of the Persian Empire (and its rule of Egypt 525–404 and 343–332 B.C.E.), Greek cities, Persia, and Egypt were linked in a triangular dynamic of shifting political and economic power that continued over several centuries.

Herodotus' lengthy ethnographic account of ancient and Archaic Egypt in his history of the wars between Persia and Greece, written in the 440s B.C.E., has indelibly marked subsequent views of Egypt. It remains a valuable source, and in later periods when access to Egypt was difficult, his description became the primary source of information. But beyond the influence of his factual description, his respectful (even reverent) picture of Egypt, emphasizing contrasts between Egyptian and Greek behavior and customs, would color later attitudes. His narrative about Egypt as a timeless, even ahistorical site of remote antiquity and great wealth, with a contained geography that could only be ruled by a powerful monarch, as a source of deep spiritual wisdom and as the inventor of essential attributes of civilization, such as writing, presents an image of Egypt that instructed later Greeks and Romans and persists today. Recent studies of Herodotus' account have illuminated his Greek-centered attitudes, purposes, and intellectual background.[3]

Alexander the Great brought Egypt under Macedonian control by conquest, and after his death in 323 B.C.E. Ptolemy I, one of his Macedonian generals, seized Egypt as his share of the empire.[4] The Ptolemies ruled Egypt, still a powerful, wealthy, and glamorous kingdom, for nearly three hundred years as active participants in the larger events of the Mediterranean. They made their rule as Macedonian Greek outsiders more acceptable to the Egyptian administrative hierarchy and the general populace by adopting for themselves the ancient apparatus of religious rituals that traditionally supported pharaonic dynasties.[5] This included ruler cults, the worship of dead (and as time went on, even still-living) rulers as gods, that provided a familiar nomenclature and clear ritual transition for dynastic authority, and emphasis on the worship of deities such as Isis, Osiris, Hathor, and then syncretic Sarapis who were believed to participate directly in Egyptian affairs and even to manifest themselves in the persons of Egyptian rulers. The Ptolemies also supported an extraordinary flowering of Greek artistic and intellectual culture centered in Alexandria. Changing circumstances eventually vitiated the dynasts' power, and by the first century B.C.E., Egyptian financial and political dealings could be manipulated by individual members of the Roman populace. The dynasty lasted until Cleopatra's death in 30 B.C.E., when Egypt became a dominion ruled by Rome.

Egyptian religion had already gained adherents in Italy, especially around the Bay of Naples, a gateway for Roman maritime trade. Pompeii's Temple of Isis was important enough to have been quickly rebuilt after the earthquake of 62, only to be destroyed in the eruption of Mt. Vesuvius in 79. Much later, in the eighteenth century, the discovery of that Temple of Isis would bring about a new burst of interest in and enthusiasm for anything Egyptian. Closer to Rome, at Praeneste, an anonymous donor financed a spectacular large floor mosaic that represents a topographical scene of the Nile in flood and the celebration of the Khoiak (New Year) festival.[6] The mosaic, laid about 110 B.C.E. in a cavelike setting just below the Sanctuary of Fortuna Primigenia, set a fashion for nilotic decorations that appears later in private houses in Pompeii and Rome. Wall painting, architecture, and sculpture in Italy show that by the late second century B.C.E., people were interested enough in Egypt to introduce its visual motifs into their daily surroundings, and by the second century C.E. distinctively Egyptian decoration, styles, architecture, and religion had become part of the cultural fabric of Roman Italy, with official imperial approval and sponsorship, especially under the emperor Hadrian.[7]

Augustus devised a new way to display imperial triumph by bringing into Rome (as a trophy of his war with Cleopatra and Marc Antony) an obelisk from Heliopolis to serve as the gnomon for his giant horologion (sun clock) in the Campus Martius.[8] He dedicated it to Sol, the sun, a continuation of its function in Egypt, but it stood as a constant reminder of his conquest of Cleopatra's Egypt. From then on, bringing an obelisk from Egypt was seen as an expression of imperial power: forty-eight are known to have existed in Rome, some of them Roman copies with fake hieroglyphic inscriptions. Others now stand in Paris, London, Istanbul, and New York.

When the struggle between Augustus and Marc Antony was still fresh, authors of the Augustan period, including the poets Horace, Virgil, and Propertius, wrote about Cleopatra as a scheming, "oriental" queen, and in this literary heritage was born an ideological dichotomy between East and West that still resurfaces.[9] Because of the prestige of Augustus' reign and admiration for him as emperor, later authors such as Pliny also elaborated the contrast between Augustus and Marc Antony, with examples of contrasting behavior (and references to Cleopatra) to illustrate the austere "uprightness" of Augustus (and the West) and the degenerate "self-indulgence" of Antony (and the East). Pliny was so widely read in the medieval period and Renaissance that his interpretation of history became a foundation for Western views of the East.

A second major phase of eager interest in Egypt arose during the Renaissance as a natural consequence of intense focus on classical antiquity and classical texts. Knowledge of Egypt was derived mostly from the ancient authors whose manuscripts were being avidly collected and read. The texts were supplemented by the Egyptian and Egyptianizing monuments of Rome, some always on view from antiquity and others newly uncovered. The obelisk, as a symbol of imperial conquest, was used and reused in Rome, repositioned in new settings, and with new meanings, under papal patronage. Egypt was revered as a source of wisdom and spiritual insight; elements of Egyptian religion, especially Hermeticism, were regarded as an anticipation of Christianity. The search for ancient precedents and the yearning to read hieroglyphs even led to forgeries of archaeological "evidence."[10] The printing press accelerated popular and scholarly interest in Egypt and especially its hieroglyphs, with the widespread distribution of books, some with extensive illustrations, such as the *Hypnerotomachia Poliphili* (1499). This medieval-style story of a hero who pursues his ideal Polia, a personification of antiquity, through a dreamscape of ancient remains is filled with Egyptian,

Hebrew, Greek, and Latin references in a style that must have seemed eccentric even when it was first published, but nonetheless recalled both Egypt and Greco-Roman antiquity with a deep nostalgia that won the book wide distribution and a long-lasting audience (it was recently reprinted).[11]

Larger architectural projects and sculptural assemblages with papal patronage deliberately recalled themes and imagery about Egypt, Cleopatra, and her Roman associates.[12] Painters took up Cleopatra as a subject of great beauty, with ideas of contemporary beauty as the model,[13] some painters, like Lavinia Fontana of Bologna (1552–1614), representing her in contemporary garb, wearing a wimple, her pose contemplative.[14] Egypt was embraced during the Renaissance more generally, without specific motives, as an extension of the classical past (as well as a setting for biblical narrative), a sophisticated antiquity antecedent to Greco-Roman antiquity.

As enthusiasm for classical antiquity brought wealthy travelers from northern Europe to Italy, Rome (and Naples) became important destinations on a route that eventually developed into the Grand Tour in the eighteenth century.[15] This cultural phenomenon of educated, well-to-do visitors exploring ancient lands, and describing and drawing what they saw and matching it with what they had read, gave impetus to the academic part of Napoleon's campaign in Egypt.

Although that campaign, undertaken in 1798, was a military disaster, and Napoleon abandoned his army in Egypt to return to France after defeat by the British, he must be credited with initiating the third major phase of European interest in Egypt. The invasion itself was crude and brutal, but because Napoleon had brought with him 167 scientists and specialists, including architects, draftsmen, engineers, linguists, humanists, and mathematicians, all equipped with the latest tools for surveying, drawing, and recording, the invaders documented a wealth of knowledge about Egypt, ancient and modern. The famous *Description de l'Egypte* was published in large folios, 1809–29, a vast corpus of new visual information that filled out the well-known texts of classical authors.

The stated purpose of the French campaign was to deliver a blow against Britain (by posing a new threat to their trade with India) and to found new French colonies, but it had been suggested earlier in revolutionary circles that France could also bring the cause of "Freedom" to Egypt and release Egyptians from their Mameluke and Ottoman Turkish overlords. Turkey at the time was in fact an ally of France.[16] The French Revolution had drawn on a wealth of icons and symbols of the classical past derived from Greek and Latin texts, and on exegeses and interpretations of them made during the Italian Renaissance, and now Napoleon was to draw upon a social and cultural standard of learning, a widespread and thorough French command of the classics.[17] He would be a new Julius Caesar, a new Augustus, conquering a distant land, Egypt itself. Moreover because that land was ruled by aristocrats, he could "liberate" Egypt just as Julius Caesar had "liberated" Gaul from the Germanic tribes.

The scholarly and scientific records collected by the French savants laid the foundation for modern Egyptology. Jean-François Champollion was encouraged by his decipherment of hieroglyphs on the Rosetta stone (taken by the British as a spoil of war) to launch another exploration of Egypt in the 1820s to collect more hieroglyphic inscriptions. The results inspired other, similar, scholarly expeditions, while the vivid memoirs and letters of private travelers stimulated other tourists to go there.[18] Meanwhile, the French antiquarian publications set a new fashion in contemporary art, architecture, interior furnishings, snuff boxes, and dishes—another round of "Egyptomania" in western Europe.[19] After the triumph of the British in Egypt, popular enthusiasm expressed in the decorative arts was also vigorous in England. Egyptian motifs were used commemoratively as well: the sculptural monuments in St. Paul's Cathedral that honor the dead heroes who defeated Napoleon in the Battle of the Nile (Aboukir Bay) refer to Egypt in their palm trees, sphinxes, pyramids, and the river god Nile in a pose based on ancient Roman versions of river gods.

An elaborate and costly Sèvres Egyptian dinner service exemplifies the European taste for Egyptian-themed objects. It includes tabletop models in porcelain of the temples at Luxor, ice buckets decorated with scenes of Egypt, seventy-two pieces in all. It was made in the years 1810–1812 for the empress Josephine as part of the divorce settlement with Napoleon, only to be rejected by her as "too severe" (despite her promotion of the Egyptian style in the arts generally). Louis XVIII gave the service, which had been stored at the factory and was now minus a few plates, to the Duke of Wellington as a thank-you present for Waterloo in 1818, though the king worried that by then the gift might seem a bit passé.[20] The mania for everything Egyptian included a new wave of interest by painters in the legends of Cleopatra, part of a long tradition of illustration stretching back to the medieval period that now took on an "Orientalist" cast. Enthusiasm for Egypt as a theme in the arts played out alongside an embedded cultural preference for Greece and Rome as models, hence the special interest in Cleopatra's confrontation with Rome. By the early nineteenth century, as France had become more "Roman" during the Revolution and especially the Napoleonic years, Britain, particularly after the Greek War of Independence, turned more to Hellenism as a model.[21]

After Napoleon's invasion, a new series of surveys and excavations, and the new field of Egyptology whose work accelerated throughout the nineteenth century, had a profound impact both on modern Egypt and on Western perceptions of ancient and modern Egypt. The development of the new discipline of archaeology in the nineteenth century was in part stimulated by this work. Meanwhile, a flood of Egyptian antiquities (looted, purchased, or excavated) poured into western European museums, making them available to a wide public. The passionate collecting activities of this era are undergoing careful scrutiny in ongoing debates about cultural heritage and cultural property.[22]

AMERICAN INTEREST IN EGYPT
AND AMERICA'S OWN OBELISK

The founders of the United States were steeped in classical learning, and the inclusion of classical values and heritage was an urgent concern in the new republic.[23] Many participants in the Constitutional Convention had a thorough knowledge of Greek and Latin historians, and details of Greek and Roman history were hotly debated in the search for workable models. During the nineteenth century, friendship with France and shared "Roman" revolutionary foundations helped maintain the same long-standing cultural interest in antiquity in the United States as in Europe generally.[24] Shifting social concerns heightened interest in Egypt, stimulated by debates about slavery, biblical narratives set in Egypt, and connections with Africa. An example illustrates the political impact of antiquarian images. For the Great Exhibition of 1851 America had sent to London a statue entitled *Greek Slave*, by Hiram Powers (1843), depicting a neoclassical nude female with chains on her wrists. *Punch* derided this statue in a cartoon and commentary by John Tenniel, showing an African woman with chains in a pose mirroring that of the statue: the hypocrisy of the statue was all too evident, and the United States was severely condemned (as it had been for decades) for not having abolished slavery.[25]

At the opening of the Suez Canal in 1869, the khedive of Egypt Ismail Pasha noticed that ships with American flags were not present. Believing that a closer connection with the United States would enhance Egypt's prosperity, he offered as a gesture of friendship an obelisk still standing near the shore of Alexandria (Fig. 1). This generosity led to a great wave of interest in Egypt when "Cleopatra's Needle," as the obelisk was now called, arrived in New York and was set up in Central Park.[26] The story of this remarkable feat of transportation, told by the hydrographer and chief engineer Henry Honeychurch Gorringe, who oversaw the project, is worth recounting here, for "Cleopatra's Needle" is the only monumental ancient Egyptian obelisk in America today, and it indelibly bears Cleopatra's name (Fig. 2).[27]

The obelisk in Central Park is one of a pair that early travelers to Egypt called "Cleopatra's Needles" out of a habit of attributing to her most of the major constructions in the area of Alexandria.[28] In fact, Cleopatra had some indirect responsibility for the placement of the pair of obelisks near the harbor. Strabo and other ancient authors mention a sanctuary that she dedicated to Julius Caesar,

FIGURE 1. The "Obelisk" cased & machinery attached for lowering. (ca. 1880). The obelisk was removed from Egypt and taken to New York after it was given to the United States by the khedive of Egypt Ismail Pasha. Photo by Geo. Wright, courtesy Library of Congress, LC-USZ62-49249.

and also a shrine and altar that she dedicated to Marc Antony. It is not clear whether these references attest one sanctuary or two.[29] One or both of these can be identified with the site of the Caesareum founded by Augustus: a temple and large precinct dedicated to the imperial cult, beginning with Julius Caesar. This site is described in ancient sources as extensive, including a temple, sacred groves, propylons, libraries, and colonnades, and its position near the harbor made it a

FIGURE 2. The obelisk in Central Park, New York, often called
"Cleopatra's Needle." Photo by Rocco Leonardis.

resort for sailors and visitors from abroad. The two obelisks were erected at the
entrance in 13 B.C.E., so that the sanctuary combined typical Hellenistic (and
now Roman) features with the Egyptian. The site of the Caesareum is fixed by the
obelisks, and partial excavations in available building lots have been conducted
recently by J.-Y. Empereur.[30]

The obelisks had been brought from the temple of Amon at Heliopolis, where
they were originally set up by Tutmoses III (1279–1212 B.C.E.) and were rein-
scribed by Ramesses II and Osorkon I. In their new positions in front of the

FIGURE 3. Detail of replacement bronze crabs, symbols of Julius Caesar's birth month.
Photo by Rocco Leonardis.

Caesareum, each was supported by four large bronze crabs, one under each
corner of the two obelisks. Gorringe found parts of two of the eight crabs, still
in position as he excavated the base of the (now) American obelisk during its
removal, and he gave them to the Metropolitan Museum in New York. The claw
of one of the crabs is inscribed in Greek and Latin with the name of the Roman
prefect of Egypt, Barbarus, and of the architect Pontius, who was responsible for
erecting the obelisks.[31]

The crabs, when intact, probably weighed about 922 pounds each (the average
weight of the replacements in Central Park) (Fig. 3). Why did the Romans include
them as supports for the obelisks? The corners of the two obelisks were very likely
already worn, probably because they had burned in a fire during the capture
of Heliopolis by Cambyses of Persia in 525 B.C.E. The crabs served as anchors
between the shaft of each obelisk and its pedestal and filled out the missing corners. Beyond serving that practical function, however, they provided symbolism
for the entrance to the Caesareum: Gorringe and Gaston L. Feuardent believed
the crabs were a symbol of Apollo Helios and suited to the original worship of the
Sun in Heliopolis. Thus the Roman choice of crabs satisfied both Egyptians and
Romans. Offering further support to this view, it has been noted that imagery
connected with Apollo was also used extensively by Augustus as part of the
imperial cult.[32] The crabs may also have been used as the astrological sign of

Julius Caesar (born in the month named after him, under the sign of Cancer), at a time when astrology was taken very seriously. Cleopatra's devotion to Julius Caesar in Egypt was thus continued and amplified by Augustus with a mixture of Egyptian and Roman symbolism.

There was great popular support in New York for Gorringe's removal of the obelisk and its installation in Central Park. In 1881 a reporter for the *New York Herald* wrote that "it would be absurd for the people of any great city to hope to be happy without an Egyptian Obelisk. Rome has had them this great while and so has Constantinople. Paris has one, London has one. If New York was without one, all those great sites might point the finger of scorn at us and intimate that we could never rise to any real moral grandeur until we had our obelisk."[33] Augustus' initial example of taking an obelisk as a trophy of his victory over Cleopatra and Marc Antony has had many emulators. The enthusiastic welcome of "Cleopatra's Needle" in New York, apart from such lofty sentiments and symbolism in the press, included advertisements and trading cards issued by manufacturers of thread showing their spools both used as capstans for shifting the obelisk and animated with human limbs and posed with the obelisk.[34]

The beginning of filmed versions of Cleopatra's story and the discovery of King Tutankhamen's tomb by Howard Carter in 1922 initiated a fourth phase of intense popular interest in Egypt throughout the world. The spectacular finds revived old legends about curses and mummies, especially after Lord Carnarvon, the financial supporter of the excavations, and then Arthur Weigall, a photographer and associate, died under odd circumstances. Concurrent growth in the distribution of photographs and film made images of Egypt and Egyptians accessible to greater numbers of people, and the legends about Cleopatra were exploited for commercial purposes.[35] Popular interest in Egypt continues to pervade the media, and ancient Egyptian history has become not only a source of education, enlightenment, and entertainment as well as a marketing tool, but also a subject for political controversy and debates over cultural and racial heritages.[36]

NEW EXCAVATIONS AND DISCOVERIES

Under Ptolemaic patronage the city of Alexandria became famous for its library and museum, Alexander's tomb and the Pharos, or lighthouse, but above all as a primary seat of scientific, historical, and literary learning. Founded by Alexander the Great in 331 B.C.E., Alexandria became the royal capital for the Ptolemies after Alexander's death. The new city attracted residents from Greece and the Levant, and the population included many ethnicities besides Egyptian. This wealthy, complex, refined Hellenistic city, with extensive marble colonnades, porticoes, canals, gardens, statuary, and granite and marble temples, must have dazzled Roman visitors at a time when Rome was still built mostly of wood, tufa,

brick and cement, and terracotta. Julius Caesar had extensive plans for refurbish-
ing Rome that were cut short by his death but carried out later by Augustus:
surely Alexandria was Julius Caesar's model for the new Rome.

Today the modern city covers most of the remains from antiquity, but underwater excavations in the harbor have expanded knowledge of the topography and
monuments of Alexandria beyond that provided by Fraser's monumental study
of 1972. The famous Pharos, one of the "seven wonders of the world," was started
by Ptolemy I and completed by his son Ptolemy II Philadelphus in 283 B.C.E.
Traditional reconstructions were based on literary descriptions, coins, and mosaics, and to them may now be added actual blocks and exterior decoration including sphinxes, Egyptian statuary, reliefs, and columns, all of colored Egyptian
granite rather than imported Greek marble.[37] Although Thiersch's three-tiered
profile of the lighthouse is still part of its reconstruction, it now appears that the
architectural decoration and statuary had a distinctively Egyptian component:
like the later Caesareum, the architecture combined Greek and Egyptian elements. Ongoing salvage excavations by J.-Y. Empereur amid the dense urban
fabric of modern Alexandria have also brought to light evidence for the grid
plan of the Hellenistic city, mausoleums (including a structure that may be one
of Alexander's tombs), and other landmarks. Other underwater excavations
have surveyed marble floors and colonnades believed to have been part of the
Ptolemaic royal quarters (i.e., "Cleopatra's palace"), a part of the city sunken by
earthquakes and tidal waves in the Late Antique period.[38]

In a recent study of Alexandrian architecture, J. McKenzie pieces together
information about the city's plan and appearance in antiquity on the basis of indirect evidence such as representations on a small scale (pottery, gems, coins) and
in late Roman mosaics.[39] She shows the wide impact, across the Mediterranean,
of architectural styles inspired by the fusion of Greco-Roman forms and age-old
Egyptian forms that began under the rule of the Ptolemies and continued well
into the late Roman period.

Because of the worldwide dispersal of Egyptian items, discoveries tied to
Cleopatra are not necessarily restricted to Egypt. An autograph of the queen has
now been identified, at the bottom of a papyrus letter that had been reused along
with other old office papers as cartonnage for a mummy, now in the collection
of the Egyptian Museum and Papyrus Collection in Berlin. Peter van Minnen's
edition of the letter, dated to February, 33 B.C.E., shows that it is a royal order
concerning tax and customs exemptions for a wealthy Roman serving as general under Marc Antony, Publius Canidius, who is mentioned by Plutarch and
included as a character by Shakespeare in *Antony and Cleopatra*. The letter is a
personal communication with a reference to exemptions from taxes paid either to
the state or to "the [private] account of me and my children," and it is signed, in
a hand different from that of the text, *genesthoi* ("so be it" or "make it happen").

An original letter and not an administrative copy, the papyrus preserves the only known autograph subscription of Cleopatra VII.[40] The letter, its unique, spectacular signature the only autograph on papyrus of a historically prominent person from antiquity, provides insight into Roman economic involvement in Egypt and into Cleopatra's dealings with Marc Antony's supporters. Furthermore, as van Minnen points out, Cleopatra must have dictated and signed thousands of such documents. The papyrus illustrates the queen at work on routine administrative concerns—a contrast to the image of her, projected over the centuries, living a life of continuous, sumptuous banqueting.

RESEARCH ON CLEOPATRA AND EGYPTOMANIA

Popular interest in Cleopatra and Egypt does not stop, and the recent excavations in Alexandria of the harbor, Pharos, and Cleopatra's palace, and the story of Cleopatra herself, have been the subjects of various documentaries and made-for-TV movies. Scholarly interest too persists: a major exhibition in Paris, Ottawa, and Vienna (1994–95) on "Egypt in Western Art, 1730–1930" was accompanied by a splendidly illustrated catalog (J.-M. Humbert et al., *Egyptomania: Egypt in Western Art, 1730–1930*, 1994); another exhibit focusing more on Hellenistic Egypt was on view in Rome, London, and Chicago (with an excellent catalog, edited by Susan Walker and Peter Higgs, *Cleopatra of Egypt: From History to Myth*, 2001). An exhibit in Hamburg, Germany, was focused on Cleopatra and the Caesars (with another excellent catalog, edited by Bernard Andreae and Karin Rhein, *Kleopatra und die Caesaren*, 2006). A scholarly monograph on Egyptomania by James Stevens Curl includes a variety of media, with an emphasis on drawings, design, and architectural motifs (*Egyptomania, the Egyptian Revival: A Recurring Theme in the History of Taste*, 1994).

The journalist Lucy Hughes-Hallett published a useful biography of Cleopatra that judiciously studies many different representations throughout history (*Cleopatra: Histories, Dreams and Distortions*, 1990), and Michael Grant's now classic *Cleopatra: A Biography* (1972) is still reprinted by Barnes and Noble. Mary Hamer published a diachronic, theoretically based cultural history (*Signs of Cleopatra: History, Politics, Representations*, 1993). A biography by Pat Southern makes Cleopatra, her Roman associates, and their historical context accessible to general readers (*Cleopatra*, 1999), as does Diana E. E. Kleiner's *Cleopatra and Rome* (2005) and Sally-Ann Ashton's *Cleopatra and Egypt* (2008). Adrian Goldsworthy highlights the relationship between Antony and Cleopatra and the historical background of their alliance (*Antony and Cleopatra*, 2010). Duane Roller's biography focuses on Cleopatra in her own period (*Cleopatra, A Biography*, 2010), while Stacy Shiff's best seller explores the complexity of writing a biography of Cleopatra (*Cleopatra, A Life*, 2010).

In her book *The Experience of Ancient Egypt* (2000) Rosalie David gives readers the social context of ancient Egypt and a history of Egyptology; the detailed scholarly examination of early Egyptology by Donald Reid, *Whose Pharaohs? Archaeology, Museums, and Egyptian National Identity from Napoleon to World War I* (2002) examines the impact of the passion for Egypt on the country itself. The Egyptian monuments in Rome, for so many centuries the primary source of visual models for Egyptian art and architecture, are now discussed conveniently in one volume by Boris de Rachewiltz and Anna Maria Partini (*Roma Egizia: Culti, templi e divinità egizie nella Roma Imperiale,* 1999), and studies on the relationship between Rome and Egypt are presented in Laurent Bricault, Miguel John Versluys, and Paul G. P. Meyboom, eds., *Nile into Tiber: Egypt in the Roman World* (2007). Papyri from Egypt, many now in collections outside of Egypt, are under study with renewed vigor, and have yielded many insights into the actual workings of Ptolemaic Egypt. J. G. Manning's *The Last Pharaohs: Egypt Under the Ptolemies, 305–30 B.C.* (2010) provides a new history of the Ptolemaic state, making use of this rich source of documentary material.

The essays presented here address various aspects of the life and death of Cleopatra VII of Egypt and her legacy. As the title of Peter Green's poem (the source of the title of this book) suggests, Cleopatra herself and her historical context remain enigmatic. Yet we visit her again and again. Rather than a complete coverage either of Cleopatra's history or of Egyptomania through the ages, the authors of the essays here provide fresh examinations of intriguing questions about Cleopatra's actions and decisions, Roman literary depictions of her story, and the reception in Rome of Egyptian culture, especially of its religion and architecture. Several of the papers address various transformations of Cleopatra and the Egyptian themes she inspired in the early modern and contemporary periods and illustrate the continuing vitality of this famous person in whom Egyptian, Greek, and Roman culture intersected in the late Hellenistic Mediterranean.

Sally-Ann Ashton presents the view of Cleopatra from the Egyptian perspective and discusses how Cleopatra used imagery modeled on her Ptolemaic ancestors, especially Arsinoe II, as well as traditional Egyptian imagery, ritual, and pharaonic practice to enhance and consolidate her claim to the throne. As the first of the Ptolemies to speak Egyptian, Cleopatra had the skill and knowledge to carry still further the policy of her predecessors, to integrate Egyptian and Greek customs. Her patronage of the cult of Isis helped to root the Hellenistic version firmly in Egypt, and after her death at least some images of Isis seem to have been inspired by representations of Cleopatra. Her posthumous images as Isis were revered in Egypt for many centuries.

In an essay originally published in 2003, Erich S. Gruen scrutinizes the evidence for Cleopatra's presence in Rome for a year and a half, 46–44 B.C.E., a long sojourn assumed to have occurred by modern historians and celebrated in modern film.[41] Gruen demonstrates that in fact Cleopatra must have made two short trips to Rome, first in 46 and again in 44, but that she spent most of the intervening time ruling in Egypt. These details change considerably the basis for the popular view of Cleopatra as a woman in love, dependent on Caesar and making a splash in Rome, suggesting instead that she was a strong and determined female ruler who properly spent most of her time managing her country.

Robert A. Gurval investigates the literary imagery of Cleopatra's death and the various permutations of meaning attributed to the bite of the asp and to her suicide. He analyzes the representation of Cleopatra's death in the poetry of Horace and examines Roman views of suicide as a bold and courageous act and a way of taking control of one's fate. The dramatic reversals in Cleopatra's life had a continuing appeal for Virgil and later authors such as Plutarch who develop the tragic aspects of using snakes and poison for death. The famous physician Galen illustrates the quick effects of an asp's poison with the dramatic story of her death. Images of snakes and death recur in Chaucer and Shakespeare, shifting Cleopatra into a Christian world. The rich and complex stories of her death give us an insight into gender-based attitudes toward feminine ingenuity and motivation and, in the end, enhance her reputation.

Sarolta A. Takács examines the evidence for the spread and growth of the cult of Isis in Rome after the defeat of Cleopatra. She first addresses whether Cleopatra's entourage (some of whom may have stayed behind in Rome when Cleopatra herself returned to Egypt) contributed to the spread of the cult of Isis. Augustus, surprisingly, was not entirely hostile to the cult but evidently wished to limit its public presence. Takács discusses the political reasons for public policies of Augustus toward the cult and for its successful propagation despite his personal dislike of anything Egyptian. His carefully orchestrated policies in fact supported the role of the emperor and the deification of Julius Caesar. In effect the lack of suppression of the cult and the tacit support it received contributed to its later success both in Rome and around the Bay of Naples, a sort of posthumous triumph for Cleopatra.

Brian A. Curran discusses the eager interest in Egyptian remains in Rome during the Renaissance, beginning with the artistic and literary circle of Alexander VI, whose antiquarian efforts deliberately recalled Alexander the Great and his conquest of Egypt. His successor Julius II continued with a program of papal imagery that glorified him as a Second Julius [Caesar] after he acquired a statue of Cleopatra so remarkable and admired that it inspired poetic discourse and became central to the papal collection of statuary. Julius II's successor Leo X continued the imperial references, undertaking serious archaeological, artistic, and philological endeavors that positioned him as a new Augustus. Thus, these three popes bolstered their regimes with obelisks, statuary, and literature that evoked the late Hellenistic period and its rulers.

Ingrid D. Rowland discusses erotica published in 1606 and widely circulated throughout Europe, the purported correspondence of Cleopatra, Marc Antony, and an Ephesian doctor, Quintus Soranus, entitled *On the Infamous Libido of Cleopatra the Queen.* The forger of these letters traded on both the reputation of Cleopatra as oversexed and insatiable (a reputation rooted in the hostile Roman literary tradition) and her later renown as an author of a text on cosmetics and gynecology. Rowland traces the original author, the motives for the publication of the forgery, and the wide success it still enjoys.

Margaret Mary DeMaria Smith discusses the limitations of Edward Said's theories about Orientalism for interpreting European paintings of Egypt in the nineteenth century. She analyzes the "Egyptian" paintings of Sir Lawrence Alma-Tadema and shows how they reflect changing views about Egypt and Egypt's role in history: while a substantial number of these works take as their subjects Roman literary accounts of Cleopatra and of her meeting with Marc Anthony, others focus less on the intersection with Rome and more on biblical topics and the concept of desolation and extinct civilization, themes of broad interest in Victorian Britain. A third group illustrates themes of "everyday life" in Egypt, thus imaginatively juxtaposing Egyptian culture and Victorian pastimes.

Alma-Tadema died in 1912, with his last painting of Cleopatra unfinished; his work almost overlaps with the production of *Cleopatra* starring Theda Bara in 1917. The early imagery of Cleopatra in twentieth-century film is investigated in the essay by Maria Wyke and Dominic Monstserrat, including tie-ins with department stores, women's magazines, and advertising campaigns. They begin with Theda Bara and discuss how the emphasis in promotional photographs changed from one aspect of Cleopatra's legend to another, and they conclude with an analysis of Elizabeth Taylor as Cleopatra and the merging of actress and role into "Lizpatra."

Giuseppe Pucci begins with the demand of Françoise de Foix (mistress of Francis I of France) for the first modern translation of Plutarch's *Life of Antony* in 1519, which stemmed from her interest in learning seductive secrets from Cleopatra. The essay examines the creation and transformation of myths and legends about Cleopatra, her appearance, her personality, and her behavior, documented by a selection from the huge number of representations in art and literature in the early modern period. Pucci concludes with brief comments on early images of Cleopatra in film, giving choice examples from Italian productions. As Pucci points out, Cleopatra is continuously "in production," in recent television and film, and in the attractions at Las Vegas.

Peter Green provides a long witty poem (with rhyme and meter) that brilliantly addresses the whole array of historical and cultural issues surrounding Cleopatra and Egyptomania, a fitting and succinct conclusion to the present volume.[42]

NOTES

1. Translation by I. Scott-Kilvers in Plutarch, *Makers of Rome* (1965): 294.

2. R. Meiggs and D. Lewis, eds., *Greek Historical Inscriptions*[2], no. 7.

3. P. Vasunia's *The Gift of the Nile: Hellenizing Egypt from Aeschylus to Alexander* (2001) is essential reading on the Graecocentric attitudes of Herodotus and other Greek authors who take up Egyptian themes; R. Thomas, *Herodotus in Context: Ethnography, Science and the Art of Persuasion* (2000), provides a stimulating examination of Herodotus' intellectual milieu.

4. See A. Bowman, *Egypt after the Pharaohs, 332 B.C.–A.D. 642*[2] (1996).

5. For their construction of traditional Egyptian temples, see D. Arnold, *Temples of the Last Pharaohs* (1999): 143–224.

6. P. Meyboom, *The Nile Mosaic of Palestrina: Early Evidence of Egyptian Religion in Italy* (1995); the mosaic is dated to 120–110 B.C.E. For discussion of other Nilotic scenes in Roman art, see Miguel J. Versluys, *Aegyptiaca Romana: Nilotic Scenes and the Roman Views of Egypt* (2002).

7. A. Roullet, *The Egyptian and Egyptianizing Monuments of Imperial Rome* (1972); M. Boatwright, *Hadrian and the City of Rome* (1987); S. Takács, *Isis and Sarapis in the Roman World* (1995), and her essay in this book; W. MacDonald and J. Pinto, *Hadrian's Villa and Its Legacy* (1995).

8. For obelisks, C. D'Onofrio, *Gli obelischi di Roma: Storia e urbanistica di una città dall' età al XX secola3* (1967–92); E. Iversen, *Obelisks in Exile, 1: The Obelisks of Rome* (1968); E. Iversen, *Obelisks in Exile, 2: The Obelisks of Istanbul and England* (1972); B. de Rachewiltz and A.M. Partini, *Roma Egizia: Culti, templi e divinità egizie nella Roma Imperiale* (1999); B.A. Curran et al., *Obelisk: A History* (2009); for Augustus' horologium, P. Zanker, *The Power of Images in the Age of Augustus* (1990): 144; its discovery, E. Buchner, *Die Sonnenuhr des Augustus* (1982); further discussion, M. Schütz, "Zur Sonnenuhr des Augustus auf dem Marsfeld," *Gymnasium* 97 (1990): 432–57. The inscription on the base of the obelisk reads: "Imperial Caesar, son of Divius (Julius), Augustus, chief priest [in 10 B.C.E.], Egypt having been brought under the will of the Roman People, gave this as a gift to Sol (the Sun)."

9. Edward Said (*Orientalism: Western Concepts of the Orient*, 1978) provides the now classic view of this dichotomy, to be read with more recent views, such as those in J.F. Codell and D.S. Macleod, eds., *Orientalism Transposed: The Impact of the Colonies on British Culture* (1998) and Andrew J. Rotter, K.E. Fleming, Kathleen Biddick, "Review Essays: Orientalism Twenty Years On," *American Historical Review* 105 (2000): 1204–49; see also Margaret Smith's article in this volume. Herodotus is the first to suggest the dichotomy, famously tracing hostilities back to the abductions of Io from Greece to Egypt and of Helen from Sparta to Troy (Hdt. 1.1–5).

10. E. Iversen, *The Myth of Egypt and Its Hieroglyphs in European Tradition* (1961, repr. 1993): 62–63; I.D. Rowland, *The Culture of the High Renaissance: Ancients and Moderns in Sixteenth-Century Rome* (1998): 46–59.

11. Iversen (1961): 67; Rowland (1998): 60–67.

12. See Brian A. Curran's essay below.

13. L. Hughes-Hallett, *Cleopatra: Histories, Dreams and Distortions* (1990): 202–16, provides a useful overview; discussed also by Giuseppe Pucci in his essay below.

14. J. Pomeroy, "Forging a Career in the Sixteenth Century: Lavinia Fontana of Bologna," *Women in the Arts* 16 (1998): 4–8.

15. For an overview, J. Black, *The British Abroad: The Grand Tour in the Eighteenth Century* (1992); also E. Chaney, *The Evolution of the Grand Tour* (1998). Early travelers to Egypt itself (before and after 1798), including Pietro Delle Valle who visited there in the years 1615–16, are discussed in P. Starkey and J. Starkey, eds., *Travellers in Egypt* (2001).

16. For an overview with extensive bibliography, D. Dykstra, "The French occupation of Egypt, 1798–1801," in M.W. Daly, ed., *The Cambridge History of Egypt*, vol. 2 (1998): 113–38; for accounts of the motivations and politics of the campaign, A. Schom, *Napoleon Bonaparte* (1997): 71–188, and

M. Jasanoff, *Edge of Empire: Lives, Culture, and Conquest in the East, 1750–1850* (2005): 117–48; also useful is J. Christopher Herold, *Bonaparte in Egypt* (1962); J. Benoist-Méchin, *Bonaparte en Égypte, ou le rêve inassouvi (1797–1801)* (1978).

17. Details of the use of classical antiquity in the Revolution: H. T. Parker, *The Cult of Antiquity and the French Revolutionaries: A Study in the Development of the Revolutionary Spirit* (1965).

18. Starkey and Starkey (2001), where P. Starkey also discusses Egyptian travelers to Europe (280–86).

19. This period is covered well by the essays in J.-M. Humbert et al., *Egyptomania: Egypt in Western Art, 1730–1930* (1994), to be read with a review by Brian A. Curran, *Art Bulletin* 78 (1996): 739–44; and by J. S. Curl, *Egyptomania: The Egyptian Revival: A Recurring Theme in the History of Taste* (1994).

20. C. Truman, *The Sèvres Egyptian Service, 1810–12*, Victoria and Albert Museum (1982); J.-M. Humbert et al. (1994): 227–35; also illustrated is a Sèvres tea service taken by Napoleon to Saint Helena (240–241). The large numbers of dinner services and dining paraphernalia from many countries, monarchs, and groups on exhibit in Apsley House in London shows that this was to be a typical offering to the Duke, but only the service from Louis XVIII features Egyptian themes.

21. Useful essays in G. W. Clarke, ed., *Rediscovering Hellenism: The Hellenic Inheritance and the English Imagination* (1989); for new ideology in Greece, E. Bastéa, *The Creation of Modern Athens, Planning the Myth* (2000).

22. A recent study investigates these issues thoroughly: Donald Reid, *Whose Pharaohs? Archaeology, Museums, and Egyptian National Identity from Napoleon to World War I* (2002); for a more general discussion of cultural property and ethical issues, see Colin Renfrew, *Loot, Legitimacy and Ownership: The Ethical Crisis in Archaeology* (2000).

23. See Carl J. Richard, *The Founders and the Classics* (1994).

24. In both the eighteenth and early nineteenth centuries in America and Europe, many prominent men were Masons (including Washington and Franklin), and Freemasonry and its images and symbols, as is well known, are prevalent in the official seal, currency, and in commemorative monuments in the United States. Freemasonry nourished interest in Egypt at least from the time of its official inception in the early eighteenth century, and its arcana has been another avenue of expression of Egyptian influence in art and architecture: see James S. Curl, *The Art and Architecture of Freemasonry* (1991).

25. J. A. Auerbach, *The Great Exhibition of 1851: A Nation on Display* (1999): 168.

26. Fullest account in Martina D'Alton, *The New York Obelisk, or How Cleopatra's Needle Came to New York and What Happened When It Got Here* (1993).

27. Henry H. Gorringe, *Egyptian Obelisks* (1882). One aspect of the project that deserves mention is that all the men involved in it, including the financial backer William Henry Vanderbilt, were Freemasons; a parade of nine thousand Masons marched up Fifth Avenue for the ceremony of laying the cornerstone. For a recent account of the entire project, see D'Alton (1993).

28. The other obelisk is now in London on the Thames embankment; it was given to the British in 1801 in gratitude for their defeat of Napoleon's army of occupation, but was not moved to London until 1877.

29. The unresolved ambiguity in the sources and the topography are discussed by P. M. Fraser, *Ptolemaic Alexandria* (1972)1: 24–25, 2: 67–71, notes 154–62.

30. J.-Y. Empereur, *Alexandria Rediscovered* (1998): 111–22.

31. I thank the Egyptian Department, especially Diana Craig Patch, of the Metropolitan Museum of Art for permission to examine the bronze crabs. For the inscriptions, see Augustus C. Merrian, *The Greek and Latin Inscriptions on the Obelisk-Crab in the Metropolitan Museum, New York* (1883). Replicas of the crabs were made for the obelisk in its present position.

32. Gorringe (1882): 75–76 (citing the research of Gaston L. Feuardent); Zanker (1990): 48–53.

33. Quoted in D'Alton (1993): 11.

34. Photographs of the advertisements and cards in D'Alton (1993): 46.

35. See the essay by Maria Wyke and Dominic Monserrat in this volume.

36. For example, the academic controversies surrounding Martin Bernal's *Black Athena: The Afrocentric Roots of Classical Civilization* 1 (1987), 2 (1981); criticism in Mary R. Lefkowitz, *Not Out of Africa: How Afrocentrism Became an Excuse to Teach Myth as History* (1996), and Mary R. Lefkowitz and Guy MacLean Rogers, eds., *Black Athena Revisited* (1996); a reply to his critics, Martin Bernal, *Black Athena Writes Back* (2001); for a study of the controversy itself, J. Berlinerblau, *Heresy in the University: The* Black Athena *Controversy and the Responsibilities of American Intellectuals* (1999).

37. The discoveries are described in Empereur (1998): 64–87. The authoritative account of the evidence for the Pharos and its reconstruction is by Hermann Thiersch, *Pharos, Antike Islam und Occident* (1909).

38. Franck Goddio, *Alexandria: The Submerged Royal Quarters* (1998). Excavations in Alexandria are also discussed in essays in the exhibition catalog M. Rausch, ed., *La gloire d'Alexandrie (7 mai–26 juillet 1998)* (1998).

39. Judith McKenzie, *The Architecture of Alexandria and Egypt, c. 300 B.C. to A.D. 700* (2007).

40. Peter van Minnen, "An Official Act of Cleopatra (with a subscription in her own hand)," *Ancient Society* 30 (2000): 29–34; "A royal ordinance of Cleopatra and related documents," in S. Walker and S.-A. Ashton (2003): 35–44.

41. Erich Gruen, "Cleopatra in Rome: Facts and Fantasies," in D. Braund and C. Gill, eds., *Myth, History and Culture in Republican Rome: Studies in honour of T. P. Wiseman* (2003): 257–74. I thank the author and the University of Exeter Press for permission to republish the essay here.

42. The poem was originally published in *Arion* 14(2006): 29–34. I thank the author and Herb Golder, editor of *Arion*, for permission to include the poem here.

1

Cleopatra, Queen of Egypt

Sally-Ann Ashton

The legendary Cleopatra the public knows—the passionate, infinitely various woman of Shakespeare's *Antony and Cleopatra* and the stylized beauty of the 1930s and 1960s films—has little to do with the historical Cleopatra, and we can gain a sense of the historical woman by considering her alongside her predecessors, the earlier Ptolemaic queens. Such an account of the last Cleopatra, who ruled Egypt from 51 to 30 B.C., can also give us a wider understanding of both the late Ptolemaic period and, to some extent, her use of earlier traditions to support her aspirations. Here I shall examine how the historical Cleopatra was presented in name and images to her several human and divine audiences: native Egyptians, the multi-ethnic and polyglot Alexandrians, the priestly hierarchy that still controlled the essential infrastructure of Egypt, the larger world of eastern Mediterranean kingdoms, and the deities of Egypt. She relied primarily on the traditional imagery and nomenclature of religious ritual developed over several millennia as a way of expressing contemporary authority, and added to that the nearer example of imagery created by earlier Ptolemaic queens, some of whom had faced dynastic challenges similar to her own. The minute iconographic details of her portraits reflect the artistic subtleties and visual sophistication of the two cultures, Greek and Egyptian, that were merged in Ptolemaic Egypt.

ARSINOE II (CA. 316–270 B.C.) AS A ROYAL MODEL

The Ptolemaic queens played an important role in both religious and political contexts from early in the dynasty: the royal pair Ptolemy II and Arsinoe II, full brother and sister as well as husband and wife, were deified as the *Theoi Adelphoi*,

FIGURE 4. Pylon of the temple of Khonsu at Karnak, with relief showing Ptolemy III making an offering to the *Theoi Adelphoi* (Ptolemy II and Arsinoe II). Photo by Sally-Ann Ashton.

or sibling gods, during their lifetimes. This was part of the effort of the Ptolemies to make their rule as outsiders, Macedonian Greeks, acceptable to Egyptians by assimilating themselves into the traditional Egyptian religious hierarchies and categories, while not denying their Greek origin and heritage. A salient feature of the old pharaonic system had been inter-family marriage, and now this pair established a precedent for the Ptolemies to continue the custom. Following Arsinoe's death, the queen was deified in her own right; textual references show that her temples in the Faiyum were distinct from those of the *Theoi Adelphoi.*[1] In dating formulas their successor Ptolemy III always refers to the *Theoi Adelphoi* as his parents, even though his mother was Arsinoe I. He advertised his respect and close association with Arsinoe II by images carved on the great portals of the temple at Karnak, where he is shown as pharaoh making an offering to her and Ptolemy II as the *Theoi Adelphoi* (Fig. 4). The promotion of the *Theoi Adelphoi* gained added impetus from a direct link with the cult of the deified Alexander the Great, who had conquered Egypt when it was under the Persians and had been declared the son of Amun-Ra by the oracle of Zeus Ammon at Siwah in 331 B.C.

In contrast, the cult of the *Theoi Soteres* or Savior Gods (titles given to the founders of the dynasty, Ptolemy I and Berenike I) had originally stood alone, and it was not until the reforms of Ptolemy IV that the cult of the founders of the dynasty was joined to the original cult of Alexander and the subsequent Ptolemaic rulers: a consolidation of ritual attentions that then linked the conquering hero, his general Ptolemy, and Ptolemy's family and successors.[2] Even after these reforms, the native priesthood chose not to add the names of Alexander and the *Theoi Soteres* to the dating formulas.[3] Thus, the *Theoi Adelphoi* became a convenient reference for assertions of dynastic authority going back to Alexander. Arsinoe II, positioned in the religious and political sphere as one of the *Theoi Adelphoi* and then deified in her own right following her death, stood as a powerful antecedent and became a model for later royal women. These names, titles, and the visual images in sculptured reliefs on temples and sculpture in the round helped establish the Ptolemies as rightful rulers in the age-old traditions of Egypt, where imagery had long held deep ritual significance and by itself (and its location) conveyed authority.

The Egyptian iconography adopted by the Ptolemaic queens drew on that of royal women from earlier dynastic periods, most especially from the eighteenth and nineteenth dynasties (sixteenth–thirteenth centuries B.C.), when powerful royal women such as Hatshepsut and Nefertiti were prominently featured as companions of their male consorts or were venerated in their own right, often depicted in specific cultic roles. Imagery and symbols associated with the goddess Hathor were especially favored for portraits, such as a headdress with double plumes, a sun disk and cow's horns, and these symbols promoted the Hathoric aspects of the queen.[4] A vulture crown was used to indicate posthumous divinity in many representations of Ptolemaic queens that served as cult statues of them as gods. (It was worn originally in images of Nekhbet, the vulture goddess and protectress of Upper Egypt.) From the time of Cleopatra III, when the queen was deified in her own right during her lifetime, the Ptolemaic queens wore vulture headdresses even in contemporary images. Finally the uraeus was added: originally this was a symbol of solar kingship, but for royal women, a uraeus also signified the cobra goddess Wadjet, protectress of Lower Egypt, and more generally, status as Hathor, the daughter and eye of Ra, as Robins suggests.[5]

Arsinoe II was the first to adopt a distinctive, more specific iconography, which then remained consistent for queens throughout the Ptolemaic period, a type illustrated by her posthumous representation.[6] This new type would have aided recognition of the ruler and also distinction among rulers, especially when they shared temples with other deities (with a ritual title, "temple-sharing goddess"). The need for an established procedure for royal portraits is reflected in the texts of the Canopus and Rosetta decrees.[7] Immediate visual recognition was especially important during the Ptolemaic period because few images were inscribed, and it is particularly useful for the identification of individuals on temple reliefs, where the cartouches often remained empty.

Fortunately, two inscribed Egyptian-style statues of Arsinoe II provide positive evidence for this new mode of representation: a statue showing Arsinoe as one of the *Theoi Adelphoi* during her lifetime, now in the Vatican Museum, and a posthumous representation of the queen (probably second century B.C.), now in the Metropolitan Museum of Art, New York.[8] The first statue shows the queen with a double uraeus and the other, with Greek attributes, shows the queen with a double cornucopia (a double horn of plenty).[9] The double uraeus appears on images of royal women from the eighteenth dynasty: in them, one cobra wears the crown of Upper Egypt and the other the crown of Lower Egypt, thus together symbolizing their unification, a constant theme in Egyptian royal imagery.[10] In the case of Arsinoe II, the double uraeus complements the double cornucopia, and they may have had a similar meaning. It should be noted, however, that the uraei of the Ptolemaic period do not wear the crowns; only once, in the case of the fragment of a sculpture from Koptos and now in the Petrie Museum of Egyptian Archaeology, are three uraei decorated, but with cow's horns. Cleaning of the crown by the British Museum Department of Conservation has revealed that the cobras were completed in stucco and then gilded, traces of which survive around the uraei, thus making the cobras the focal point of the headdress. Details such as the cobras and their crowns formed part of a visual language in an era when literacy—especially in Egyptian languages—was limited to a few.[11]

THE STRUGGLES OF CLEOPATRA II (CA. 185–116 B.C.) AND CLEOPATRA III (D. 101 B.C.)

Cleopatra II, like her far more famous namesake Cleopatra VII, suffered difficult political and dynastic struggles after the death of her mother, Cleopatra I, in 176 B.C., and her response to her situation helps illustrate the vital authority and evident skill for dynastic survival exercised by Ptolemaic queens. She had two brothers and was married to the elder, Ptolemy VI, in 176 B.C., probably in an attempt to avert potential family feuds.[12] Cleopatra II and Ptolemy VI took on the title *Philometores*, Mother-loving Gods, thus honoring Cleopatra I and establishing continuity with her. Six years later the younger brother, Ptolemy VIII, joined his siblings so that the three became joint rulers of Egypt.[13] The union was short lived, since Ptolemy VI was removed from power after outside intervention from the Seleucid king Antiochos IV, and Ptolemy VIII and Cleopatra II were set up as joint rulers.[14] According to Livy (45.11.6) it was Cleopatra II who brought about peace, and the three siblings attempted to rule together once more. But problems continued to vex the reign and indeed this entire period of Ptolemaic rule: not just the Seleucids but also Roman generals became involved in the internal struggles between the siblings and their factions, and between Alexandrians and the rest of Egypt.[15] Each time, however, Cleopatra II is shown to be the constant member of any alliance, her seemingly unenviable role in fact allowing her more flexibility and power than either of her brothers. Following the death of Ptolemy VI, Cleopatra II ruled jointly with Ptolemy VIII. Conflicts continued and in 132/1 B.C. the queen organized a revolt against her brother and declared herself queen in Upper Egypt, taking the titles Queen Cleopatra, *Philometor* ("mother-loving") goddess, *Soteira* ("savior"), thus resurrecting the title that she had used with Ptolemy VI.[16] Diodorus (34–5.14) and Justin (38.12–13) record her brother's response: he murdered their son, and sent the body to his sister. Such terrible dynastic strife threw the country into a state of civil war. Yet Cleopatra II continued to rule with Ptolemy VIII, even though he had her son Ptolemy VII executed, and despite his rape of and subsequent marriage to her daughter, Cleopatra III. This resulted in a second triple rule, equally fraught with troubles and power struggles.

Even from the grave it seemed that Ptolemy VIII was capable of wreaking havoc: Egypt was effectively left to Cleopatra III (Justin 39.3.1), although her mother was still alive and ruled with her daughter for the first year following their husband's death. This placed the younger queen in an apparently strong and yet still vulnerable position, since according to the will of Ptolemy VIII she was permitted to choose which of her sons would be her co-ruler. In reality, she was forced to alternate her allegiance between the two, and she depended initially on her mother's favorite and then on whomever was most popular with the Alexandrians.[17] She was finally murdered for her trouble in 101 B.C. by Ptolemy X. The queen herself is generally depicted by historians in a sympathetic light, as a victim of her uncle Ptolemy VIII's lust in her early years, which resulted in the unhappy joint rule of her mother Cleopatra II, herself, and one of her sons (Justin 38.8).

Behind these later literary impressions, however, existed an Egyptian queen who clearly aimed to advance her power and status. Papyri indicate that Cleopatra III believed herself to be Isis and that she adopted the priestly roles, such as priest of the cult of Alexander the Great, typically held by the male ruler. She promoted her own cult as herself, in addition to herself as Isis, Cybele, and Aphrodite.[18] The queen also claimed five out of the nine Alexandrian eponymous priesthoods for her own cults.[19] Her visual images also reveal an ambitious response to her individual power: Cleopatra III can be found to take the dominant position on relief scenes, such as standing in front of Ptolemy IX, her son, in an offering scene at the Karnak temple.[20] Interestingly, this particular queen adopted a more masculine image in both her Greek and Egyptian-style sculptural representations.[21] The use of the religious apparatus of ruler-cults, hieratic nomenclature, and official sculpture in temples was an important expression of ruling authority for Cleopatra III and her mother Cleopatra II, and formed part of the royal heritage for Cleopatra VII.

THE CHALLENGE OF REPRESENTING
ROMAN PARTNERS

In comparison with those predecessors, Cleopatra VII managed to escape her marital and family ties more easily: her alliance with Julius Caesar freed her from Ptolemy XIII, and Ptolemy XIV's young age put him at a disadvantage in the face of her strengthened position and her son Ptolemy XV (Caesarion).[22] Like all her predecessors, Cleopatra VII was obliged to have a male consort, essential to the pharaonic system, which depended on male and female pairing, and when she is shown in images making an offering to the gods herself, her consort can be found in a parallel register doing the same.

The actual circumstances of her life were more complicated than this suggests, and the complications gave rise to artistic dilemmas and problems in official nomenclature. In the Hellenistic Greek tradition it seems to have been possible to present an extended family and the queen's lovers, but Egyptian priests and indeed even artists must have felt at the least confused and stymied, since some of her official relationships really had no traditional parallel in pharaonic imagery. Her male associates included her father Ptolemy XII, her brothers Ptolemy XIII and XIV, Julius Caesar, Marc Antony, and her son Ptolemy XV Caesarion. Paternal, maternal, and sibling relationships all had visual and titular precedents earlier in the Ptolemaic period, as illustrated by the titles *Philopator*, *Philometor*, and *Philadelphos*, but Julius Caesar and Marc Antony created a new problem for the Egyptian priesthood (and for the queen): how should her association with these two Romans in Egypt be represented, particularly since they were the fathers of royal children? This truly mattered, because of the deep symbolism attached to visual representation in Egyptian religion: the visual stood directly for the actual and had to be conveyed by a formulaic, conservative tradition then at least 3,000 years old.

CLEOPATRA'S EMULATION OF ARSINOE II

The images of Cleopatra VII do not offer the same masculine interpretation as those of Cleopatra III, and unlike earlier queens such as Hatshepsut, she did not appear in the guise of a pharaoh.[23] Her youthful, idealized image, found in both the Greek and Egyptian-style representations of Cleopatra VII, is very different from those of what might have seemed the most logical role models, Cleopatra II and III. Instead, Cleopatra VII associated herself with Arsinoe II, stylistically and iconographically in both reliefs and sculpture in the round.

Cleopatra's choice of the esteemed and successful Arsinoe II as a model may also have had ideological implications. Arsinoe's secure reign and close relationship with her brother and consort in no way resembled that of Cleopatra with Ptolemy XIII or XIV but it does accord with the presentation of the queen with her son Caesarion, Ptolemy XV. Yet Cleopatra's imagery did move in bold directions, since she was sometimes depicted by herself, such as her appearance alone in scenes on the temple at Armant that may designate her divine status as much as her role as ruler.[24] In contrast, at the temple at Philae, Arsinoe II stands behind Isis receiving offerings from Ptolemy II as a goddess but never appears by herself as one of the *Theoi Adelphoi* making an offering.

A link with Arsinoe II may be seen again in that Cleopatra is also described in official nomenclature as "Daughter of Geb," a title used only by the two queens, since other Ptolemaic queens preferred to be associated with Ra.[25] The association with Geb the creator god was probably chosen deliberately, and in the case of both queens, the title was used during their lifetimes. For Arsinoe II, this meant she held the title before she was deified in her own right, since the epithet appears on her statue now in the Vatican Museum.

Earlier in the dynasty, when deification of individual rulers was made posthumously, there was little confusion in this official imagery in the temples. But later rulers can be found making an offering to themselves in temple imagery, after the Ptolemies took on the role of priest or priestess for their own cults beginning in the second century B.C. (as had earlier rulers in the eighteenth and nineteenth dynasties).[26] By the first century B.C. the age-old assimilation between ruler and god had expanded. Now the royal family was considered to be divine in its own right, as illustrated by the adoption of the title *Thea* ("goddess") by Cleopatra at the start of her reign and the title *New Isis* (Plutarch, *Life of Antony* 54).

CLEOPATRA'S DIVINE STATUS

Cleopatra adopted the role traditionally fulfilled by the pharaoh as the one who makes offerings to the gods, but she did so not only as regent and guardian of her son. On the bark shrine at Koptos, the queen and her consort, probably Ptolemy XIV, make offerings as individuals and not together, thus stressing their equality and independent roles.[27] The titles adopted by the queen stress her links with particular members of her family. The most commonly used, *Philopator*, refers of course to her father Ptolemy Auletes, with whom she probably co-ruled toward the end of his reign.[28] The title *Thea* ("goddess") may literally have referred to her divine status; the epithet had been used by Cleopatra Thea, sister of Cleopatra III, and the masculine equivalent *Theos* was used by Ptolemy XII, Cleopatra VII's father. Caesarion also took the title *Philopator* and *Philometor* in honor of his parents.

The role of protectress is echoed in a title that appears in demotic script during her reign, "Glorification of Cleopatra Philopator," and, it has been suggested, refers to her good deeds for Egypt and addresses her as the divine protectress of the country.[29] This is echoed by the presentation of her son Caesarion in representations, both Egyptian and Greek, that promote him as her rightful heir and successor, at the possible expense of her own power. In fact, the close and apparently amicable relationship that Cleopatra and Caesarion enjoyed seems novel in comparison with the preceding turbulent years of Ptolemaic rule. Could this bond have lasted, if Cleopatra and Marc Antony had been victorious at the battle of Actium?

There is only one mention of Cleopatra adopting the title "King of Egypt." This title was recorded by C. R. Lepsius at Armant and is of considerable interest, particularly because of the scene in relief that accompanies it.[30] Despite the title, Cleopatra does not appear in the guise of a male ruler or even with the crown of a pharaoh; instead, she wears a crown that is modeled on the headdress associated with Geb and worn earlier in representations of Arsinoe II.[31] The association with Geb seems to have been deliberate and is repeated elsewhere: Cleopatra VII appears with the same crown on a stele now in Turin and on the walls of the temple of Hathor at Denderah.[32]

It was not necessary for Cleopatra to appear as a male pharaoh, since role models such as Arsinoe II offered an accepted presentation for a queen without losing the power that the reigning pharaoh possessed. The popularity of Arsinoe II's cult over that of the *Theoi Adelphoi* is testimony to the importance of the Ptolemaic royal women. While earlier Egyptian artists perhaps had struggled to convey this change in roles, their successors in the Ptolemaic period were, it seems, able to deal with the many challenges that the royal family gave them in accurately representing their specific roles. Within Egypt Cleopatra VII was presented as the Egyptian queen, mother and protectress and goddess, who promotes her son as her consort and rightful heir, but the queen's representation in the Greek world offers a different insight into her aspirations.[33] There is no preserved evidence for the presentation of Cleopatra's Macedonian Greek inheritance in Egypt, perhaps a result of the Roman conquest, since the victors would purvey their own view of her. Yet possibly the absence of the Macedonian connection reflects the queen's desire to be seen as an Egyptian, and ironically it is this particular face that has been emphasized in more recent times.

DOUBLE OR TRIPLE URAEUS FOR CLEOPATRA'S CROWN

Cleopatra's assimilation of the iconography used by Arsinoe II has led to some confusion among modern scholars. Even in the case of the inscribed crown from

Koptos, it was naturally assumed by scholars that the titles "King's Daughter," "King's Sister," "Great Royal Wife" must refer to Arsinoe.[34] These titles are valid for many later Ptolemaic queens, however, including Cleopatra VII, married to her brother at the time of her dedications at Koptos. The key in this confusing issue may well be the number of uraei. As previously noted, Arsinoe is shown with two cobras, but recent research on the Ptolemaic royal image has shown that the triple form of uraeus may be associated with Cleopatra VII.[35] Six statues of Cleopatra represent the first use of the triple form of the uraeus in Egyptian royal sculpture, its meaning still unclear. Initially it was suggested that the triple form of the uraeus represented a triple rule, although the double, as mentioned previously, typically represents the unification of Upper and Lower Egypt. Recently it has been suggested that for Cleopatra VII, the three cobras could represent (1) Cleopatra's title of "Queen of Kings"; (2) territorial gains, following the Donations of Alexandria; or (3) the divine triad Horus, Isis, and Osiris, as a means of representing Caesarion, Cleopatra, and Ptolemy XII her father, who not only called himself the "New Dionysos" but inspired the queen to adopt the title *Philopator* ("father-loving").

There are ideological problems with the latter hypothesis because Auletes was not the father of Caesarion and while Julius Caesar is known to have associated himself with Dionysos, he did not rule Egypt as pharaoh, and so to associate him with Osiris may not have been deemed appropriate.[36] This interpretation would accord with the queen's relationship with her brothers Ptolemy XIII and XIV, however, since both would be assimilated to Horus as pharaoh of Egypt. This also corresponds to the early appearance of the triple uraeus on the Koptos crown, assuming that this statue was dedicated at the same time as the bark shrine at the site.

The triple uraeus may have been used simply to suggest Cleopatra's connection with Arsinoe II, while keeping the image distinctive, since all other queens wore the single cobra on their brow.[37] The choice of Arsinoe II as role model might therefore have been politically motivated. Imagery that evokes purely Egyptian themes would also seem more appropriate than the three cobras representing foreign territories, since at home Cleopatra was very much an Egyptian. Two stylistically similar statues in the same proportions as the fragment in the Petrie Museum show the queen with a single uraeus. The statues, now in the Royal Ontario Museum, Toronto, and the Greco-Roman Museum, Alexandria, are unusual because the crowns were carved from the same block of stone as the figure. The statue in Alexandria (originally in Fouah) represents a late Ptolemaic queen wearing a single uraeus, a tripartite wig, and a stylized knotted garment.[38] The features are stylized, and archaizing in the carving of the mouth and eyes, and suggest that the statue dates to the late first century B.C. The statue in Toronto is purely Egyptian in style and also has stylized features but is sufficiently different from the masculine portraits of Cleopatra III to indicate that it may be an early portrait of Cleopatra VII.[39] It is possible, then, that the triple uraeus was used following the death of Ptolemy XIII, or at the time around the birth of Caesarion. The crown of the piece in the Petrie Museum is significant because it is the only datable example and, if it was connected with the dedication of the bark shrine, it illustrates that from relatively early in her reign Cleopatra wished to distinguish herself from her immediate predecessors, and to offer an image that referred to Arsinoe II but was made distinctive by the third cobra.

IMAGES OF PTOLEMAIC ROYAL WOMEN AS QUEENS AND GODDESSES

The images of Ptolemaic royal women are divided into two groups: those that represent the queens in their role in the dynastic cult or as queens, and those that show them as goddesses in their own right. The purely Egyptian-style images may have been intended to represent them as dynastic queens, as we see in the inscribed example of Arsinoe II now in the Vatican Museum, whereas the second group, showing them as goddesses, consists of Egyptian-style images with Greek features. These two types of statues were once thought to reflect a chronological distinction, the purely Egyptian early and those with Greek features later, but it is now understood that they served different functions. The Greek features include a corkscrew wig and the attribute of a cornucopia.[40] Some statues show traits of a Greek "archaizing" style, with snailshell curls along the fringes of the wigs, while others have a more Egyptian style in the sheathlike drapery. In the case of one subgroup, Greek-style corkscrew curls are replaced by the more traditional Egyptian tripartite wig.

One of these statues may help us interpret Cleopatra's use of the triple uraeus. Now in the Hermitage Museum, the statue depicts a queen in a sheathlike dress, wearing a tripartite wig and triple uraeus and holding a double cornucopia in her left arm.[41] Because double cornucopiae are associated with Arsinoe II in both Greek and Egyptian contexts, earlier scholars assumed that the image represented this queen (like the Koptos crown). Coins minted in Cyprus by Cleopatra VII, however, also have a double horn of plenty on the reverse. If the statue represents Cleopatra, this reidentification would explain the triple uraeus in place of the double uraeus that was associated with the earlier queen, Arsinoe II: it was now a necessary distinctive feature for Cleopatra. A second, purely Egyptian-style statue with a triple uraeus had also been dated to the third century B.C., because of its presumed association with Arsinoe II; it is now in San Jose at the Rosicrucian Museum.[42] A more recent, detailed study of Ptolemaic royal statuary has shown that some first-century B.C. images were retrospective in that they copy the stylistic features of third-century B.C. representations.

FIGURE 5. Marble portrait of
Cleopatra VII, before 31 B.C.E.
Inv. 1976.10. Antikensammlung,
Staatliche Museen, Berlin.
Photo Bildarchiv Preussischer
Kulturbesitz/Art Resource, NY.

The portrait features on the Rosicrucian statue fit most comfortably in the first
century B.C.[43]

What the details of the uraeus crown, cornuacopiae, and stylized features
indicate is a deliberate link not just with Arsinoe II but also with portrait types
of the third century B.C. Only the changes in facial features betray the later date
of the purely Egyptian-style images of Cleopatra VII: the wig and drapery are
consistent with those from the early Ptolemaic period. Such subtle quotations
may be found in the Greek-style portraits of Cleopatra too; they are youthful
and idealized, again inspired by the images of third-century B.C. Ptolemaic
queens (Fig. 5). This visual sophistication and artful recall of powerful predecessors is completely lost in the general modern perception of the queen, still
largely based on the Roman view of her as overly sexed, insatiably ambitious,
and manipulative.

CLEOPATRA AS ISIS

A long-standing, legendary assimilation that does seem to have been founded
upon historical fact is that of Cleopatra and Isis. Plutarch says that the queen
presented herself as Isis during the Donations of Alexandria, a pageant staged to

emphasize and celebrate Egypt's territorial claims (Plutarch, *Life of Antony* 54). The close association between the queen and the goddess is illustrated on the back wall of the temple of Hathor at Alexandria, where Cleopatra and her son make offerings to the goddess. Mother and son were also likely represented in a colossal pair of statues from the Hadra region of the city. Although the fragments of the colossal images have long been identified as Cleopatra and Marc Antony, the representation of Antony in any Egyptian role is extremely unlikely, because he did not rule as king, while the youthful appearance of the male portrait accords well with images of Caesarion.[44] Once again the female statue is closely similar in style to royal and divine representations from the third century B.C. This is especially true of the facial features, which are rounded and stylized with drill holes at the corners of the mouth: all features found on early Ptolemaic sculpture. Furthermore, a careful inspection of the iconography of the female statue reveals that it is a type used for representations of goddesses rather than queens: there is only a vulture's head rather than a uraeus. Unusually (for the canons of Egyptian art) the fragments of the statues show that the two figures, most likely mother and son, held hands, thus stressing a close personal bond.[45] It would therefore seem that in this representation we see Cleopatra as Isis, promoted from her royal or even personal divine status to that of a long-established deity, and here in Isis' role as protectress of the ruling king, her own son Caesarion.

A colossal statue of a queen from Canopus, now housed in the Greco-Roman Museum at Alexandria may also represent Cleopatra VII and provide further significant evidence for how the queen was represented around Alexandria.[46] The face of the statue appears to have been deliberately removed and so it is not possible to know whether the subject wore a single, double, or triple uraeus. The over-life scale of this statue (2.35 meters tall) may be compared with the colossal statue of the queen from Hadra, which in its fragmentary form is three meters tall from the modius of the crown to the upper torso. The two images in Alexandria and Hadra represent the two divine roles of the queen, as goddess in her own right and as Isis, supporter of Caesarion as pharaoh; and yet it was the Canopus type in Alexandria that was later adopted to represent the goddess by the Romans, as we shall see.

CLEOPATRA AS THE ROMAN ISIS?

A Greek-style representation of an Egyptian goddess now in Rome, from the area in the city of the ancient Roman sanctuary of Isis and Serapis, may also represent Cleopatra as Isis (Fig. 6).[47] The statue's head (for many years identified as Isis) has portrait features that are similar to the Vatican Cleopatra but shows Cleopatra with an Egyptian tripartite wig and vulture headdress, although the head of the vulture and the small crown, which were attached separately, are now lost. The

FIGURE 6. Ptolemaic Queen with vulture headress, probably Cleopatra as Isis. Musei Capitolini, Rome. Photo Alinari/Art Resource, NY.

use of inlaid eyes is a characteristic more commonly found in Egyptian stone representations of the first century B.C., and this feature, along with the style of carving, may indicate that the sculptor had knowledge of the Egyptian artistic tradition. The presentation of the queen as an Egyptian goddess accords well with her presentation in Egypt. Ironically perhaps, this recent research has added historical support for the Hollywood images of Elizabeth Taylor and Vivian Leigh playing the part of the queen, because this particular head shows her in Egyptianizing rather than purely Egyptian or purely Greek attire.

Here in this statue in Rome, as in Egypt, Cleopatra was shown as a divine being in her own right. Her role as protectress and mother, always in the guise of a divine queen or goddess, and usually accompanied by Caesarion, was promoted to the Egyptians, with Caesarion simultaneously fulfilling an independent role as pharaoh. This divine Cleopatra is radically different from the temptress and harlot, the negative view rooted in Augustan literary propaganda. The youthful appearance of the Capitoline queen with her Egyptian regalia, dignified and solemn in her official capacity, also seems quite distant from the "hateful" virago conjured by Roman authors such as Cicero. Although the portrait may not accurately represent the queen's true appearance, it evokes Plutarch's description

(*Life of Antony* 27): "Her actual beauty was not in itself so remarkable; it was the charm of her presence that was irresistible." Her "presence" on which Plutarch comments was manifested in various celebratory and ritual roles and related images, and these indicate a strategic policy of presentation that surpassed any perceived need to represent this particular queen in the guise of a male pharaoh. Cleopatra VII effectively elevated herself beyond this, by becoming the goddess Isis, thus protecting her son and consort, but at the same time retaining her own personal power and status.

The imagery of Cleopatra as a living queen and goddess in Egypt shows the visual means of confirming her authority through religious iconography, rooted in ancient tradition and the more recent past but carefully shaped to new realities. Her posthumous images are equally interesting, not only as evidence of the continued worship of the goddess Isis but also because they made a lasting impression on Egyptianizing cults in the Imperial Roman world more broadly. This latter accomplishment may have been inadvertent, but the evidence for the queen's influence on the presentation of Isis is of considerable importance, as we have seen in the colossal images from Alexandria and Rome. The iconography adopted for the goddess Isis during the Imperial Roman period was clearly taken from statues representing Ptolemaic queens, in particular those wearing a corkscrew wig, with a knotted costume, and holding a cornucopia. These statues, originally intended to represent Ptolemaic queens, found their way to Italy and were perhaps reused as images of Isis. Following the death of Cleopatra VII, the iconography of Isis associated specifically with her became confused, and the triple uraeus on representations of Isis was replaced with varying elements.[48] This confusion between the identity of Cleopatra and Isis nevertheless ensured her continued worship in the guise of a popular Egyptian goddess.

The earlier Greek and Roman cult statues of the goddess Isis are generally shown as archaizing Greek statues (as illustrated by the statue from the Temple of Isis at Pompeii) but they are later replaced by Egyptianizing images with the knotted costume, corkscrew locks, and cornucopia; in Egypt, however, the assimilation of Ptolemaic queen into Isis probably occurred still earlier. At the very least, this association formulated the iconography for the goddess in the Roman world: perhaps the ultimate accolade for a queen who was effectively finished by the Empire! In Egypt, it was not only as Isis that Cleopatra continued to be worshipped, for a demotic inscription at the temple of Isis at Philae suggests that the veneration of Cleopatra as a deity herself and her cult continued until at least the fourth century A.D.[49] While the queen's Roman reputation lives on and has taken many forms, her original, intended images have survived, and give us a far more accurate idea of how the queen herself wished to be portrayed, in several guises for her many audiences.

NOTES

1. J. Quaegebeur, "Cleopatra VII and the Cults of the Ptolemaic Queens," in R. S. Bianchi, R. A. Fazzini, and J. Quaegebeur, eds., *Cleopatra's Egypt: Age of the Ptolemies* (1988): 43–44 and P. M. Fraser, *Ptolemaic Alexandria*, (1972) 1: 228. For a general overview of Hellenistic ruler cults, see P. Green, *From Alexander to Actium: The Historical Evolution of the Hellenistic Age* (1990): 396–419; of its imagery, J. J. Pollitt, *Art in the Hellenistic Age* (1986): 271–75, and R. R. R. Smith, *Hellenistic Royal Portraits* (1988); for the essential antecedent Alexander, see A. F. Stewart, *Faces of Power: Alexander's Image and Hellenistic Politics* (1993). Some of the observations here have been developed further in my book *Cleopatra and Egypt* (2008).

2. G. Hölbl, *A History of the Ptolemaic Empire* (2001): 169–70 and Fraser (1972) 1: 218.

3. L. Koenen, "The Ptolemaic King as a Religious Figure," in A. Bulloch et al., eds., *Images and Ideologies: Self-Definition in the Hellenistic World* (1993): 89.

4. G. Robins, *Women in Ancient Egypt* (1996): 24.

5. G. Robins (1996): 23–24.

6. S.-A. Ashton, *Ptolemaic Royal Sculpture from Egypt* (2001): 116–17, no. 66; S. Walker and P. Higgs, eds., *Cleopatra of Egypt: From History to Myth* (2001): 166–67, nos. 165, 166.

7. Ashton, *Ptolemaic Royal Sculpture* (2001): 13–19 for summary.

8. Ashton, *Ptolemaic Royal Sculpture* (2001): 37–38; 108–9, no. 54; 100–101, no. 35; also in S. Walker and P. Higgs (2001):166–67, no. 166.

9. Ashton, "The Ptolemaic Influence on Egyptian Royal Sculpture," in A. McDonald and C. Riggs, eds., *Current Research in Egyptology* (2000): 4.

10. J. G. Griffiths, "The Death of Cleopatra VII," *Journal of Egyptian Archaeology* 47 (1961): 50–51; E. R. Russmann, *Representation of the King in the XXVth Dynasty* (1974): 39; G. Robins (1996): 24.

11. S. Walker and P. Higgs (2001): 171, no. 170.

12. J. Whitehorne, *Cleopatras* (1994): 89.

13. Whitehorne (1994): 93–96 for discussion.

14. G. Hölbl (2001): 183–86.

15. For an account of Roman interventions, see Erich Gruen, *The Hellenistic World and the Coming of Rome* (1984): 712–16.

16. J. Whitehorne (1994): 118.

17. G. Hölbl (2001): 205.

18. J. Whitehorne (1994): 146.

19. G. Hölbl (2001): 280 and 285.

20. J. Quaegebeur (1988): 51, note 60.

21. Vienna (AS I 406) and Paris (Louvre, Ma 3546). See S. Walker and P. Higgs (2001): 59–60, nos. 25, 26, respectively, for bibliography and identification, and Ashton, *Ptolemaic Royal Sculpture* (2001): 106–7, no. 47 for the Vienna queen.

22. G. Hölbl (2001): 231–39.

23. For representations of Hatshepsut, see J. Vandier, *Manuel d'archéologie égyptienne, 3: Les grandes époques, la statuaire* (1958); G. Robins (1996): 45–52; and C. H. Roehrig, ed., *Hatshepsut: From Queen to Pharaoh* (2005). Since writing this paper a stele with an image of Cleopatra appearing as a male pharaoh has been found in a collection in China. There are no details currently available.

24. C. R. Lepsius, *Denkmaeler aus Aegypten und Aethiopien nach den Zeichnungen der von seiner Majestät dem koenige von Preußen Friedrich Wilhelm IV nach diesen Ländern gesendeten und in den Jahren 1842–1845 ausgefuehrten wissenschaftlichen Expedition* (1901) 4.1:11.

25. L. Troy, *Patterns of Queenship in Ancient Egyptian Myth and History* (1986): 178–79; see also H. Gauthier, *Le livre des rois d'Égypte* (1916): 410–18.

26. P. Köln 81 lists all of Cleopatra III's cult titles; see also G. Hölbl (2001): 285 for a list of eponymous Alexandrian priesthoods.

27. C. Traunecker, *Coptos, Hommes et Dieux sur le Parvis de Geb* (1992): 272–303 for a translation of the texts and discussion on the bark shrine. Traunecker suggests that the identity of the male ruler might be Ptolemy XIV.

28. M. Grant, *Cleopatra: A Biography* (1972): 30.

29. E. A. E. Reymond, "Demotic Literary Works of Graeco-Roman Date in the Rainer Collection of Papyri in Vienna," in *Papyrus Erzherzog Rainer (P. Rainer Cent.). Festschrift zum 100-jährigen Bestehen der Papyrussammlung der Österreichischen Nationalbibliothek* (1983): 46, and J. Quaegebeur (1988): 51–52.

30. J. Quaegebeur (1988): 52, quoting C. R. Lepsius (1849–1959) part 4: pls. 63–64.

31. P. Dils, "La couronne d'Arsinoé II Philadelphe," in W. Clarysse et al., eds., *Egyptian Religion, The Last Thousand Years: Studies Dedicated to the Memory of Jan Quaegebeur* 2 (1988).

32. B. Porter and R. L. B. Moss, *A Topographical Bibliography* (1927) 1.2: 714.

33. Ashton, "Cleopatra: Goddess, Ruler or Regent?" in S. Walker and S.-A. Ashton, eds., *Cleopatra Reassessed* (2003): 25–30.

34. Ashton, *Ptolemaic Royal Sculpture* (2001): 42 and 67 for full bibliography and previous identifications.

35. Ashton, "Identifying the Egyptian-style Ptolemaic Queens," in S. Walker and P. Higgs, eds., *Cleopatra of Egypt: From History to Myth* (2001): 152–55, and Ashton, *Ptolemaic Royal Sculpture* (2001): 40–42.

36. G. Hölbl (2001): 289–90.

37. Ashton, "The Use of the Double and Triple Uraeus in Royal Iconography," in A. Cooke and F. Simpson, eds., *Current Research in Egyptology* 2 (2005): 1–9.

38. This idea was originally mooted by R. S. Bianchi in "Not the Isis Knot" (1980) and was re-iterated by me in "The Ptolemaic Influence on Egyptian Royal Sculpture," in A. McDonald and C. Riggs, eds., *Current Research in Egyptology 2000* (2000), and in fuller detail with a full catalog of this type of image in my *Ptolemaic Royal Sculpture* (2001): 45–53.

39. R. S. Bianchi, R. A. Fazzini, and J. Quagebeur, eds., *Cleopatra's Egypt: Age of the Ptolemies* (1988): 181, no. 73.

40. Ashton, "The Ptolemaic Influence on Egyptian Royal Sculpture" (2000): 2.

41. S. Walker and P. Higgs (2001): 160, no. 160.

42. Ashton, *Ptolemaic Royal Sculpture* (2001): 41–42, 102–3, no. 39; S. Walker and P. Higgs (2001): 162, no. 161.

43. Ashton, *Ptolemaic Royal Sculpture* (2001): 42, and S. Walker and P. Higgs (2001): nos. 161, 162.

44. Alexandria, Greco-Roman Museum 11275, illustrated in Ashton, *Ptolemaic Royal Sculpture* (2001): 98–99, no. 34; for the female fragment in Mariemont, Musée de Mariemont E49, see 102–3, no. 42. The site of the temple has recently been investigated and will be published in the *Journal of Egyptian Archaeology* by Ashton et al.

45. For a reconstruction based on the Mariemont and Alexandrian fragments see R. R. R. Smith (1988): pl. 50.I.

46. Ashton, *Ptolemaic Royal Sculpture* (2001): 48, 114–15, no. 62.

47. Rome, Musei Capitolini 1154; S. Walker and P. Higgs (2001): 216–17, no. 194, and compare no. 195 for an impression of how the statue appeared with its crown.

48. Ashton, *The Last Queens of Egypt: Cleopatra's Royal House* (2003): 143–52, and Ashton, *Roman Egyptomania* (2004): 52–65 and 180–85.

49. J. Quaegebeur (1988): 41 and 53.

2

Cleopatra in Rome

Facts and Fantasies

Erich S. Gruen

CLEOPATRA'S CINEMATIC ENTRY INTO ROME

The fascination of Cleopatra continues to cast a spell on the public imagination. Few, if any, figures from antiquity have so wide a name-recognition.[1] Popular books, novels, movies, and television specials that feature this ruler of Egypt appear with regularity and can count on a large market for their wares. The subject, of course, entranced even Shakespeare and Bernard Shaw who produced two very different but still enthralling plays. Perhaps no one has had a broader impact upon the present perception of Cleopatra, however, than Joseph Manciewicz, whose spectacular film, which broke all financial records—for expenditure— and paraded Elizabeth Taylor as the preening and seductive queen, still enjoys repeated reruns on television and a steady business at the video stores.[2] Yet serious scholarship on Cleopatra lags woefully behind, perhaps reluctant to confront the tide of popular imagery and myth-making that would overwhelm it. Peter Wiseman's keen eye for the manipulation of myth and the manufacture of legends would have a grand field to survey here. It may be a useful—and occasionally amusing—exercise to penetrate a select segment of those fables.

Manciewicz's film, still impossible to evade or escape on this subject, contains numerous lavish and spectacular scenes. One stands out as especially striking and memorable: the entry of Cleopatra into Rome. She arrives, preceded by lithe, dark dancing girls, sitting in imposing grandeur on a lofty platform in the lap of

Republished with permission of the author and the University of Exeter press from *Myth, History and Culture in Republican Rome: Studies in Honour of T. P. Wiseman* (2003): 257–74.

a gigantic sphinx, drawn through the gates of the city by dozens of slaves, moving at a measured pace to allow the queen, bedecked in magnificent splendor, to be gawked at every step along the way by thousands of awe-struck Romans, who then burst into wild applause and loud cheers. The scene provides an imposing display of royal majesty, dazzling the spectators and commanding their deference and obeisance. No one who has viewed the film is likely to forget that spectacle. Is there any reason to believe it?

In fact, it is all imaginary. None of our testimony, even that which is most hostile to, or critical of, Caesar or Cleopatra, describes such an event. The very notion of staid and sturdy Romans lining the streets of their venerable city to gaze with pleasure upon the pomp and ostentation of an eastern queen is hard to swallow. Of course, no blame should be laid at the doorstep of Manciewicz. Artistic license shields him from scholarly nit-picking. Nor did he pull this idea out of thin air. Cleopatra did come to Rome, in the autumn of 46 B.C.E., and she set up house there, in Trastevere, in Caesar's own estate. She returned to Egypt shortly after the Ides of March in 44 B.C.E.—in a hurry. The situation was a little too explosive for her in Rome after the assassination of Julius Caesar.

CLEOPATRA'S STAY IN ROME

This stay in Rome has stimulated the imaginations of many: not just novelists and film-makers, but some eminent scholars as well. It led to inventive surmise about the powerful and baleful influence exercised by Cleopatra over the Roman dictator. As the embodiment of royalty and luxury, it was conjectured, the queen induced Caesar to aspire after a Hellenistic monarchy of his own, thereby helping to explain the extravagant honors and titles he acquired in the last months of his life, some of them royal, some even divine in character.[3] The visit in Rome induced certain researchers to put credence in the rumors that circulated (then or later) about Caesar's elaborate plans for the future. He allegedly planned to transfer his capital from Rome to Alexandria.[4] Indirect hints surfaced that Caesar proposed to marry Cleopatra, although he already had a wife and Roman law forbade polygamy. Report had it that Caesar even gave instructions to the tribune Helvius Cinna to propose a measure that would permit the dictator to marry whoever—and however many—he wished for the purpose of procreation.[5] This gossip has largely, and rightly, been discounted by recent scholars.[6]

Another item, however, continues to enjoy the status of truth and reliability. Appian, writing in the second century C.E., records that Caesar installed a statue of Cleopatra in the Temple of Venus Genetrix, right next to the goddess herself, his own advertised ancestress, an image, so Appian asserted, that still stands in his day.[7] That piece of information has gone almost unquestioned in the scholarly literature.[8] Yet it is difficult to imagine that an honorific statue of Cleopatra in

Rome would have survived the battle of Actium and the acquisition of supreme power by Octavian, especially in the house of a goddess who was progenitor of the line to which Octavian now belonged.[9] A more likely scenario deserves preference. Dio Cassius later mentions the statue in the context of spoils taken by Octavian from Alexandria and dedications placed in Roman temples.[10] That makes good sense. The statue represents a token of victory, dedicated to the ancestral deity, not, as Appian mistakenly assumed, a token of Caesar's infatuation.

The speculative particulars, however credible or implausible, do not alter the larger fact: Cleopatra's presence in Rome. She was there, ostensibly for a year and half, ensconced in luxury in Caesar's private quarters, an affront to almost all Romans. Historians have never contemplated seriously the extraordinary nature of this episode; indeed, they have not seen fit to question it. Yet the escapade, once one reflects upon it, veritably bursts with questions. What did Caesar think he was doing by installing the queen of Egypt, with her entire entourage, in Trastevere, there to wander conspicuously about his estate and gardens for an indefinite period of time, while Calpurnia looked on as his tolerant, forbearing, and long-suffering wife? If he were to do it at all, why in 46 B.C.E., when civil war against the Pompeians still raged, with significant forces under the command of Pompey's son in Spain? Would Caesar risk alienating the Roman aristocracy and a host of his own potential supporters by flaunting his bedecked and bejeweled foreign mistress? It all makes very little sense.

Quite apart from what Caesar may have thought he was doing, what did Cleopatra think *she* was doing? This sojourn in Rome, when it is contemplated at all by modern scholars, has been viewed only from a Caesarian vantage point: what was Cleopatra's value to him, or how was he to use her in furthering his royal aspirations, in controlling Egypt, or in assuring a hereditary succession. That represents a skewed and narrow vision. Cleopatra was no mere instrument of Caesarian policy, no mere ornament for his ambitions, no mere plaything for his sexual desires. One would do well to recall that she had only just regained her throne in Egypt, after considerable upheaval and turbulence. What was she doing in Rome for months at a stretch while her own hold upon loyalty in Alexandria must have been very shaky? The volatile Alexandrians had already demonstrated their displeasure with Caesar in no uncertain terms when he had set up his headquarters in their city. They would certainly take no more kindly to Cleopatra's establishing a household in the dictator's dwelling in Rome.

How to explain it? Had Cleopatra become heedlessly enamored of Caesar, gripped by a fervor to spend all her time at his side? If so, she would not enjoy his company for long. A month or so after Cleopatra arrived in Rome, Caesar went off to the wars in Spain.[11] None could predict how long he would be gone—or if he would ever return. Was Cleopatra planning to wait patiently, no matter how long it took? As it happened, Caesar's expedition abroad lasted for about six months.

What was Cleopatra doing during that long absence? How long did she plan to stay? As we know, she left in a hurry after the Ides of March in 44 B.C.E. But the slaying of Caesar could not have been anticipated. Would she, otherwise, have remained indefinitely? Who was running the country in Egypt?

An even more intriguing question suggests itself. How is it that, when Cleopatra did return, after having left Egypt in an unsettled condition, having been away for more than a year and a half, and with her powerful paramour now dead, she apparently picked up the pieces in her homeland without encountering dissent or difficulty?

No one has bothered to pose these questions. But once posed, they make clear that something must be wrong with this picture. A closer inspection is warranted.

THE BACKGROUND TO THE ROMAN VISIT

Cleopatra, it should be emphasized, was a formidable figure in her own right. She possessed considerable intellectual gifts, great resourcefulness, and high ambition. Plutarch reports that the queen had a mellifluous voice, like a many-stringed instrument, a woman of great charm and wit, not perhaps a dazzling beauty (as coins and portrait busts confirm), but an engaging conversationalist and a person of wide-ranging intellect. He adds that she was fluent in nine languages—none of which, interestingly enough, was Latin. (She doubtless conversed with Caesar in Greek.) However embellished this portrait might be, it indicates a woman of real accomplishment.[12] The Roman perspective, inescapably, presents her as part of a duo, whether with Caesar or with Antony, either as being manipulated by them for their purposes or as manipulating them for hers. Neither analysis does full justice to the woman or to the circumstances in which she found herself.

Cleopatra VII stood in the long line of the Ptolemies who for two and a half centuries had ruled Egypt and, for much of the time, Cyrene, Cyprus, Palestine, Coele-Syria, parts of Asia Minor, and the Aegean. The Ptolemies enjoyed the most enduring and proudest of the Hellenistic kingdoms. Born to the purple, Cleopatra saw her mission as maintaining the (best) traditions of her royal line, and indeed as reviving the ancient glories of that line. She faced an arduous struggle. Intrigues within the family, court cabals, and civil strife made her quest an uphill battle from the start. This is not the place to rehearse those details. It needs only be stressed that Cleopatra had to call upon substantial ingenuity and to resort to both internal and external resources well before Julius Caesar came on the scene.

A brief review of her prior experience, or at least its highlights, can illustrate that resourcefulness. Cleopatra ascended the throne in 51 B.C.E. at the age of seventeen or eighteen. She succeeded her father, the mercurial and rather questionable character Ptolemy XII Auletes (the "Piper").[13] She shared that throne with her half-brother, Ptolemy XIII, only ten years old at the time, a boy whom, as convention dictated, she duly married. The situation already held the potential for danger and disruption. Conflict soon arose in the court. The advisers of young Ptolemy, portrayed in our sources as sinister and ambitious ministers, one of them (inevitably) a eunuch, succeeded in driving Cleopatra out of Alexandria, in order to give themselves free rein in the exercise of influence over the king and the kingdom. The expulsion, it appears, occurred some time around spring 48.[14] Soon after, the two contending parties confronted each other in arms: the troops of Ptolemy XIII arrayed against the forces assembled by Cleopatra near Pelusium on the Mediterranean in the easternmost part of Egypt.

A greater international crisis, however, supervened: the Roman civil war. Pompeius Magnus, defeated by Caesar at Pharsalos, fled to Egypt, where he might hope to find rescue and support from the Roman troops who had served with his lieutenant and political ally A. Gabinius, who were now settled in Egypt, and who formed part of the army of Ptolemy under the command of Achillas. It proved to be a fatal miscalculation. A party met Pompey when he landed on the coast and treacherously murdered him, one of the assassins being a former Pompeian officer. For that deed, young Ptolemy, now just thirteen years old, earned a place among arch-traitors in Dante's *Inferno*—together with such distinguished company as Cain and Judas.[15] If Ptolemy or his advisers expected that this deed would earn some credit with Julius Caesar or, more likely, that it would induce Caesar to bypass Egypt, his mission accomplished by others, they were soon disillusioned. Caesar arrived in Alexandria at the beginning of October 48, spurned the grisly head of Pompey (duly embalmed in Egyptian custom) that was offered to him, wept when he saw it, but did not leave. The Roman *imperator*, instead, announced that he would take it upon himself to arbitrate the dispute between Ptolemy and Cleopatra. That is not exactly what the ministers of Ptolemy had been hoping for. The young teenager turned up to make his case, to induce Caesar to leave, and to forestall the arrival of Cleopatra. But the ever resourceful queen, according to the most celebrated of Cleopatra stories, reached the palace concealed in a carpet, and popped out at the most opportune moment when the carpet unrolled at the feet of Caesar. The event triggered momentous upheaval. Civil war soon erupted in the streets of Alexandria, during the course of which Caesar barely escaped with his life when he had to swim two hundred yards to safety, clad in full armor. The outcome is no secret. Caesar emerged victorious, the advisers of young Ptolemy were slain, the king himself drowned in the Nile, and Cleopatra was declared queen of Egypt, co-ruler with her surviving younger brother Ptolemy XIV, who was a mere twelve years of age. Caesar and Cleopatra then enjoyed a leisurely trip up the Nile in the early months of 47, the stuff of which many later legends were made.[16]

So much for the narrative, up to this point. It will be salutary to pause and ponder some interesting features of it, especially as they relate to the accomplishments and influence of Cleopatra. She had been driven out of Alexandria and toppled from her throne by a palace cabal in spring 48. Yet, just a few months later, she managed to show up with an army to confront the forces of her enemy at Pelusium.[17] Obviously, the queen had not suffered the fate of a homeless and impotent refugee in the meantime. She must have had substantial resources to call upon, and a strong base of support for her endeavors in Egypt or its environs. Just where did this backing come from? The sources do not specify, an infuriating omission and a frustration to inquiry. The question rarely surfaces in the scholarship.[18]

Cleopatra, as we happen to know, had taken steps at the beginning of her reign to show concern for, and interest in, the native traditions of the Egyptian populace. Her first act as queen of which we have knowledge was involvement in the installation of the Bucchis bull, the sacred animal of Hermonthis in Upper Egypt, in March 51. An inscription carved on a stele informs us of Cleopatra's presence at the ceremony of transporting the sacred bull to its shrine and installing it there. She proceeded at a later date to finance a birth temple at Hermonthis, entrenching further her connections with the rituals and priesthood of Upper Egypt.[19] The queen showed similar consideration to the shrine of the Apis bull at Memphis. As other epigraphic evidence declares, she provided generous financial support for the Apis cult, confirmed by priestly requests for the god's blessing at the birth of Cleopatra's son.[20] Papyrological testimony takes us a little further, disclosing Cleopatra's solicitude for the population in Alexandria. A decree guaranteeing a supply of grain for the city during a period of drought and potential famine supplies that information.[21] That is not much to go on. But it would be reasonable to infer that gestures and actions of this sort permitted the queen to develop a base of support in the capital and in the countryside. It did not hurt that she had a fluent command of Egyptian, the first Ptolemaic ruler ever to learn the native language of the realm.[22]

When the counselors and officers of Ptolemy drove Cleopatra out of Alexandria in 48, she, evidently, had somewhere to go and had sympathetic supporters to receive her. Unfortunately, we have no firm information as to where she went. The Byzantine historian John Malalas reports, from sources unidentified and now lost to us, that she went to the Thebaid in Upper Egypt.[23] That is a plausible enough destination, in view of her earlier overtures to the dwellers of that region. But trust in so late a source is risky. Moreover, since Cleopatra eventually turned up with an army in Pelusium, Upper Egypt is hardly the most obvious route. This would not rule out recruitment by supporters in the Thebaid, or even a brief appearance by the queen in the region. But the main gathering of troops must be from elsewhere. Appian's account, that Cleopatra collected forces in Syria, makes logical sense in terms of geography.[24] That notice also corresponds to the independent testimony of Strabo, who has Cleopatra make for Syria upon her expulsion from Alexandria.[25] Just what is meant by "Syria" here eludes our grasp. The notice appears in a segment of Strabo's *Geography* devoted to Egypt, and he is not concerned to be any more specific. He might well refer to Coele-Syria, Phoenicia, Palestine, or the area in general that lies eastward of Egypt and in the direction of Syria.[26] It may be relevant that the coinage of Ascalon, an important coastal city of Palestine, north of Gaza, includes the issue of a tetradrachm in the year 49 B.C.E. that displays a portrait of Cleopatra, one in a long series of coins honoring Ptolemaic rulers.[27] A suggestion that Ascalon formed the base of Cleopatra's operations can be no more than speculation. But the coinage, certainly, confirms her prestige and authority in areas lying within Egypt's sphere of influence. Whatever the location and whatever the means, the fact that Cleopatra recruited a military force of some size and in a relatively short time is quite striking testimony to the extent of her effectiveness and the power of her appeal. Cleopatra, though just twenty-one in 48 B.C.E., was a figure of esteem and a force to be reckoned with.

CAESAR AND CLEOPATRA IN ALEXANDRIA

This takes the tale to the notorious episode of Cleopatra's initial appearance before Caesar. Nothing is likely to eradicate the memorable image of the queen smuggled into Caesar's headquarters rolled up in an oriental rug. Countless movies and television specials have accorded that image canonical status. Scholars have made no effort to undo the impression.[28] Few would pay attention if they did. But skepticism has a place here. One ought at least to underscore the fact, for it is not generally known, that the carpet caper appears in one source only: Plutarch's *Life of Caesar*. Nor does he actually mention anything as elegant as a carpet: Cleopatra was wrapped up in bed clothes![29] The event receives no mention in Appian, nor in Suetonius, fond as he is of pretty stories. It failed to make it even into Dio Cassius' narrative, although that historian does speak of Cleopatra employing every feminine wile, beautifying herself to the hilt, in order to exercise her charms on Caesar.[30] The nearest approximation to Plutarch's version comes in the poet Lucan's fanciful invention that has Cleopatra bribe Ptolemy's guards to give her access to the harbor, slip through in a small boat, and thus reach Caesar. But there is no rug.[31]

The unassailable fact is that Caesar elected to arbitrate differences between Ptolemy and Cleopatra, based on the authority of the will of Ptolemy Auletes, their father, who had left the kingdom to both jointly. The will had provided that the Roman people should have responsibility for seeing that his wishes were fulfilled. Caesar, as representative of Rome, showed no reluctance to take on the role of arbiter and enforcer. To that end he summoned both brother and sister before his tribunal in Alexandria to resolve the matter without arms.[32] So Cleopatra, if she made an appearance at all at that point, did not have to arrive surreptitiously in folds of bedding. Indeed, the very idea that the queen of Egypt, claimant to that proud and commanding kingdom, heir to the ancient dynasty of the Ptolemies, and a devotee of formal ceremonies and ritual, would make her initial appearance to Julius Caesar wrapped in a rug is virtually unthinkable.[33]

Caesar faced formidable difficulties in bringing stability to the tumultuous political scene in Egypt. He doubtless knew (or was soon advised) that a settlement in that land had little chance of success without acknowledging the claims of Cleopatra. Politics took priority. That is not to deny a love-match between Caesar and the queen of Egypt. These were two highly gifted, engaging, and passionate people, no mere calculating machines. But Caesar had to confront the political realities on the ground in Egypt. His small band of soldiers was in no position to control the situation. A settlement that sought to reconcile the parties, divide authority, and encourage harmony reflected long-standing Roman practice in arbitrating differences among royal rivals in the east.[34] It is striking that Caesar not only endorsed the joint rule of Cleopatra and Ptolemy XIII over Egypt but awarded the island of Cyprus to their younger siblings, Arsinoe and Ptolemy XIV, despite the fact that Cyprus was a Roman province! The *imperator* had now resigned it to the Ptolemies. The decision, plainly, did not derive from infatuation with Cleopatra. Indeed, she may have well bridled at this distribution of territory to all her siblings. Nonetheless, the ceding of Cyprus represented a notable gesture in the direction of reviving the glory days of Ptolemaic Egypt, and the queen could take pride in that.[35]

All these plans, in any case, came to naught. Civil war broke out in Alexandria, Ptolemy XIII drowned in the Nile, and his younger sister Arsinoe was placed under arrest by Caesar. Cleopatra's principal rivals had now been removed, and her support in the land was doubtless undiminished, perhaps enhanced. She did not need a trip up the Nile with Caesar to shore up her position. That brief holiday may, indeed, have been more passion than politics.[36] The birth of a child, the future Caesarion, came some time later.[37]

The passion, however, was not all-consuming. Caesar himself left shortly after, in the summer of 47, to pursue his civil war against the followers and supporters of Pompey in Asia Minor and in North Africa, campaigns that lasted several months. He then returned to Rome to celebrate four triumphs in the autumn of 46.[38] He had not seen Cleopatra for a year. Indeed, he had made certain to leave a large garrison in Alexandria in the meantime, thus to exercise surveillance in the area.[39] Caesar does not appear to have been obsessed by lust for Cleopatra. The queen arrived in Rome probably in the late autumn of 46, and, as we have seen, about a month later Caesar went off to Spain for half a year. Cleopatra had, doubtless, brought her infant child with her to Rome. But Caesar never acknowledged him as his son during his lifetime—and did not name him in the will.[40]

CLEOPATRA'S STAY IN ROME RECONSIDERED

The critical question now resurfaces. What was Cleopatra doing in Rome? Dio Cassius supplies an important bit of information that needs to be taken seriously. The historian reports that Caesar enrolled Cleopatra and her new husband, that is the young boy, her brother Ptolemy XIV, as friends and allies of the Roman people.[41] That notice makes eminently good sense. The establishment or reiteration of formal bonds between Rome and foreign principalities had long held a central place in the diplomatic conventions of Rome and the Hellenistic states, particularly when the situation was an unsettled one. Eastern kings and pretenders whose hold on their thrones was shaky or contested found it eminently useful to obtain Roman endorsement for their claims, a convenient instrument to parade before their countrymen. Such negotiations often occurred through an exchange of diplomatic missions. But royal visitors to Rome for the purpose of affirming official diplomatic relationships were by no means unknown. We have ample testimony for rulers or would-be rulers of Pergamum, Bithynia, Cappadocia, and Syria who traveled to Rome in the second century B.C.E.[42] In each instance they came to seek recognition of their claims or acknowledgment of their legitimacy. More tellingly, the practice was by no means unknown to the Ptolemies themselves. In the mid second century, when the two brothers Ptolemy Philometor and Ptolemy Euergetes vied for power and territory, each found himself at different times in Rome, presenting his own case and pressing it upon the Roman senate. Philometor even used the ploy of taking up lodging in a cheap rental in Rome, far from the posh districts of the city, thereby shaming the senate, once they learned of it, into plying him with gifts, presenting him with a royal robe, and setting him up in properly luxurious quarters.[43] Caesar's generous hospitality to Cleopatra would ensure that no similar embarrassment to Rome would take place this time. Philometor's rival Euergetes had used a rather different route in his effort to secure influence in Rome. He offered himself in marriage to that most aristocratic of Roman widows, Cornelia, daughter of Scipio Africanus and mother of the Gracchi. The noble lady, to her credit, turned him down flat.[44] So Cleopatra's presence and objectives in Rome had some very pertinent precedents.

But one need not reach back to the second century B.C.E. for suitable models. Ptolemy Auletes, Cleopatra's father, had distributed a significant amount of cash in Rome in order to secure recognition of his hold on the Egyptian throne. The strategy backfired badly, for it stirred considerable negative publicity and widespread unpopularity in Alexandria. The reaction prompted an expulsion of the king from his kingdom. Auletes then turned up again in Rome, there to plead his cause and to furnish more funds to Roman leaders, borrowing heavily in order to finance this endeavor.[45] It is noteworthy that, among other things, he obtained official recognition as friend and ally of Rome in 59, and he was housed in the comfortable Alban estate of Pompeius Magnus.[46]

In short, clear precedents existed for the arrival, the aims, and even the housing of Cleopatra in Rome. She knew the value of an official recognition by Roman authorities, a treaty of friendship and alliance, and all the proper diplomatic niceties that would accompany it—reasons enough for Cleopatra to spend time in Rome. This form of certification would substantially shore up her position at home. The respect paid to foreign dignitaries, including the provision of lodging commensurate with their status, fits the conventional expectations of diplomatic practice. No need to conjure up sexual longings to explain the visit.[47]

The likelihood of an ostentatious, luxury-laden, and opulent entrance into the city diminishes dramatically. The fanciful re-creation of Manciewicz, however memorable, has no warrant or plausibility. Such a procession would have given gratuitous offense, and was in the interests neither of Caesar nor of Cleopatra. The visit itself, in fact, did not make much of a splash at all. None of our sources mentions a notable or conspicuous arrival by the queen. She was simply another foreign ruler arriving on a diplomatic mission. Most Romans may have failed to notice her.

So far, so good. Cleopatra came on an appropriate mission: to receive formal recognition, to obtain a treaty, and to bolster her authority in Egypt. But why then did she stay? The official ceremonies could not have required an extended stretch of time. It would be difficult to imagine a lengthy and boisterous debate in the senate on this matter while Caesar ran the show. What then would be the point of Cleopatra remaining in Rome for a year and half, indeed, presumably, much longer had it not been for the Ides of March?[48] If she wished to solidify her position in Egypt, she could hardly do so very effectively at that distance and with so long an absence. The frequent religious rituals, ceremonies, and festivals in her home country demanded or expected the presence of the ruler. To abandon them indefinitely would cost Cleopatra dearly and bring a loss of favor with gods and subjects alike. Could she run the risk of leaving the government and administration of the land in the hands of others? Who was minding the store in Egypt?

The solution may lie elsewhere. A very different possibility merits consideration. Perhaps Cleopatra did not, in fact, stay in Rome for those eighteen months or more. A return to Egypt shortly after obtaining a formal alliance with Rome would be practical and logical, thereby allowing her to resume control of the government. Why should we believe that she remained in Rome—especially after Caesar left for Spain?

The critical evidence comes from Cicero, a contemporary and an eyewitness, providing seemingly incontrovertible information. Cicero's letters provide unimpeachable testimony to the date of Cleopatra's departure from Rome, that is shortly after the Ides of March 44. A continued presence in Rome would be uncomfortable, possibly hazardous, for the queen. The first reference to her exit comes in a letter of mid-April, just a month after Caesar's assassination.[49] Cicero then alludes to the event in a number of subsequent letters to Atticus over the next two months. This would seem to be decisive for the length of stay, as all historians have assumed. Yet Cicero never breathes a word about Cleopatra during the whole of her supposed eighteen-month sojourn. Is this a weak argument from silence? Not really. We possess about two hundred letters of Cicero that fall in this very period from the autumn of 46 to the spring of 44, none of which indicates that Cicero was even aware of Cleopatra's existence.

Another piece of testimony bears, interestingly, on this question. Suetonius, in his biography of Caesar, makes an intriguing and largely unnoticed remark: that Cleopatra had been summoned to the city, that Caesar provided her with the highest honors and rewards, and *that he sent her back*![50] The mention of distinctions bestowed upon the queen must refer to the titles accorded her of "friend and ally of Rome" and to the customary gifts provided for visiting royalty. But more important is the notice that she evidently departed with Caesar's blessing. The return to Egypt may well have come not long after Cleopatra got her official imprimatur from Roman authorities—and before Caesar went off to Spain. If that reconstruction is right, it would explain very nicely why matters remained stable and under control in Egypt. The queen was there.

A letter of Cicero may, indeed, offer a hint to that effect. He wrote to Atticus in June 44, venting some spleen against Cleopatra. "I hate the queen," he exploded. Just why is unclear. Cicero expressed great irritation at the queen's haughty demeanor when she dwelled in her gardens across the Tiber.[51] But the specific complaint remains obscure. Cicero makes a cryptic remark about some literary material, perhaps manuscripts, promised to him but never delivered. What matters, however, is that Cicero takes a particular jab at a certain Ammonius, evidently a minister of the queen, who guaranteed the carrying out of her promises but failed to implement them.[52] That statement could well imply that, at the time Cicero received his promises, Cleopatra was no longer around in person and that her agents were acting for her. One might even take the conjecture a step further, with due caution and tentativeness, and suggest that Ammonius pledged the delivery of manuscripts (or copies thereof) from the library in Alexandria and that Cleopatra never brought them.[53] But there is no need to press that speculation further.

Cleopatra was, of course, back in Rome before the Ides of March in 44. But we do not know how long she had been there. It may, indeed, not have been very long at all. One might bear in mind that Caesar himself had only returned to Rome from the Spanish wars and from a stay in Gaul in October of 45.[54] What brought Cleopatra back to Rome (on this reconstruction) can only be guessed at. But an educated guess is possible. Now that Caesar's foes abroad had at last been defeated, the dictator could undertake a wholesale set of institutional and administrative reforms in earnest. Among them, as we know, were major plans for the Roman provinces, including a wide-ranging policy of colonization, both east and west. These involved, among other things, structural changes in provincial administration.[55] Another item of significance in this connection needs to be taken into account. It had not been very long before, in the 60s to be precise, that some Romans seriously discussed the possibility of annexing Egypt as a province.[56]

Under those circumstances, Cleopatra's reappearance in Rome seems almost mandatory. She needed to reiterate her claims on the realm of her forefathers. Even if the queen did not fear the conversion of Egypt into a province, she would surely have a stake in any discussion of the fate of Cyprus. Caesar, as we have seen, had awarded the island in 48 to Cleopatra's younger siblings, Arsinoe and Ptolemy XIV.[57] The situation had changed markedly since then. Arsinoe had been arrested by Caesar and had marched in his triumph, and young Ptolemy was now Cleopatra's husband. The queen would, understandably, be concerned about a possible Roman re-annexation of Cyprus, a jewel in the crown of Ptolemaic overseas possessions.[58]

Good reasons, therefore, existed for a return visit to Rome. A logical time would come after Caesar's triumphant re-entry and after his plans for reorganizing the empire began to take shape and receive public notice. The queen arrived perhaps early in the year 44.[59] Of course, she would not stay after the stabbing of Caesar. Protection of the homeland at a time of such uncertainty and potential upheaval in the Mediterranean was vital. Cicero describes her exit as "flight" (*fuga*), perhaps a rhetorical flourish. But he certainly does not make much of it, even telling Atticus that her departure is a matter of no great concern.[60] Subsequent Ciceronian references to her withdrawal from Rome are equally brief and elliptical, with an obscure allusion to some rumor whose meaning is never elucidated.[61] The rumor may have touched, in some way, on the situation and future of her son Caesarion and the supposed paternity of Caesar, an issue that would inevitably have been raised by the absence of any mention of him in the dictator's will. Cicero does, in any case, hint darkly that there is something he would wish to know about the queen and "that Caesar."[62] The reference surely points to Caesarion, who evidently left the city with his mother. In that connection it may be significant that Cicero says nothing about Ptolemy XIV, Cleopatra's consort and young brother. We know that he accompanied her on the trip to Rome in the autumn of 46.[63] The fact that he goes unmentioned in 44 supplies some support for the idea that this was a separate trip on Cleopatra's part. The teenager, in any case, perished in the summer of 44, allegedly poisoned by Cleopatra.[64] Perhaps he had attempted, or been a figurehead for, an attempted coup in her absence.

So much for speculation. The results can be summed up with brevity. The eighteen-month sojourn of Cleopatra in Rome, so peculiar, puzzling, and paradoxical, though accepted almost unquestioningly by modern scholars, may be a phantom. It belongs in the same category with fantasies about Cleopatra holding court in Caesar's gardens, having her gilded statue set up in the temple of Venus Genetrix, and turning Caesar's dictatorship into a Hellenistic monarchy—not to mention the Hollywood fantasy of Cleopatra entering the portals of Rome in a dazzling splendor and a grandiose eastern ostentation that no Roman would have tolerated for a moment. Once one dispenses with these ornate trappings, and with the extremely implausible (even nearly inconceivable) notion that Cleopatra dawdled for more than a year and half in Rome while her own kingdom rocked rudderless, a very different and more comprehensible scenario emerges.

It might be reconstructed as follows. Cleopatra came to Rome in 46 to secure official recognition, a signed and sealed treaty of alliance that would strengthen her hand in Egypt and accord her international esteem in the Near East. That she may have resumed her dalliance with Caesar, after not having seen him for over a year, is perfectly possible, but probably irrelevant. Caesar, in any case, left Rome for Spain a month later. Cleopatra did not even have an erotic motive for staying. She had accomplished her mission very satisfactorily and could return home, with treaties, honors, and gifts in her luggage, as undisputed ruler of the Ptolemaic lands. When she next visited Rome, a similar purpose prompted the trip: to press the claims of her dynastic privileges at a time when the Caesarian government was reconsidering provincial policy in the eastern Mediterranean. Although Cleopatra may have had to leave earlier than anticipated when Caesar was treacherously murdered, she appears to have accomplished what she intended anyway. Egypt stood intact and even Cyprus remained under the authority of the queen. Cleopatra was no mere sexual predator, and certainly no plaything of Caesar, lolling about his gardens in Trastevere and loyally awaiting his return. She was queen of Egypt, Cyrene, and Cyprus, heir to the long and proud dynasty of the Ptolemies, and now professed mother of Caesar's son, a passionate but also very astute woman who had maneuvered Rome—and would maneuver Rome again—into advancing the interests of the Ptolemaic legacy.

NOTES

1. On the views of Cleopatra in antiquity, see I. Becher, *Das Bild der Kleopatra in der griechischen und lateinischen Literatur* (1966) and, with particular attention to Augustan writers, M. Wyke, "Augustan Cleopatras: Female Power and Poetic Authority," in A. Powell, ed. *Roman Poetry and Propaganda in the Age of Augustus* (1992): 98–140. On the modern reception of Cleopatra, see L. Hughes-Hallett, *Cleopatra: Histories, Dreams and Distortions* (1990): 113–307.

2. On Elizabeth Taylor and the Manciewicz film, see Hughes-Hallett (1990): 276–92; M. Wyke, *Projecting the Past: Ancient Rome, Cinema and History* (1997): 100–109.

3. See A. Bouché-Leclercq, *Histoire des Lagides* (1904): 2.220–22; E. Meyer, *Caesars Monarchie und das Principat des Pompeius* (1922): 521–522; L. R. Taylor, *The Divinity of the Roman Emperor* (1931): 61–62, 75–76; J. H. Collins, "Caesar and the Corruption of Power," *Historia* 4 (1955): 462–465; H. Volkmann, *Cleopatra: A Study in Politics and Propaganda* (1958): 79–82; J. H. Collins, "On the Date and Interpretation of the Bellum Civile," *American Journal of Philology* 80 (1959): 125–30; cf. M. Grant, *Cleopatra: A Biography* (1972): 88–89; P. Southern, *Cleopatra* (1999): 57–58. On the honors and distinctions themselves, see H. Gesche, *Die Vergottung Caesars* (1968): 12–55; M. Gelzer, *Caesar: Politician and Statesman* (1968): 307–22; S. Weinstock, *Divus Iulius* (1971).: 270–341; E. Rawson, "Caesar: Civil War and Dictatorship," in J. A. Crook, A. Lintott, and E. Rawson, eds., *Cambridge Ancient History²*, vol. 9 (1994): 461–67. A useful survey of scholarship in H. Gesche, *Caesar* (1976): 162–172.

4. Nicolaus Damascenus, *FGrH* 90 F 68; Suetonius, *Divus Iulius* 79.3. See Meyer (1922): 520–21.

5. Suetonius, *Divus Iulius* 52.3; cf. Dio Cassius 44.7.3; Aulus Gellius 16.7.12. This is accepted, e.g., by Meyer (1922): 525–26; Volkmann (1958): 87–88.

6. E.g., J. P. V. D. Balsdon, "The Ides of March," *Historia* 7 (1958): 86; Gelzer (1968): 323; Grant (1972): 92; C. Meier, *Caesar* (1995): 477.

7. Appian, *Bella Civilia* 2.102.

8. See, e.g., Volkmann (1958): 80–81; Gelzer (1968): 287; Grant (1972): 87–88; Z. Yavetz, *Caesar in der öffentlichen Meinung* (1979): 199; P. Green, *From Alexander to Actium: The Historical Evolution of the Hellenistic Age* (1990): 669; Meier (1995): 446; Southern (1999): 57–58.

9. Would Cleopatra's image have been installed in the temple as a reincarnation of Isis, and hence a counterpart of Venus? So, e.g., Grant (1972): 88. Not very likely. Roman officialdom had frowned on the cult of Isis in recent years. See Dio Cassius 40.47, 42.26; Varro, *apud* Tertullian, *ad Nationes* 1.10. Cf. the discussion of S. Takács, *Isis and Sarapis in the Roman World* (1995): 56–67. Note also that Cleopatra's official presentation as the new Isis occurred only in 34, according to Plutarch, *Life of Antony* 54.

10. Dio Cassius 51.22.3. It should be observed that the forum of Caesar, where the temple of Venus Genetrix stood, was itself only brought to completion by Octavian. Hence, the dedication of a captured statue of Cleopatra would be most suitable for the new conqueror.

11. Caesar himself had returned to Rome from the wars in the East and in North Africa in July 46 and had celebrated four triumphs in late September. Cleopatra, probably, arrived shortly thereafter. Caesar left Rome again around November. See Gelzer (1968): 286–87, 293.

12. Plutarch, *Life of Antony* 27.3–5. C. B. R. Pelling, *Plutarch: Life of Antony* (1988): 191, questions the mastery of so many languages, citing Valerius Maximus 8.7.ext.16 on Mithridates as commanding twenty-two tongues. But this is not a common literary convention. The absence of Latin from the repertoire (not remarked upon by Plutarch) lends some credibility. Whatever exaggeration exists in Plutarch's account, Cleopatra's charms and conversational skills are noted also by Dio Cassius, 42.34.4.

13. On the reign of Aulètes, see Bouché-Leclercq (1904): 2.116–76; E. Bevan, *A History of Egypt under the Ptolemaic Dynasty* (1927): 342–58; E. Olshausen, *Rom und Aegypten von 116 bis 52 v. Chr.* (1963); E. Bloedow, *Beiträge zur Geschichte des Ptolemaeus XII* (1963); P. M. Fraser, *Ptolemaic Alexandria* (1972): 1.124–26; 2.222–27.

14. Caesar, *Bellum Civile* 3.103, with reference to September or October 48, places the expulsion "a few months earlier." Cf. Appian, *Bella Civilia* 2.84. The effort of Grant (1972): 52–53, accepted by Green (1990): 664, to set this in 50 B.C.E., is unpersuasive. See the cogent arguments of C. Peek, "She, Like a Good King: A Reconstruction of the Career of Kleopatra VII" (diss. 2000).

15. Dante, *Inferno* 33.124.

16. On the civil war in Alexandria, see the fullest treatment, in P. Graindor, *La Guerre d'Alexandrie* (1931), with a useful summary in J. Carcopino, *Jules César* (1968): 415–30. A more detailed study of particular aspects is given by H. Heinen, *Rom und Ägypten von 51 bis 47 v. Chr.* (1966): 69–165.

17. Caesar, *Bellum Civile* 3.103; Strabo 17.1.11; Appian, *Bella Civilia* 2.84; Livy, *Periochae* 111; Plutarch, *Life of Caesar* 48.3; *Life of Pompey* 77.1; Dio Cassius 42.3.1.

18. It is treated now, in sound and sensible fashion, by Peek (2000).

19. R. Mond and M. Myers, *The Bucheum* (1934): 2.12; Grant (1972): 46–47.

20. D. Thompson, *Memphis under the Ptolemies* (1988): 124–25; Peek (2000).

21. *BGU* 1730; cf. Peek (2000).

22. Plutarch, *Life of Antony* 27.4–5.

23. Malalas, *Chron.* 10.

24. Appian, *Bella Civilia* 2.84.

25. Strabo 17.1.11. Green's (1990: 664) reconstruction of the route is pure conjecture.

26. Cf. Strabo 16.2.1–2. See the excellent treatment by Peek (2000).

27. *British Museum Catalogue*, Palestine, 107–8; A.B. Brett, "A New Cleopatra Tetradrachm of Ascalon," *American Journal of Archaeology* 41 (1937): 452–63; Grant (1972): 53; Peek (2000).

28. See, e.g., Volkmann (1958): 66; Heinen (1966): 82–85; Grant (1972): 63; Green (1990): 663; Meier (1995): 408; Southern (1999): 32.

29. Plutarch, *Life of Caesar* 49.

30. Dio Cassius 42.34.3–6.

31. Lucan, 10.37.

32. Caesar, *Bellum Civile* 3.105–7: "He made it known that he wanted King Ptolemy and his sister Cleopatra to disband their armies and to settle their disputes before his tribunal rather than by force of arms between themselves." Ostendit sibi placere regem Ptolemaeum atque eius sororem Cleopatram exercitus, quos haberent, dimittere et de controversiis apud se potius quam inter se armis disceptare; Dio Cassius 42.35.4–6. Cf. Strabo 17.11. Caesar may have claimed a standing here on the grounds of Auletes' will that had granted Rome a guardianship (ἐπιμέλεια) over his children; Dio Cassius 42.35.5. See D. Braund, *Rome and the Friendly King* (1984): 137. Dio Cassius, 42.34.3–6, reports that Cleopatra took the initiative and contacted Caesar first; accepted by Heinen (1966): 82.

33. Heinen (1966): 84, also worries about the propriety of appearances here but suggests that Cleopatra emerged from the bedclothes at an outer door—before Caesar saw her!

34. On Roman arbitration and mediation in the Greek East, see E.S. Gruen, *The Hellenistic World and the Coming of Rome* (1984): 101–26.

35. Dio Cassius 42.35.4–6. Not surprisingly, Caesar passes over this in his own account.

36. The trip took place, probably, in the spring of 47; Appian, *Bella Civilia* 2.90; Suetonius, *Divus Iulius* 52.1. Cf. Heinen (1966): 148–49.

37. On the date of Caesarion's birth and the paternity of Caesar, much disputed matters but not of relevance here, see J.P.V.D. Balsdon, "Review of Volkmann, *Cleopatra*," *Classical Review* 10 (1960): 68–71; H. Heinen, "Cäsar und Kaisarion," *Historia* 18 (1969): 181–203, with earlier bibliography; Grant (1972): 83–85.

38. Sources in T.R.S. Broughton, *The Magistrates of the Roman Republic* (1952): 2.293.

39. *Bellum Alexandrinum* 33; Suetonius, *Divus Iulius* 76; Appian, *Bella Civilia* 4.59.

40. Nicolaus Damascenus, *FGrH* 90 F 68. It was, of course, in Antony's interests later to claim that Caesar had acknowledged the paternity; Suetonius, *Divus Iulius* 52.2.

41. Dio Cassius 43.27.3. Dio adds that Caesar incurred displeasure by housing the royal family

in his personal estate. But courtesy and hospitality to foreign dignitaries had a long history in the Republic.

42. Gruen (1984): 573–75, 580–92, 665–67.

43. Valerius Maximus 1.1.1f; Diodorus Siculus 31.18.1–2.

44. Plutarch, *Life of Tiberius Gracchus* 1.4.

45. Cicero, *Pro Rabirio Postumo* 4; Dio Cassius 39.12.1–2.

46. Cicero, *Pro Rabirio Postumo* 6; Caesar, *Bellum Civile* 3.107; Strabo 17.1.11; Suetonius, *Divus Iulius* 54; Dio Cassius 39.12.1.

47. Caesar, in fact, had had yet another affair since leaving Cleopatra in Egypt, this one with the wife of the king of Mauretania, while he was on campaign in Spain; Suetonius, *Divus Iulius* 52.1. He was rarely idle on this front.

48. Even a year and a half is a conservative estimate. Caesar's reform of the calendar in 46 required the addition of approximately two months between November and December of that year. See Gelzer (1968): 289, with references. Cleopatra would have had quite a long stay. Thanks are due to Tim Cornell for making the point in discussion.

49. Cicero, *ad Atticum* 14.8.1.

50. Suetonius, *Divus Iulius* 52.1: "Having summoned her to the city and bestowed the greatest distinctions and gifts upon her, he sent her back again." Accitam in urbem non nisi maximis honoribus praemiisque auctam remisit. Insofar as scholars have taken note of this passage, they have usually dismissed it as inaccurate or wrong; e.g. Bouché-Leclercq (1904) 2.222; Meyer (1922): 522; Gelzer (1968): 287 note 2. Grant (1972: 91) allows for the possibility of a "short visit to Egypt" but does not pursue the matter.

51. Cicero, *ad Atticum* 15.15.2: "I cannot recall without intense pain the arrogance of the queen herself when she lived in the gardens across the Tiber." Superbiam autem ipsius reginae, cum esset trans Tiberim in hortis, commemorare sine magno dolore non possum.

52. Cicero, *ad Atticum* 15.15.2: "I hate the queen. Ammonius knows that I have good reason to do so, that guarantor of her promises. The promised writings suited my position and I would have ventured to declare it in a public forum." Reginam odi. Id me iure facere scit sponsor promissorum eius Ammonius, quae quidem promissa erant φιλόλογα et dignitatis meae, ut uel in contione dicere auderem.

53. The Library had not burned down, as is often thought, during the Alexandrine war. See E. A. Parsons, *The Alexandrian Library* (1952): 188–319; L. Canfora, *The Vanished Library* (1989): 66–82.

54. Velleius Paterculus 2.56.3.

55. On Caesar's measures concerning the provinces, see Gelzer (1968): 288–89, 296–99, 311–12; Yavetz (1979): 109–10; E. Rawson (1994) 442–48.

56. Cicero, *de rege Alexandrino* fr. 1–2, 6–7; *de lege Agraria* 1.1, 2.41–44; Plutarch, *Life of Crassus* 13.1–2; Suetonius, *Divus Iulius* 11. Cf. T. P. Wiseman, "The Senate and the Populares, 69–60 B.C.," in J. A. Crook, A. Lintott, and E. Rawson, eds., *Cambridge Ancient History* 2, vol. 9 (1994) 345–46.

57. Dio Cassius 42.35.5.

58. Cleopatra still held the island in 43, under the control of one of her military appointees; Appian *Bella Civilia* 4.61. We also possess a bronze coin representing Cleopatra with a baby, presumably Caesarion, and the monogram KUPR for Cyprus; *British Museum Catalogue*, Cyprus, CXVII. This was evidently minted in 47 or early 46 when Caesarion was a baby, and indicates that Cleopatra controlled the island in those years. See Heinen (1969): 189. The effort of P. J. Bicknell, "Caesar, Antony, Cleopatra, and Cyprus," *Latomus* 36 (1977) 325–34, to deny that Cleopatra possessed the island before 44, based on Strabo 14.6.6, is unconvincing. Strabo clearly conflates material here. See Heinen (1966): 91, 145; T. Schrapel, *Das Reich der Kleopatra* (1996): 106–24.

59. This would require a trip outside the normal season and one that might occupy two or three

months. If Cleopatra left Alexandria after Caesar's return to Rome, she could hardly have arrived before the beginning of 44. The northwesterly winds, even in the sailing season, made the trip from Alexandria to Rome much longer than that from Rome to Alexandria, as few as nine days for the one and as many as seventy days for the other; L. Casson, *Ships and Seamanship in the Ancient World* (1971): 282–83, 289, 297–99.

60. Cicero, *ad Atticum* 14.8.1: "The queen's flight does not bother me." Reginae fuga mihi non molesta est.

61. Cicero, *ad Atticum* 14.20.2, 15.1.5: "The rumor about the queen is losing strength." De regina rumor extinguitur; 15.4.4: "I would like the story about the queen to be true." De regina verum velim.

62. Cicero, *ad Atticum* 14.20.2: "I would like to know the truth about the queen and about that Caesar too." De regina velim atque etiam de Caesare illo.

63. Dio Cassius 43.28.3.

64. Josephus, *Antiquitates Judaicae* 15.89; Josephus, *Contra Apionem* 2.58; Porphyry, *FGrH* 260, F 2.16.

3

Dying Like a Queen

The Story of Cleopatra and the Asp(s) in Antiquity

Robert A. Gurval

The sultry actress Barbara Stanwyck never played the role of the Egyptian queen, Cleopatra. The accomplished director, Howard Hawks, best known today for his light comedies like *Bringing up Baby* (1938) and *His Girl Friday* (1940) and suspenseful film-noirs like *To Have and Have Not* (1944) and *The Big Sleep* (1946), never made a film about ancient Rome. But in their most famous collaboration, *Ball of Fire* (1941), the death of Cleopatra makes a surprising appearance. In a brief but cleverly scripted scene the Hollywood film intimates popular culture's familiarity with the legendary queen and at the same time its befuddlement at the manner and meaning of her death. The classic screwball comedy casts eight bachelor professors in the seclusion of a New York brownstone, writing what their chief and the film's male romantic lead, Gary Cooper, describe as a work that endeavors to catalog all human knowledge—an encyclopedia to rival Britannica's. A garbage man from the Bronx, seeing all those books in the windows, interrupts their serious intellectual pursuits to find out something about Cleopatra. A "quizzola" on the radio, "a corn crunches quiz-quiz"—to give some flavor of the era and the film's dialogue—invites participants to send cereal box-tops and answers, asking a multiple-choice question. Cleopatra died: (A) from swallowing a needle; (B) from a snake-bite; (C) from hiccups.[1]

The history professor, looking more like an amiable, pot-bellied Hollywood-type Roman senator, takes up the challenge with assurance and a ready entry: "Cleopatra, born in 69 B.C., daughter of Ptolemy XIII [*sic* Hollywood's reckoning], killed herself on the 29th day of August 30 B.C. by placing an *asp* to her bosom." The anxious sanitation worker is left puzzled. "A what?" The slow repetition of the exotic-sounding reptilian's name, *as-p*, followed at once by the clipped explanation, "a small snake," eventually satisfies the would-be contestant and leads to a second question on English grammar. The subsequent arrival of Stanwyck (in the saucy role of a brazen burlesque singer who seduces the sexually timid Cooper) evokes comic associations between ancient and modern femme fatales.

But the story of Cleopatra and the asp is hardly the stuff of trivia questions. Students of ancient history, readers of Shakespearean drama, and fans of Hollywood epic films would have no problem choosing the correct response. Historians may investigate the ambition and political strategies of the cunning Egyptian queen, while others, like the seventeenth-century French philosopher Pascal, may doubt her legendary beauty by casting aspersion on the length of her nose.[2] Yet others may question her incestuous Greek ethnicity and racial identity,[3] but we all know how Cleopatra met her demise. She killed herself with an asp (or two).[4] The ancient literary tradition, so rich and so diverse in its authors and texts, later transformed into an even more potent and enduring cultural depository of poetry, drama, and film, from the fourteenth century to the twentieth, from Chaucer to Claudette Colbert, leaves only the most skeptical of us still in the dark.

We know that Cleopatra died by a snake-bite but what did that mean? The ancients, both contemporaries and later generations, favored this story, though many were inclined to reserve doubts. Aelian, who wrote a seventeen-book study of animals, wearing several caps at the same time, philosopher, zoologist, and amateur coroner, considered the manner of the queen's death "a puzzle" (αἴνιγμα) that could only be solved by the careful observation of two faint puncture marks on her corpse and the discovery of an asp's trail in the sand (*On the History of Animals* 9.11). The geographer Strabo, a contemporary of the events, offered two standard alternatives for the cause of death (*Geography* 17.1.10): either the bite of an asp or poison applied directly into her body. On one critical point, however, all the ancient sources agreed. Cleopatra took her own life. In the last century before the birth of Christ, not unlike our own, where foul play and the fantastic sensationalize almost every famous death, this absence of suspicion is in itself astonishing. Modern historians are more dubious, tempted to suspect compulsion, intrigue, and murder. Such speculations I leave to others. Instead I want to explore not the historical truths of Cleopatra's death but its ancient literary fictions—historical, poetic, and scientific. This inquiry will be more selective and illustrative than exhaustive. My choice of texts for analysis will privilege a lyric ode, a papyrus fragment, a biography, and a medical treatise. By such a pattern of representation, I wish to explore some of the various and diverse ways that the ancients saw Cleopatra's death, interpreted its meaning, and incorporated its image into the thematics of their own works. I would like to conclude this inquiry with a forward glance at Chaucer and the makings of a medieval tradition of a Cleopatra who died for love. But before literary representations, the asp as symbol.

FIGURE 7. (*top*) Bronze coin of Cleopatra VII. Diademed portrait of Cleopatra, holding her son Ptolemy XV, Caesarion. British Museum, London. Photo credit the Trustees of the British Museum/Art Resource, NY.

ASP AS SYMBOL

In the heyday of the 1920s Egyptomania, following Howard Carter's discovery of a tomb and boy-pharaoh in the Valley of the Kings, a German scholar, Wilhelm Spiegelberg, first posed the scholarly question of why Cleopatra died by a snake-bite. Less than four pages in length, the discussion was brief but its impact was profound and long lasting.[5] In sum, Spiegelberg argued that by selecting the bite of an asp as a means of suicide, Cleopatra was seeking to die in a noble fashion befitting her royal position and divine ancestry. The asp was the uraeus, the sacred serpent of the Sun-god Re, which, raised aloft on the royal crown as an emblem, protected its regal holder from the harm of enemies. The bite of this snake, according to a passage in Josephus,[6] conferred immortality upon its hapless victims. No descendant of the Macedonian Ptolemies, Cleopatra was the last daughter of an ancient and illustrious line of Pharaohs. Cleopatra's final deed was thus a symbolic ritual act that returned the queen to her heavenly father and by a public spectacle, however privately achieved, proclaimed an apotheosis to her native peoples and foreign conquerors.[7]

To borrow a current metaphor of political journalism, the snake symbolism doesn't have legs. First, in the tradition of the Ptolemaic queens before her, even those who did not rule in their own right, Cleopatra associated herself closely with both Aphrodite and Isis and was even worshipped as goddess in her own lifetime. Like her father, Ptolemy Auletes, the "New Dionysos" (*Neos Dionysos*) and her son Caesarion, the "New Horos" (*Neos Horos*), Cleopatra was the "New Isis" (*Nea Isis*).[8] On dedicatory stelai and public inscriptions, which fused Pharaonic tradition and Greek text, she was Queen Cleopatra, the Goddess

FIGURE 8. (*bottom*) Silver denarius of Cleopatra VII and Marc Antony, 32 B.C.E.
Diademed portrait of Cleopatra, at lower right, stem of prow. British Museum, London.
Photo credit the Trustees of the British Museum/Art Resource, NY.

(*Thea*), the Younger (*Neotera*). On Cleopatra's coins, the obverse of one of the
earliest extant specimens depicts a bust of Cleopatra nursing an infant Caesarion
(perhaps suggestive of Isis and Horus, or Aphrodite and Eros), without inscription. Its reverse offers a double cornucopia and identifies her simply as "Queen
Cleopatra" (ΒΑΣΙΛΙΣΣΑΣ ΚΛΕΟΠΑΤΡΑΣ) (Fig. 7).[9] Later, on one of Antony's
Roman issues, the heads of the Roman *triumvir* and Egyptian queen are featured
on opposite sides. Antony vaunts his conquest over Armenia by a military slogan
(ANTONI ARMENIA DEVICTA) and a king's tiara on one side, and Cleopatra
receives her titles "Queen, the Daughter of Kings, the Mother of Sons Who Are
Kings" (CLEOPATRAE REGINAE REGVM FILIORVM REGVM) on the other
(Fig. 8).[10] In sum, Cleopatra didn't need a snake to proclaim herself a goddess or
queen.

Second, the authority of Flavius Josephus is surely suspect (*Against Apion* 2.7.86).

Nos itaque asinis neque honorem neque potestatem aliquam damus, sicut Aegyptii
crocodillis et aspidibus, quando eos qui ab istis mordentur et a crocodillis rapiun-
tur felices et deo dignos arbitrantur.

And so we (i.e., the Jews) afford no honor or power to jack-asses, such as the
Egyptians do to crocodiles and asps, since they believe that men bitten by them or
carried off by crocodiles are blessed and deemed worthy in the eyes of God.

The philhellenic Jewish historian is hardly a credible or unbiased witness
to Egyptian practice and religious belief. His attitude to Cleopatra, no friend
to Judaea, is pointed in his solitary comment about her death ("but she indeed

suffered the punishment that was due," *sed illa quidem poenam subiit compe-tentem, Against Apion* 2.60). To be sure, Herodotus as early as the fifth century B.C.E. testifies to the Egyptian custom that the bodies of those who drown in the Nile or are killed by crocodiles, whether Egyptian or foreign, cannot be touched except by priests of the Nile, and that they must be embalmed and buried in a consecrated place (Herodotus 2.90). But the early Greek historian says nothing about asps, and, in any case, neither Herodotus nor even Josephus speaks of apotheosis.[11]

Finally, Cleopatra's death is not unique. Demetrios of Phaleron (born ca. 350 B.C.E.), Athenian *strategos*, peripatetic philosopher, and court librarian of Ptolemy I Soter, also perished by the bite of an asp. The circumstances are curiously similar. Having advised Ptolemy I unsuccessfully to bequeath his throne to the children of Eurydice, Demetrios soon fell into disfavor with the new ruler (Ptolemy II Philadelphus), the son of Berenice, who had supplanted Eurydice as queen. The exact circumstances of Demetrios' death are unclear but Diogenes Laertius explains that before his death he was kept under guard in a confined space and in despair took up the asp.[12] But the manner of his death was well known. The Roman orator Cicero could allude to it in a public speech ("but in that same kingdom of Egypt, he was deprived of his life when an asp was applied to his body," *in eodem isto Aegyptio regno aspide ad corpus admota vita esse privatum, On Behalf of Rabirius Postumus* 23), and an epigram even survives in the Greek Anthology (7.113).

Ἀνεῖλεν ἀσπὶς τὸν σοφὸν Δημήτριον
   ἰὸν ἔχουσα πολὺν
ἄσμηκτον, οὐ στίλβουσα φῶς ἀπ' ὀμμάτων,
   ἀλλ' ἀίδην μέλανα

An asp killed the philosopher Demetrios,
   a snake that had much poison
   that could not be smeared off,
darting not light from its eyes but black death.

The asp then was not reserved for only Pharaohs and queens. Like hemlock in classical Athens, the snake venom might even have been a condemned man's choice of suicide in Hellenistic Egypt. Or even public execution, as documented in an ancient medical text, where the author records that he witnessed many of these deaths in Alexandria.[13]

What then did the *aspis* suggest to the ancient Greeks and Romans? In general, throughout the Mediterranean world, snakes were a source of both reverence and mortal fear, often associated with the protection of sacred places, tombs, altars, and the home. Seen as portentous creatures who lurk underground and emerge on a sudden from their lairs, snakes also betokened ill omen and death. The asp

FIGURE 9. Guido Reni, *Cleopatra* (ca. 1638–39). Galleria Palatina, Palazzo Pitti, Florence. Photo credit Scala/Art Resource, NY.

was a foreign snake, indigenous to the north African coast and first attested in ancient classical literature in Herodotus' account of Libya (4.191). Already in Aristophanes, puns played upon the two meanings of the word (*Wasps* 23), as the noun ἀσπὶς, since Homer, had more commonly signified a warrior's circular shield. In a Hellenistic poem on the remedies against poisonous animals, the asp's epithet is "blood-red" (φοινήεσσαν, Nicander, *Theriaca* 158), alluding more to its deadly bite than to its color. In modern biological terms, the ancient asp is most likely the Egyptian cobra, the *Naja Haje*. No puny snake such as Guido Reni imagined in his seventeenth-century painting, now in the Palazzo Pitti in Florence (Fig. 9), the Egyptian cobra is large and thick bodied, with a broad head and big eye.

For Cicero, the foreign word *aspis* evoked Egypt and supplied a handy example of ethnic perversity (*Tusculan Disputations* 5.78).[14]

> Aegyptiorum morem quis ignorat? quorum imbutae mentes pravitatis erroribus quamvis carnificinam prius subierint quam ibim aut aspidem aut felem aut canem aut crocodilum violent.

> Who does not know of the custom of the Egyptians? Their minds are infected with depraved delusions and they would sooner submit to torture than do harm to an ibis or asp or cat or dog or crocodile.

Pliny the Elder, the chronicler of an ancient encyclopedia to rival Britannica's in thirty-seven books, sums up the ancient knowledge about the asp (*Natural History* 29.65).

Aspides percussos torpore et somno necant, omnium serpentium minime sanabiles. Sed venenum earum, si sanguinem attigit aut recens volnus, statim interemit; si inveteratum ulcus, tardius. De cetero potum quantalibet copia non nocet. Non enim est tabifica vis.

The asps kill those they strike by numbness and sleep, the least curable of all snakes. But the poison of these snakes, if it penetrates the blood or recent wound, kills at once, if an old sore, more slowly. On the other hand, if the poison is drunk, whatever the quantity, it's harmless. For it is not a force that consumes or wastes the body.

Significantly, the observations of science, most of all of the likeness of the poison's effects to sleep (*somnus*), function as a recurrent, meaningful literary motif in accounts of the queen's death. The elegist Propertius, a contemporary witness, watched the image of the queen as it was carried in the triumphal procession along the Sacra Via (*Elegies* 3.11.53–54).

bracchia spectavi sacris admorsa colubris
    et trahere occultum membra soporis iter.

I saw her arms bitten by the sacred snakes and her limbs draw sleep's hidden path.

Even in the truncated epitome of the historian Florus, Cleopatra is described as released in death as if in sleep (*sic morte quasi somno soluta est*, 2.21.11). And finally, by the third century C.E., the ancient typology of African snakes, classified by size and color, included the *hypnale*, so named because of its somniferous death and identified by its most famous victim, Cleopatra (C. Iulius Solinus, *A Collection of Memorable Facts* 27.31).

Hypnale, quod somno necat, teste etiam Cleopatra emitur ad mortem.

The hypnale, which kills by sleep, is procured for death, as even Cleopatra can attest.

One other feature of Pliny's prosaic description of symptoms merits mention at this point, namely, the swiftness and potency of the poison when the victim is bitten. Death by asp-bite is not immediate but most victims usually do not live more than a few hours.[15] The snake's poison is a powerful neurotoxin, where yields are typically of 175–300 mg., and a lethal dose for humans is 15–20 mg. Aelian also testifies to the asp's deadly bite (*On the History of Animals* 1.54), where men survive only by drastic measures such as excision or cautery (*On the History of Animals* 2.5). Historical records and modern science might refute the high mortality rate of stricken victims,[16] but for the ancients the only effective recourse is sucking out the venom. Indeed, a race of North African men, the Psylli, was distinguished simply for their immunity to the bite of snakes. In historical narratives of Cleopatra's death, the Psylli are prominently featured but arrive too late (Suetonius, *Life of Divus Augustus* 17.4).

> Et Antonium quidem seras condiciones pacis temptantem ad mortem adegit viditque mortuum. Cleopatrae, quam servatam triumpho magno opere cupiebat, etiam Psyllos admovit, qui venenum ac virus exsugerent, quod perisse morsu aspidis putabatur.

> Though Antony tried to make terms for peace at the final hour, he [i.e., Octavian] forced him to commit suicide and viewed his dead body; as for Cleopatra, whom he greatly desired to be kept alive for his triumph, he brought in even Psylli, men who suck out poison and venom, because it was thought she died from the bite of an asp.

The account from the Roman biographer is probably taken directly from the *Memoirs* of Augustus, repeated in later sources (Cassius Dio, *Roman History* 51.14.4–6, and Orosius, *Histories Against the Pagans* 6.19). Its purpose, if, in fact, it derives from the victor himself, is twofold. It not only lent credence to the belief in the snake-bite,[17] but it also, perhaps more importantly, serves to testify to her conqueror's efforts—or the *appearance* of these efforts—to keep the queen alive and put her in his triumphal parade. So too the record from the otherwise lost historical narrative of Livy (Porphyrio, *On Horace's Odes* 1.37.30).

> Nam et Titus Livius refert illam cum de industria ab Augusto in captivitate indulgentius tractaretur identidem dicere solitam fuisse: 'οὐ θριαμβεύσομαι.'

> For also Titus Livius says that when Cleopatra was kept under guard and handled by Augustus with diligence and special care, she was accustomed to say over and again: "I will not be led in triumph."

The phrase "I will not be led in triumph" (οὐ θριαμβεύσομαι—a striking example of the first-person verb, middle form but passive in meaning) constitutes the Egyptian queen's last words, spoken appropriately in Greek. The opposing dynamics of compulsion and freedom reflected conversely in the deaths of Antony and Cleopatra may be understood in the complex arrangement of political strategies and competition set out in Paul Plass' engaging study of suicide, *The Game of Death in Ancient Rome: Arena Sport and Political Suicide* (1995).[18] In Plass' theoretical model of Roman suicide and reciprocity, the players are emperor and his opposition. Outcomes of their "games" can be tabulated in columns, where contestants score a win, loss, or draw, depending upon their preemptive moves, method of death, and subsequent reputation. Plass, who was more interested in exploring the tactics and language of political suicide practiced by the Roman aristocracy in the age of the emperors, omits from his discussion Cleopatra. But I would like to suggest that Horace, a contemporary lyric poet, chalks one up for the Egyptian queen in his poetic fiction of her suicide and confrontation with Octavian.

THE POLITICS OF SUICIDE AND HORACE'S ODES 1.37

Nunc est bibendum, nunc pede libero
pulsanda tellus, nunc Saliaribus
   ornare pulvinar deorum
     tempus erat dapibus, sodales.

antehac nefas depromere, Caecubum
cellis avitis, dum Capitolio
   regina dementes ruinas
     funus et imperio parabat

contaminato cum grege turpium
morbo virorum, quidlibet impotens
   sperare fortunaque dulci
     ebria. sed minuit furorem

vix una sospes navis ab ignibus,
mentemque lymphatam Mareotico
   redegit in veros timores
     Caesar ab Italia volantem

remis adurgens, accipiter velut
mollis columbas aut leporem citus
   venator in campis nivalis
     Haemoniae, daret ut catenis

fatale monstrum; quae generosius
perire quaerens nec muliebriter
   expavit ensem nec latentis
     classe cita reparavit oras;

ausa et iacentem visere regiam
vultu sereno, fortis et asperas
   tractare serpentes, ut atrum
     corpore combiberet venenum,

deliberata morte ferocior,
saevis Liburnis scilicet invidens
   privata deduci superbo
     non humilis mulier triumpho.

Now we should drink, now with foot free we should beat the ground, now with Salian banquets it was the time to deck the gods' sacred couches, my friends. Before it was wrong to take down the Caecuban wine from cellars of old, while against the

Capitol the queen was plotting crazed ruin and destruction to our empire, with her polluted flock of men, foul with disease, unrestrained to hope for whatever and with the sweetness of Fortune intoxicated. But her madness weakened when scarcely one ship was saved from the fires, and her mind, sloshed with Mareotic wine, was driven to true fears. As she flew from Italy, Caesar pressed on with oars, just as a hawk hunts soft doves or the swift hunter chases the hare in the fields of snowy Haemonia, in order to put in chains the fateful prodigy of death. But she, more nobly, sought to perish, and not like a woman feared the sword nor gained hidden shores with her swift fleet. Daring to gaze upon her fallen kingdom with tranquil composure, she handled the fierce serpents to drink into her body their black poison. The more emboldened deliberating on death, she scorned to be led in cruel Libernian galleys, unqueened and in haughty—no lowly woman, she!—triumph.

In its thirty-two verses, Horace's *Odes* 1.37 is the earliest literary document that records the death of Cleopatra. Better known today as simply Horace's Cleopatra Ode, the poem has evoked a wide range of modern critical response. What had once been disparaged as an "almost perfect example of bad taste in the field of 'applied patriotism'" at the end of the Second World War gave way in the late 1950s to "a kind of manifesto of the Horatian imagination," as Steele Commager described it, where the poet's treatment of the foreign queen reflects his "fondness for seeing every situation in a double aspect."[19] This double aspect aptly characterizes the inherent tensions and tight dichotomy of the lyric composition's overall structure and shifting moods. Reckless abandon and dissolute conduct yield to sober reflection and a noble death. However much the ode purports to be a jubilant song of triumph, blending a rich encomiastic tradition of Greek poetry and Roman symposia, sifting elements of public ritual and private ceremonies, the "transfiguration of the vanquished," to take the phrase from one recent critic,[20] commands our attention.

Horace's poem commences with a twofold allusion. First, the emphatic, *nunc est bibendum*, borrows from the opening of an ode of Alcaeus, a sixth-century B.C.E. Greek lyric poet: "Now we must get drunk and drink with some force, since Myrsilus is dead."[21] Like the suicide of Cleopatra, the death of the tyrant who once ruled the city of Mytilene occasioned the celebration. Second, the thrice repeated *nunc* also gives an impassioned intertextuality to the anxious question that began Horace's own ninth epode (*Quando . . . bibam*, "When, blessed Maecenas, will I drink with you . . . the Caecuban wine, stored away for festal banquets?"). The poet now makes it clear that not the successful outcome of the Actian victory, but rather the death of the foreign enemy brought an end to the bitter conflict and a more fitting reason to celebrate. Supported by her flock of foul and degraded men, the *regina* assails the Capitol, the very center and symbol of Rome; she lacks restraint or is reckless (*impotens*) to hope for everything (*quidlibet . . . sperare*), and she is intoxicated (*ebria*) with the sweetness of fortune. It is a recurrent motif of drinking ("we should drink" *bibendum*, line 1; "intoxicated" *ebria*, line 12; "sloshed" *lymphatam*, line 14; "to drink into" *combiberet*, line 28), a drinking both literal and metaphorical, that impels the dramatic action of the ode, linking celebrant and conquered. The pointed contrast, however, is not between drunken queen and symposiastic poet, but between the conflicting emotions of the queen who at the end of the ode drinks in her body the black poison.

This stark transition in attitudes expressed toward the queen is precipitated by her defeat. Appearing in the very center of the ode, the victor Octavian is the catalyst who forces the queen into a realization of her own situation. Steele Commager once deemed this description of Actium as "the poet's alchemy of historic fact." Historians have not been so flattering. Not "scarcely one ship" escaped the fires of destruction, but the entire fleet of the queen (sixty ships) and with it her royal treasury returned intact and safe to the harbor of Alexandria. The ever cautious Octavian did not attempt immediately to pursue the vanquished pair to Egypt. In fact, it was almost eleven months to the day from the date of the battle before Octavian entered Alexandria. And as every Roman reader was fully aware, the naval battle was not waged in Italy, but off the coast of northwestern Greece. Despite the potent phrase *ab Italia*, Cleopatra did not flee from Italian shores.

In lines 17–20, the similes of the chase between hawk and tender dove, between swift hunter and hare, are Homeric and as such they are encomiastic in nature, extolling the Roman victor to heroic heights. But the epic imagery, however laudatory on one level, intensifies a chase that was not really a chase, and exaggerates an ambition to shackle the queen in chains that was never fulfilled. The heavy-sounding chains, marking off the stanza with two long syllables, slow down the pace of action and take the reader out of the Thessalian landscape and back to the aftermath of Actium. The *catenae*, of course, allude to the claims of Octavian's desire to lead the defeated in his triumphal procession,[22] but coming so abruptly after the simile of tracking a hare in the snow (*leporem*), the chains leave at least modern readers disquieted by the harsh contrast of images.

In his influential study, *Polyhymnia: The Rhetoric of Horatian Lyric Discourse* (1991), Gregson Davis alerts us to the encomiastic techniques practiced in the Horatian odes, articulating the view that the noble suicide of the queen merely serves to exalt the Roman victor; in *The Sorrows of the Ancient Romans* (1993), Carlin Barton aptly reminds us that the importance of an equal opponent or worthy adversary to the Romans can never be overstressed.[23] So too the ancient rhetorical term *amplificatio* augments this reading of the ode. According to Quintilian, an aspiring orator should magnify one thing by an allusion to another. The *virtus* of Scipio is thus increased by extolling the fame of Hannibal in war, and the courage of the Germans and Gauls serves only to enhance the *gloria* of Caesar (*Oratorical Institutions* 8.4.20).[24] The rhetorical impulse of the poem certainly enhances the queen (and Caesar too) but her nobility is found neither in battle nor in her famous name but in death, or more precisely in her preparation and method of death.

In the political world of recurrent civil war and public violence in the late Republic, suicide emerged as a powerful tool of opposition. By the early Empire in the first century of this era, it had become a way of life, or of death, one might even say, for an aristocratic elite and the enemies of the Caesars. Philosophers, orators, and historians provided the moral values, rhetorical tropes, and narrative examples to fashion what may legitimately be called a "culture of suicide." Some have even used the term "cult." If a cult, the hero of worship was none other than Cato the Younger, the ever obstinate, unrelenting foe of Julius Caesar, who defiantly spurned the gesture of *clementia* by the victor and took his own life. Almost at once, the realities of his suicide at Utica gave way to a myth. As Miriam Griffin put it, Roman suicide had its own "etiquette and style," and the dying moments of famous men (and women) became a popular literary topos in imperial Rome. Death was not only the moment but the means by which a sullied life could be redeemed and ennobled. The emperor Otho, almost a century later, found admirers even among his enemies when he fell on his dagger. An effeminate senator, Caninius Rebilus gains the historian Tacitus' attention (*Annals* 13.30) in an obituary brief: "distinguished in legal learning and wealth, he escaped the miseries of decrepit old age by opening his veins. No one believed that he could muster the resolve to take his own life since he was branded like a woman for his sexual passions." But, to the Stoic adherents in the principate of Nero, Cato provided the paradigmatic exemplum on the topic of "disdaining death" (*ad contemnendam mortem*, Seneca, *Moral Epistles* 24.6). In the philosopher's view, Cato took the necessary provisions for the two instruments required at the end (*duo haec in rebus extremis instrumenta prospexerat*). The first is the will or moral resolve to die (*ut vellet mori*), and the other is the means to do so (*ut posset*).

Like Cato, Cleopatra faces death with calmness and defiance. The arresting, ambiguous *fatale monstrum* (line 21) is the focus of multiple and disputed meanings—less of our English "monster" and more of the Latin "prodigy," something of supernatural awe or wonder. With this phrase and with the nominative relative *quae*, Cleopatra replaces Caesar as subject. The poet's description of events in Alexandria prepares us for the queen's final act. She seeks to die in a manner more befitting her race (*generosius*). The comparative adverb intimates the options that befall the defeated Roman general on the battlefield: to fall upon the sword or to escape in flight. Cleopatra disdains both, showing no fear, in denial of her gender (*nec muliebriter*). Instead she dares to accept her situation as she gazes upon her fallen kingdom (*iacentem . . . regiam*). Her mind once described as frenzied (*lymphatam*) now displays signs of inner, almost Stoic tranquility (*voltu sereno*, line 26).

Poison (*venenum*, line 27) emphatically concludes the penultimate stanza. If the subject of his poem was merely the demise of the queen, Horace could have chosen to leave the reader with the melodramatic final scene of suicide. The transfiguration of Cleopatra from drunken whore to noble queen would have been complete at line 28. But Horace's ode ends instead on a powerful note of steadfast defiance and dubious victory. *Triumpho* is the poem's final word. With its displaced adjective, "haughty" (*superbo*), the triumph literally encircles the phrase *non humilis mulier*, but even as the victor holds the queen in his grasp, ever eager to lead her in chains, she eludes him. Like Cato's, Cleopatra's death is a liberation. In the final act of her life, Cleopatra takes control of her own fate and mitigates the nature of her public defeat by a private act of self-control and self-imposed death. The ode, which began as a song of triumph, leaves the reader reflecting not upon the victor, his glorious conquest, and the public occasion, but upon the queen, her resolve, boldness in taking up the deadly snakes, and private victory. In the end, it is the *non humilis mulier* who usurps the claim of *triumphator.*[25]

SUICIDE AS MELODRAMA: CLEOPATRA AND POISON

The dramatic reversals of Cleopatra's life and death appealed to other poets. The Egyptian queen makes a startling appearance in Virgil's *Aeneid*, where she leads barking Anubis against the might of Rome but whose death is foreshadowed with a multiplicity of emotions. And in at least one, perhaps two, historical epic poems, she and Antony were featured.

The meager papyrus fragments of a Latin epic poem have not fared well since the report of their discovery in a villa at Herculaneum in the eighteenth century. Most of the scholarly attention has fallen, not unfairly, on the charred but more copious Greek texts of the Epicurean philosopher Philodemos. A recent author of a history of Latin literature deemed the fragments "wretched" (whether he meant their quality of verse or extant condition is left unclear).[26] He attributes them with almost indifference to the obscure Augustan poet Gaius Rabirius. Once commonly known as *The Poem on the Actian Battle* (*Carmen de Bello Actiaco*), the fragments instead depict the last days of Antony and Cleopatra in Alexandria.[27] Two columns are of interest here, the fifth and sixth.

column V   [dele]ctumqu[e loc]um quo noxia turba co[i]ret
praeberetque suae spectacula tri[s]tia mortis.
qualis ad instantis acies cum tela parantur,
signa tubae classesque simul terrestribus armis,
est facies ea visa loci, cum saeva coirent
instrumenta necis, v[a]rio congesta paratu.
und[i]que sic illuc campo deforme co[a]c[t]um
omne vagabatur leti genus, omne timoris.

And the place was chosen where the throng of criminals might assemble and offer grim spectacles of their own deaths. Just as when for pressing battles, weapons are prepared, standards, war-trumpets, fleets along with land armies, so the appearance of this place seemed when the cruel instruments of murder were assembled, heaped up in various preparations: thus on all sides gathered together there on the field every foul kind of death, every kind of fear wandered.

column VI   [hic i]acet [absumptus f]erro, tu[m]et [il]le ven[eno]
aut pendente [su]is cervicibus aspide mollem
labitur in somnum trahiturque libidine mortis:
percutit [ad]flatu brevis hunc sine morsibus anguis,
volnere seu t[e]nui pars inlita parva veneni-
ocius interem[i]t, laqueis pars cogitur artis
in[t]ersaeptam animam pressis effundere venis,
i[n]mersisque f[r]eto clauserunt guttura fauces.
[h]as inter strages solio descendit et inter

This one lies cut off by the sword, that one is swollen with poison or another, with an asp hanging from his own neck, slips into slumber and is dragged by the desire of death. A small snake kills this one with its breath without a bite, some whose wounds are smeared with a fine amount of poison perish quickly, others are forced to pour forth their choked spirit from blocked passageways, and the throats of those drowned in water closed their openings. Amid these slaughters she descends from her throne and among . . .

The poet of the papyri fragments describes preparations of death: a chosen place (*delectum locum*), a guilty crowd assembled (*noxia turba*), and grim spectacles (*spectacula tristia*). They are likened to a battlefield of armaments and men. Victims of various deaths are listed in an eerie series (death by the sword; poison; snakes; choking; and drowning), which is then is cut off by the torn edges of the roll as the queen descends from her throne amidst these slaughters (*has inter strages*). Critics react with moral disgust or aesthetic disparagement. It has been argued that these macabre stories stem from a hostile propaganda to implicate Cleopatra with the cruelty and inhumanity of the Hellenistic kings.[28] If propaganda, it is interesting that the later sources that describe the same incident do not vilify the queen but speak instead of a woman resolved to find a way to die. Aelian remarks simply, "as Augustus came near, she made tests at her banquets for a painless death" (ὅτε τοῦ Σεβαστοῦ προσιόντος ἀνώδυνον θάνατον ἐν τοῖς συμποσίοις ἐβασάνιζε, Aelian, *On the History of Animals* 9.11). Plutarch offers a fuller account (*Life of Antony* 71.6–8).

Κλεοπάτρα δὲ φαρμάκων θανασίμων συνῆγε παντοδαπὰς δυνάμεις, ὧν ἑκάστης τὸ ἀνώδυνον ἐλέγχουσα, προὔβαλλε. τοῖς ἐπὶ θανάτῳ φρουρουμένοις. ἐπεὶ δ᾽ ἑώρα τὰς μὲν ὠκυμόρους τὴν ὀξύτητα τοῦ θανάτου δι᾽ ὀδύνης ἐπιφερούσας, τὰς δὲ πραοτέρας τάχος οὐκ ἐχούσας, τῶν θηρίων ἀπεπειρᾶτο, θεωμένης αὐτῆς ἕτερον ἑτέρῳ προσφερόντων. ἐποίει δὲ τοῦτο καθ᾽ ἡμέραν· καὶ σχεδὸν ἐν πᾶσι μόνον εὕρισκε τὸ δῆγμα τῆς ἀσπίδος ἄνευ σπασμοῦ καὶ στεναγμοῦ κάρον ὑπνώδη καὶ καταφορὰν ἐφελκόμενον, ἱδρῶτι μαλακῷ τοῦ προσώπου καὶ τῶν αἰσθητηρίων ἀμαυρώσει παραλυομένων ῥᾳδίως, καὶ δυσχεραινόντων πρὸς τὰς ἐξεγέρσεις καὶ ἀνακλήσεις ὥσπερ οἱ βαθέως καθεύδοντες.

Cleopatra was collecting all kinds of deadly poisons. She tested the painless action of each one by giving them to men sentenced to death. But when she learned that swift poisons involved a sharpness of death through pain but the mild did not have quickness, she made trial of venomous beasts, watching with her own eyes as they were applied, one creature to the body of another. And this she did daily, and from nearly all of them she found that the bite of an asp alone was without convulsion or groaning, bringing on a sleepful torpor and lethargy, with a gentle perspiration on the face where the senses were easily relaxed and difficult to be awakened or aroused like those who are in a deep sleep.

The biographer here speaks dispassionately of experiments and results, carefully preparing his reader for the queen's death and the asp. Cleopatra sought a death, swift, painless, and without harm to her body. To the ancients, the bite of an asp exactly fit such requirements. Greek writers of medicine and science privilege the story of the snake-bite by incorporating Cleopatra into their discussions of the asp, but, of course, these discussions may not actually reflect a queen's resolve to die; they merely validate such a resolve and perpetuate the myth of a dignified and defiant suicide. By the second century of this era this myth, disseminated and codified in various kinds of prose and poetic texts, identified Cleopatra in a Greco-Roman world as a celebrated figure of regal power shrouded in mystery and eroticism.

The queen's death is missing from the fragments but in another badly mutilated column the Fate Atropos (whose very name means "cannot be turned back"), watches her unseen.

column VII   haec regina gerit. procul hanc occulta videbat
              Atropos inrid[e]ns [in]ter diversa vagantem
              consilia interitus, quam iam qua fata manerent.

The queen does these things. Hidden at a distance, Atropos saw her as her mind wandered among different plans of death, the woman whom already some fate awaited.

The foreboding of the queen's death, anticipated without knowledge, recalls the Virgilian ekphrasis of the hero's shield at the end of the eighth book of the *Aeneid*. The poet/craftsman offers three distinct glimpses of the queen that offer conflicting portraits of Rome's hated enemy. It is the second of these where the queen's death is intimated as she is marshalling her forces into battle (8.696–97).

regina in mediis patrio vocat agmina sistro
necdum etiam geminos a tergo respicit anguis.

The queen in the midst calls her troops with her ancestral rattle, not even yet does
she look back at the twin snakes behind her.

The suicide of the Egyptian *regina* has no logical function or place in the
description of Actium. Neither the historical circumstances nor the geographic
locale allows it. But Virgil alludes to her death with a melodramatic scene of dire
foreshadowing. The snakes are, of course, the asp(s) by which the queen kills
herself but to any reader of the epic poem these twin snakes (*geminos anguis*) are
familiar creatures betokening death and destruction. In their most memorable
appearance in book two, the paired monsters emerge from the depths of a calm
sea and make their way to the shores of Troy to slay the priest Laocoön and his
sons (2.203–5).

ecce autem gemini a Tenedo tranquilla per alta
(horresco referens) immensis orbibus angues
incumbunt pelago pariterque ad litora tendunt.

Behold however from Tenedos over the still deep (I shudder in telling it) twin snakes
with huge coils press upon the sea and together they head to the shore.

Like Laocoön, Cleopatra falls victim to the inescapable destiny of the gods.
Her ignorance of forthcoming doom parallels the other tragic victims of the
Aeneid, above all, the Carthaginian queen, Dido, who is introduced in the epic
as "unknowing of fate" (*fati nescia*, 1.299) and later called "unlucky" (*infelix*,
1.749).

The final vignette of the battle of Actium portrays Cleopatra in flight where
hostile rumors of her cowardice and betrayal of Antony circulated in the victor's
propaganda (*Aeneid* 8.707–13).

ipsa videbatur ventis regina vocatis
vela dare et laxos iam iamque immittere funis.
illam inter caedes pallentem morte futura
fecerat Ignipotens undis et Iapyge ferri
contra autem magno maerentem corpore Nilum
pandentemque sinus et tota veste vocantem
caeruleum in gremium latebrosaque flumina victos.

The queen herself is seen calling upon the winds, spreading sails and now, almost
now slackening the ropes. Amid the slaughter the god of fire had fashioned her
pale at her approaching death, borne off by the waves and by the western wind.
But opposite was the Nile, grieving with his great body and expanding his folds
and with all his garment calling into his dark-blue bosom and hidden streams the
conquered.

Significantly, the queen is caught in flight after the appearance of Apollo Actius, the god, who in the preceding lines struck fear into all the Egyptians and foreign races who fled (*omnis eo terrore Aegyptus et Indi / omnis Arabs, omnes vertebant terga Sabaei*, 8.705–6). Not as the treacherous woman who abandons Antony, Cleopatra flees to the grieving Nile in the company of the conquered (*victos* abruptly cuts off the scene in line 713). The poet's last words to describe Cleopatra, "pale at her approaching death" (*pallentem morte futura*), appropriately echo an earlier climactic scene in the epic where Dido prepares to kill herself (*pallida morte futura*, 4.644). The legendary Carthaginian queen, who ruled a foreign people in a distant land and seduced the Trojan hero as he lingered on the coast of north Africa, prefigures the historical Cleopatra. The parallels would be striking even if Virgil had not altered the perhaps duplicitous character of Dido found in earlier Roman epic.[29] Virgil's complex image of the Carthaginian queen mixes initial admiration with final sorrow and pity. She is no sorceress or shameless seducer but a tragic victim of divine intervention whose frenzied passion gives way to irrational action and self-destruction. Virgil's Dido destabilizes the Roman chauvinism and confidence that had constructed the Egyptian queen as a hated figure of sexual perversity, female dominance, and ruin. By recalling the poignant suicide of Dido at the very moment of Cleopatra's flight from Actium, Virgil takes the first literary steps in shaping Cleopatra as a figure of romance and epic melodrama. It is an irony of literature and culture that the enemy of Rome informed Virgil's portrait of the Carthaginian queen, but the literary Cleopatras such as appear in the papyrus fragment are inspired as much by the poetics of the Virgilian character of Dido as by the realities of the historical event or Augustan propaganda surrounding the historical figure.

NARRATIVES OF DEATH: PLUTARCH AND GALEN

"Plutarch tells it magnificently."[30] So C. B. R. Pelling, the Cambridge commentator on the Greek biographer's *Life of Antony*, exclaims in his prefatory remarks on Cleopatra's suicide. The merits of Plutarch *qua* narrator have long been acknowledged. Narratological analysis of his text, however, is less common. One reading interprets the final scenes as a dramatic mimesis of the Isis-Osiris myth.[31] Plutarch, who is also the author of a monograph *On Isis and Osiris*, calls attention to the queen's assimilation to Isis at key moments earlier in the biography of her Roman lover but significantly refrains from an explicit association or even inference of divinity in the depiction of Cleopatra's death.

The final act is played out in three dramatic scenes: (1) the death of Antony; (2) the encounter with Octavian; and (3) the death of Cleopatra. Plutarch includes familiar themes of deceit and guile in his characterization of Cleopatra but unlike the third-century Greek historian Cassius Dio, for example, the biographer strains to explain them. When Cleopatra sends false word of her death to Antony, it is because she feared his anger and madness when he was deserted by his forces. Antony cries out that Cleopatra betrayed him but Plutarch's narrative does not implicate the queen. After her capture when she meets her conqueror in an interview, Dio constructs a scene of failed seduction. Plutarch, on the other hand, who acknowledges that the queen still retains her charm and boldness of beauty despite her mournful condition, subverts the outcome of the exchange into a victory for the queen: "And so Octavian departed, thinking that he had deceived her but he was deceived instead" (ἐξηπατημένος δὲ μᾶλλον, 83.5).

Later, Cleopatra laments her dead Antony, and her final words intimately entwine the lovers in death. A text in contrast, the subsequent narrative by the historian Cassius Dio, offers similar declarations of her love and desire to be buried beside Antony. The words, however, are spoken to Octavian in guile to win his favor. Plutarch's Cleopatra, like a tragic character, prays instead to the spirit of her lover, invoking the power of the Roman gods, that he not abandon his wife (γυναῖκα) nor permit a triumph to be celebrated over himself in her person (μηδ' ἐν ἐμοὶ περιίδῃς θριαμβευόμενον σεαυτόν, the same verb that the Roman historian Livy recorded). But Plutarch takes this legendary gesture of defiance ("I will not be led in triumph"), softens its tone by applying the verb to Antony in the passive voice and inserts it into the queen's funereal dirge to her Roman husband. At the final moment Cleopatra is more the lover of Antony than the enemy of Octavian. Having wreathed and kissed his urn, Cleopatra, like a Roman Cato, prepares for death with a bath and sumptuous meal.

A man from the country enters with a basket of figs. The guards, impressed by their size and beauty, take a sample. Cleopatra dines and sends off a tablet to Octavian. After the queen is found dead, the narrative digresses for an explanation of the asp story, inviting one recent scholar to express his disdain at Plutarch's apparently reckless change of style.

> Having wound his readers up to such a marvellous finale, at this point Plutarch does a sort of Jekyll and Hyde act. In an abrupt and disconcerting change of character he exchanges the bow tie and velvet smoking jacket of the literary historian for the lab coat of the criminal pathologist and embarks upon a scientific discussion of the exact cause of Cleopatra's death.[32]

Putting aside the doctor and his other monstrous self, we might also observe that Plutarch already shut off the reader's view of Cleopatra's death when the queen literally closed the door to die (τὰς θύρας ἔκλεισε, 85.2). The scene shifts suddenly to Octavian (Caesar's name, Καῖσαρ, begins the next sentence), who is seen in the author's narrative opening the queen's message. From the opposite verbal forms "she closed" (ἔκλεισε) to "having opened" (λύσας), we shift from closure to revelation. But this revelation comes significantly only *after* the event.

The death scene suggests the rituals of a mystery cult. As the non-initiated, we, the readers, are not allowed to view the ceremony. Instead we may only read the tablet with Octavian and view the queen as she was found, "lying on a golden couch and arrayed like a queen" (βασιλικῶς). The two faithful women, Iras and Charmion, as Plutarch names them, were not yet both dead. The one lay at her feet, the other struggled to arrange the diadem about her head. The last words do not belong to Cleopatra, for we are not permitted this intimacy. In reply to the rebuke, "a fine thing is this, Charmion" (καλὰ ταῦτα, Χάρμιον), the dying slave gives the superlative "truly most fine" (κάλλιστα μὲν οὖν) and the explanation "befitting the descendant of so many kings" (καὶ πρέπουτα τῇ τοσούτων ἀπογόνῳ βασιλέων).

Plutarch's dramatic narrative recalls elements of Greek tragedy, and a medical text, most likely erroneously ascribed to the famous physician Galen and known in antiquity by the title *On Poisonous Animals Dedicated to Piso,* includes the story of the queen's suicide and makes the comparison with tragedy explicit (8).

Siquidem ferunt, Cleopatram inventam fuisse dextra manu regium gestamen in capite detinere, ut mortua quoque spectantibus regina appareret: id quod de Polyxena tragicus poeta scribit. Nam etiam si a Pyrrho iugularetur, tamen mentem adhibuit, ut cum decore caderet.

Some even say that Cleopatra was found with her right hand holding her royal crown on her head so that even dead she might seem a queen to those viewing her body, which is what the tragic poet writes about Polyxena. For even if she was going to be strangled by Pyrrhus, nevertheless she had the intention to die with grace and dignity.

Polyxena is the daughter of Priam who in Euripides' fifth-century B.C.E. Athenian tragedy, *Hecuba,* is sacrificed on the tomb of Achilles by Pyrrhus (also called Neoptolemus) to appease his father's ghost. One might expect to find few parallels between the Trojan virgin and Antony's Egyptian lover, but both die as free women, befitting their noble births, and in the spectacles of their deaths ("so that she might die nobly" *ut cum decore caderet*) they may be compared. The medical text varies in several respects (the queen experiments on her two female companions of slightly different names, for example, not on condemned men) but it also serves a double purpose in telling Cleopatra's death. The story is both a source of pleasure in its narration (*non sine animi voluptate narravimus*), fulfillling the students' longing (*desiderium*), and at the same time a didactic tool to learn how quickly the asp bears death. Like the physicians whom Lucretius says smear honey on the rim of the cups to entice children to drink the nasty wormwood (*On the Nature of Things* 1.936–38), so the medical author beguiles his students with the story of the queen's death so they may learn the symptoms of an asp-bite.

EPILEGOMENON AND CHAUCER

As the centuries after those last hours in Alexandria rolled by, and a pagan era passed into a Christian, the legendary name of Cleopatra endured. The *exemplum* of the queen oscillated between moral reproach and perverse fascination. The details of the queen's suicide, surviving more and more in epitomes and anecdotes, strove ever more for the fantastic. The asp remained as a symbol of the queen's identity. To the Christian apologist of the early third century C.E., Tertullian, Cleopatra and her asps may be likened to the acts of the martyrs of a new religion (*To the Peoples* 1.18.2).

> regina Aegypti bestiis suis usa est.

> The queen of Egypt applied wild animals to herself.

She is, in fact, even more courageous, as the asps are snakes more terrifying than the bull or bear (Tertullian, *To the Martyrs* 4.6).

> Bestias femina libens appetiit et utique aspides serpentes tauro vel urso horridiores, quas Cleopatra immisit sibi, ne in manus inimci perveniret.

> The woman willingly sought out the wild beasts, in fact, the asps, snakes more horrible than a bull or bear which Cleopatra applied to herself lest she fall into the hands of her enemy.

Most classical authors do not specify where the asp bit the queen, but Propertius and the few Greek narratives that do, mention the arm(s) explicitly. For Orosius, it was the left arm (the most practical and obvious if the queen were right handed). But with the advent of the Christian era, the bite moves up from the arm to the breast. Fulgentius, the author of *On the Ages of the World and of Man*, perhaps from the early sixth century, represents an early Christian eroticism of the pagan queen's death (14).

> Primus namque universae terrae limites imperiali maiestate subiecit, Britannicas ultra mare Atlanticum sitas insulas mira felicitate repressit, Actiacae pugnae certamine triumphans exstitit atque Aegyptiacam superatam reginam lactandas praebere mammas serpentibus persuasit.

> For he (i.e., Augustus) was the first to place the boundaries of the whole world under Rome's imperial rule and he subdued the islands of Britain located beyond the Atlantic Ocean with a wondrous prosperity, and he showed himself triumphant in the struggle of the battle of Actium and forced the Egyptian queen whom he conquered to submit her breasts to be suckled by the snakes.

Chaucer, writing almost a thousand years later, continues the reception of the Egyptian queen into a Christian world. His literary invention of her death in his *Legend of Good Women* is bold, and its stark divergence from the classical tradition is illustrative of the new ways of reading and viewing Cleopatra in the late Middle Ages. Modern critical response judges the poem either playful Ovidian fun or harsh satire and misogyny. Instructed by Cupid, in penance to his heresy of offending women, the poet surprisingly begins his hagiography of pagan feminine virtue with Cleopatra. In Chaucer's both serious and mocking eulogy, addressed to multiple audiences, Antony becomes a shining knight and Cleopatra his courtly queen, where she is described "fayr as is the rose in May" (613). The legend concludes with the queen's suicide (696–702).

> And with that word, naked with ful good herte,
> Among the serpents in the pit she sterte,
> And ther she chees to han hir buryinge;
> Anoon the neddres gonne hir for to stinge,
> And she hir deeth receyveth with good chere,
> For love of Antony, that was hir so dere:
> And this is storial sooth, hit is no fable.

No royal diadem, no faithful servants, no act of cunning. Cleopatra dies naked. Gone too is the asp, replaced by a pit full of serpents and Old English adders. In his iconographical study of the Chaucerian poem, V. A. Kolve suggested that this final act evoked, in the medieval mind, images of human flesh eaten by worms in the grave (where *pit* and *grave*, and *serpent* and *worm* may be synonymous terms).[33] Centuries later, Shakespeare too played with the words *worm* and *serpent* when the queen speaks to the clown (*Antony and Cleopatra* 5.2.300–301):

> *Clown.*   Look you, the worm is not to be trusted but in the keeping
> of wise people, for indeed there is no goodness in the worm.

Whether serpent or worm, the characteristic aspect of the Egyptian snake, as we have seen, is now mostly lost.

On the ancient theatrical stage of Cleopatra's death, the asp functioned as an important prop. In Caesar's triumphal show, an image of her death, with arms bitten by the sacred snakes (*sacris colubris*), entertained the Roman spectators. For Horace, taking hold of the harsh serpents (*asperas serpentes*, where the Latin adjective *asperas* may pun on the foreign-sounding name *aspis*) demonstrated the queen's courage and defied the will of a Caesar. For Virgil, the asps were twin serpents (*geminos anguis*) whose ominous appearance in the Actian waves foreshadowed Cleopatra's demise and associated her even more intimately with the fate of Troy and Dido, the epic's other *regina*. For Plutarch, Aelian, and the author of the treatise *On Poisonous Animals*, the bite of an asp was the method, tested by experimentation, to find a "painless death" (ἀνώδυνον θάνατον). Embedded in their texts are gender-based cultural attitudes toward feminine ingenuity and motivation. Whether the asp (or its venom) killed the queen or not, a myth, in its richness and multiplicity, political, literary, and cultural, served both the Roman victor and foreign queen well. And if we still laugh at the ignorance of the garbage man from the Bronx in Howard Hawks' comedy, who does not know an asp when he hears one, the curt reply of the smug history professor that it was a "small snake" suggests that he didn't know much more.

NOTES

1. The absurdity of the choices, namely (A) swallowing a needle and (C) hiccups, make the correct response easier for the film's audience to recognize but at the same time (B) the snake-bite, when inserted between these two outrageous alternatives, suggests the manner of the queen's death was almost equally bizarre or even inexplicable to twentieth-century America. The incorrect choices are not haphazard. The needle, of course, refers to the famous Egyptian obelisk in Central Park, New York (chosen as an opening scene of the film), which earned the erroneously popular nickname of Cleopatra's Needle. The suggestion of hiccups is a playful allusion to a comic episode in the well-known seduction scene of the 1934 film *Cleopatra*, with Claudette Colbert in the lead role. Here the queen, trying to seduce Antony with wine and what was then a novel idea of reverse psychology, finds herself stricken by an amusing seizure of unqueenly burps.

2. Blaise Pascal, *Pensées* 32 (1662–63): "Had Cleopatra's nose been shorter, the whole face of the world would have changed" (*Le nez de Cléopâtre s'il eût été plus court toute la face de la terre aurait changé*).

3. Werner Huss, "Die Herkunft der Kleopatra Philopator," *Aegyptus* 70 (1990): 191–203, has argued that Cleopatra's mother may have belonged to a high-ranked Egyptian family. But the evidence remains dubious.

4. Adrian Thornton, "Vergil, the Augustans, and the Invention of Cleopatra's Suicide—One Asp or Two?" *Vergilius* 44 (1998): 31–50, also examines the cultural myth of Cleopatra's suicide in ancient literature and attributes the ancient origins of the myth of two asps to the famous passage in Virgil's *Aeneid* (8.696–97). To counter the inevitable difficulty that the contemporary poets Horace and Propertius, who also refer to asps in the plural and whose works were written *before* (certainly, for Horace's three book of *Odes* and most likely for Propertius' third book of *Elegies*) the publication of the *Aeneid*, Thornton must be forced to conclude that the ekphrasis of the shield of Aeneas was written almost ten years before the death of Virgil and the posthumous circulation of the epic and that the passage was known by some public reading "fairly soon after Actium." It is more likely that all three poets, as Propertius himself attests in *Elegies* 3.11.53–54, refer to an actual image of Cleopatra displayed in the triumphal ceremonies with asps curled around her arms as is evident in several extant cult representations of Isis.

5. Wilhelm Spiegelberg, "Weshalb wählte Kleopatra den Tod durch Schlangenbiss?" *Ägyptologische Mitteilungen* (1925): 1–6. Citing Spiegelberg's article in a footnote and defending it from criticism by E. Hermann, W. W. Tarn, the original co-author of the *Cambridge Ancient History* 10 (1934: 110), expressed confidence in the interpretation: "of the manner of her death no doubt should now exist, for it is known why she used an asp." The popular biographers Hans Volkmann (*Cleopatra: A Study in Politics and Propaganda*, 1958: 206–7); Jack Lindsay (*Cleopatra*, 1971: 433–36); and Michael Grant (*Cleopatra*, 1972: 225–28) followed this view.

6. Josephus, *Against Apion* 2.7.86.

7. M. A. Levi, "Cleopatra e l'aspide," *Parola del Passato* (1954) interpreted the manner of death as an effort by the queen to demonstrate a continuous and sacred line of succession from the Egyptian

pharaohs whereby each sovereign returns to his or her father while Horos continues on the throne with the successor.

8. For the title of New Isis, unattested by extant inscriptions, see Plutarch, *Life of Antony* 54.9. For discussion of such honors, see Volkmann (1958): 147–48; M. Wyke, "Augustan Cleopatras: female power and authority," in A. Powell, ed., *Roman Poetry and Propaganda in the Age of Augustus* (1992): 95–98; and F. E. Brenk, "Antony-Osiris, Cleopatra-Isis. The end of Plutarch's Antony," in P. Stadter, ed., *Plutarch and the Historical Tradition* (1992): 160–61.

9. *Roman Provincial Coinage*: nos. 4094–6.

10. M. H. Crawford, *Roman Republican Coinage*: no. 543. Experts may distinguish between obverse and reverse but ancient users of these coins only saw two "heads" of authority, a striking (no pun intended) decision that illustrated a unique sharing of power.

11. The Latin phrase *deo dignos* means "worthy in the eyes of God" (dative case), not "worthy of godhood" (ablative).

12. Diogenes Laertius, *On the Lives of Famous Philosophers* 5.78.

13. The pseudo-Galen text, *On Poisonous Animals Dedicated to Piso* (*De Theriaca ad Pisonem*) 8, reports that he personally had witnessed many victims die by asp bite ("for truly these snakes kill quickly as I often have witnessed in Alexandria," *nam re vera serpentes isti velociter interficiunt, sicut ego saepe in magna Alexandria spectavi*). Presumably, this death was a form of public execution or scientific experimentation, or both. Either possibility would suggest that the death by an asp-bite was not as rare or perverse at least in Alexandria as it may have seemed to the Romans.

14. Cf. Cicero, *On the Nature of the Gods* 3.47, where the interlocutor Cotta postulates that if Isis and Osiris should be included among the traditional gods of worship, then the gods of foreigners (*barbarorum deos*) should not be scorned—oxen, horses, ibises, hawks, asps, crocodiles, fishes, dogs, wolves, cats, and many other beasts.

15. Aelian, *On the History of Animals* 6.38, contends that victims may live up to four hours and suffer from choking and convulsions and retching.

16. For a fascinating scientific account of the snake's venom, see Thornton (1998): 34–36. Thornton cites evidence, contrary to ancient opinion and other modern observations, that the cobra's venom remains toxic even if taken orally.

17. Suetonius used the verb *putabatur* ("it was thought"), which reflects the doubts of Greek writers.

18. Paul Plass (1995).

19. The critics are respectively W. H. Alexander ("*Nunc Tempus Erat*: Horace, *Odes* 1.37.4," *Classical Journal* 39, 1944: 233), and Steele Commager ("Horace, *Carmina* 1.37," *Phoenix* 12, 1958: 55 *bis*).

20. Gregson Davis (1991): 233–42. The title of his discussion on the Cleopatra Ode is "From Dispraise to Praise: The Transfiguration of the Vanquished (C. 1.37)."

21. Athenaeus, *Scholars at Dinner* 10.430a–c = Alcaeus [lyric poet] 332.

22. Similarly, Horace, *Epode* 7.6–7: "or so that the British captive might descend the Sacra Via in chains" (*aut Britannus ut descenderet/Sacra catenatus via*) and Propertius 2.1.33–34: "or the necks of kings bound with golden chains and the prows won at Actium running along the Sacra Via" (*aut regum auratis circumdata colla catenis/Actiaque in Sacra currere rostra Via*).

23. Carlin Barton (1993): 182–86.

24. Cf. Aulus Gellius, *Attic Nights* 5.6.21 on occasions when it is not proper to award a formal triumph: "it is not fitting when the victory was achieved against a just enemy nor when the name of the enemy is lowborn, as in the case of slaves or pirates" (*neque cum iusto hoste gesta sunt, aut hostium nomen humile et non idoneum est, ut servorum piratarumque*).

25. Michèle Lowrie (*Horace's Narrative Odes*, 1997: 138–64) places her analysis of the ode in a nuanced and cogent reading of three consecutive poems at the juncture of Horace's first two books

(*Odes* 1.37, 38 and 2.1). Building upon earlier feminist readings of the ode, she argues that the foreign enemy's gender represents "the breakdown of categories in civil war." As a woman, Cleopatra masks the reality of the civil conflict and power struggle with Antony. But it is only as a man that she can dignify his victory in Rome. Declining to take sides in the modern readings of the ode's final praise of Cleopatra as either genuine sympathy or unmitigated glorification of the victor (extreme points of view she rightly judges untenable in Horatian lyric discourse), Lowrie emphasizes instead the poem's *multiplex*—as she describes it—associations that evoke varied contradictions inherent in the nature of civil war and the Roman propaganda against the queen.

26. Gian Bagio Conte, *Latin Literature: A History* (1994): 430.

27. The text comes from the edition of Edward Courtney (*The Fragmentary Latin Poets*, 1993), under Rabirius. I have added the much-emended first verse of column VI. For an earlier bibliography on this mutilated epic poem, see Gurval, *Actium and Augustus: The Politics and Emotions of Civil War* (1995): 15, note 26.

28. Gabriele Marasco, "Cleopatra e gli esperimenti su cavie umane," *Historia* 44 (1995): 317–25.

29. N.M. Horsfall, "Dido in the Light of History," in S.J. Harrison, ed., *Oxford Readings in Vergil's Aeneid* (1990): 143, has argued that Naevius' *Punic War* fashioned the Carthaginian queen as "evil, treacherous, insidious, a magician." The fragmentary evidence seems inconclusive.

30. C.B.R. Pelling, ed., *Plutarch: Life of Antony* (1988): 320.

31. Brenk (1992): 170–73.

32. John E.G. Whitehorn, *Cleopatras* (1994): 190–91.

33. V.A. Kolve, "From Cleopatra to Alceste: An Iconographic Study of the *Legend of Good Women*," in J.P. Hermann and J.J. Burke, Jr. eds., *Signs and Symbols in Chaucer's Poetry* (1981): 130–78.

4

Cleopatra, Isis, and the Formation of Augustan Rome

Sarolta A. Takács

The bright mirror I braved: the devil in it
Loved me like my soul, my soul:
Now that I seek myself in a serpent
My smile is fatal.

Nile moves in me; my thighs splay
Into the squalled Mediterranean;
My brain hides in that Abyssinia
Lost armies foundered towards.

Desert and river unwrinkle again.
Seeming to bring them the waters that make drunk
Caesar, Pompey, Antony I drank.
Now let the snake reign.

A half-deity out of Capricorn,
This rigid Augustus mounts
With his sword virginal indeed; and has shorn
Summarily the moon-horned river

From my bed. May the moon
Ruin him with virginity! Drink me, now, whole
With coiled Egypt's past; then from my delta
Swim like a fish toward Rome.

Ted Hughes, *Cleopatra to the Asp*

The English poet laureate Ted Hughes' poem *Cleopatra to the Asp* succinctly captures the essence of Cleopatra's Egypt as a potent influence on the formation of Augustan Rome. This essay investigates the historical basis for that influence, part of the stimulus for the Augustan remodeling of the Roman Republic into the Principate. Whether this modeling was deliberate or unintentional is not my concern. I will argue, however, that the religious apparatus that supported succession in Cleopatra's dynasty, in which the goddess Isis played a pivotal role, influenced and, in some ways, shaped Augustus' political innovations. Ancient authors, papyri, and inscriptions are the basis for this historical analysis, which has two geographical and chronological foci, Egypt (pre-Ptolemaic and Ptolemaic) and Rome (Republican and Augustan), and two societal aspects, religious and political.

Egypt became the personal province of Octavian Augustus in 30 B.C.E. after he defeated Egypt's last Ptolemaic ruler, Cleopatra VII, the New Isis, and Marc Antony, her Dionysian lover, at Actium. Thus, Augustus saved the Roman state from falling into the hands of a degenerate country whose inhabitants worshipped animals and vegetables. Although I mean that tongue in cheek, the Egyptian as animal and vegetable worshipper is a well-known topos in Latin literature.[1] This notion that oriental influences weakened the Roman Empire, and might have brought it to its knees, still lurks in secondary literature. After all, it was in Augustus' hands that Rome had been strengthened against the oriental influences that eroded the core of Roman self-definition based on the *mos maiorum*, ancestral patterns of behavior. But these "oriental" (read Egyptian) influences judged so negatively by authors of the Augustan period are not assessed in the same way by those writing in the Flavian or Hadrianic periods. No tone of dismay accompanies the account of the austere Vespasian accidentally healing a lame and a blind man in the name of Sarapis (Isis' Ptolemaic consort), after he was proclaimed emperor in Alexandria (Tacitus, *Historiae* 4.81). Vespasian's son Domitian rebuilt the temple of Isis in Rome after it burnt down in the fire of 80. No author hesitates to remark on the philhellene Hadrian's (whose beloved Antinous drowned in the Nile) great interest in Egypt or his visits there.

In fact, it was Augustus who permitted the integration of the worship of Isis and her consort Sarapis into the array of Roman cults, with both political and dynastic aspects attached. Ancient authors and, consequently, modern scholarship ignore this and simply follow the clichéd view of Rome combating oriental decadence propagated and perpetuated by the circle of authors writing for the first *princeps*. But how did Isis come to Rome and into the mental and religious landscape of Romans at the height of supposed anti-Egyptian feelings? How did pharaonic and Ptolemaic dynastic concepts mesh with Roman ideology? The assimilation of two systems of representation, Ptolemaic Egyptian and Republican Roman, stimulated the imperial Roman culture described in general history books, a creation of Augustus.[2]

AUGUSTUS IN EGYPT

Augustus, the conqueror, stayed in Egypt for several weeks only and never returned to the province. Dio Cassius (51.16.3–5) writes that:

περὶ μὲν δὴ τοὺς ἄλλους τοιαῦτα ἐγίγνετο, τῶν δὲ Αἰγυπτίων τῶν τε Ἀλεξανδρέων πάντων ἐφείσατο ὥστε μὴ διολέσαι τινά, τὸ μὲν ἀληθὲς ὅτι οὐκ ἠξίωσε τοσούτους τε αὐτοὺς ὄντας καὶ χρησιμωτάτους τοῖς Ῥωμαίοις ἐς πολλὰ ἂν γενομένους ἀνήκεστόν τι δρᾶσαι· πρόφασιν δὲ ὅμως προυβάλλετο τόν τε θεὸν τὸν Σάραπιν καὶ τὸν Ἀλέξανδρον τὸν οἰκιστὴν αὐτῶν, καὶ τρίτον Ἄρειον τὸν πολίτην, ᾧ που φιλοσοφοῦντί τε καὶ συνόντι οἱ ἐχρῆτο. καὶ τόν γε λόγον δι' οὗ συνέγνω σφίσιν, ἑλληνιστί, ὅπως συνῶσιν αὐτοῦ, εἶπε. καὶ μετὰ ταῦτα τὸ μὲν τοῦ Ἀλεξάνδρου σῶμα εἶδε, καὶ αὐτοῦ καὶ προσήψατο, ὥστε τι τῆς ῥινός, ὥς φασι, θραυσθῆναι· τὰ δὲ δὴ τῶν Πτολεμαίων, καίτοι τῶν Ἀλεξανδρέων σπουδῇ βουληθέντων αὐτῷ δεῖξαι, οὐκ ἐθεάσατο, εἰπὼν ὅτι "βασιλέα ἀλλ' οὐ νεκροὺς ἰδεῖν ἐπεθύμησα." κἀκ τῆς αὐτῆς ταύτης αἰτίας οὐδὲ τῷ Ἄπιδι ἐντυχεῖν ἠθέλησε, λέγων θεοὺς ἀλλ' οὐχὶ βοῦς προσκυνεῖν εἰθίσθαι.

He spared Egyptians and Alexandrians and put none to death. In truth, he did not want to harm those who could be useful to the Romans in many ways. Likewise he put forth as a pretext their god Sarapis and Alexander, their founder, and, thirdly, their fellow citizen Arius. He philosophized with him and was acquainted with him. He gave the speech in which he pardoned them in Greek, so that they could understand him. Afterwards, he viewed the body of Alexander and he touched it breaking off a piece of the nose. What is more, he did not view the bodies of the Ptolemies, although the Alexandrians were anxious to show them to him, and he said: "I desired to see a king, not corpses." And for this same reason he did not want to make a visit to see the Apis bull, saying that he was accustomed to worship gods not cattle.

Since Dio Cassius reports that Augustus delivered this speech in Greek, the imagined audience was Greek speaking, with the implication that they were assimilated (hellenized) Egyptians. More likely they were Greeks and Macedonians, that is, Alexandrians. But unlike the Greek inhabitants of Alexandria, native Egyptians might not have had as much interest in Sarapis, the syncretic god and patron deity of the Ptolemies, and the city's founder Alexander. The target audience in Augustus' speech as Dio Cassius imagines it were those involved in Egyptian politics. Augustus' actions described here were clearly political. He did not view the mummified Ptolemies, for he did not want to give the impression that he continued their rule and their tradition. If there was someone worthy of *imitatio*, it was Alexander alone, the great conqueror whose body one could consider "a sacred relic."[3] While earlier rhetorical views of the Egyptians, again recorded by Dio Cassius, reveal a deep dislike for them and their religious customs,[4] such views should not be taken at face value. This rhetorical discourse had a distinct purpose, the slandering of Cleopatra and Marc Antony.[5]

The Apis bull was well known throughout the Roman world, and Augustus' Roman sensibility is unlikely to have been offended had he participated in the ceremonial viewing of the divine bull.[6] Since Augustus' legitimacy as the new ruler of Egypt did not depend on the Memphite clergy, he may have felt it quite unnecessary to undertake the ceremonial visit to Apis.[7] Furthermore, the high priest in Memphis, Imouthes/Petobastis IV, had died two days before Alexandria fell to Augustus on 3 August 30 B.C.E. Even Imouthes' fate as a mummy seems linked to Augustus and his consolidation of power. Imouthes lay in the House of Embalming for close to seven years, until 23 B.C.E., when on 9 April, he was finally buried. A successor was not appointed until 27 B.C.E.[8] The significance of this appointment is noted by Thompson: "This new high priest, Psenamounis II, was cousin of Imouthes/Petobastis IV. The appointment, made thus within the family, was traditional and, like his predecessor, the new high priest of Ptah had duties in the ruler cult. The title of 'prophet of pharaoh' was modified to that of 'prophet of Caesar.'"[9]

Dio Cassius leads us to believe that Augustus' visit to the tomb of Alexander and the refusal to visit the Apis bull happened in close chronological proximity, but Suetonius, while relating both events in his *Life of Augustus*, mentions Augustus' refusal to visit the Apis bull in Memphis only *en passant* and as part of his "journey through Egypt."[10] Memphis was the city "which gave birth to gods."[11] It was a "a sacred city, the home of Ptah and of his emanation Apis."[12] Jan Assman writes:

> Here, Ptah, the god of the Earth, god of the *Ur*-hill and god of artisans, is put before the older god of heaven, god of light and time, Re. Here Ptah created by reflecting the cosmos in his heart before Re moved up to the heavens and through his light and movement created all things. In all of this a reflection is forged of one's own history and one's own origins. Memphis is Egypt's first capital, the place of the oldest monuments. . . . Memphis became synonymous with a past, which for the first time was something whole (coherent), big and made visible separate from the present.[13]

Apis had been known in Egypt as early as the Old Kingdom and the cult of Apis was a significant part of royal ritual.[14] The relationship between the Ptolemies and the Memphite priests of Ptah was also close.[15] Augustus, however, did not feel that he had to continue it: we may assume that he simply had no interest in following the lead of the Ptolemies, including Cleopatra, in this particular ritual.

Like Alexander, his regime was the start of a new era. Augustus postponed his formal assumption of power until the Egyptian New Year, 1 Thoth. In this he followed tradition, although the coronation was omitted and thereby Augustus managed to satisfy Egyptian and Roman sensibilities. In contrast to the doubts that had been raised about Marc Antony's motives and actions in Egypt, this man's rule over Egypt would not prevent his emergence as Rome's premiere citizen. Since there was no coronation, Augustus demonstrated that he adhered to Republican principles. Indeed, at least in the minds of scholars such as the very learned and still influential Franz Cumont, Augustus' task in keeping Rome free from external religious and cultural pollution was monumental:

> At the beginning of our era there set in that great movement of conversion that soon established the worship of Isis and Sarapis from the outskirts of the Sahara to the vallum of Britain, and from the mountains of Asturias to the mouths of the Danube.

The resistance still offered by the central power could not last much longer. It was impossible to dam in this overflowing stream whose thundering waves struck the shaking walls of the *pomerium* from every side. The prestige of Alexandria seemed invincible.[16]

A futile struggle had begun. "A purely African faith," in Reginald Witt's analysis, was to become a world religion and pave the way for Christianity.[17]

THE IMPACT OF ISIS

According to the Heliopolite theology, Isis, who was possibly the personification of the throne, and Osiris, god of the dead, were the children of the sky-goddess, Nut, who daily devours the heavenly bodies and bears them again, and Geb, the procreative Earth-god. Isis and Osiris had a son, Horus, represented in the form of a falcon. With the advent of Macedonian rule over Egypt, Sarapis, an oracular god, became Isis' companion. Osiris still held the central position in the mysteries, however. The foundation myth of Isis, i.e., Isis' search for the pieces of her husband's/brother's body, its mending, Horus' revenge on the murderer Seth, and Horus' consequent accession to the celestial throne, represents the aetiology of Egyptian dynastic ritual. This myth furnished the structure for Egypt's religious and daily life, and shaped the perception of the ruler as the embodiment of Horus, who ascends to the throne because of his divine parents and because he avenged his murdered father.[18] Thus, the pharaoh was a living myth.

While Alexander associated himself with Ammon-Ra, Ptolemy I Soter chose the syncretic Sarapis as the dynasty's new patron deity. Sarapis was connected with Memphis, whose priests (of Ptah) wielded tremendous political power; they, in essence, made and unmade pharaohs. The name of the god allowed linguistic connections outside Egypt. Some could believe that Sarapis' place of origin was the Black Sea city Sinope, others could associate *-apis* with the Greek king Apis, who had died in Egypt. The Ptolemies successfully integrated into the ancient system something new: Sarapis became part of the dynastic ritual that furnished the structure for Egypt's religious and daily life.[19]

Isis and her Alexandrian consort Sarapis became new members of the elastic and inclusive Roman pantheon. On a political level Sarapis, most especially, was bound to the *domus Augusta*. But this triggered no immediate, intense devotional outpouring to Isis and Sarapis. Ladislav Vidman collected all inscriptions mentioning Isis and Sarapis, and even with newly found ones, the number remains small, about 80 from Rome.[20] Géza Alföldy, who studied the epigraphical material preserved from the western provinces of the empire, calculated that names of all oriental deities do not comprise more than 10 percent. The percentage preserved in inscriptions from the eastern provinces, excluding Egypt, is higher, but in no way do they dislodge the Greco-Roman deities.[21]

Yet scholarly myths do not die easily, especially under the influence of the mythic views, derived from later literature and film, of the cast of *dramatis personae*, the seductive Cleopatra VII, her powerful lovers, Julius Caesar and Marc Antony, and the awfully young, yet politically astute Augustus, all in the context of a rapidly disintegrating political system, the waning Republic. These are the ingredients of a great epic filled with passion, political intrigue, maneuvering and, ultimately, a paradoxically heroic death. It was after all Octavian Augustus who supplied the powerful sequel, since his "propaganda" still shapes most general views of the history of the late Republic and early Principate. In this version of events, his fight was on behalf of the Roman Republic against the utterly un-Roman oriental embodied in the persons of the new Isis, Cleopatra, and her consort, the reckless new Dionysos, Marc Antony. Yet since Romans were already fascinated by Egyptian culture and adopted part of its religion in the worship of Isis, bias against Cleopatra as its representative still seemed to be restricted to her, as an isolated historical event; shortly after the reign of Augustus, the worship of Isis flourished in Rome and elsewhere in the Mediterranean. Cleopatra as a glamorous but temporary enemy seems to have stimulated even more acceptance of Egyptian culture in its Ptolemaic forms.

CLEOPATRA AND ISIS IN ROME

Cicero, a paragon of Roman virtue, hated Cleopatra ("reginam odi"[22]), who visited Rome with her son by Julius Caesar, Caesarion, in the summer of 46 B.C.E. He hated her arrogance (*superbia*). The reason was not because she was the lover of the man who just celebrated four triumphs and was moving ever more quickly and steadily outside the politically acceptable. It was because she had not produced, by way of her servants, one of whom Cicero calls *hominem nefarium*, the promised *philologa* (manuscripts, one assumes). These *philologa* might have been tokens to sweeten the negative opinion of Rome's *pater patriae*.[23] The terms *regina, superbia,* and *nefarius* are loaded ones and point to the regal past, whose last king (*rex*) was Tarquinius Superbus. Nevertheless, Cicero's complaint seems, as it often happens with him, petty. On April 16, 44 B.C.E., when Cleopatra is said to have departed, her "flight" (as he puts it) does not distress him a bit. Why not imagine a sigh of relief?

Joseph Burel believed that Egyptians who had followed Cleopatra stayed behind in Rome and intensified the propagation of the cult of Isis.[24] This now outdated explanatory model is very much in line with what Tibullus, Propertius, and Ovid have to say about the adherents of the cult of Isis. These worshippers came from the *monde des courtisanes*, the immoral demi-monde. In this view, their lack of moral purity made these women and their lovers susceptible to Isis. Clearly, someone possessing such purity would not think of seducing a Roman matron wearing a dog-mask nor would a pure matron fall for someone wearing such a thing.[25] Undoubtedly, there must be some love-spell at work, for how could the average Roman resist these Isiac poisons, when even the successful general Marc Antony could not?[26]

There is no need to postulate an increased presence of expatriate Egyptians or Alexandrians in Rome because of Cleopatra's stay in Rome. Successful propagation of the cult depended neither on them nor on Egypt's last pharaoh, since the popularity of Isis throughout the Mediterranean is well attested. While it is true that in Greek cities the first generation of priests tended to be Egyptians, subsequent ones were Greek.[27] The aspect of the worship of Isis that involved initiations closed to the public, much like a mystery cult, was probably fashioned along the lines of the Eleusinian Mysteries in Athens.[28] Then there was the Ptolemaic fusion with the hellenized deity Sarapis, added by Ptolemy Soter. As the eastern Mediterranean world struggled to redefine itself after Alexander's death, the hellenized Egyptian deities found many adherents outside Egypt. In the propagation of the cult, the island Delos played an important role, as it was a tax-free commercial center that attracted wealthy merchants from all over the Mediterranean, especially those involved in trading slaves. The island consequently became a significant conduit for various cultural expressions in art, architecture, and religious customs, since the merchants, proud to advertise their home cities, spent lavishly in support of the sanctuaries and for amenities in the local town.

The earliest inscription concerning Isis from Rome, dated to 90–60 B.C.E., mentions a group of eight freedmen and freedwomen and five freeborn ones.[29] Their names point to large and well-connected families, far from the sordid world of prostitutes. These families had connections with Delos and were engaged in slave trading. The first senatorial actions against the cult of Isis in Rome seemed to have been taken less than a generation after the fall of Delos into the hands of Mithradates VI of Pontus.[30] Moreover, a detailed study of inscriptions from the provinces along the Rhine and Danube shows that dedicators who named Isis and Sarapis in their inscriptions were mostly administrative employees and military officials, representatives of the central administration. This documentation casts into doubt the common but now outdated assumption that worshippers of Isis were members of the demi-monde.

ROMAN RECEPTION OF EGYPTIAN ISIS

András Alföldi was the first to link Isiac symbols to Roman politics and propagation of ideas.[31] He postulated that the subaltern personnel working the mint was "an always battle-ready revolutionary vanguard of Isiacs."[32] They inserted Isiac symbols without consulting the moneyer in charge to further a socio-revolutionary mass movement. While Alföldi's conjecture goes too far, it can certainly be argued that the appearance of Isiac symbols on coins of the late Republic point to an awareness, or maybe even an interest, among the senatorial class in the symbolism connected with the goddess Isis. It is more likely, however, that this was an expression of interest in Egypt. Roman political relations with Egypt included senators who deemed it fit and profitable to meddle in her internal politics. In the 50s B.C.E., the senatorial order was also very much divided, and its internal rivalries were played out in foreign countries.

Egypt under Ptolemy XII Auletes was one of these countries. The citizens of Alexandria had expelled their flute-playing pharaoh in 58 B.C.E. for his pro-Roman relations. Gabinius, one of the consuls of 58 B.C.E., however, reinstated Auletes in 55 B.C.E. after receiving a sizable bribe. Cicero despised Gabinius, once a legate of Pompey, for his bribe taking, yet despite Gabinius' weakness for bribes and his support of Caesar and Clodius, Cicero, with lawyerly detachment, eventually defended Gabinius against extortion, although unsuccessfully. The various senatorial actions against the cult of Isis in the 50s B.C.E. were not so much repeated efforts to quell a mass-favored cult, or attempts to cleanse the state of religious pollution, as they were demonstrations of senatorial power, a power that was steadily and increasingly disintegrating from within. Nevertheless, on matters of religion the Senate could act cohesively. Their actions against the cult of Isis may be interpreted as efforts to reinforce what they saw as an intact socio-political system, and to make clear who was in charge. It was the Senate who, in effect, had the traditional political right to introduce a cult officially. As the Republic became the Principate, it was the *princeps* who exercised this right. Augustus' relationship toward Egypt was not unlike that of the Senate, even before the 50s B.C.E. The relationship was usefully ambiguous.

There were three Augustan actions that dealt with Isis and Isiacs. The first one might surprise, for it was a vote by the second triumvirate in favor of a temple of Isis (Dio Cassius 47.15). Then, there were two prohibitions, issued first in 28 B.C.E., and a second time in 21 B.C.E., against carrying Egyptian cult-images inside the *pomerium*, the religious city limit. Augustus' chief concern was, as always, with the public and not the private sphere. He did not intend to inhibit cultic activities that took place inside a private temple structure or on private property. While Augustus prohibited the carrying of Egyptian cult-images inside the *pomerium* in 28 B.C.E., he also "made provisions for the restoration of their temples" (Dio Cassius 53.2.4–5). The intention behind Augustus' prohibitions was the relocation of the cultic procession route from public streets to private locations.

In the 20s B.C.E. Augustus continued to demonstrate a resolute political (public) stand against anything as identifiably Egyptian. This showed him to be a protector of Roman values without provoking any deities or their worshippers since the worship was, in reality, not strictly curtailed. Finally, these actions removed a potentially attractive nuisance from public streets. All public action was to be directed instead toward securing Augustus' own political program. Possible danger came not from the cult of Isis and Sarapis itself, but from its adherents congregating together with varying purposes. That the Senate and then subsequent emperors passed various laws prohibiting or curtailing *collegia* leaves no doubt about the apprehensions of the political leadership and the caution it exercised toward any group. The measures of 28 and 21 B.C.E., forbidding the transport of Egyptian cult-images inside the city of Rome, and limiting them to circumscribed places, illustrates this anxiety; it enforced control and eliminated emotional crowds.

Scholars have cited these measures as additional proof of Augustus' deep dislike for anything Egyptian and, above all, his sincere devotion to the *mos maiorum*. If we look at these two prohibitions, however, within the contexts of Augustus' political intent or "program," which could only be effective in an ordered political and religious environment, they read differently. Friction had to be avoided and this meant, among other things, a guarded acknowledgment of the Alexandrian deities. This was part of a guarantee for the *pax deorum* and the resulting *pax hominum*. In addition, Augustus had at least to appear consistent in his pronouncements and decrees. Inconsistency would have meant a loss of confidence, and confidence in his person was the guarantee of stability.

RECEPTION OF EGYPTIAN MOTIFS IN CAMPANIA

The political measures against public display of "Egyptian cults" within the city limits did not prohibit the inclusion of Egyptian motifs in Roman art and literature, nor were they ever intended to. Interest in exotic African animals and plants, and scenes of the Nile, was already established in visual representations at least as early as the end of the second century B.C.E.: the best known early example is the enormous floor mosaic laid near the Sanctuary of Fortuna

Primigenia at Praeneste, with an almost scholarly illustration of the Nile in flood, and careful labels for many of the figures.[33] In the private sphere, Roman houses and villas in the Bay of Naples (Campania) had displayed nilotic landscapes and Isiac symbols since the same period. Even at the time of intensive political anti-Egyptian diatribes before the battle of Actium in the 30s B.C.E., the artistic use of Egyptian motifs in private settings did not cease. In the Roman mind political and private interests did not have to coincide, and Egyptian motifs presented an exotic world that was politically very much in Rome's sphere of interest, in addition to being fun and interesting variations. Furthermore, landscapes and Isiac symbols had been elements of Roman art long before Cleopatra and Marc Antony were declared public enemies. Isis and Sarapis, too, were no strangers to Campania and Rome. In Campania, their cult had been introduced in the second century B.C.E. when the agriculturally rich region had frequent maritime trade and other close economic ties with Delos and Ptolemaic Egypt. The divine couple were not only Egyptian deities, but they also symbolized Egypt and as such they or their attributes were integrated into the paintings. These gods and their attributes found their way onto murals in illusionistic settings, but they illustrated a part of experienced reality in Roman Campania.

RECEPTION AND USE OF EGYPTIAN MOTIFS IN ROME

After the defeat of Cleopatra and Marc Antony at Actium and the consequent integration of Egypt as a province of Rome, Egyptian artistic motifs were used even more extensively than before: now Egypt belonged to the emperor.[34] The best examples of this are Augustus' and Livia's houses on the Palatine, the *aula Isiaca*, and the villa della Farnesina, probably the home of Agrippa and Julia. The wall decorations of the upper *cubiculum* of Augustus' house include Egyptian landscapes with obelisks, lotus flowers, *uraei*, and *situlae*.[35] Livia's suite incorporates similar motifs and depicted an Egyptian sun theme.[36] Suetonius (*Life of Augustus* 72) reports that Augustus' "palace was remarkable neither for his size nor for elegance," and indeed, in comparison to Nero's Golden House or Hadrian's extensive Tiburine villa, the first *princeps'* house might have seemed small and modest. Yet, his house abutted a temple of Apollo. Augustus had vowed the temple's construction in 36 B.C.E., and the building was dedicated eight years later on October 9, 28 B.C.E.

Augustus' temple of Apollo on the Palatine was a response to Gaius Sosius, who had rebuilt the ancient temple of Apollo Medicus,[37] after his Judean triumph of 34 B.C.E. Sosius, who had been proconsul of Syria 38–35 B.C.E. and consul in 32 B.C.E., had commanded the left wing of Marc Antony's fleet at Actium. Egypt's conqueror could hardly be outdone by a supporter of Marc Antony. Augustus knew something about *Realpolitik*. He chose Apollo as his divine guardian and neighbor on the Palatine and replaced his original signet ring, which sported a sphinx, with a depiction of Apollo. T. P. Wiseman notes that Augustus "upstaged [Sosius' building] in two ways. He put the huge theatre of Marcellus right in front of it; and he built his own temple of Apollo, inside the *pomerium*, on the Palatine."[38] The spot for the new temple was special, since lightning had struck it, and the *haruspices* declared that Apollo wished to reside there.[39] This Apollo was the guardian of Actium, the place of the naval battle that had sealed the political demise of Cleopatra and Marc Antony.

In the *Aeneid*, Virgil juxtaposes Rome's Olympian gods with Egypt's dog-faced god Anubis and marks Egypt's last pharaoh as a nameless *sistrum*-beating queen (*regina patrio sistro*), an enduring poetic creation that provides a vivid picture of the battle of Actium (8.696–713):

> Regina in mediis patrio vocat agmina sistro
> necdum etiam geminos a tergo respicit anguis.
> omnigenumque deum monstra et latrator Anubis
> contra Neptunum et Venerem contraque Minervam
> tela tenent. Saevit medio in certamine Mavors
> caelatus ferro tristesque ex aethere Dirae,
> et scissa gaudens vadit Discordia palla,
> quam cum sanguineo sequitur Bellona flagello.
> Actius haec cernens arcum tendebat Apollo
> desuper: omnis eo terrore Aegyptus et Indi,
> omnis Arabs, omnes vertebant terga Sabaei.
> Ipsa videbatur ventis regina vocatis
> vela dare et laxos iam iamque inmittere funis.
> Illam inter caedes pallentem morte futura
> fecerat Ignipotens undis et Iapyge ferri,
> contra autem magno maerentem corpore Nilum
> pandentemque sinus et tota veste vocantem
> caeruleum in gremium latebrosaque flumina victos.

The queen / amidst the battle called her flotilla on / with a sistrum's beat, a frenzy out of Egypt / never turning her head as yet to see / twin snakes of death behind, while monster forms / of gods of every race, and the dog-god / Anubis bark-ing, held their weapons up / against our Neptune, Venus, and Minerva. / Mars, engraved in steel, raged in the fight / as from high air the dire Furies came / with Discord, taking joy in a torn robe, / and on her heels, with bloody scourge, Bellona. / Overlooking it all, Actian Apollo / began to pull his bow. Wild at this sight, all Egypt, Indians, Arabians, all / Sabaeans put about in flight, and she, / the queen, appeared crying for winds to shift / just as she hauled up sail and slackened sheets. / The Lord of Fire had portrayed her there, / amid the slaughter, pallid with death to come, / then borne by waves and wind from northwest, / while the great length of mourning Nile awaited her / with open bays, calling the conquered home / to his blue bosom and his hidden streams.[40]

This epic struggle was waged between Roman and foreign gods, one of them a queen who was considered a god. Whomever this child of Isis chose as her consort would also have to be placed within the Egyptian dynastic system. Hence, it was quite understandable that the Ephesians (as Plutarch records) greeted Marc Antony as Dionysos,[41] for Dionysos was equated with Osiris.[42] Augustus set out to eliminate a Roman rival of impeccable patrician lineage, who had served with distinction as a general under Julius Caesar and was very popular among his troops; he found it expedient to have the rival depicted as part of an oriental, absolutely un-Roman, power-hungry couple. Thus what was really a civil war (after many decades of bitter civil wars among Romans) became, under Augustus' manipulations, a battle between a defender of true *Romanitas* and two people pretending to be Egyptian gods. Hence the construction of a temple honoring Actian Apollo next to his own house emphasized his claims of destiny and divine support.

Also near Augustus' housing complex on the Palatine (*domus Augusti*), was the temple of Victory, which once housed the sacred stone of the Great Mother, the Mater Magna, until her own temple was built and dedicated in 191 B.C.E. The Sibylline Books, which had originally instructed the Romans to fetch the Great Mother to Rome, were deposited in Augustus' new temple of Apollo Palatinus. These books had been newly edited under the *princeps'* auspices. The Palatine temple of Apollo and the temple of Victory are in close proximity. Below the western corner of the Palatine was the Lupercal with the *Ficus Ruminalis*, the sacred fig tree, where the she-wolf suckled Rome's twin founders, Romulus and Remus. Augustus had surrounded himself with the symbols of Trojan ancestry, Roman foundation, and victory.[43]

In 25 B.C.E., Augustus connected his house directly with the temple of Apollo by way of colonnades called the *porticus* of the Danaids. These mythological figures, daughters of Danaus, like their father and his twin brother, Aegyptus, were born in Egypt to the king Belus, but they traced their lineage back to Io of Argos. When the Danaids were expected to marry Aegyptus' sons, they fled with their father to Argos, the family's ancestral home, where they asked for and received asylum; eventually, however, they were asked by their father to kill their husbands on the wedding night, and 48 of the 50 did so.[44] In the underworld they spend eternity carrying water in sieves. The myth of the Danaids integrates an Egyptian theme into the Greek cultural system, embraced in turn by Romans. The Danaids' cultural ambiguity made them a useful (even brilliant!) choice as a cultural emblem, and here statues (presumably of all fifty daughters and fifty sons) lined the colonnades. They were Egyptians but of Greek lineage who, in flight, returned home; collectively, their fate could be read as a warning about the sanctity of marriage. Rome's first citizen at the same time introduced and did not introduce Egypt into Rome's own mythological center, perhaps with an instructive social message.

By a senatorial decree an altar and a statue of Vesta were placed at the end of

Augustus' house, opposite to Apollo Palatinus. They were dedicated on April 28, the festival day of Vesta, in 12 B.C.E., after Augustus became *pontifex maximus*. Vesta, the goddess whose fire was never let out (*ignis inextinctus*), symbolized the state, saved by Augustus from destruction. The temple of Apollo formed the axis of the whole complex. To the left of it were the apartments of the imperial family on two levels, right of it the library and public space, and the *aedicula* of Vesta. Augustus' Palatine complex seems to be a reinterpretation, a Roman adaptation, of the Ptolemaic and Attalid concept of the palace structure, especially with respect to the temples and libraries that connect to the private quarters.[45] As always the case with Augustus, there was a decisive Roman or "indigenous" element. In this case, a house (*domus*) was a status symbol that represented a man's public status, his *existimatio*. And, that *dignitas* dictated that one's house appropriately reflected one's public *existimatio*. There were striking yet basic parallels between a Roman house and a temple, as Wiseman has shown: "[. . .] the house of a Roman senator was itself partly public in function, and his *vestibulum* and *atrium* could advertise his glory to the Roman people as effectively as a temple with his name on the architrave."[46]

THE TRIUMPH OF ALEXANDRIANISM?

The adaptation of Egyptian themes was subtle. In the end it was not "Alexandrianism in all its forms . . . that had completely permeated Roman civilization," which in particular worried Burel and his intellectual followers.[47] There were no Egyptian artists and merchants, ardent believers of Isis, who ignored the emperor's policies and acted as apostles of her faith inside the city and spread this "Alexandrianism" among the morally weak. It was the Roman elite itself that found Egypt, and especially Alexandria, so culturally attractive. Here was a sophisticated Hellenistic city that presided over an ancient and exotic country, now firmly placed within Rome's political landscape. When celebrating the general Messalla's triumph over Aquitania, for example, Augustus' contemporary Tibullus did not shy away from introducing Egyptian motifs into his poem (1.7). The poet moves from Messalla the *triumphator* to the land that had been molded to be Rome's greatest conquest and triumph: Egypt. Tibullus' patron is, in fact, indirectly to be compared with the normative *triumphator* Augustus (1.7.5–8, 21–28).

> . . . novos pubes Romana triumphos
> vidit et evinctos bracchia capta duces:
> at te victrices lauros, Messalla, gerentem
> portabat nitidis currus eburnus equis.
> qualis et, arentes cum findit Sirius agros,
> fertilis aestiva Nilus abundet aqua?

Nile patre, quanam possim te dicere causa
aut quibus in terris occuluisse caput?
te propter nullos tellus tua postulat imbres,
arida nec pulvio supplicat herba Iovi.
te canit atque suum pubes miratur Osirim
barbara, Memphiten plangere docta bovem.

The Roman youth has seen new triumphs and leaders with captured arms bound: but you, Messalla, used to wear the victory laurels, carried in an ivory chariot by white horses. . . . And how, when Sirius cleaves the scorched fields, the fertile Nile abounds with summery water? Father Nile, in what way may I utter the cause or in which lands you have hidden your head? Because of you your land does not request any showers, nor does the parched stalk yield to rain-giving Jupiter. The foreign youth, taught to bewail the Memphite bull, celebrates you in song and admires you as their own Osiris.

Tibullus then connects Osiris and the Memphite bull, Apis, with Messalla's *genius.* He wishes that Messalla be blessed with descendants (*at tibi succrescat proles quae facta parentis / augeat et circa stet veneranda senem*); thus, more directly, Egypt's fertility guaranteed by the Nile and its gods is linked to Augustus' general. Any negative overtones associated with Egypt are absent here. Cleopatra's country had been conquered and integrated. The god Osiris pays homage to Messalla. Augustus' placing of obelisks in Rome shows, on a more monumental scale than Tibullus' poem, that leading Romans saw themselves not only as conquerors but also as heirs of Egypt's tradition. The incorporation of these originally Egyptian monuments equipped with Latin inscriptions visually expressed both Augustus' claim to power and Rome's political superiority.

As with so many things in regard to Augustus, there was a carefully orchestrated relationship toward Egyptian gods and Egyptian symbols of power, one that is not easily separated into the public and private sphere. In the end, though, there were three Augustan actions that helped prepare the successful integration of Isis and Sarapis into the political sphere: first, the institutionalization of the emperor worship; second, the deification of Julius Caesar, which began the line of the *divi imperatores*; and third, the manufacture of carefully directed images and signs. The systematic propagation of the concept of the emperor as the central social, political, and religious force of the state set him apart from all the other inhabitants of the Empire. An emperor was a *divi filius* (son of a god) and this status had an inherent dynamic. Each subsequent emperor could place himself among gods more easily than his predecessor and thus expect appropriate treatment. The *princeps* gradually became a living exemplar of this myth that furnished the structure of Rome's religious and political life. The extraordinary position of the *princeps* eventually matched that of the Ptolemaic rulers, whose dynastic myths of succession, based on apotheosis and divine honors, suited well the emerging political realities at Rome. And Augustus, once thought to be the bulwark against Egyptian influences, was the one whose policies ultimately led to an integration of the goddess Isis and her consort, Sarapis.

Horace's poem 1.37 (*nunc est bibendum*) captures the irony that the hated *fatale monstrum* is herself instrumental for Roman history and its development. This poem, filled with dichotomies and layered paradoxes, in the end turns the *monstrum* into something brave, something acceptable.[48] The *uraeus* (sacred serpent) on the headdress of Egyptian pharaohs signified their sovereignty. Cleopatra chose the venomous bite of a formidable Egyptian asp (*uraeus*) to end her life[49] and with her death the pharaonic system ended. While Ted Hughes' Cleopatra sought herself in a serpent undergoing a transformation from the female to the masculine sphere of power and authority, and while the modern poet hails the snake's reign, her impact was in truth not that immediate. Augustus made sure that Rome and its political institutions were perceived as intact and supreme. In creating and preserving that perception, however, Ptolemaic Egypt's dynastic etiology and ideology swam ever so gently toward Rome.

NOTES

I would like to thank Margaret Miles for her enthusiasm and commitment in putting together the Egyptomania conference at the University of California at Irvine and shepherding the editing process ever so gently and skillfully. A version of this paper was given at All Soul's College, Oxford, in a lecture series on "Culture and Language in Greco-Roman Egypt" headed by John Adam and Jane Lightfoot. Their and the audience's comments and inquiries were invaluable as was Maureen McGeary's inestimable input at later stages. I am grateful to Mary DiLucia who gave me Ted Hughes' *Cleopatra to the Asp* to read and to Gregory Dundas whose work on the imperial cult in Egypt I have found inspiring ever since we talked about it as graduate students.

1. For example, Cicero, *Res publica* 3.9 and Juvenal 15.10. A more detailed discussion of the material in K. A. D. Smelik and E. A. Hemelrijk, "Who Knows Not What Monsters Demented Egypt Worships? Opinions on Egyptian Animal Worship in Antiquity as Part of the Ancient Conception of Egypt," *ANRW* II 17.4 (1987): 1852–2000.

2. Here with the word *culture* I include the sharing and propagation of ideological information, and religious and historical data, in order to cultivate a people's basic and coherent belief of itself.

3. G. Dundas, "Pharaoh, Basileus and Imperator: The Roman Imperial Cult in Egypt" (diss. 1994): 60; F. Pfister, *Der Reliquienkult im Altertum* (1909–12, repr. 1974): 529ff; D. Kienast, "Augustus und Alexander," *Gymnasium* 76 (1969): 430–56; and E. Gruen, "Augustus and the Ideology of War and Peace," in R. Winkes, ed., *The Age of Augustus* (1985): 51–72.

4. Dio Cassius 50.24.6–7: "Alexandrians and Egyptians who worship reptiles and other beasts as if they were gods, who embalm their bodies for an appearance of immortality, and . . . those being the boldest [i.e., men] prostrate themselves and those being the weakest [i.e., women] play the man . . ."

5. Dio Cassius 50.24–27.

6. See, for example, G. J .F. Kater-Sibbes and M. J. Vermaseren, *Apis* (1975).

7. C. Maystre, *Les grands prêtres de Ptah de Memphis* (1992). On the linkage of the Apis bull to

royal ritual see Dundas (1994): 63, with reference to D. J. Thompson, *Memphis under the Ptolemies* (1988) and "The High Priests of Memphis under Ptolemaic Rule," in M. Beard and J. North, eds., *Pagan Priests* (1988): 97–116. It should be noted that the Roman authors who mention Augustus' refusal of ceremonies centered on the Apis bull were probably well aware of the notorious account of the Persian king Cambyses' sacrilegious treatment of the bull (jeering at it and then stabbing it fatally in its thigh) after he conquered Egypt in the late sixth century B.C.E., behavior believed to have driven him mad (Hdt. 3.27–29); the later Persian king Ochos was said to have roasted and eaten the bull (Plutarch, *De Iside et Osiride* 11). Even Augustus himself possibly might have known that behavior toward the Apis was regarded by Egyptians as a sort of litmus test of legitimacy to rule, one that the Ptolemies had used to their advantage.

8. According to Thompson (1988), probably after the events in Rome of 13 January.

9. Thompson (1988): 271. Dundas (1994): 82, note 101, gives a translation of a "'composite' titulary of Augustus" reconstructed by J.-C. Grenier, "Traditions pharaoniques et realités impériales: Le nom de couronnement du Pharaon à l'époque romaine," in L. Criscuolo and G. Geraci, eds., *Egitto e storia antica dall'ellenismo all'età araba* (1989): 403–20: "Strong of arm, smiter of foreigners, great of power, Champion of Egypt, the handsome youth, lovable, the king of kings, elect of Ptah-Tenen the great Nun, father of gods; who has taken possession of the kingship of Rè on the throne of Geb in order to protect the throne of Shu, who enters Egypt to the rejoicing of the people and in the joy of the gods and goddesses, who takes possession of the power like Rè shining in the horizon, sovereign, king, son of a king, whose commands reach the limits of the heavens; rampart of bronze around Egypt, the living Apis, heir of Ptah who loves him and announces for him a long era full of happiness, (for) he has made offerings to the gods, he has protected all the sacred animals of Egypt, and he has (thus) confirmed the laws of the Universe, as Thoth, twice great, lord of Hermopolis, who offers maat to Rè; who watches over the prosperity of Egypt, whose power is incomparable in the city *par excellence* which he loves, Rome."

10. Suetonius (*Life of Augustus*) mentions the viewing of Alexander's body in chapter 18, and the omission of visiting the Apis bull in chapter 93.

11. *P. Oxy.* 2332.531. Thompson (1988): 4, note 6: "*theotokos Memphis*, the otherwise Christian imagery is striking." The editors of the papyrus text dated the piece to 311 C.E. The Christian imagery should not seem too striking for Egypt even in the early fourth century C.E.

12. Thompson (1988): 4.

13. J. Assmann, *Stein u. Zeit* (1991): 312: "Ptah, der Gott von Memphis, wird . . . dem traditionellen Schöpfergott Re, dem Sonnengott, vorangestellt. Ptah, der Gott der Erde, des Urhügels und des Handwerks ist älter als der Gott des Himmels, des Lichts und der Zeit. Noch bevor Re sich zum Himmel erhob und durch sein Licht und seine Bewegung alle Dinge schuf und ordnete, schuf Ptah, der memphitische Urgott, indem er das All in seinem Herzen ersann. In all dem prägt sich eine Besinnung auf die eigene Geschichte und die eigenen Ursprünge aus. Memphis ist die erste Hauptstadt Ägyptens, die Stätte der ältesten Denkmäler . . . Memphis wurde zum Inbegriff der Vergangenheit, die nun erstmals als etwas Ganzes, Großes und von der Gegenwart Abgesondertes sichtbar gemacht wurde . . ." The original text (with German translation) can be found in H. Junker, *Die Götterlehre von Memphis: Schabaka-Inschrift* (1940).

14. J. Vercoutter, *Textes Biographiques du Sérapéum de Memphis* (1962).

15. Thompson (1988): 114–25 and (1990): 107–16; D. J. Crawford, J. Quaegebeur, and W. Clarysse, eds., *Studies on Ptolemaic Memphis* (1980).

16. Franz Cumont, *Oriental Religions in Roman Paganism* (1911): 83–84.

17. Reginald Witt, *Isis in the Ancient World* (1971, reprint 1997).

18. Augustus' personal story has some obvious parallels to the story of Horus: he was the (adopted) son of Julius Caesar, whose Julian clan traced its ancestry back through Aeneas' son Iulius

to Aeneas' mother the goddess Venus; Augustus too had tracked down the assassins of Julius Caesar and defeated them, and celebrated their defeat with a temple to Mars Ultor (the Avenger) in his new forum, vowed on the eve of the battle and dedicated in 2 B.C.E.

19. For further discussion and bibliography see Sarolta A. Takács, *Isis and Sarapis in the Roman World* (1995).

20. L. Vidman, *Sylloge inscriptionum religionis Isiacae et Sarapiacae* (1969). Today there are about 800 inscriptions recorded of which approximately 10 percent come from Rome and 25 percent from Delos.

21. G. Alföldy, "Die Krise des Imperium Romanum und die Religion Roms," *Religion und Gesellschaft in der römischen Kaiserzeit, Kölner Historische Abhandlung* 35 (1989): 53–102.

22. Letter written in 44 B.C.E.

23. I. Becher, *Das Bild der Kleopatra in der griechischen und lateinischen Literatur* (1966): her discussion of Cicero, pp. 17–18.

24. Joseph Burel, *Isis et les Isiaques sous l'Empire romain* (1911).

25. This refers to the scandal concerning Paulina and Decimus, in the reign of Tiberius (Josephus, *Antiquitates Judaicae* 18.66–80).

26. Dio Cassius 50.5.3.

27. Discussed in F. Dunand, *Le culte d'Isis dans le basin oriental de la Méditerranée* (1973) 2: 4, 83–115.

28. W. Burkert, *Ancient Mystery Cults* (1987): 6–27, 38–41, 97–98.

29. *CIL* I2 1263 = VI 227 = *SIRIS* 377:

A. Caecili(us) A. l(ibertus) Olipor| Cn. Caecili A. [l(iberti)] Silonis| Caeci[li]a A. et Cn. l(iberta) Asia| A. Caecili A. Cn. l(iberti) Alexsandri|5 Polla Caecilia Spuri [f(ilia)]| A. Cae[c]ili A. f(ilii) Pal(atina) Rufi| T. Sulpici T. f(ilii) {Caecili} sac(erdotis) Isid(is) Capitoli(nae)| Porcia T. l(iberta) Rufa {sac(erdos)} Sulpici {Capitoli(nae)}| T. Porcius T. f(ilius) Col(lina) Maxsimus|10 T. Sulpicius T. l(ibertus) Primus| C. Valerius C. l(ibertus) [P]hilar[g]urus| Q. Lolius Q. [f(ilius)] H]or(atia) Rufus| D. Aurelius D. l(ibertus) Stella (?)| H(oc) m(onumentum) <h>e(redes) non seq(uetur)

30. For a more detailed analysis of the integration of Isis and Sarapis and the political aspects touched upon throughout this paper see Takács (1995).

31. A. Alföldi, "Isiskult und Umsturzbewegung im letzten Jahrhundert der römischen Republik," *Schweizerische Münzblätter* 5 (1954): 25–31.

32. Alföldi (1954): 30: ". . . stets kampfbereite revolutionäre Stoßgruppe der Isiaci."

33. For discussion of the famous Barberini mosaic and its date (between 120 and 110 B.C.E.), see P. G .P. Meyboom, *The'Nile Mosaic of Palestrina: Early Evidence of Egyptian Religion in Italy* (1995).

34. M. De Vos, *L'Egittomania in pitture e mosaici Romano-Campania della prima età imperiale* (1980).

35. G. Carettoni, *Das Haus des Augustus auf dem Palatin* (1983): 67–85.

36. M.-Th. Picard-Schmitter, "Bétyles Hellenistiques," *Fondation Eugène Piot Monuments et Mémoires* 57 (1971): 43–88.

37. This temple, which stood outside the *Porta Carmentalis*, was dedicated in 431 B.C.E.

38. T. P. Wiseman, "Cybele, Virgil, and Augustus," in T. Woodman and D. West, eds., *Poetry and Politics in the Age of Augustus* (1984): 125.

39. Dio Cassius 49.15.5. The interpretation of the omen is in itself a reversal, for lightning is usually interpreted as a negative omen. The temple of Apollo on the Palatine and Augustus' ideology are discussed by P. Zanker, *The Power of Images in the Age of Augustus* (1988): esp. 65–70.

40. Trans. Robert Fitzgerald (1990): 254–55.

41. Plutarch, *Life of Antony* 24.

42. Plutarch, *De Iside et Osiride* 362a.

43. Here, as well as below, I follow T. P. Wiseman's excellent discussion of Augustus' Palatine

complex (1984). For details of its topography and the archaeological remains, L. Haselberger, ed., *Mapping Augustan Rome* (2002): 104–6, s.v. *Domus: Augustus*.

44. This version of the myth is represented in Aeschylus' *The Suppliant Maidens*. For an analysis of the Greek views of Egypt and Egyptians implicit in this play, see P. Vasunia, *The Gift of the Nile: Hellenizing Egypt from Aeschylus to Alexander* (2001): 33–58. In early versions of the story, only Hypermnestra does not kill her new husband and shows herself to be a faithful wife; her motives and exceptional status attracted the attention of Augustan poets: her heroism is praised by Horace (*Odes* 3.11) and Ovid (*Heroides* 14). For architectural details, see C. K. Quenemoen, "The Portico of the Danaids: A New Reconstruction," *AJA* 110 (2006): 229–50.

45. A more detailed discussion of the Alexandrian and Pergamene library in G. Nagy, "The Library of Pergamon," in H. Koester, ed., *Pergamon: Citadel of the Gods, Harvard Theological Studies* 46 (1998): 185–232, esp. 194–99.

46. T. P. Wiseman, "*Conspicui Postes Tectaque Digna Deo*: The Public Image of Aristocratic and Imperial Houses in the Late Republic and Early Empire," in *L'Urbs, Espace Urbain et Histoire* (1987): 395.

47. Burel (1911): 8: ". . . l'Alexandrisme sous toutes formes . . . envahit totalement la civilisation romaine."

48. Michèle Lowrie, *Horace's Narrative Odes* (1997) offers an insightful discussion on this poem.

49. See R. Gurval in this volume as well as M. Guarducci, "La 'morte di Cleopatra' nella catacomba della Via Latina," *Atti della Pontificia Accademia Romana di Archeologia*, ser. 3, vol. 37 (1964–65): 259–81.

5

Love, Triumph, Tragedy

Cleopatra and Egypt
in High Renaissance Rome

Brian A. Curran

In the 1963 film version of *Cleopatra*, the part of Julius Caesar is played by the suave British stage and screen actor, Rex Harrison (1908–90).[1] Seeing the film on the big screen at the symposium that inspired these papers, I was once again impressed by the urbanity and worldliness that this fine performer brought to the role. His sure touch is missed in the second part of the film, where the romance between Cleopatra and Antony tends to drag, despite the legendary behind-the-scenes romance of Harrison's co-stars.[2] Two years later, Harrison took a leading role in another cinematic epic, Sir Carol Reed's production of the *Agony and the Ecstasy* (1965), an adaptation of Irving Stone's best-selling novel about Michelangelo and the painting of the Sistine Ceiling. Charlton Heston played the tortured but inspired artist, while Harrison essayed the role of his implacable patron and sometime nemesis, Pope Julius II. Harrison works hard to convey the ambition and impatience of this famously "terrible" pontiff, whose ferocity is provoked by the artist's stubborn claims to autonomy. His best scenes come at the end of the film, when painter and pontiff find solace and vindication in the sublimity of the finished ceiling. But there is a further irony in Harrison's essaying the roles of the Roman general Julius Caesar and the Roman pontiff Julius II only a couple of years apart. For it was a recurring conceit of the later, the "warrior" pope and self-styled "second" Julius, to compare himself (or to have others compare him) to his most distinguished political and military namesake. The broader implications of this association, and their relevance to an episode in the cultural "afterlife" of the Egyptian Queen who was Caesar's most celebrated romantic and political "conquest" (if conquest it can be called) will be the focus of this chapter.

JULIUS II, THE PAPACY, AND THE REMAINS
OF ANTIQUITY

As the pope most associated with the flowering of the "classical" style of the High Renaissance in Rome, Julius II (Giuliano della Rovere, b. 1443, pope 1503–11) seems an unlikely Egyptian revivalist, especially when compared to his predecessor, Alexander VI Borgia (Rodrigo Borgia, ruled 1492–1503), who claimed descent from the Egyptian Osiris (see more below).[3] Julius' grandiose projects— the rebuilding of St. Peter's Basilica, the construction of the vast Cortile del Belvedere, the much-delayed plan for his own papal tomb, and the celebrated fresco projects for the Sistine Ceiling and the Vatican *stanze*—are directed to a revival of an explicitly Roman *imperium*, and seem as far as they can be from contemporary dabblings in "Egyptian" mysticism and fantasy. As it turns out, however, Julius' pontificate does not represent a hiatus in the revival of Egyptian themes so much as a redirection of them to the Julian themes of triumph and imperial restoration.[4]

But before considering Julius' cultural and "Egyptianizing" agendas in detail, a little historical background would seem to be in order. As is generally well known, by the time that Julius came to the papal throne in 1503, the papacy as an institution had only recently emerged from a period of conflict and uncertainty. After the disastrous conflicts that afflicted the would-be "imperial" papacy of Boniface VIII (ruled 1294–1303), his successors took the drastic step of moving the papal residence to Avignon in southern France, the better to escape the depredations of the fractious and warlike Roman barons. The ensuing "Babylonian exile" had catastrophic consequences for the Eternal City, and the return of the papacy in 1377 appeared, briefly, to hold the promise of restoration. But the election of rival popes in the wake of Gregory XI's death in 1377 inaugurated a period of even greater confusion, which ended only after an agreement was reached at the Council of Constance (1414–18), which forced the rival popes to resign and elected the Roman Oddone Colonna, who took the name Martin V, the first pontiff of the newly "unified" church (he ruled from 1417 to 1431).

Martin V may rightly be considered the first "Renaissance" pope, and key elements of his policies—the renewal and rebuilding of Rome, the consolidation of the papal states, the promotion of papal primacy in European political, cultural, and religious life—were taken up, with varying success and emphasis, by his successors. In promoting their right to authority in matters worldly and religious, the popes emphasized their inheritance of the throne of St. Peter the Apostle, who had been selected by Christ himself as the "rock" upon which he would build his church. Since Peter had come to Rome to be martyred and had been buried on the site of the Vatican basilica, the popes could claim to have inherited the right to rule in Rome from him. But this was not enough for the founders of the medieval papacy, who claimed, through promotion of the so-called Donation of Constantine, to have inherited the Imperial authority of the Roman emperors as well. During the fifteenth century, the legitimacy of this claim was challenged by the deconstruction of the eighth-century Donation by Lorenzo Valla, but the Roman pontiffs from Martin's successor Eugenius IV to Julius and his successors, the Medici Popes Leo X and Clement VII, continued to base their claims to inherited *imperium* on this tradition.[5]

In the cultural sphere, the Renaissance papacy promoted this ideology through the systematic appropriation of Roman imagery and rhetoric.[6] By the second half of the fourteenth century, a new tool for the reclamation of Rome's ancient legacy began to emerge in the new "humanist" movement. As scholars dedicated to the study of Latin literature and the renewal of ancient culture, the humanists and their agents scoured the monasteries of Europe and the Greek east for the "lost" manuscripts of the ancient authors. At the same time, they began to approach the battered fabric of the Eternal City as a kind of three-dimensional text, whose monuments, if properly understood, could likewise provide valuable testimony for the greatness of the ancients. Pope Martin's return to Rome in 1420 brought new opportunities—and a sense of political urgency—to the studies of the humanists in his employ. Inscriptions were copied and collected in volumes of *syllogai*, and the ruins were scrutinized to determine their original appearance, date, and function. Over time, a virtual "cult" of antiquity emerged among humanists whose livelihood depended, not always reliably, on the patronage of the popes and other princes of the church who hoped to *become* pope. Palaces filled with ancient statues, libraries with copies of the works of the ancient authors, the "authorities" consulted for information on all things antique.[7]

HIEROGLYPHS AND OBELISKS

One by-product of this humanist-antiquarian movement was the emergence of a kind of Egyptology. The ancient authors had a lot to say about Egyptian history, culture, and religion. Indeed, as Stanley Burstein has observed, "references to Egypt and its culture occur in the works of almost every surviving classical author."[8] What intrigued the early humanists most, however, were their accounts of the Egyptian hieroglyphs, which the authors described with confident unanimity as a system of allegorical picture-writing that the Egyptians had devised in remote antiquity to preserve the memory of their knowledge and accomplishments for later generations. According to this tradition, the Egyptian priests had jealously guarded the secret of the hieroglyphs, the better to conceal the details of their most sacred doctrines from the eyes of the ignorant masses. But since the symbolic meanings of the individual signs had been inspired by their inventors'

profound knowledge of the essential meaning of things, it was theoretically possible that they might be understood by the most enlightened minds of later times
and cultures. If only some specimens of this amazing form of writing could be
identified and examined, they might begin to reveal some of the lost wisdom of
the Egyptians.[9]

As it turned out, of course, the humanists did not have to look far for examples
of the hieroglyphs. For prominent among the Roman monuments that they studied with such passion and care were any number of Egyptian obelisks and other
pharaonic and Egyptianizing antiquities—including statues, cult objects, and
Isiac and nilotic wall decorations.[10] Some of these had come to Rome as spoils of
the Roman conquest of Egypt (and the defeat of Cleopatra), most notably the pair
of Heliopolitan obelisks that Augustus raised in the city in 10 B.C., to mark the
twentieth anniversary of his Egyptian triumph.[11] Others made their way to Rome
to provide suitable ornament for the Roman sanctuaries of Isis and Serapis, or
to lend an exotic element to the decoration of the houses and gardens of Roman
patricians.[12] And so, during the Imperial period Rome became a kind of open-
air Egyptian museum. According to the sources, there were some 48 obelisks
in the city by the middle of the fourth century. But over the ensuing centuries,
as they fell prey to vandalism, earthquake, and other ravages, the obelisks fell
into the debris of the ruined city. By the early 1400s only three remained standing upright in Rome. Two of these were small, hieroglyph-covered monuments
from the Roman temple of Isis near the Pantheon (see below). But the third was
something else again: the towering, 82-foot monolith called the *guglia* or "needle"
at the Vatican. The *Vaticanus* was unique in many ways. It was the only obelisk
in the city that still rose on its original ancient base over the ruins of the circus
on the south flank of St. Peter's Basilica, where it had been set up after its removal
from Alexandria by order of the emperor Caligula in ca. 37 B.C.[13] It was also, along
with the still-buried pair at the Mausoleum of Augustus, one of the small number
of obelisks that lacks a hieroglyphic inscription. The only carving on its surface
was a curious and partially eradicated Latin inscription on its lower east and west
faces that records its dedication to Caligula's predecessors—the deified Augustus
and Tiberius:

DIVO CAESARI DIVI IU.I.F. AUGUSTO, TI CAESARI DIVI AUGUST.F.
AUGUSTO, SACRUM

Sacred to the Divine Caesar Augustus, son of the Divine Julius, and to Tiberius
Caesar Augustus, son of the Divine Julius.[14]

By the twelfth century, presumably as a result of this dedication, the obelisk
had become widely identified as the Tomb of Julius Caesar, whose ashes were
believed to be interred in the bronze sphere at the monument's summit (an alter-

nate tradition associated the obelisk with the martyrdom of St. Peter). Although it was discredited by the middle of the Quattrocento (thanks in large part to the somewhat garbled passage in Pliny the Elder's *Natural History* describing its transport to Rome) the Caesarian tradition retained its hold on the imagination of popes and humanists well into the sixteenth century, and was not entirely discredited until 1586, when the globe was removed and pronounced empty by Pope Sixtus V's team of experts.[15]

But as noted above, the *Vaticanus* was not the only obelisk that could be seen in Rome in the early fifteenth century. There were the two previously mentioned obelisks from the Iseum Campense, both of them inscribed in hieroglyphs for the pharaoh Rameses II, that stood in the Piazza di San Macuto (near the Pantheon) and on the north side of the Campidoglio Piazza on the Capitoline Hill. Broken but partially unburied obelisks, also inscribed with hieroglyphs, could be seen on the Pincian hill and in the ruins of the extramural circuses near the Via Labicana and the Via Appia. There were also a number of Egyptian statues that could be seen in the city, the most prominent being the pair of grey granite lions of Nectanebo I that reclined on their hieroglyph-covered bases in the Piazza della Rotunda, where they provided fitting frontispieces for the great columnar porch of the Pantheon.[16]

Recognition of these monuments' Egyptian origins was made possible by some fortuitous manuscript discoveries in the early fifteenth century. In the late 1410s and early 1420s, copies of Horapollo's *Hieroglyphica* and Ammianus Marcellinus' fourth-century Roman history came into the hands of the Florentine humanists Niccolò Niccoli and Poggio Bracciolini. The great scholar of Renaissance hieroglyphic studies, Karl Giehlow, has identified the convergence of these persons in Rome ca. 1422–24, as the historical moment when the carvings on the obelisks were recognized as the "sacred letters" of the Egyptians. Poggio was the first to identify them "in print," in his *De varietate fortunae* of 1448.[17]

Thanks to the work of these scholars, devotees of the antiquities of Rome "awoke" one day to find themselves in a landscape seasoned with Egyptian monuments and inscriptions. Fired with the excitement of recognition, did they rush to put their sources to the test and attempt to decipher these enigmatic carvings themselves? If so, their efforts must have met with frustration, since the record is virtually silent on this point. But the idea of the hieroglyphs was too compelling to be abandoned by a humanist culture obsessed with the restoration and emulation of the lost arts of the ancients. The problem of decipherment was set aside in favor of a more promising project: the *reinvention* of the "Egyptian" method for the creation of modern hieroglyphs. One of the earliest and most influential formulations of this idea is found in Leon Battista Alberti's *De re aedificatoria* (1452–72, printed 1485). In the course of a discussion of funerary monuments and inscriptions, Alberti suggests that the hieroglyphs could provide appropri-

FIGURE 10. *Roman Scene
with the Vatican Obelisk,*
from Giovanni Marcanova,
Collectio antiquitatum (ca. 1465),
Princeton University Library,
MS Garrett 158, fol. 6v. Photo
courtesy Princeton University
Library.

ate ornaments for contemporary monuments, since, as a potentially "universal"
system of image-writing, their meanings could be accessible to later generations
even if the meaning of alphabetic inscriptions became lost (as had happened, he
observed, with the writing of the Etruscans). Indeed, Alberti argues, the ancient
Greeks and Romans had understood this principle when they added reliefs and
emblems their own monuments. What was good enough for the Romans, of
course, was good enough for Alberti and his readers, and from the 1450s on, the
enthusiasm for the hieroglyphs contributed in no small part to the Renaissance
taste for emblems and *imprese.*[18]

In his capacity as architect and archaeologist, Alberti was probably involved in
the project, initiated by Pope Nicholas V (1447–55), to move the Vatican obelisk to
the piazza in front of St. Peter's basilica. According to Nicholas' secretary, Gianozzo
Manetti (1396–1459), the obelisk was to be raised on life-sized bronze figures of
the Evangelists and topped with a bronze figure of the risen Christ. This fantastic
scheme was quickly abandoned after Nicholas' death, although preliminary studies
for its transport were reportedly drawn up, and the base of the monument itself was
partially cleared, as drawings of the 1460s reveal (see Fig. 10).[19] The plan was revived

briefly toward the end of the pontificate of Paul II (ca. 1471) and was entertained by a succession of later pontiffs, notably Leo X and Paul III. But despite the best intentions of these popes and their architects, the obelisk remained in its original location until 1586, when its removal was successfully realized by Sixtus V and Domenico Fontana in a feat that was considered an engineering miracle of its day.[20]

NEW SETTINGS AND FRESH MEANINGS FOR ROME'S "EGYPTIAN EXILES"

The "Egyptian Revival" of the Renaissance entered a new phase with the discovery and dissemination of the philosophical/religious writings attributed to the Egyptian sage Hermes Trismegistus.[21] This collection of Greek texts was translated into Latin in 1463 by Marsilio Ficino, who provided commentaries emphasizing its apparent prefigurations of Christian doctrine. Through this work and a series of translations (including those by Iamblichus and Plotinus), Ficino established the reputation of Hermes as a pagan prophet who stood at the forefront of a divinely inspired ancient theology or *prisca theologia* that descended from the Egyptians to the Greeks and found its fulfillment in Christian revelation.[22] So successful was Ficino's promotion of the Hermetic "idea" that by the 1490s the Egyptian gods were respectable enough to be admitted to the private chambers of the pope himself.

On the vault of the Sala dei Santi in the Appartamento Borgia of the Vatican palace, above a set of richly gilded scenes of some of Alexander VI's patron saints, Bernardino Pinturicchio painted the first monumental Egyptian mythological cycle since antiquity. Working in the period ca. 1493–95, Pinturicchio covered the entire ceiling with scenes from the myths of Isis, Osiris, and the sacred bull Apis. The narrative details are culled from the best ancient sources, including Ovid, Diodorus Siculus, and (possibly) Plutarch. The story of Osiris and Apis unfolds on the eight triangular compartments of the vaults. The northern vaults represent Osiris' activities as the benefactor of mankind, including his marriage to Isis and his institution of the arts of agriculture, including the cultivation of the vine and the use of the ox-driven plow. On the southern vault, Osiris is murdered and dismembered by his treacherous half-brother Typhon and his limbs are reassembled by Isis for burial in a gold and jewel-encrusted pyramid-tomb. The final scenes show the appearance of Apis before the mourners at Osiris' tomb and the institution of his cult, as a shrine with a golden statue of the sacred bull is carried in procession by a group of worshippers (Fig. 11). The parallel story of the bovine transformation and later apotheosis of Io as the Egyptian Isis is depicted on the panels of the central arch.[23]

The primary motivation for this unexpected exercise in Egyptian mythography was recognized years ago: to provide a mytho-poetic gloss on the origins

FIGURE 11. Pinturricchio, *Procession of Apis* (1493–95). Vault of the Salal dei Santi in the Appartamento Borgia, Vatican Palace. Alinari/Art Resource, New York.

of the heraldic ox of the Borgia arms (a figure that appears hundreds of times in these rooms). The most obvious clue is provided by a detail in the fresco of the *Disputation of St. Catherine of Alexandria* that dominates the southern wall. In the background, the Gate of the Temple of Serapis is represented by a modified Arch of Constantine, topped by a golden bull and dedicated in gold letters "To the Cultivator of Peace," a motto adopted by the pope on a medal in 1494.[24] A specific dynastic and genealogical connection to the pope's family is suggested in the final scene. One of the Apis worshippers is marked by the Aragonese double-crown, a preferred device of the Borgia, while an acroterial figure of Heracles, Borgia's supposed ancestor, appears at the top of the Apis-shrine.[25]

The heraldic Egyptology of Pinturicchio's frescoes has long been associated with one of the most notorious figures in Alexander's court circle, Giovanni Nanni, better known as Annius of Viterbo (ca. 1432–1502).[26] A Dominican friar who dabbled in prophecy, astrology, and historical and archaeological forgery, Annius was appointed *Magister Sacri Palatii* (theologian to the papal court) by Alexander VI in 1499.[27] But his connection to the Borgia pope dated back at least to the autumn of 1493, when Alexander was present at Annius' fortuitous discovery of an Etruscan tomb in Viterbo whose contents included, according to Annius, a statue of Isis.[28]

But this was not Annius' only Egyptological discovery. As early as 1491–92, he announced that a marble relief that he "discovered" on the pulpit of the Viterbo's cathedral was nothing less than a fragment of a triumphal column inscribed in "the sacred letters of the Egyptians" to commemorate the victory of Osiris over the giants in Viterbo in remote antiquity.[29] It is difficult for modern observers to grasp how Annius came to identify this assemblage—preserved and recently restored in the Museo Civico of Viterbo (Fig. 12)—as an Egyptian or hieroglyphic monument. Present-day scholars have identified the central panel as a lunette of twelfth-to-thirteenth-century date, and the accompanying profile heads (which Annius identified as portraits of Osiris and his cousin Sais Xantho, the "muse of Egypt") to be later, perhaps fifteenth-century work.[30]

Annius' most extensive discussion of the *columna*—including his sign-for-sign "translation" of its so-called hieroglyphs—appears in the pages of his *magnum opus*, the *Commentaria . . . super opera diversorum auctorum de Antiquitatibus* ("Commentaries on Works of Various Authors Discussing Antiquities"), published in Rome in 1498 with the privilege of Alexander VI himself (and reprinted in many later editions).[31] The core of the work consists of a collection of ancient texts—attributed to Berosus of Chaldea and the Egyptian Manetho, among others—that were purportedly rediscovered, but actually forged by Annius himself, but the description appears in Annius' commentary. This excerpt gives an idea of its character and content:

> And Pliny, in his *Natural History* says that these images that you see are Egyptian sacred letters. Therefore, on this column there is a space, in the middle of which is the trunk of an oak tree, resembling a compounded scepter, the tops of whose branches form the image of an eye. These images are particular to Osiris, as Xenophon affirms. Both he and Macrobius, in the first book of the *Saturnalia*, confirm this, saying that to express Osiris in the sacred letters they carved a scepter, and they [also] represented him with the image of an eye. And by this sign they

FIGURE 12. "Columna Osiriana," Museo Civico, Viterbo. Photo by Brian Curran.

showed Osiris. Moreover, they placed on this tree trunk not one but many scepters, because he ruled not only one, but every part of the world, as Diodorus writes . . . Therefore, these . . . effigies may be read in this fashion: "I am Osiris the king, who was called against by the Italians and hastened to fight against the oppressors of the Italian dominion . . . I am Osiris, who taught the Italians to plow, to sow, to prune, to cultivate the vine, gather grapes, and make wine, and I left behind for them my two nephews, as guardians of the realm from land and sea."[32]

For all their display of real and spurious learning, Annius' labors were motivated by a rather simple agenda: to prove the importance of his hometown of Viterbo in the earliest history of Italy and human civilization.[33] The main thrust

of his narrative can be summarized as follows. Noah, whom Annius identified with the Etruscan founder-god, Janus, retired to Italy after dividing the
kingdoms of the world among his sons. Settling on the future site of Viterbo, he
founded an enlightened kingdom based on the doctrines imparted to him by
God. Among his most distinguished descendants was the Egyptian king Osiris,
also known as Apis, who was the son of Noah's least favorite offspring, Cham.
In the sixth century after the flood, Osiris was called to Italy to liberate the
colonies established by his grandfather from a race of cannibalistic giants. Osiris
campaigned with the help of his son, Heracles the Egyptian (called Libyus or
Aegyptius). Victorious, Osiris ruled in Viterbo for ten years, then returned to
Egypt, where he was killed and dismembered by his jealous brother Typhon.
Heracles and his mother Isis began another war against Typhon and his allies
(another gang of evil giants). Heracles' campaign brought him to Libya (where he
killed the giant Antaeus), to Spain (where he founded the ancient line of Spanish
kings, including the Borgia), and eventually to Italy, where he restored the kingdoms of his forefathers.[34]

Annius' Euhemeristic conception of history, which explains the mythical
figures of antiquity as "famous men" and rulers whose contributions to civilization led to their deification by later generations, was applicable to genealogy as
well as to history.[35] In one such case, Annius apparently traced the origins of the
Farnese family (important local patrons in Viterbo) all the way back to Heracles
and Osiris.[36] He probably provided a similar genealogy for the Borgia, whose
origins could be traced to the ancient kings of Spain and the same Egyptian
Heracles.[37]

The Egyptological fantasies of Pinturicchio and Annius prompted one scholar
to remark that the Renaissance fascination with Egypt "reached its peak in
Rome in the years around 1500."[38] The virtually simultaneous appearance of
that most celebrated of all Renaissance exercises in hieroglyphic *fantasia*, the
Hypnerotomachia Poliphili of 1499, has inspired a number of attempts—most
notably by Maurizio Calvesi—to link the elusive author of this work to the same
Roman milieu.[39] But, as I have argued elsewhere, these efforts have been unconvincing, and while it is evident that its illustrator had access to drawings and
description of monuments in Rome, the *Hypnerotomachia* is best understood in
traditional terms as the work of a Venetian friar whose approach was rooted in
the local tradition of close trade and cultural ties to Egypt and the East.[40]

POPE JULIUS II AS THE SECOND JULIUS CAESAR

The 1490s may have marked an early peak, but the Roman/Renaissance taste
for things Egyptian did not fade into the shadows after Alexander's passing in
August 1503. After the month-long interlude of Pius III, the Borgia pope was

succeeded by his mortal nemesis Giuliano della Rovere, who, so far as we know, made no claim to descend from Egyptian or any other mythical gods or heroes. But he certainly shared the warlike and imperial proclivities of his predecessor, and it was for these reasons that he was more than willing to have himself identified, in word and image, as a "Second Julius Caesar."

The most explicit representation of this theme appears on a small bronze medal issued to commemorate Julius' return to Rome on March 28, 1507, following his victory over the rebellious papal client city of Bologna. On the obverse face of the medal, a profile portrait of the pope is accompanied by an inscription IVLIVS. CAESAR. PONT. II. ("Julius Caesar Pontifex Maximus II"). As studies by Roberto Weiss, Charles Stinger, and Nicholas Temple have shown, this bold proclamation of Julius' Caesarian status is echoed in contemporary literary sources.[41] But Julius also asserted his status as a *triumphator* in public ceremonial, by staging his entry into Bologna (on 11 November 1506) and his subsequent return to Rome as triumphal processions in the Roman manner. Desiderius Erasmus, who witnessed the pope's passage through the streets of Bologna, made the connection when he expressed his personal disgust for this pope who "wages war, conquers, triumphs, and acts wholly like Julius [Caesar]."[42] In both cities, ephemeral triumphal arches were erected, and triumphal cars were decked out with appropriately all'antica emblems of victory, as well as devices and heraldry of the pope and his family. The Roman ceremonies, in particular, must have resembled, in their richness and general character, the spectacle depicted in Andrea Mantegna's great canvases of *The Triumphs of Caesar*, which had been painted for the Gonzaga of Mantua a few years earlier.[43] The staging of the pope's Roman entry on Palm Sunday provided a further association, which both Julius and his audience would have certainly recognized, with Christ's triumphal ride into Jerusalem. The inscription on the reverse of the Roman medal, "Blessed is he who comes in the name of the Lord," refers directly to the Palm Sunday liturgy, making that connection as explicit as it could be. [44]

In a recent study, Nicholas Temple has argued that the urban projects initiated by Julius II in the Vatican and other parts of Rome (including the laying out of the Via Julia and Via della Lungara on the east and west banks of the Tiber) may be understood as part of a broader scheme to renew the fabric of the modern city by restoring or emulating the routes associated with the ancient Via Triumphalis, the route of which had been studied by the great curial humanist Flavio Biondo (*Roma triumphans*, 1459).[45] It would seem then that a degree of consensus has emerged regarding this pontiff's conscious association of himself (and various aspects of his policy and public representation) with his most celebrated Roman namesake. But before proceeding, I should acknowledge that at least one prominent Julius II scholar, Christine Shaw, has expressed strong reservations on this point.[46] While she acknowledges the "imperial" scale of Julius' building projects and provides additional evidence for the "Caesarian" interpretation of his 1507 procession, Shaw's principle objection seems to be that, while writers, artists, and other interested parties may indeed have compared the "warrior" pope to Julius Caesar (and it cannot be denied that they did so), "what was said of Julius by other people, cannot be taken as evidence of his own motives."[47] The problem here may be a matter of culture vs. history, or intention vs. reception. It is, of course, completely plausible and even likely that (as Shaw argues) Julius may not have viewed his "imitation" of Julius Caesar as a defining motive in matters of political or ecclesiastical policy. And it is certainly true that his staging of "Roman" triumphs was not, in itself, especially original or innovative. As Shaw points out, Cesare Borgia had processed through the city in a comparable manner under his own appropriately "Caesarian" motto ("Caesar or nothing").[48] Indeed, throughout the fifteenth and sixteenth centuries, rulers of states routinely staged "triumphs" in this manner and laid claim to any number of associations with ancient conquerors, heroes, and gods.

Shaw proposes that the key figure with whom Julius "wished to be identified" was his uncle, Francesco della Rovere (1414–84), who as Pope Sixtus IV (r. 1471– 84), preceded Julius on the papal throne and raised the young Guiliano della Rovere to the cardinalate.[49] This may well be the case, of course, but it should be pointed out that identification with one does not in itself exclude a parallel association with the other. Sixtus IV was himself more than capable of comparing himself to the ancient rulers of Rome, as he did on the inscription appended to the fresco (which includes portraits of Sixtus along with his nephews Guiliano/ Julius and Raffaele Riario) commemorating his founding of the Vatican Library and provision of Rome with "churches and palace restored, and the streets, fora, city walls, bridges," the Aqua Virgo, and other urban amenities befitting the public works of a Roman emperor.[50]

My point here is that, whatever the inner motivations of a ruler like Julius II della Rovere may (or may not) have been, it clear that as pope, he was operating within a well-established set of cultural and political assumptions. And prominent among these was the idea, which he may have deliberately sought to emphasize through his choice of a papal name, that the papal rulers of Rome had inherited a legacy of power and authority formerly claimed by the ancient rulers of the city and its empire.

JULIUS II AND EGYPT

As a committed enemy of the Borgia pope, Giuliano della Rovere spent almost a decade in self-imposed exile from Rome before his return in the fall of 1503. Then, after the 26-day pontificate of Pius III (Francesco Todeschini Piccolomini), Giuliano was elected and took possession of the papal residence in the Vatican.

According to the papal Master of Ceremonies, Paris de Grassis, it was the constant sight of the image and *imprese* of his enemy Alexander VI in the Borgia Apartment that drove Julius to move his apartment upstairs to the Vatican *stanze*, whose redecoration by Raphael would be one of the cultural jewels of his pontificate.[51] In an article published in 1951, Ernst Gombrich suggested that Julius' distaste was not limited to the specific imagery of the Borgia decorations, but extended more broadly to a rejection of their fascination with Egypt and its hieroglyphs, and to theories about these things emanating from the general direction of Viterbo.[52]

I shall address some of Gombrich's specific arguments below. For the moment, however, it is important to note that attitudes toward Annius and his "Egyptian" theories at the Julian court were a bit more nuanced than his characterization suggests. Annius had his critics at the time, to be sure. The Florentine humanist and hieroglyph-expert Pietro Crinito (1475–1507) was perhaps the prominent among them. But there were others only too willing to accept his theses as genuine.[53] Perhaps the most important of these enthusiasts in the Julian context was Annius' fellow-townsman Egidio da Viterbo (1469–1532).[54] Inspired by the research of Ficino, Egidio embraced the idea of the *prisca theologia* and shared Ficino's view of the hieroglyphs as a mystical system devised to encode the "secret wisdom" of the Egyptians and their spiritual descendants.[55] Egidio was a close associate of Julius II, who favored him as an engaging preacher and propagandist, and appointed him vicar general of the Augustinian order. Indeed, as John O'Malley and Ingrid Rowland have shown, Egidio's synthesis of Annius' universal history with the Ficinian *prisca theologia* made a direct appeal to Julius' own ambitions as pontiff. How could the pope possibly argue with a man whose learned orations proclaimed his election to the throne of St. Peter as the fulfillment of Rome's primordial destiny? According to Egidio, the new pontiff was not only a new Julius Caesar, but a new Janus as well, and as such, represented the true and long-awaited successor to Annius' sacred, Etruscan kingdom.[56]

Gombrich extrapolated Julius' hostility to things Egyptian by linking two incidents where the pope rejected, seemingly out of hand, some Egyptianizing schemes proposed by his architect, Donato Bramante. The first of these must have occurred during the preliminary stages of the planning for the new St. Peter's. Our informant in this case is none other than Egidio da Viterbo, who reports that Bramante, frustrated by the challenge of moving the Vatican obelisk, recommended that the axis of the basilica be shifted from west-east to north-south, so that the facade could be aligned with the obelisk in its original position. But the pope, recognizing that this would require moving the tomb of the Apostle from its venerated location at the crossing of the basilica, rejected this proposal, and resisted Bramante's sycophantic argument that his plan would align the temple of the new Julius with the obelisk of his namesake, Julius Caesar. With Egidio's support, the matter of the obelisk was put aside (yet again).[57] A few years later (ca. 1506), Bramante presented a second project for Julius' approval. Our informant this time is Bramante's biographer, Giorgio Vasari:

> The fancy took Bramante to make, in a frieze on the outer facade of the Belvedere, some letters after the manner of ancient hieroglyphics (*a guisa di ieroglifi antichi*), representing the name of the Pope and his own, in order to show his ingenuity; and he had begun thus: "Julio II, Pont. Max.," having caused a head in profile of Julius Caesar to be made, and a bridge with two arches, which signified "Julio II, Pont," and an obelisk from the Circus Maximus to represent "Max." At which the point the Pope laughed, and caused him to make the letters in the ancient manner, one *braccio* in height, which are still there to this day, saying that he had copied this folly from a door at Viterbo. There one Maestro Francesco, an architect, had placed his name, carved in the architrave, and represented by a St. Francis (*Francesco*), an arch (*arco*), a roof (*tetto*), and a tower (*torre*), which interpreted in his own way, denoted "Maestro Francesco Architettore."[58]

There may be some truth to this anecdote, since the decision was taken to put a more traditional but still impressive Latin inscription (in gilt-bronze letters) in the same place.[59] It was Gombrich's view that Bramante's hieroglyphs were inspired by the *Hypnerotomachia*, and in particular by the hieroglyphic dedication of the obelisk of Caesar that appears in the Poliandrion cemetery in the later part of the book. The obelisk stands on a base with bizarre "hieroglyphic" medallions and a dedication, also in hieroglyphs, to Julius Caesar (Fig. 13).

> DIVO IULIO CAESARI SEMP. AUG. TOTIUS ORB. GUBERNAT OB ANIMI CLEMENT ET LIBERALITATEM AEGYPTII COMMUNI AER.S. EREXERE.

> To the Divine Julius Caesar, ever Augustus and ruler of the whole world, for his qualities of mercy and liberality, the Egyptians have erected this from their public funds.[60]

It is obvious that the *Hypnerotomachia* inscription—or its "translation" at the very least—was modeled on the Latin dedications of the Vatican obelisk. And there is no reason to believe that Bramante was not familiar with, or even inspired by, this imaginative adaptation.[61] On closer inspection, however, it becomes clear that Bramante's "hieroglyphs" are fundamentally different in conception from the ones in the *Hypnerotomachia*. Indeed, they may best be described as a rebus, since they function as pictorial puns, and not as allegorical image-signs. Whatever the degree of inspiration from the Venetian romance, it seems clear that Bramante relied on his own, rather different conception of the hieroglyphs for the Belvedere plan.[62]

Gombrich's suggestion that the reference to Viterbo represents a Julian swipe

numifmati in circo. Vno facello cum patefacta porta,cum una ara i me-
dio. Nouiffimamente erano dui perpendiculi. Lequale figure i latino cu
fi le interpretai.

DIVO IVLIO CAESARI SEMP. AVG.TOTIVS ORB.
GVBERNAT.OB ANIMI CLEMENT.ET LIBERALI
TATEMAEGYPTII COMMVNIA ERE.S.EREXERE.

Similmente in qualūque fron
te del recenfito fuppofito qua-
drato,quale la prima circulata
figura,tale unaltra fe pftaua a li
nea &ordie della prima a la de
xtra planitie dūque mirai an-
cora tali eleganti hieroglyphi,
primo uno uiperato caduceo.
Alla ima parte dilla uirga dil-
quale, & de qui,& deli,uidi u-
na formica che fe crefceua i ele
phanto. Verfo la fupernate æ-
qualmente dui elepháti decref
ceuano in formice. Tra quefti
nel mediaftimo era uno uafo PACE,AC CONCORDIA PAR-
cum foco,& dal altro lato una VAER'ESCRESCVNT,DISCOR
conchula cum aqua.cufi io li DIAMAXIMAEDECRESCVNT.
interpretai. Pace,ac concordia
paruæ res crefcūt,difcordia ma
xima decrefcunt.

FIGURE 13. Hieroglyphs
of the Obelisk of Caesar.
Hypnerotomachia Poliphili,
Venice, 1499, fol. p. vi–v. SAX
NE910.I8 C6 1499, Marquand
Library of Art and Archaeology,
Princeton University. Gift of
Frank Jewett Mather, Jr. Photo
courtesy Marquand Library,
Princeton University.

at Annius and the Borgia seems to have been compromised by a discovery that
was unknown to him. In the 1940s, a "hieroglyphic" lintel similar to the one
referenced by Vasari was discovered in Viterbo. Displayed today in the atrium
of the Cassa di Risparmio in Viterbo, this *peperino* slab has been connected to
the Vasarian anecdote by Enzo Bentivoglio.[63] While the original context of the
piece seems to be lost, its imagery corresponds in significant ways to Vasari's
description. Moving from the left to the right, the Franciscan monogram HIS is
followed by "hieroglyphic" images of an arch, a roof, and a tower (*architettore*)
and the word *faciebat*. Bentivoglio interpreted the monogram as an architect's
"signature" with the name, Francesco, denoted by the monogram, and it is hard
to imagine that Vasari had anything other than this lintel, or one similar to it, in
mind. Although there are problems—Bentivoglio has dated the lintel to the time
of Leo X—it would seem that Julius' retort to Bramante—however anachronistic
or anecdotal it may be—has little to do with Annius and his *columna*.[64]

A NEGLECTED OBELISK

Gombrich was also apparently unfamiliar with a another incident that would appear, at first glance, to support his "anti-Egyptian" thesis. This was the discovery of the large, broken obelisk, originally raised in the Campus Martius by Augustus as a token of his Egyptian victory, where it functioned as the *gnomon* of a gigantic sundial or *Horologium*.[65] Thanks to the account of Pliny the Elder (*Natural History* 36.14.72–73), the general location of this monument was familiar to Roman antiquarians of the fifteenth century. The earliest mention of its discovery comes from the text of an archaeological "tour" conducted between 1484 and 1498 by Pomponio Leto (1428–98). Passing through the Campus Martius, Leto observes that the base of the obelisk and pavements inscribed with "lines of gilt metal" and mosaics of the four winds could be seen in the cellars of the chaplains' house at the church of S. Lorenzo in Lucina.[66] These pavements are also noted in Francesco Albertini's *Opusculum de mirabilibus novae et veteris urbis Romae*, printed in 1510 and dedicated to Julius II. Albertini also mentions that the shaft of the obelisk had also been seen in his time, but had been abandoned "half-buried" in the debris.[67]

A date of 1512, appended to a schematic drawing of the obelisk in the *Codex Coner*, suggests that the obelisk was rediscovered again at about this time, that is, toward the end of Julius' reign.[68] The most detailed account is provided by the Bellunese humanist Antonio Lellio (known as Laelius Podager: "the Gouty"), writing in the margins of his copy of Jacopo Mazzocchi's *Epigrammatica antiquae urbis* (1521):

> In the *regio* of the Campus Martius in the time of Julius II, while a certain barber was digging a latrine in the garden of his little house between S. Lorenzo in Lucina and the house of Cardinal Grassi, he discovered the pedestal of the biggest obelisk that has ever been seen in the city. The obelisk had been thrown down, and it was not possible to see whether it was in one piece, since all of it could not be seen. On the base was an inscription that I read but did not remember correctly. It gave the name of the divine Augustus, followed by these words: "He dedicated it to the sun when Egypt had been brought under the sway of the Roman people." I recognized at once that this obelisk was the very famous *gnomon* mentioned by Pliny long ago. I learned from people living in the neighborhood that every time they excavated the ground for their wine-cellars or drains, they had come across various celestial signs, wonderfully designed in bronze, which were in the pavement around the *gnomon*. Applications were made to Julius II to have the pavement cleared and the obelisk set up in its former place, but he was, as usual, too distracted by his wars to mind these things. The barber finally lost his patience and buried this miracle of antiquity all over again.[69]

Lellio makes it reasonably clear that in this case, at least, the pope had little interest in raising obelisks. We may surmise that the excavation remained accessible for a few days or weeks, since the inscription was copied and found its way into the sketchbook of Giuliano da Sangallo (ca. 1512-13) and the afore-mentioned *Codex Coner*.[70] After this the trail runs cold, but the memory of the find was never entirely lost, and during the mid-sixteenth century, Pirro Ligorio or someone in his circle sketched a section of it under the house of the banker Spandocchi.[71] After years of further neglect, the obelisk was finally excavated in 1748 and, after more years of delay, its remnants were restored and erected in the Piazza di Montecitorio in 1792.[72] As recently as 1979–81, a section of travertine pavement with a meridian strip and Greek inscriptions in bronze letters was discovered in the area, confirming the Renaissance identification of the site.[73]

THE DISCOVERY OF THE *LAOCOÖN*

It is important to note at this point that despite his reported neglect of the Campus Martius obelisk and hostility to Bramante's reorientation plan, there is no reason to doubt Julius' appreciation for antiquity and ancient art as a whole. As the patron of so many grandiose projects, Julius surely understood, and was more than willing to appropriate, the imagery and scale of Rome's ancient monuments. And we must remember that it was Julius who founded the ancient sculpture col-lection in the Vatican Belvedere, and even before this he pursued the collection of ancient works of art, such as the celebrated Apollo Belvedere, which he kept in his private gardens at SS. Apostoli or S. Pietro in Vincoli until its transfer to the Vatican (ca. 1509).[74]

For evidence of Julius' enthusiasm for ancient art and responsiveness to new discoveries, we need only cite his acquisition of the celebrated *Laocoön*, whose discovery in the Esquiline *vigna* of Felice de Fredis on January 14, 1506 was greeted by artists and poets alike as a virtual second coming of antiquity.[75] According to a later account, even before it had been extracted from the earth, Michelangelo and Giuliano da Sangallo were called to the site, where the latter reportedly hailed the find as "*Laocoön*, of which Pliny speaks!"[76] After much dis-cussion and a certain tension between potential buyers, the group was purchased by Julius (March 23, 1506), who had it installed in the Belvedere in June of the same year.[77] Not long after, the curial humanist Jacopo Sadoleto composed his famous verses hailing the discovery of the statue as a metaphor for the revival of antiquity itself after centuries of slumber in the Roman earth:

From heaped-up mound of earth and from the heart
Of mighty ruins, lo! Long time once more
Has brought Laocoön home, who stood of old
In princely palaces and graced thy halls,

Imperial Titus, wrought by skill divine
(Even learned ancients saw no nobler work),
The statue now from darkness saved returns
To see the stronghold of Rome's second life.
. . . It is noble still to seize what chance is given
For praise, and strive the highest peak to gain.
It is yours with living images to quicken stone,
To give hard marble feeling till it breathes.[78]

The clamor attending the discovery of the Laocoön stands in stark contrast to the pope's neglect of the Campus Martius obelisk. On the simplest level, the difference may only reflect the relative ease of retrieving a piece of marble statuary from a shallow pit, as compared to the excavation of a colossal obelisk that lay half-buried under an occupied city block. But it is also possible that what distinguished the discovery of Laocoön was the sense of a once-in-a-lifetime rediscovery of a work of art that had been praised by Pliny, the best-known ancient authority on the subject, as "a work to be preferred to all others, either in painting or in bronze."[79] Sadoleto's praise for the accomplishment of the three sculptors (named by Pliny as Hagesander, Polydorus, and Athenodorus of Rhodes), who worked together to create a work so marvelous that it seemed to live and to breathe, continued to echo through the literature regarding the piece from the sixteenth century on, and was even referenced on the tomb slab commissioned in 1529 for the burial of Felice de Fredis in the church of S. Maria in Aracoeli in Rome, where we read that the deceased "has merited immortality for his own virtue and for having discovered the divine image of Laocoön that is seen in Vatican almost to breathe."[80]

JULIUS II PURCHASES A STATUE OF CLEOPATRA

That Julius could be receptive to Egyptianizing allusions when they suited his own agenda is suggested by his acquisition of another ancient statue, the Vatican Cleopatra (Fig. 14), which has been reidentified in modern times as a figure of the "Sleeping Ariadne."[81] Julius acquired the statue rather late in his pontificate, sometime before February 2, 1512, after months of negotiation with its previous owner, the Roman patrician Angelo Maffei.[82] The statue was apparently already highly regarded in artistic and antiquarian circles, and the pope paid such a substantial fee for it that it was still being paid off during the pontificate of Paul III (1534–49).[83] After being moved to the Vatican, the Cleopatra was installed atop an ancient sarcophagus in a fountain in the northeast corner of the Belvedere statue court. The result was described by Giovanni Pico della Mirandola in a letter of August 1512:

FIGURE 14. *Sleeping Ariadne*, also called the Belvedere *Cleopatra*, Musei Vaticani.
Alinari/Art Resource, New York.

In one of the corners you also see the image of Cleopatra, bitten by the snake, from
whose breasts, as it were, the water floes in the manner of the ancient aqueducts
and falls into an antique marble sarcophagus on which the deeds of the Emperor
Trajan are related.[84]

This installation followed an established type of "nymphaeum fountain" that
joined a fountain grotto with a figure of a sleeping nymph or goddess.[85] Gombrich
noted the resemblance to a fountain of this type in the *Hypnerotomachia*, but
there were other models, as we will see presently.[86] As for the identification of
the Vatican figure as an image of the Egyptian queen, the process is fairly easy to
reconstruct. The humanists in Julius' court were undoubtedly familiar with the
classical accounts of Cleopatra's death, and in particular with descriptions of an
image or effigy that had been displayed in Octavian's Egyptian triumph.[87] Dio
Cassius reported that an "effigy of Cleopatra on a couch" was carried in procession along with the queen's surviving children.[88] Plutarch alludes to this image in
his famous description of Cleopatra's suicide:

Some also say that Cleopatra's arm was seen to have two slight and indistinct
punctures; and this Caesar [Augustus] also seems to have believed. For in his

triumph an image of Cleopatra herself with the asp clinging to her was carried in the procession.[89]

In the verses of the Augustan poet Propertius, the suicide of the queen is presented in "eyewitness" terms, perhaps inspired by the memory of the effigy:

> I saw her (Cleopatra's) arms bitten by the sacred asps, I saw her limbs take in the hidden journey of slumber.[90]

Turning to the Vatican statue, we observe that the languorously reclining figure may certainly be interpreted as dead, or dying, or at the very least falling into a deep, deathlike sleep (thus the later identification with Ariadne).[91] But it was her attribute of the snake armlet, coiled around her upper left arm, that Pico and his contemporaries interpreted as the poisonous instrument of Cleopatra's suicide.[92]

POETRY IN HONOR OF (THE VATICAN) CLEOPATRA

As was the case with the *Laocoön*, the poetic and dramatic implications of the ancient descriptions associated with the *Cleopatra* were seized upon by contemporary writers and artists. In the visual sphere, the statue almost immediately provided a widely accepted model for portrayals of the queen's passionate (and frequently erotic) suicide.[93] Composed during the pontificate of Julius' successor, Pope Leo X (pope from 1513–21), the poem dedicated to the statue by Baldassare Castiglione (1478–1539) became so well known that it inspired the later compositions by Bernardino Baldi (1553–1617) and Agostino Favoriti (1624–82), all three of which were later carved onto the pilasters framing the statue when it was installed in the Vatican museum.[94] Castiglione's poem, which was printed and widely circulated from 1530 onward, honors Pope Julius and his successor for the sympathetic "reception" they granted to the petrified image of the tragic queen:

CLEOPATRA

Whoever you are who sees arms bitten by harsh snakes and eyes grown dim in eternal night carved in this marble, do not believe that I lay down in death unwilling. For a long time my conquerors forbade me to break off my life, doubtless so I, a captive queen, might be borne in a thronging triumphal procession, and, turned slave, wait upon Roman daughters-in-law. I, that scion descended from so many ancient kings, whom the favored race of Pharian Canopus worshiped, and Egypt fostered with her luxuries, and all the Orient deemed worthy of honors fit for gods. But virtue and noble desire for an honorable death overcame shameful life and the tyrant's snares, for freedom was achieved by death, and I felt no chains: I went down to the waters of the Underworld a free shade.

The faithless foe raged that this had been granted to me, and his rage blazed up with the mad goads of his cruelty; for he, unconquered in his triumphal chariot, between the blazoned inscriptions and enslaved peoples, led through the Capital

the luckless image of a dead woman. And, so ancient, long ages would not destroy
the fame of the deed, nor my lot be unknown to late-born descendants, he ordered
an image to be carved from breathing marble, to testify wretchedly to my fate and
misfortunes.

Thereafter Julius, marveling at the splendid genius of the artist, placed it in a
celebrated place among the figures of ancient heroes, and set the stone beneath
eternal tears, the solace of a grieving heart: not so I might lament the happiness of
longed-for death—since for me the serpent with its lethal bite drove away tears, and
death itself held no fear—but so I could bestow eternal tears upon the dear ashes
and shade of my beloved husband, as a pledge of love eternal, a sorrowful and mel-
ancholy gift for the helpless dead. Yet even these the bitter Romans snatched away.

But you, great Leo, sprung from the gods, under whom the golden age and honors of ancient glory have returned, if the all-powerful Father sent you down from
heavenly Olympus as a guardian for wretched mortals, and if your immeasurable
virtue is matched by your power and you dispense divine gifts with a beneficent
hand, nod to my humble prayers, and do not let me pray in vain. What I seek is
little. Restore those tears, excellent father. Restore, I beg, that weeping, a weeping
which is almost a gift for me, since now heartless fortune has left me nothing else.

Even Niobe, who dared insult the gods with her wicked tongue, her heart
encased in hard marble, is still permitted tears, and an unceasing trickle drips from
the marble. My life was different, I lived blamelessly, unless you call it a crime to
love. Tears are lovers' sole consolation. And more, my tears are a delightful pleasure
to those in torment, and invite sweet sleep with their murmuring. When the hound
of Icarus bakes the thirsting fields, birds come here to drink, and hop among the
branches around and above. Then the fertile earth burgeons with young grass, and
golden apples redden amid their branches, here where the fragrant grove rising
over dense shadows does not grudge gardens the rich trees of the Hesperides.[95]

Castiglione's poem is notable for its tone of pathos and tragedy. He emphasizes
the queen's powerful but doomed love for Antony—a characterization drawn
from Plutarch, whose relatively sympathetic portrayal contrasts sharply with the
virulent anti-Egyptian and anti-Cleopatra rhetoric of the Augustan poets and
Lucan. In this sense, Castiglione's poem represents a shift from the Augustan
"nationalist" image of Cleopatra as a harlot and seductress, a portrait that had
dominated medieval and early Renaissance conceptions of the character (as evi-
denced by her treatment by Dante, Petrarch, Boccaccio, and others).[96]

Apparently written a few years earlier than Castiglione's poem is a collection of epigrammatic verses composed for the statue by the Roman humanist Evangelista Maddalena de' Capodiferro, also known as Faustus or "Fausto
Romano" (d. ca. 1527).[97] These verses, preserved in a pair of manuscripts in the
Vatican library, are especially relevant to our discussion since they connect the
presumed subject of the statue (Cleopatra) directly to its purchaser, Julius II, and
through comparison to his ancient namesake, Julius Caesar.

ON THE FOUNTAIN OF CLEOPATRA

I, weary Cleopatra, delight in the sleep-inducing whisper of the clear, sweet, cool water. Approach in silence, bathe in silence, drink and depart in silence, lest sleep desert me. As much as, while I lived, Caesar, ruler of the world, burned for love of me, so much a second Julius loves me, now marble.

ON THE SAME SPRING

I who held the Nile have now become the tenant of a little spring, and teach men that great power is not to be trusted. I, who, conquered, refused by death to follow the triumphal procession of Augustus, now, stone, serve your waters, Julius.

ANOTHER

Come and depart, and wash and drink in silence, while I, wretched Cleopatra, savor sleep. Julius II, surpassed by none in his devotion, placed me fittingly beside the spring he has drawn forth. For, just as that water before you flows away, so flow the kingdoms of mortals, and those grown great fall with greater violence.

DIFFERENTLY EXPRESSED

Fitting that it is a tiny spring. Pretend it is the Nile, and I the real Cleopatra who savors these waters. Caesar tamed the Nile's waves, while Julius drew forth these: he was second only in years.

ANOTHER

Do not touch me, pray, do not wake me from sweet sleep. I am alive; only the chill water keeps me from growing warm. Caesar bound me to the mighty waves of the Nile, and the second Julius made me keeper of his waters.

DIFFERENTLY EXPRESSED

A. You fall faint, Cleopatra, either from sleep or sleep-bearing poison; the waters' murmur mingles your cares with dreams.

B. Oh, if only these were the waters of deadly Lethe, then you would not be gazing with me on the ruin of my kingdom. Better today to have fallen sooner, still happy, than to be weighed down by a miserable death after three centuries.[98]

Like Castiglione, Capodiferro puts his verses into the voice of the statue, which speaks for the represented subject (Cleopatra). As Leonard Barkan and others have pointed out, this poetic device of the "speaking statue" is rooted in the Classical tradition, most notably in the collection of epigrams known as the *Greek Anthology*, which had been rediscovered and circulated in Roman human-ist circles during the second half of the Quattrocento.[99] The genre enjoyed some-thing of a vogue during the Renaissance, and turned up in a variety of contexts, many of them specific to Rome and its "second population" of antique statues.[100] Perhaps the most famous example is Michelangelo's response (ca. 1544–46) to an epigram by Giovanni Strozzi, where the master gives voice to his figure of *La notte* on the tomb of Giuliano de' Medici.

> Sleep is dear to me, and being of stone is dearer,
> As long as injury and shame endure;
> Not to see or hear to hear is a great boon to me;
> Therefore, do not wake me, pray, speak softly.[101]

Michelangelo's epigram shares a common source with Castiglione and Capodiferro's *Cleopatra* in a much-cited epigram, allegedly copied from an antique on the Danube, but now identified as the work of the Roman humanist Gianantonio Campano (ca. 1470).[102] Alexander Pope is our translator:

> Nymph of the grot, these sacred springs I keep,
> And to the murmur of these waters sleep;
> Ah, spare my slumbers gently tread the cave!
> And drink in silence, or in silence leave![103]

Widely accepted as antique and duly recorded in collections of ancient inscriptions, this epigram enjoyed something of a vogue in the early sixteenth century. Sometime after 1513, it was inscribed on the basin of Angelo Colocci's "sleeping nymph" fountain, a modern work inspired by the installation of the Vatican Cleopatra.[104] Capodiferro, as a member (with Castiglione) of the group that assembled in the gardens of Colocci and Goritz, was positioned to draw on all these traditions to produce his own minor masterpiece of sycophantic flattery.

The central conceit of Capodiferro's verses is his comparison of Julius "the second" with the "first" Julius (Caesar), the lover and "conqueror" of the *real* Cleopatra.[105] In a neat twist, Julius' ownership of the statue is associated with Caesar's "conquest" of the Nile and Augustus' subsequent defeat of the Egyptian queen. Thus, according to Brummer, the fountain and its statue becomes a triumphal monument glorifying Pope Julius II as the second Julius Caesar.[106] In a further extension of this reading, Brummer and others have argued that the entire statue court be read as a poetic representation, in Virgilian terms, of Julius' (and the papacy's) fulfillment of Rome's destiny. In this formulation, the *Laocoön* stands for the fall of Troy and Aeneas' journey to Italy, the *Venus Genetrix* is the progenitor of Aeneas and the Julian lineage of Caesar, and the *Apollo Belvedere* represents Actian Apollo, the Olympian protector of Rome in the struggle against Cleopatra and the "monstrous gods" of Egypt at Actium.[107] As Brummer points out, Capodiferro composed a poem to the Apollo Belvedere praising the statue in precisely these terms.[108] In a second poem, the *Laudes Iulii II Pont. Max.*, Capodiferro characterizes the Belvedere statues (Apollo, Laocoön, Venus, and Cleopatra) as *marmoreos lares*: the "household gods" of Pope Julius, the "new Aeneas."[109]

These readings are both compelling and convincing, but I would suggest that a measure of caution is warranted. After all, a collection of statues is a fluid thing. As more works were added, the potential meanings of the ensemble were subject to new and unanticipated interpretations limited only by the poetic imaginations of its audience. Thus, we must allow for the possibility, even the likelihood, of multiple readings of the Vatican and other sculptural displays.

Whatever the more grandiose meanings of the Vatican statue court as a whole, Julius' acquisition of the *Cleopatra* and its poetic interpretation by Capodiferro suggest that the pope had a "situational" openness to Egyptian subjects and imagery in cases where they served his tastes and the agenda of the moment. The fact that Julius took such pains to add this statue to the Vatican collection at a relatively late date in his pontificate (see above) suggests that he was cognizant of its symbolic as well as its aesthetic value.

AN EPHEMERAL OBELISK FOR JULIUS II

It was perhaps in this same spirit that Julius did not object to the most explicit Egyptianizing "monument" produced during his pontificate: the ephemeral, float-borne obelisk that was a featured attraction in the carnival celebrations of February, 1513.[110] On the four faces of the obelisk were painted inscriptions in Greek, Latin, Hebrew, and "Egyptian letters" (*lettere egyptie*) that took the following form: "At the top, a sheaf of corn, then an ape, an oak, and a hawk, with a palm on the left and an eye on the right, with a stork at the bottom" signifying (along with the other inscriptions) "Julius II Pont. Max: Liberator of Italy and expeller of the schismatics."[111] We have no information about the hieroglyphic method employed, or the identity of its author, but the apparently "allegorical" inscriptions (and their association with inscriptions in Greek and Hebrew) seem much closer in spirit to the "multicultural antiquarianism" of the *Hypnerotomachia* than Bramante's Belvedere hieroglyphs would have been.

Julius' belated "conversion" to the authoritative power-imagery of obelisks and hieroglyphs may have been inspired, in part, by a revival of the plan to move the Vatican obelisk to the Piazza S. Pietro (an eventuality more or less ensured by Julius' rejection of Bramante's proposed reorientation of the basilica). Evidence for the renewed plan is scarce, and derives mainly from a drawing of the obelisk (datable to ca. 1513) in the Vatican album of Giuliano da Sangallo.[112] An earlier rendition of the obelisk in the same album (and datable to ca. 1465–88) is accompanied by a set of approximate measurements, which presumably derive from the mid-fifteenth-century project.[113] The second drawing is provided with much more precise measurements, as well as an estimated weight of the shaft, an obvious prerequisite for any attempt to raise and move the monument.[114] Significantly, Sangallo has added a figure of an eagle to the bronze globe at its summit, an embellishment never executed but that may be understood as an "Imperial" reference appropriate to a monument of Julius Caesar. Even before he became pope, Julius demonstrated an appreciation for this Imperial creature when he mounted an ancient relief sculpture of one of these birds "saved from so many ruins" on the porch of his titular church of SS. Apostoli.[115] In its position atop the obelisk, the eagle also functioned as a kind of visual pun, suggesting all at once the Imperial *aguglia* (eagle), the *guglia* ("needle") of Caesar, and the pontiff's name, *Giulio* or Julius.[116] If the traditional dating is accepted, Sangallo's drawing could have been made soon after his return to Rome at the election of Leo X, where he took a post with Bramante at the *fabbrica* of St. Peter's (January 1, 1514).[117] It is possible, therefore, that the drawing reflects a renewed obelisk project initiated toward the end of Julius' pontificate (ca. 1512–13).

POPE LEO X AS THE NEW AUGUSTUS

The election of Giovanni de' Medici as Pope Leo X in 1513 heralded a new phase in the humanist and antiquarian culture of Rome. Leo continued to add to the sculpture collection in the Belvedere and oversaw an ambitious program of archaeological study and restoration that took on distinctly Egyptianizing, even pharaonic airs. If the Borgia pope envisioned himself as an heir to Osiris and Alexander the Great, and Julius' projects embodied their patron's image as a new Julius Caesar, Leo X completed the "line of succession" by fashioning himself a second Augustus, the peaceful and enlightened ruler of the new Christian empire. In keeping with this general theme, and in stark contrast to Julius' apparent disinterest and inaction, Pope Leo soon showed himself more than willing to support the restoration of Rome's Egyptian monuments. He had the Nectanebo lions restored and reinstalled on high pedestals before the Pantheon of Agrippa, added the great statue of the Nile to the Belvedere statue court, and was probably responsible for setting a pair of late dynastic sphinxes before the steps of the Senator's Palace on the Campidoglio (in 1513). When an obelisk was uncovered during roadwork near the Mausoleum of Augustus in the summer of 1519, it was immediately excavated and ambitious plans for its restoration at the center of an Egyptianizing ensemble were drawn up by the pope's architects, Antonio da Sangallo il Giovane and Raphael. The project was abandoned soon after Leo's death, but the intended proclamation of the Medici pontiff as a reincarnation of Augustus and an Egyptian triumphator in his own right cannot have been clearer.[118] It seems ironic then, that it is in the guise of a kinder and more enlightened successor to the cruel Augustus that Leo takes the place of his predecessor in Castiglione's poem on the Vatican *Cleopatra* (see above).

The Cleopatra poems of Castiglione and Capodiferro show (better than any proclamation to that effect that I can fashion) how the worlds of poetic imagination and political ideology could co-exist in the sphere of Renaissance culture. Christine Shaw grudgingly admits this when she concludes that "to deny that Julius saw himself as a second Caesar or the reviver of the splendors of Imperial Rome is not to say that he could not appreciate, perhaps even enjoy, the literary parallels of his courtiers of the grandeur of Bramante's dreams."[119] Indeed. But as I hope to have shown in this paper, dreams and myths may, in some cases, be able to provide more than mere "entertainment." In some cases, they might even provide an insight into the processes whereby a "pragmatic politician" like Julius II found the motive to give concrete form to the grandiose "dreams" of his artists—Bramante, Michelangelo, and Raphael among them.[120] Without dreams like these, and I would include the dreams of the sleeping Cleopatra among them, achievements such as the ones they passed down to us would hardly have been possible.

NOTES

1. The author extends his thanks to Professor Margaret Miles for the invitation to present an early version of this paper at the symposium in 1999, and for her support and valuable suggestions throughout the process of bringing it to publication. In the time that lapsed between the original presentation and the final revision of this chapter, related treatments of this material appeared in my book, *The Egyptian Renaissance: The Afterlife of Ancient Egypt in Early Modern Italy* (2007). This chapter has been updated to reflect the latest scholarship and revised to address some historiographic issues regarding Julius II's patronage.

2. Jon Solomon, *The Ancient World in the Cinema*, 2nd ed., (2001): 68–75.

3. For the life and pontificate of Julius II, see Ludwig von Pastor, *The History of the Popes from the Close of the Middle Ages* 4–6 (1894–1998); Christine Shaw, *Julius II: The Warrior Pope* (1993).

4. For Julius II as patron of art and culture, see Pastor, *History of the Popes* 6, 455–607; Loren Partridge and Randolph Starn, *A Renaissance Likeness: Art and Culture in Raphael's Julius II* (1980); George L. Hersey, *High Renaissance Art in St. Peter's and the Vatican* (1992); Michael Koshikawa and Martha J. McClintock, *High Renaissance in the Vatican: The Age of Julius II and Leo X* (1993); Ingrid D. Rowland, *The Culture of the High Renaissance: Ancients and Moderns in Sixteenth-Century Rome* (1998): 141–92.

5. For papal ideology in relation to humanist culture and notions of *imperium*, see the fundamental study by Charles L. Stinger, *The Renaissance in Rome* (1998).

6. For general discussion, see Mary Hollingsworth, *Patronage in Renaissance Italy: From 1400 to the Early Sixteenth Century* (1994): 227–315; Loren Partridge, *The Art of Renaissance Rome, 1400–1600* (1996).

7. For early humanist activity in Rome, see Christopher S. Celenza, *Renaissance Humanism and the Papal Curia: Lapo da Castiglionchio the Younger's "De curiae commodes"* (1999) and Elizabeth McCahill, "Humanism in the Theater of Lies: Classical Scholarship in the Early Quattrocento Curia" (diss. 2005). For further discussion of these themes, see Stinger (1998): 1–82, 235–91; Rowland (1998): 7–41; and Anthony T. Grafton, "The Renaissance," in Richard Jenkyns, ed., *The Legacy of Rome: A New Appraisal* (1992): 97–123. For archaeological studies and excavations during the Renaissance, see Rodolfo Lanciani, *Storia degli scavi di Roma e notizie intorno le collezione romane di antichità* (1989–94); Roberto Weiss, *The Renaissance Discovery of Classical Antiquity* (1988); Phillip Jacks, *The*

Antiquarian and the Myth of Antiquity: The Origins of Rome in Renaissance Thought (1993). For the discovery and collection of ancient sculpture, see Frances Haskell and Nicholas Penny, *Taste and the Antique: The Lure of Classical Sculpture 1500–1900* (1981); Phyllis Pray Bober and Ruth Rubinstein, *Renaissance Artists and Antique Sculpture: A Handbook of Sources* (1987); and Leonard Barkan, *Unearthing the Past: Archaeology and Aesthetics in the Making of Renaissance Culture* (1999).

8. Stanley M. Burstein, "Images of Egypt in Greek Historiography," in A. Loprieno, ed., *Ancient Egyptian Literature: History and Forms* (1996): 591–604, esp. 592.

9. For Egyptian and hieroglyphic studies in the Renaissance, see Karl Giehlow, "Die Hieroglyphenkunde des Humanismus in der Allegorie der Renaissance," *Jahrbuch der Kunsthistorisches Sammlungen des Allerhöchsten Kaiserhauses* 32 (1915) 1–229; Erik Iversen, *The Myth of Egypt and Its Hieroglyphs in European Tradition* (1961, repr. 1993): 57–87; Maurice Pope, *The Story of Decipherment from Egyptian Hieroglyphs to Maya Script* (1999): 11–84; Rudolf Wittkower, "Hieroglyphic Studies in the Early Renaissance," in *Allegory and the Migration of Symbols* (1977): 114–28; Charles Dempsey, "Renaissance Hieroglyphic Studies and Gentile Bellini's 'Saint Mark Preaching in Alexandria,'" in I. Merkel and A. G. Debus, ed., *Hermeticism and the Renaissance: Intellectual History and the Occult in Early Modern Europe* (1988): 342–65; and Brian Curran, *The Egyptian Renaissance: The Afterlife of Ancient Egypt in Early Modern Italy* (2007).

10. For catalogs and general discussion, see Anne Roullet, *The Egyptian and Egyptianizing Monuments of Imperial Rome* (1972); Mariette de Vos, *L'egittomania in pitture e mosaici Romano-Campani della prima età imperiale* (1980); O. Lollio Barberi, G. Parola, and M. P. Toti, *Le antichità egiziane di Roma imperiale* (1995); Sally-Ann Ashton, *Roman Egyptomania* (2004). For the obelisks, the basic sources are Erik Iversen, *Obelisks in Exile* 1 (1968), and Cesare D'Onofrio, *Gli obelischi di Roma: Storia e urbanistica di una città dall' età al XX secolà* 3 (1992).

11. For the Augustan obelisks, see Iversen (1968): 65–75, 142–60; D'Onofrio (1992): 260–66, 369–421.

12. For the numerous Egyptian monuments discovered on the site of the Roman Iseum Campense, see Katja Lembke, *Das Iseum Campense in Rom: Studie über den Isiskult unter Domitian* (1994).

13. For the complex history of this obelisk, see Iversen (1968): 19–46; D'Onofrio (1992): 121–36; Géza Alföldy, *Der Obelisk auf dem Petersplatz in Rom: Ein historisches Monument der Antike* (1990).

14. For the many problems posed by this inscription, see Iversen (1968): 19–21; D'Onofrio (1992): 121–36.

15. For these points, see Iversen (1968): 23–25, 31–32. For further discussion of the medieval context of the obelisk, see John Osborne, "St. Peter's Needle and the Ashes of Julius Caesar," in Maria Wyke, ed., *Julius Caesar in Western Culture* (2006): 95–109.

16. For these obelisks, see Iversen (1968): 76–92, 101–14; D'Onofrio (1992): 29–81, 288–301; 106–14.

17. See Giehlow, "Hieroglyphenkunde," 12–40; Iversen (1961): 64–66.

18. *De re aedificatoria*, 8. 4; see Leon Battista Alberti, *On the Art of Building in Ten Books*, ed. J.Rykwert, N. Leach, and R. Tavernor (1988): 256–57. For discussion, see Giehlow (1915): 29–37; Claudio Finzi, "Leon Battista Alberti: Geroglifiche e gloria," in C. M. Govi, S. Curto, and S. Pernigotti, eds., *L'Egitto fuori dell'Egitto: Dalla riscoperta all'Egittologia* (1991): 205–8.

19. See Brian Curran and Antony Grafton, "A Fifteenth-Century Site Report on the Vatican Obelisk," *Journal of the Warburg and Courtauld Institutes* 58 (1995): 234–48.

20. Iversen (1968): 27–44; D'Onofrio (1992): 137-185.

21. See Brian P. Copenhaver, *Hermetica: The Greek "Corpus Hermeticum" and the Latin "Asclepius"'in a New English Translation with Notes and Introduction* (1992).

22. See Frances W. Yates, *Giordano Bruno and the Hermetic Tradition* (1964): 1–83; M. J. B. Allen,

"Marsilio Ficino, Hermes Trismegistus and the Corpus Hermeticum," in John Henry and Sarah Hutton, eds., *New Perspectives on Renaissance Thought: Essays in the History of Science, Education and Philosophy in Memory of Charles B. Schmitt* (1990): 38–47.

23. For the Sala dei Santi, see Fritz Saxl, "The Appartamento Borgia," in F. Saxl, *Lectures* 1 (1957): 174–88; N. Randolph Parks, "On the Meaning of Pinturicchio's Sala dei Santi," *Art History* 2 (1979) 291–317; Paola Mattiangeli, "Annio de Viterbo inspiratore di cicli pittorici," in G. Baffioni and P. Mattiangeli, eds., *Annio da Viterbo: Documenti e ricerche* 1 (1981): 257–303; Sabine Poeschel, "Age Itaque Alexander: Das Appartamento Borgia und die Erwartungen an Alexander VI," *Römische Jahrbuch der Bibliotheca Hertziana* 25 (1989): 129–65; Rowland (1998): 46–53; Sabine Poeschel, *Alexander Maximus: Das Bildprogramm des Appartamento Borgia im Vatikan* (1999): 131–81. For this section of the cycle, see Saxl (1957): 182–83; Parks (1979): 299–302, notes on 314–16; Mattiangeli (1981): 290–96; Poeschel (1989): 156–60.

24. Parks (1979): 296, 309, note 29 (for the medal); Poeschel (1989): 151.

25. Saxl (1957): 182–83; Parks (1979): 299–302, notes on 314–16; Mattiangeli (1981): 290–96.

26. Annius' influence was proposed by Giehlow (1915): 40–46; followed by Saxl (1957) and most convincingly by Mattiangeli (1981). My discussion here draws to some extent on a previously published study, B. Curran, "*De sacrarum litterarum aegyptiorum interpretatione*: Reticence and Hubris in Hieroglyphic Studies of the Renaissance: Pierio Valeriano and Annius of Viterbo," *Memoirs of the American Academy in Rome* 43/44 (2000): 139–82.

27. For Annius and his work, see Roberto Weiss, "Traccia per una biografia di Annio da Viterbo," *Italia medievale e umanistica* 5 (1962): 425–41; Walter Stephens, "Berosus Chaldaeus: Counterfeit and Fictive Editors of the Early Sixteenth Century" (diss. 1979); Edoardo Fumagalli, "Aneddoti della vita di Annio da Viterbo, O. P.," *Archivium Fratrum Praedicatorum* 50 (1980): 167–99; W. Stephens, *Giants in Those Days: Folklore, Ancient History, and Nationalism* (1989): 58–138; Anthony Grafton, "Invention of Traditions and Traditions of Invention in Renaissance Europe: The Strange Case of Annius of Viterbo," in A. Grafton, *Defenders of the Text: The Traditions of Scholarship in an Age of Science, 1450–1800* (1991) 76–103; Rowland (1998): 53–59.

28. See Stephens (1979): 155–63; Rowland (1998): 56–57; and Adriana Emiliozzi, *Il Museo Civico di Viterbo: Storia delle raccolte archeologiche* (1986): 19–36.

29. See Roberto Weiss, "An Unknown Epigraphic Tract by Annius of Viterbo," in C. P. Brand et al., *Italian Studies Presented to E. R. Vincent* (1962): 101–20; Amanda Collins, "Renaissance Epigraphy and Its Legitimating Potential: Annius of Viterbo, Etruscan Inscriptions, and the Origins of Civilization," in Alison E. Cooley, ed., *The Afterlife of Inscriptions: Reusing, Rediscovering, Reinventing, and Revitalizing Ancient Inscriptions* (2000): 57–76.

30. For the date and components of the tablet, see Weiss, "Unknown Epigraphic Tract" (1962): 119, n. 53; Mattiangeli (1981): 297–98; Emiliozzi (1986): 29–31.

31. Giovanni Nanni (Annius of Viterbo), *Commentaria Fratris Ioannis Annii Viterbensis ordinis praedicator, theologiae professoris super opera diversorum auctorum de Antiquitatibus loquentorum* (1498); *Berosi sacerdotis chaldaici, antiquitatum Italiae ac totius orbis libri Commentariis Joannis Annii Viterbensis . . .* (1552); and the Italian translations by Pietro Lauro, *I cinque libri de la antichità de Beroso . . . con lo commento di Giovanni Annio da Viterbo* (1550). For a list of editions, see Stephens (1989): 344–45 (Appendix II).

32. Annius (1552): 380; translation from Curran (2000): 172–73.

33. For Annius' nationalistic motivations, see E. N. Tigerstedt, "Ioannes Annius and Graecia Mendax," in C. Henderson, ed., *Classical, Mediaeval, and Renaissance Studies in Honor of Berthold Louis Ullman* 2 (1964): 293–310.

34. Annius (1552): 108–79; see Giehlow (1915): 40–42; Stephens (1989): 134–35.

35. See John Daniel Cooke, "Euhemerism: A Mediaeval Interpretation of Classical Paganism,"

Speculum 11 (1927): 396–410; Jean Seznec, *The Survival of the Pagan Gods: The Mythological Tradition and Its Place in Renaissance Humanism and Art* (1953): 11–36.

36. Annius' treatise on the origins of the Farnese, *De Viterbii viris et factis illustribis*, was completed ca. 1491 and dedicated to Cardinal Ranuccio Farnese. See Mattiangeli (1981): 266–68.

37. For the thesis of an Annian Borgia genealogy, see Giehlow (1915): 44–46; Saxl (1957): 183–88; Mattiangeli (1981): 260–69. For more on genealogies of this type, see Roberto Bizzocchi, *Genealogie incredibili: Scritti di storia nell'Europa moderna* (1995).

38. Stinger (1998): 303.

39. See Maurizio Calvesi, *Il sogno di Poliphilo prenestino* (1980); and Maurizio Calvesi, *La "pugna d'amore in sogno" di Francesco Colonna Romano* (1996).

40. B. Curran, "The 'Hypnerotomachia Poliphili' and Renaissance Egyptology," *Word and Image* 14 (1998): 156–85. For further discussion see Patricia Fortini Brown, *Venice and Antiquity: The Venetian Sense of the Past* (1996): 686–705. The text is now available in English translation; see Francesco Colonna, *Hypnerotomachia Poliphili: The Strife of Love in a Dream*, trans. by Joscelyn Godwin (1999).

41. See Roberto Weiss, "The Medals of Julius II (1503–1513)," *Journal of the Warburg and Courtauld Institutes* 28 (1964): 163–82; Stinger (1998): 235–46; Stanislaus von Moos, "The Palace as a Fortress: Rome and Bologna under Julius II," in Henry A. Millon and Linda Nochlin, eds., *Art and Architecture in the Service of Politics* (1978): 46–79; Paul Gwynne, "'Tu alter Caesar eris': Maximilian I, Vladislav II, Johannes Michael Nagonius, and the 'renovatio Imperii,'" *Renaissance Studies* 10 (1996): 56–71; and Nicholas Temple, "Julius II as Second Caesar," in Maria Wyke, ed., *Julius Caesar in Western Culture* (2006), 110–27.

42. Translation from Stinger (1998): 236, 382, note 3, citing Desiderius Erasmus Roterodami, *Opera omnia: Ordinis primi, Tomus primus* (1969): 573: "Summus Pontifex Iulius belligeratur, vincit, triumphat, planeque Iulium agit."

43. For descriptions and sources regarding the 1506–7 triumphs, see Stinger (1998): 235–38. For the connection to Mantegna's triumphs, see Temple (2006): 113. For more on Mantegna's paintings, see Andrew Martindale, *The Triumphs of Caesar by Andrea Mantegna in the Collection of Her Majesty the Queen at Hampton Court* (1979), and Stephen J. Campbell, "Mantegna's Triumph: The Cultural Politics of Imitation 'all'antica' at the Court of Mantua, 1490–1530," in Stephen J. Campbell, ed., *Artists at Court: Image-Making and Identity 1300–1550* (2005): 91–105, 216–19.

44. See Shaw (1993): 205, for the Palm Sunday reference. For more on this theme, see Brent Kinman, "Parousia, Jesus' 'A-Triumphal' Entry, and the Fate of Jerusalem (Luke 19:28–44)," *Journal of Biblical Literature* 118 (1999): 279–94.

45. Temple (2006): 110–20.

46. See Shaw (1993): 204–7.

47. Shaw (1993): 205.

48. Shaw (1993): 205.

49. Shaw (1993): 206–7.

50. Rowland (1998): 32.

51. Paris de Grassis, *Diaries*, Nov. 26, 1507; British Library Add. Ms. 8441, fol. 170r; cf. V. Golzio, *Raffaello nei documenti, nelle testimonianze dei contemporanei e nella letteratura del suo secolo* (1936): 14; partial translation in Julian Klaczko, *Rome and the Renaissance* (1903), 151.

52. E. H. Gombrich, "Hypnerotomachiana," in E. H. Gombrich, *Symbolic Images* 3 (1985): 102–8.

53. Giehlow (1915): 84, n. 1. For others who rejected Annius' forgeries, see Weiss, "Traccia" (1962): 437–38; Grafton (1991): 93.

54. For Egidio's acceptance and expansion of Annius' theories, see John W. O'Malley, *Giles of Viterbo on Church and Reform* (1968): 30–32, 88–89, 123–27; Amanda Collins, "The Etruscans in the

Renaissance: The Sacred Destiny of Rome and the 'Historia Viginti Saeculorum' of Giles of Viterbo (ca. 1469–1532)," *Studi e materiali di storia delle religione* 65 (1998): 337–65; Rowland (1998): 148–50.

55. O'Malley (1968): 120–24.

56. For further discussion, see John W. O'Malley, "Fulfillment of the Golden Age under Pope Julius II: Text of a Discourse of Giles of Viterbo," *Traditio* 25 (1969): 265–338; Marjorie Reeves, "Cardinal Egidio of Viterbo: A Prophetic Interpretation of History," in M. Reeves, ed., *Prophetic Rome in the High Renaissance Period* (1992): 91–109.

57. The controversy is described in Egidio's *Historia viginti seculorum*, Biblioteca Angelica Lat. 502, fol. 194r. See Gombrich (1985): 103–4; O'Malley (1968): 123–27.

58. Translation by Gombrich (1968): 102; cf. Giorgio Vasari, *Le vite de' più eccellenti pittori, scultori ed architettori*, in G. Gaetano Milanesi, ed., *Le opere di Giorgio Vasari* (1906, repr. 1981): 4.158–59.

59. See Michael Koshikawa and Martha J. McClintock (1993): 40, cat. no. 24.

60. Translation derived from Gombrich (1985): 102; Colonna (1999): 244–45.

61. Giehlow (1915): 53–55.

62. For the rebus in Bramante's work, see Peter Murray, "'Bramante milanese': The Printings and Engravings," *Arte Lombarda* 7 (1962): 25–42. For rebuslike images in the Renaissance, see Jean Céard and Jean-Claude Margolin, *Rébus de la Renaissance: des images que parlent* (1986).

63. See Enzo Bentivoglio, "Bramante e il geroglifico di Viterbo," *Mitteilungen des Kunsthistorischen Instituts in Florenz* 16 (1992): 167–74.

64. Bentivoglio (1992): 170–74.

65. For this obelisk, see Iversen (1968): 142–60; D'Onofrio (1992): 369–421.

66. For the text, see Cesare D'Onofrio, ed., *Visitiamo Roma nel Quattrocento: La città degli Umanisti* (1989): 278; Iversen (1968): 144–47.

67. Francesco Albertini, *Opusculum de mirabilibus novae et veteris urbis Romae* (1510), fol. Hiv–Hiir.

68. *Codex Coner*, Sir John Soane's Museum, London, fol. 56: "rep[er]to fuit año D. 1512 in canpo Martio"; see Thomas Ashby, *Sixteenth-Century Drawings of Roman Buildings Attributed to Andreas Coner* (1904): 39–40, fig. 69; R. Lanciani (1984–2002) 1: 177–80, fig. 105.

69. A. Laelius Podager, in A. Mazzocchi, *Epigrammata antiquae urbis* (Rome, 1521), Vat. lat. 8492, fol. 21 r: "Sub Iulio II pont. max. in regione Campi Marti post aedem D. Laurentii in Lucina, et prope domum cardinalis Crassi, in domunculae cuiusdam tonsoris horticulo, dum in eo pro conficienda latrina foderetur, detecta est basis obelisci omnium, qui in urbe extent, ut conspicari erat maximi. Obeliscus jacebat, nec videri poterat an totus integer esset, quippe cuius ima tantum pars videbatur. In basi erat inscriptio, quam ego legi, sed non recte de ea memini, quamque de nomine divi Augusti, & de his verbis . . . AEGYPTO IN POSTESTATEM POPULI REDACTA SOLE DONUM DEDIT. In hoc obelisco gnomon olim ille erat percelebris de quo Plinius memnit. Quin vicini, qui circa illum insulas habent, asseverabant omnes pene se ipsos, dum pro conficiendis cellis vinariis alias fodissent, invenisse varia signa caelestia ex aere. artificio mirabili, quae in pavimento circa gnomonem hunc erant. Iulio principi in bellis tunc, ut semper, implicitissimo, ut obeliscum hunc iterum erigi . . . facere, suasere quidem permulti, persuasit autem nemo. Ideo tantum antiquitatis miraculum a tonsore illo iterum sepultum est." The text is transcribed in Lanciani, *Storia degli scavi* (1984–2002) 1:178; partial translation in Lanciani, *The Ruins and Excavations of Ancient Rome* (1897): 465–68. See also Iversen (1968): 147–48; D'Onofrio (1992): 387–88; and Anthony Grafton, ed., *Rome Reborn: The Vatican Library and Renaissance Culture* (1993): 119, pl. 94.

70. Biblioteca Comunale, Siena, Ms. S. IV. 8, fol. 3. See Rodolfo Falb, *Il taccuino senese di Giuliano da Sangallo* (1902): 30, pl. 3.

71. Pirro Ligorio describes the monument in his *Libro XIIII delle Antichità di Roma di Pyrro Ligorio Pittore, il qual tratta degli obellischi et varie cose degli Egitti*, Oxford, Bodleian Library, Ms.

Bodl. Canon. ital. 138, fol. 76v. Lanciani connected Ligorio's investigation to a sketch in the Codex Ursinianus, Biblioteca Apostolica Vaticana, Vat lat. 3439, fol. 2v; see Lanciani (1984–2002): 1.179–80, fig. 106.

72. For the later history of the obelisk, see Iversen (1968): 148–60.

73. See E. Buchner, *Die Sonnenuhr des Augustus, Nachdruck aus "RM" 1976 und 1980 und Nachtrag über die Ausgrabung 1980/81* (1982); Michael Schütz, "Zur Sonnenuhr des Augustus auf dem Marsfeld," *Gymnasium* 97 (1990): 432–57.

74. For the Belvedere statue court (and Julius as a collector) see A. Michaelis, "Geschichte des Statuenhofes im Vaticanischen Belvedere," *Jahrbuch des Kaiserlich Deutschen archäologischen Instituts* 5 (1890): 5–72; Hans Brummer, *The Statue Court in the Vatican Belvedere* (1970): 20–42; Frances Haskell and Nicholas Penny (1981): 7–10; G. Daltrop, "Nascita e significato della raccolta delle statue antiche in Vaticano," in M. Fagiolo, ed., *Roma e l'antico nell'arte e nella cultura del Cinquecento* (1985): 111–29; D. Brown, "The Apollo Belvedere and the Garden of Giuliano della Rovere at SS. Apostoli," *Journal of the Warburg and Courtauld Institutes* 49 (1986): 235–38; and the essays in Matthias Winner, Bernard Andreae, Carlo Pietrangeli, eds., *Il cortile delle statue: der Statuenhof des Belvedere im Vatikan* (1998).

75. For description and documents regarding the discovery and reception of the statue, see C. C. van Essen, "La decouverte du Laocoön," *Mededelingen der Koninklijke Nederlandse Akademie van Wetenschappen* 18, no. 12 (1955): 291–308; Brummer(1970): 75–119; Matthias Winner, "Zum Nachleben des Laokoon Der Renaissance," *Jahrbuch der Berliner Museen* 16 (1974): 83–121; Haskell and Penny (1981): 10, 243–47, cat. no. 52; Bober and Rubinstein (1987): 151–52, cat. no. 121; Barkan (1999): 1–17; Sonia Maffei, "La fama di Laocoonte nei testi del Cinquecento," in Salvatore Settis, ed., *Laocoonte, fama e stile, con un apparato documentario a cura di Sonia Maffei su La fama di Laocoonte nei testi del Cinquecento* (1999): 85–230; Michael Koortbojian, "Pliny's Laocoön?" in Alina Payne, Ann Kuttner, and Rebekah Smick, eds., *Antiquity and Its Interpreters* (2000): 199–216.

76. This story is recounted in a letter of Francesco da Sangallo, written more than half a century after the event, but earlier letters make it clear that the association with Pliny and Michelangelo's consultation were part of the original reception. See Maffei (1999): 99–111; Koortbojian (2000): 199–203.

77. Pastor (1891–1928): 6.489; Brummer (1970): 75–78; Haskell and Penny (1981): 243.

78. Jacopo Sadoleto, *On the Statue of Laocoön*, trans. by H. S. Wilkinson, in John Hollander, *The Gazer's Spirit: Poems Speaking to Silent Works of Art* (1994): 97–105. Latin text in Alessandro Perosa and John Sparrow, eds., *Renaissance Latin Verse: An Anthology* (1979): 184–86; Latin with prose translation in Michael Baxandall, "Jacopo Sadoleto's Laocoön," in M. Baxandall, *Words for Pictures: Seven Papers on Renaissance Art and Criticism* (2003): 98–116, esp. 98–101.

79. Pliny the Elder, *Historia Naturalis* 36.37, trans. from K. Jex-Blake, *The Elder Pliny's Chapters on Art* (1896, repr. 1968), cf. Koortbojian (2000): 199.

80. Latin transcription and Italian translation in Maffei (1999): 114–15.

81. For the history and reception of the statue, see A. Michaelis (1890): 18–20; W. Amelung, *Die Sculpturen des Vaticanischen Museums* (1903): 2.636–43, cat. no. 414; W. Helbig, *Führer durch die öffentlichen Sammlungen klassischer Altertümer in Rome* (1963): 1.109–10; Brummer (1970: 154–85; Haskell and Penny (1981): 184–87, cat. no. 24; Bober and Rubinstein (1987): 113–14, cat. no. 79; Leonard Barkan, "The Beholder's Tale: Ancient Sculpture, Renaissance Narratives," *Representations* 44 (1993): 133–66; Barkan (1999): 233–47; and Claudia Maria Wolf, *Die schlafende Ariadne im Vatikan: Ein hellenistischer Statuentypus und seine Rezeption* (2002).

82. See Brummer (1970): 154, n. 1 (document recording the transfer); Wolf (2002): 68–70.

83. Eugene Müntz, *Les antiquités de la ville de Rome aux XIVe, Xve, et XVIe siècles* (1886): 48–49.

84. G. F. Pico della Mirandola, *Illustrissimi ac doctissimi principis Jo. Francisci Pici Mirandu-*

lae . . . de Venere & Cupidine expellendis carmen ; item eiusdem Laurentius & Geminianus hymni . . .
(Rome: Iacobus Mazochius, 1513), fol. b IVr, translation from Gombrich (1985): 106.

85. The literature on the Cleopatra/Sleeping Nymph theme is extensive. See Otto Kurz, "Huius Nympha Loci," *Journal of the Warburg and Courtauld Institutes* 16 (1953): 171–77; Brummer (1970): 165–71; Elizabeth MacDougall, "The Sleeping Nymph: Origins of a Humanist Fountain Type," *Art Bulletin* 57 (1975): 357–65; Phyllis Pray Bober, "The 'Coryciana' and the Nymph Corycia," *Journal of the Warburg and Courtauld Institutes* 40 (1977): 223–39; Barkan (1999): 237–43.

86. Gombrich (1985): 106, fig. 107.

87. For the sources, see J. Gwyn Griffiths, "The Death of Cleopatra VII," *Journal of Egyptian Archaeology* 47 (1961): 113–18.

88. Dio Cassius 51.21; trans. Earnest Carrey, *Dio's Roman History* (Cambridge, Mass. 1995).

89. Plutarch, *Life of Antony* 86.3; trans. B. Perrin, *Plutarch's Lives* (Cambridge, Mass. 1920).

90. Propertius, 3.11.52–56; trans. Robert Alan Gurval, *Actium and Augustus: The Politics and Emotions of Civil War* (1995): 201.

91. Thus the interpretation of Ulisse Aldrovandi, "Delle statue antiche che per tutta Roma in diversi luoghi, e case si veggono," in Lucio Mauro, *Le antichità della città di Rome breviussima raccolte da chiunque ne ha scritto* (1557): 117: "A man manca di Antinoo si vede la statua di Cleopatre, che pare che tramortisca e venga meno." For PDF, see Margaret Daly Davis, ed., *Documents for the History of Art 1350–1760.29* (2009), http://archiv.ub.uni-heidelberg.de/artdok/volltexte/2009/704/. For discussion of the statue in relation to ancient images of Ariadne, see Sheila McNally, "Ariadne and Others: Images of Sleep in Greek and Early Roman Art," *Classical Antiquity* 4 (1985): 152–92.

92. For examples of the "snake bracelet," see R. S. Bianchi, R. A. Fazzini, and J. Quagebeur, eds. *Cleopatra's Egypt: Age of the Ptolemies* (1988): 201–2, cat. nos. 95, 96; and C. Ziegler in Jean-Marcel Humbert, Michael Pantazzi, and Christiane Ziegler, eds., *Egyptomania: Egypt in Western Art 1730–1930* (1994): 563–64, cat. no. 381.

93. Perhaps the most dramatic of the early responses is Rosso Fiorentino's panel of the *Dying Cleopatra*, painted ca. 1525–26 and now in the Herzog Anton Ulrich-Museum, Braunschweig; see David Franklin, *Rosso in Italy: The Italian Career of Rosso Fiorentino* (1994): 148–53. For other images inspired by the statue, see Silva Urbini, "Il mito di Cleopatra. Motivi ed esiti della sua rinnovata fortuna fra Rinascimento e Barocco," *Xenia Antigua* 2 (1993): 181–222; and Claude Ritschard, Allison Morehead, Mieke Bal, and Bettina Baumgärtel, *Cléopâtre dans le miroir de l'art occidental* (2004): 82–83, cat. no. 3, 86–87, cat. no. 7, 98–99, cat. no. 14 (Rosso), 102–5, cat. nos. 16–17, and others.

94. Haskell and Penny (1981): 186–87.

95. Latin text in Alessandro Perosa and John Sparrow, eds., *Renaissance Latin Verse: An Anthology* (1979): 193–95:

CLEOPATRA

Marmore quisquis in hoc saevis admorsa colubris
bracchia et aeterna torpentia lumina nocte
aspicis, invitam ne crede occumbere leto.
Victores vetuere diu me adrumpere vitam
regina ut veherer celebri captiva triumpho
scilicet et nuribus parerem serva Latinis,
illa ego progenies tot ducta ab origine regum
quam Pharii coluit gens fortunata Canopi
deliciis fovitque suis Aegyptia tellus
atque Oriens omnis divum dignatus honore est.
Sed virtus pulchraeque necis generosa cupido
vicit vitae ignominiam insidiasque tyranni:

libertas nam parta nece est, nec vincula sensi,
umbraque Tartareas descendi libera ad undas.
Quod licuisse mihi indignatus perfidus hostis
saevitiae insanis stimulis exarsit et ira;
namque triumphali invictus Capitolia curru
insignes inter titulos gentesque subactas
exstinctae infelix simulacrum duxit, et amens
spectaculo explevit crudelia lumina inani.
Neu longaeva vetustas facti famam aboleret
aut seris mea sors ignota nepotibus esset,
effigiem excudi spiranti e marmore iussit
testatri et casus fatum miserabile nostri.
Quam deinde, ingenium artificis miratus Iulus
egregium, celebri visendam sede locavit
signa inter veterum heroum, saxoque perennes
supposuit lacrimas, aegrae solatia mentis:
optatae non ut deflerem gaudia mortis—
nam mihi nec lacrimas letali vipera morsu
excussit nec mors ullum intulit ipsa timorem—
sed caro ut cineri et dilecti coniugis umbrae
aeternas lacrimas, aeterni pignus amoris,
maesta darem, inferiasque inopes et tristia dona;
has etiam tamen infensi rapuere Quirites.
At tu, magne Leo, divum genus, aurea sub quo
saecula et antiquae redierunt laudis honores,
si te praesidium miseris mortalibus ipse
omnipotens Pater aethereo demisit Olympo,
et tua si immensae virtuti est aequa potestas
munificaque manu dispensas dona deorum,
annue supplicibus votis, nec vana precari
me sine; parva peto: lacrimas, Pater optime, redde.
Redde, oro, fletum, fletus mihi muneris instar,
improba quando aliud nil iam Fortuna reliquit.
At Niobe, ausa deos scelerata incessere lingua,
induerit licet in durum praecordia marmor,
flet tamen, assiduusque liquor de marmore manat.
Vita mihi dispar; vixi sine crimine, si non
crimen amare vocas; fletus solamen amantum est.
Adde, quod afflictis nostrae iucunda voluptas
sunt lacrimae, dulcesque invitant murmure somnos:
et cum exusta siti Icarius canis arva perurit,
huc potum veniunt volucres, circumque superque
frondibus insultant; tenero tum gramine laeta
terra viret, rutilantque suis poma aurea ramis;
hic ubi odoratum surgens densa nemus umbra
Hesperidum dites truncos non invidet hortis.

96. For Plutarch as a "sympathetic" source, see L. Hughes-Hallet, *Cleopatra: Histories, Dreams and Distortions* (1990): 70–110. For medieval and Renaissance conceptions of Cleopatra, see Beverly

Taylor, "The Medieval Cleopatra: The Classical and Medieval Tradition of Chaucer's Legend of Cleopatra," *Journal of Medieval and Renaissance Studies* 7 (1977): 249–69; Hughes-Hallett (1990): 36–69; Mary Hamer, *Signs of Cleopatra: History, Politics, Representation* (1993): 24–44.

97. For Capodiferro, see Osvaldo Tommasini, "Evangelista Maddaleni de' Capodiferro accademico . . . e storico," *Atti della Regia Accademia dei Lincei, serie IV: Scienze morali storiche e filologiche* 10 (1893): 3–20; G. Ballistreri, "Capodiferro, Evangelista Maddaleni (Maddalena) de', detto Fausto," *Dizionario biografico degli Italiani*, vol. 18 (1975): 621–25; Rowland (1998): 87–90.

98. Cod. Vat. Lat. 3351 fols. 122r-v; clearer in Cod. Vat. Lat. 10377 fols. 90–92. I have followed the transcription published by Brummer (1970): 221–22; and I thank Charlotte Stanford and J.R.T. Holland for assistance with the translation:

DE FONTE CLEOPATRAE
Fessa soporifero Fontis Cleopatra susurro
    Perspicui, dulcis, frigidulique fruor.
Accaedas tacitus tacitusque lavere bibasque
    Et tacitus, cesset ne mihi somnus abi.
Quantum me, vivam, Caesar mundi arbiter arsit
    Marmoream tantum Iulius alter amat.

DE EODEM FONTE
Quae Nilum tenui, parvi facta accola fontis
    Edoceo summis rebus abesse fidem.
Vincta sequi Augusti renui quae morte triumphos
    Servio nunc limphis, saxea, Iule tuis.

ALIUD
Accaedas et abi tacitusque lavere bibasque
    Infaelix somno dum Cleopatra fruor
Iulius invicta nulli pietate secundus
    Quam duxit statuit me bene propter aquam.
Nam veluti fluit ista fluunt mortalia regna:
    Maiorique cadunt impete magna satis.

ALITER
Fons parvus licet est: simulatum credite Nilum
    Veraque sum limphis, quae, Cleopatra fruor.
Niliacas Caesar domuit, has Iulius undas
    Duxit: solum annis iste Secundus erat.

ALIUD
Ne me tange, precor, dulci ne me excute somno.
    Vivo ego: ni caleo, frigida lympha facit.
Niliacas Caesar me vinxit magnas ad undas
    Prefecitque suis Iulius alter aquis.

ALITER
Somno an somnifero langues Cleopatra veneno;
    Immiscet curis somnia murmur aquae.
O utinam haec essent fatalis flumina Lethes,
    Non mecum aspicerem regna perire mea.
Utilius hodie est cito et occubuisse beata,
    Post tria quam misera saecula morte premi.

99. See J. Hutton, *The Greek Anthology in Italy to the Year 1800* (1935): 3; MacDougall (1975): 358; Kenneth Gross, *The Dream of the Moving Statue* (1993): 139–46; Barkan (1993) and Barkan (1999): 237–43.

100. For this concept, see Leonard Barkan, "Rome's Other Population," *Raritan* 1, no. 2 (1991): 66–81.

101. Translation from James M. Saslow, *The Poetry of Michelangelo* (1991): 419. For discussion, see Gross (1993): 92–99; Norman E. Land, *The Viewer as Poet: The Renaissance Response to Art* (1994): 77–80; Hollander (1994): 45–47.

102. For the history of the epigram, see Kurz (1953): 171–77, and MacDougall (1975): 357–59 (for the present attribution). See also Brummer (1970): 168; and Bober (1977): 224.

103. John Butt, ed., *The Poems of Alexander Pope: A One-Volume Edition of the Twickenham Text with Selected Annotations* (1963): 474; trans. of inscription, *CIL* VI 5. 3. For a modern translation, see Rowland (1998): 183.

104. Brummer (1970: 167–71, fig. 152.

105. Brummer (1970): 220–23.

106. Brummer (1970): 163, 216–49.

107. See Stinger (1998): 271–76; Arnold Nesselrath, "Il Cortile delle Statue: luogo e storia," in M. Winner, B. Andreae, and C. Pietrangeli (1998): 1–16; Hans Brummer, "On the Julian Program of the Cortile delle Statue in the Vatikan Belvedere," in M. Winner, B. Andreae, and C. Pietrangeli (1998): 67–75.

108. The verse is preserved in Cod. Vat. Lat. 10377, fol. 63v, see Brummer (1970): 225–27.

109. Cod. Vat. Lat. 10377, fol. 98v; see Nesselrath (1998): 1, n. 4.

110. For the carnival, see Klaczko (1903): 360–66.

111. The obelisk is described in a letter to Isabella d'Este and dated February, 1513, published by Alessandro Luzio, "Federico Gonzaga, ostaggio alla corte di Giulio II," *Archivio della Reale Società Romana di Storia Patria* 9 (1886): 580. For discussion, see Brummer (1970): 222–23; Stinger (1998): 58.

112. Giuliano da Sangallo, Biblioteca Apostolica Vaticano, Cod. Barb. lat. 4424, fol. 70r; cf. C. Hülsen, *Il Libro di Giuliano da Sangallo. Codice Vaticano Barberiniano Latina 4424* (1910): 1.72; vol. 2, pl. 62r; Stefano Borsi, *Giuliano da Sangallo. I disegni di architettura e dell'antico* (1985): 75–78.

113. Cod. Barb. lat.. 4424, fol. 8r; Hülsen (1910): 1.xxvii-viii, 16; vol. 2, pl. 10r; Borsi (1985): 76.

114. Vat. Barb. lat., fol. 70 r. Giuliano's Sienese album, Biblioteca Comunale, Siena, Ms. S. IV. 8., fol. 9v, includes a measured study of "la punta de la guglia di Vatichano in Roma" and its "pala," see Falb (1902): 33, pl. X.

115. Stinger (1998): 235.

116. For these associations, see Iversen (1968): 24, fig. 11a, b, who does not connect the eagle's imagery to Julius II.

117. Sangallo remained on the job after Bramante's death in April 1514, but returned to Florence in 1515. See Giorgio Vasari, *Le vite de' più eccellenti pittori, scultori ed architettori*, in Milanesi (1906): 4.286–87, 297.

118. See B.A. Curran, "The Sphinx in the City: Egyptian Monuments and Urban Spaces in Renaissance Rome," in Stephen J. Milner and Stephen J. Campbell, eds., *Artistic Exchange and Cultural Translation in the Italian Renaissance City* (2004): 294–326.

119. Shaw (1993): 207.

120. For the characterization of Julius as a "pragmatic politician," see Shaw (1993): 206.

6

The Amazing Afterlife of Cleopatra's Love Potions

Ingrid D. Rowland

I wish you all joy of the worm.
WILLIAM SHAKESPEARE, *Antony and Cleopatra*, ACT 5, SCENE 2

The death of Elizabeth I of England in 1603 may help to explain northern Europe's sudden resurgence of interest, in the early seventeenth century, in a very different queen, Cleopatra of Egypt.[1] In London, for example, Samuel Daniel "newly altered" his tragedy *Cleopatra* for performance and republication in 1607; William Shakespeare followed with his own *Antony and Cleopatra*, first performed in 1608.[2] Meanwhile, German scholars reported the discovery of an old manuscript containing the texts of *Letters on the Infamous Libido of Cleopatra the Queen*, exchanged among three people: Marc Antony, the famous physician Quintus Soranus of Ephesus, and the monarch herself. This correspondence was first published in Frankfurt, just before the fall book fair of 1606, a fitting scholarly prelude to the salacious scripts that would soon be sweeping the stages of London.[3] Taken together, the two new plays and the ancient letters presented a picture of Egypt's last sovereign that diverged as drastically from the image of England's recently deceased Virgin Queen as the goddess of love ever differed from chaste Diana.

THERAPEUTIC SEXUAL ADVICE FOR CLEOPATRA AND MARC ANTONY?

Shakespeare eloquently described Cleopatra's charms (*Antony and Cleopatra* 2.2.):

> Age cannot wither her, nor custom stale
> Her infinite variety. Other women cloy
> The appetites they feed, but she makes hungry

Where most she satisfied; for vilest things
Become themselves in her . . .

If Shakespeare conveyed the queen's powers of seduction by dramatic suggestion, the *Letters* revealed them outright. They revealed Cleopatra as a woman of
insatiable physical appetites, as well as a sovereign of such overpowering natural
authority that she could reduce Rome's toughest soldiers—all but Augustus—to
abject thralldom. Marc Antony's first letter to Quintus Soranus has the tough
Roman general shifting responsibility in mid-sentence (through an egregious
dangling participle) from his own adulterous impulses to the Alexandrian
queen's aggressive allure:[4]

> Smitten by love of Cleopatra and delighting in her extraordinary beauty, softened
> by her caresses beyond what becomes a manly spirit, I so relaxed the marital bond
> [he was still married to Fulvia Flacca Bambula] that, disdaining both myself and
> fear of the law, she stained herself with me in adultery; and in no mean wise, rather,
> subordinating her womanly modesty to desire, she broke into such impatience for
> crime that in a single night, after donning a hood, she accepted, in a brothel as a
> prostitute, the embraces of one hundred and six men.[5]

His letter continues by supplying explicit clinical details about Cleopatra's
physical state—just what an ancient Roman physician might want to know when
giving advice by correspondence from one side of the Mediterranean to the other.
Soranus replied with an equally graphic prescription after this tantalizing preface:[6]

> When I was undergoing instruction in the Temple of Venus on the island of Chios, I
> discovered a book that contained the recipe and applications of this reliable ointment,
> which I send to you. . . . The power of this ointment is such that by it any woman will
> be so attracted to the man with whom she lies that she will forget every other love.

After a preliminary rub of milk of wild fig and root of spurge-laurel, Antony
was advised to apply the secret ointment, whose additional virtues, especially
when combined with the eating of "hot" foods like pepper, eggs, cheese, and
strong wine, included a capacity to expand any man's "extension" to ten Roman
inches, "which if you do not have by nature, you should have by medicine."[7]
Cleopatra's response to the special Grecian formula was spectacular and immediate, as she wrote to Soranus with glowing gratitude:[8]

> To the many thanks I owe the greatness of your good will, my conscience bears
> witness, which manifestly perceives the great danger and great infamy from which
> I have been freed by your wisdom. And Antony testifies as well, whom, thanks to
> your intervention, I now cherish exclusively.

Soranus, in his reply, furnished the queen with a disquisition on female anat-
omy (including identification of the ovaries as "testiculi") as well as a series of

recipes for the couple's future use: for Antony, a poultice of pepper, catnip, and pear, and another of chamomile, rue, and radish boiled in oil, left to macerate for three days, mixed with wax, and applied "from knee to navel when it is time to go to bed." For Cleopatra, with her hot nature, he advised a diet of spelt bread, lettuce with vinegar and a little salt, rough wine, meat, and "frigid things"; for the more sluggish Antony, spicy radishes.

THE *LETTERS* PUBLISHED WITH *PRIAPEIA*?

Whatever the satisfaction this story of balanced diet and balanced love may have given its readers, in the hierarchical society of the seventeenth century, the familiar tone of the *Letters* would have seemed most peculiar for queenly correspondence. Taken together with the precise sexual references in the letters of Antony and Soranus, only the distance of antiquity and the exchange's avowed clinical purpose might readily distinguish it from sheer pornography. More peculiar still was the company these letters kept when they first saw publication, for they were tacked on to an edition, with scholarly commentary, of the collection of poems known as the *Priapeia*, a series of ancient verses addressed to the Greco-Roman world's phallic god of fertility and sometimes ascribed to Virgil.[9]

In the 1606 printed edition of the *Priapeia*, an introductory letter (dated 1596) identified that work's scholarly commentator as a certain Caspar Schoppe, who at the age of thirty had achieved some notoriety in Europe. The son of a prominent family of Nuremberg pastors, Schoppe had converted to a vehement brand of Catholicism in 1598 and emigrated to Rome, where he arrived on New Year's Eve of the same year. In a pair of letters posted on October 21 of 1606, this pious convert denied any connection to the little book that was sparking such attention at the Frankfurt book fair, although he would later confess that he had made some learned conjectures about the text of the *Priapeia* in his student days.[10] Another possible candidate for the commentary's real author, however, was easy enough to find, for the *Letters* of Cleopatra were said to have come from a manuscript in the possession of Schoppe's former friend and fellow student, Melchior Goldast von Haiminsfeld, who, in addition to maintaining a staunch Calvinist faith, had also revealed himself as a versatile and ingenious forger. In a massive broadside of 1607, *Scaliger Hypobolimaeus*, an outraged Schoppe claimed that Goldast had fabricated the *Priapeia* commentary himself.[11]

THE FORGER REVEALED: A FELLOW STUDENT

Schoppe's accusation, bold though it was, made sense. Goldast's previous foray into forgery had targeted a converted Catholic as its victim: the Flemish scholar

Justus Lipsius (1547–1606), whose religious affiliation tended to change with his academic appointments (he was Lutheran in Jena, Calvinist in Leiden, Catholic in Louvain).[12] In 1600, using a printer in Zürich, Goldast published a speech "On the Double Concord of Letters and Religion" claiming that Lipsius had delivered it in Jena in 1574, and offering the booklet for sale at Frankfurt's spring book fair.[13] Clever marketing, however, proved a two-edged sword. When some learned book-buyers questioned the authenticity of the speech, its Swiss printer became suspicious and asked for some learned advice. A commission of scholars convened in Zürich to authenticate the material, but they could not determine the authorship of the speech on the basis of its style alone; on the whole, they concluded, it sounded just like Lipsius. But when Lipsius himself protested from Louvain that he had neither composed nor delivered the speech, and asked, furthermore, that it be removed from the fair's catalog, the commission decided that the speech must be forged, and that Goldast must be the forger. To save his own honor, Goldast retaliated against Lipsius by writing an anonymous pamphlet that hurled invective against one of Lipsius' (real) works written in defense of the Catholic faith.

Goldast and Caspar Schoppe had known each other since 1594, when both were enrolled at the university of Altdorf, a Protestant establishment connected to the city of Nuremberg. There they had both studied with the eminent Lutheran jurist Conrad Rittershausen, becoming good friends with their mentor and with one another. (Goldast, in fact, lived with Rittershausen as a boarder.) At Rittershausen's urging, Schoppe had transferred in the winter of 1595–96 to the Catholic university of Ingolstadt in order to attend the lectures of another illustrious legal scholar, Hubert Giffen (Hubertus Giphanius), and there began to waver in his Lutheran faith. Alarmed by this development, Schoppe's father ordered him back to the safely Lutheran setting of Altdorf, but the young man's religious doubt proved overpowering; after further readings in the Church fathers and the just-published *Ecclesiastical History* of Cesare Cardinal Baronio, he left Ingolstadt without taking a degree, heading first to Venice and thence to Prague, where he underwent a full-scale conversion in the city's gorgeous cathedral.

With a convert's enthusiasm, Schoppe then set out for Rome, where he was taken up by some of the Curia's guiding lights: the church historian Cardinal Baronio, and Cardinal Madruzzo, protector of the German nation and head of the Inquisition. Schoppe subscribed zealously to the repressive policies of Pope Clement VIII Aldobrandini, with whose family he forged close ties. Letters back to his friends in Germany now pressed them insistently to convert to Catholicism. He dedicated special energy to proselytizing his former mentor Rittershausen, and it is in the course of that correspondence that Schoppe provided eyewitness testimony in February of 1600 to the trial and execution of the Italian philosopher Giordano Bruno, who was gagged, stripped naked, and burned alive at the stake for "obstinate and pertinacious heresy," a procedure that met with Schoppe's vociferous approval.[14] The insufferable complacency of Schoppe's tone as he writes of Bruno's cruel execution, as well as his letter's implicit threats of eternal damnation for anyone who disagreed with it, were enough to alienate the normally patient Rittershausen forever. As another of Schoppe's detractors would say: "all his writings seem to be bloodthirsty, and have nothing of the spirit of Jesus, that is, of gentleness, modesty, humility, and temperance. Yet he is such a Pharisee that he prides himself on Stoic practice, eating no meat nor drinking wine, wearing a discipline and sleeping on the floor and other things of this kind; in short, I think he is perhaps a Catholic, although a bad one and of low degree."[15]

THE FORGER'S OTHER VICTIM

Goldast's forgery of Justus Lipsius, then, was fueled by his onetime friend Caspar Schoppe's departure for Italy and continual self-righteous needling from Rome. We may never know precisely why Goldast chose to focus on Lipsius as his particular victim, but the general reasons for his attack are surely clear: the whole intellectual community at Altdorf had been nurtured on Lipsius' work in history and philology, and Goldast may have regarded Lipsius' turn to Catholicism, like Schoppe's, as a kind of betrayal. Lipsius' conversion had exerted an equal and opposite influence on Schoppe: at the very moment when Goldast was commending his false speech of Lipsius to book-buyers in Frankfurt, Schoppe was republishing a real work of Lipsius in Rome: his 1596 guidebook to the Eternal City.[16] Schoppe had already become a variety of high-class tour guide to German visitors in Rome, with a special mission to convert the Protestants among them; the reissued Lipsius guidebook (which was published together with a second guidebook by the English Catholic Thomas Stapleton) must have aimed especially at the influx of visitors and pilgrims expected for the Holy Year of 1600. For all his Catholic piety and ascetic practices, however, Schoppe had also managed to amass a considerable body of expertise in scholarly erotica. Whether or not he drafted a commentary on the Priapeia in his youth, he certainly published comments on Apuleius and the Satyricon of Petronius in this early period of his life as a Catholic expatriate.[17]

FALLOUT FROM THE FORGERY

This, then, was the background of religious and scholarly rancor against which Goldast would have fabricated the "Schoppe" commentary on the Priapeia. The 1606 edition began, as mentioned above, with a prefatory letter, dated Ingolstadt 1596, whose contents must have been particularly galling to Schoppe in Rome; at exactly the time when he had made his first tentative steps toward joining the

Roman Church, Europe's learned readers would now believe that he had really been poring over racy ancient poetry, gazing out his window at mating sparrows, his mind thoroughly occupied with pagan bawdry rather than Christian piety.

Furthermore, any scholarly pretensions the *Priapeia* commentary may have claimed were thoroughly compromised by its coupling with the *Letters*—taken in tandem, each work only served to emphasize the risqué aspects of the other. It was a thoroughly effective way to brand Schoppe as an eager consumer of pornography. But Goldast did not stop there. Although the little book was designed to suggest that Schoppe had been its editor and author, the preface to the *Letters* took pains to note that the letters had come from a manuscript in Goldast's personal library—for Schoppe, this information would have been as good as a signature by Melchior Goldast von Haiminsfeld himself.

Schoppe certainly regarded the book as a personal attack by his former friend, and he retaliated as viciously as he knew how. The letters he cited in his own *Scaliger Hypobolimaeus* reported that Goldast was dead, broken on the wheel as a convicted murderer. And this story struck uncomfortably close to home, for Goldast's brother Sebastian had indeed been executed by this horrific means in Strasbourg in 1603, for killing a local woman.[18] Informed that he had mistaken one Goldast brother for another (which he must have known all along), Schoppe seized the opportunity to add insult to injury by "not giving up hope that one day [Melchior] would experience the same fate as his brother, and rot on high rather than underground."[19] Goldast, in turn, tried to sue Schoppe for libel, but the distances between Protestant Germany and papal Rome were too great for any legal process to transfer from one venue to the other. Besides, over the long course of time, Goldast had gotten as rich a satisfaction from his imposture as any forger could have hoped. The *Priapeia* and the *Letters* have stuck together like conjoined twins through countless reprintings into the eighteenth century, sometimes joined by Schoppe's commentary on Petronius' *Satyricon*, sometimes by other works, but always regarded as a standard component of any well-stocked library of erotica. Cheap, yet bristling with learned references, these various editions of the two texts satisfied several scholarly appetites at once: avarice, lust, and pride in erudition. No less than Goethe wrote about the pleasure he took in the book (the 1646 edition) during his own Italian travels.[20]

THE FORGER GOLDAST'S LEARNED PUBLICATION IN HIS OWN NAME

Goldast was as well prepared a man as any (including Schoppe himself) to draft an edition of the *Priapeia* and forge the letters of Cleopatra, for at precisely this moment he was busily at work on an annotated scholarly edition of an authentic and more famous ancient erotic text, Ovid's *Art of Love*. This he published under his own name in 1610, once again aiming for the clientele at the Frankfurt book fair.[21] Ironically, much of his research must have been done in a religious house, for Goldast, perpetually short of cash, had taken lodging in 1606 with the Discalced (i.e., barefoot) Carmelites in Frankfurt. Publishing the "Schoppe" edition of the *Priapeia* and the *Letters* may well have been a scheme intended to earn him money, as well as striking a clever sidelong blow for Protestant integrity against a Catholic apostate.

Goldast had particular reason to resent the Catholic cause in these first years of the seventeenth century. To make ends meet, he was working as an editor for the Frankfurt publisher Peter Kopff, who had been appointed by the Frankfurt city council to draw up the lists for the two annual book fairs. The success of the fairs in these troubled times depended in large measure on a resolute policy of religious neutrality, but in the early years of the seventeenth century, a Jesuit-backed Imperial Book Commission had been attempting with increasing insistence to gain control of the fair's publication lists. Any sectarian shift would have had a devastating effect both on the thriving local print industry and on the marketing of books throughout Europe; on a smaller scale, the shop of Peter Kopff would have felt particularly vulnerable, and Melchior Goldast along with it.[22] Goldast's small effort with the *Priapeia* could not do something as grand as dismantling the Catholic-leaning Book Commission, but it did brand one Catholic apologist as a hypocrite and Pharisee. For Schoppe, at last, confessed that he had indeed written some conjectures on the *Priapeia* in his youth. With characteristic venom, he pinned the blame on his Protestant rival (and fellow commentator on the *Priapeia*) Joseph Justus Scaliger:[23]

> But I was only a boy of seventeen, and educated in heretic schools, and invited to do it by your example.

THE FORGER'S CRAFTY COMMENTARY ON SPARROWS

Although scholars have debated the issue since 1606, there can be little doubt that any work young Caspar Schoppe may have done on the *Priapeia* had been generously expanded by the time Goldast prepared a commentary on the work for publication. He had also given the scholarly apparatus a wicked twist. With fine-tuned pomposity, the book's prefatory letter to an otherwise unknown Nicolaus Popponius, allegedly drafted in Ingolstadt in 1596 (when Schoppe was twenty rather than seventeen), insists upon the little work's educational purpose:[24]

> For inasmuch as these poems can affect this republic, either by increasing learning, or by aiding virtue, they should not be destroyed. About learning, I think there is no point in discussing it here, when any half-educated person can see it from our very Commentaries and the index. They have information that Physicians can

consult to find terms by which they can refer to the less respectable parts of the body conveniently and modestly, and many other things that are observed by us in the Commentaries. Lawyers have material pertinent to the correct meaning of words. And you will be amazed, but even Theologians will have what is necessary for them to know. For how can they speak truly and surely about the terrible crimes of the nations, of that buggery which we call Sodomy, and thoroughly detest it, unless they know it from these writings?[25] But what need is there for words? Who will dare to deny that the *Priapeia* are necessary to aid virtue?

His bona fides thus established, "Schoppe" proceeds to elucidate various passages of the *Priapeia* by explaining obscure terms and comparing its relentlessly phallic poems with other works of ancient literature. Neither the text itself nor the commentary is distinguished by subtlety of touch; both text and notes dwell at length on rape and, especially, masturbation. But the scholarly remark that would earn "Schoppe" the greatest notoriety had to do with sparrows:[26]

> In springtime, every creature is more prone to Venus, but the sparrow is more so than any other. When I was in Ingolstadt I observed a sparrow from my study who mated repeatedly, and then was so overtaken by lassitude that when he tried to fly off, he fell to the ground.

This passage, together with a few references to memories of Schoppe's professor Hubert Giffen, has sometimes been taken as proof that Schoppe must have written the *Priapeia* commentary himself.[27] Yet the references to Giffen are precisely the means by which a forger (i.e., Goldast) could most convincingly have established Schoppe's putative authorship. As for the languorous sparrow, its long life in subsequent literature, most conspicuously in Pierre Bayle's influential eighteenth-century *Dictionnaire Historique et Critique,* suggests the work of an ingenious prankster rather than an earnest Catholic apologist. The *Priapeia* as we have them are more persuasive as a collaborative effort between an unwitting Schoppe and a wickedly inspired Goldast than as a work that a young Schoppe would have consigned to the hands of his erstwhile friend before setting out for Venice, Prague, Rome, and conversion.[28]

ERUDITION FUELS THE DECEPTION

As for the *Letters,* forged although they certainly are, bluntly erotic though their chief purpose may be, they also, like most successful forgeries, begin from a solid basis in fact, and not only reveal, but indeed actively flaunt their author's considerable grounding in classical literature. That author, as Anne Baade was first to point out, can only have been Goldast himself.[29] Goldast uses ancient medicine as the excuse by which he can touch on the particulars of sexual congress and by which he can also claim redeeming social importance for his erotic exercise.

By an expedient common to forgers and the writers of fiction, he presents his creation by telling an infinitely regressing series of stories within stories.

The outermost layer belongs to an anonymous "Paduan printer" who, according to his prefatory letter, had decided to publish a manuscript from Goldast's personal library. Padua would have evoked thoughts of its famous medical school, whose elegant wooden anatomical theater had been installed not long before, in 1594. There was, of course, no Paduan printer who read over Goldast's parchment codex. There were only Wolfgang Richter and Conrad Nebenius, printers of Frankfurt, who in 1605 had delivered themselves of Goldast's *Some Ancient Swabian Writers*, a pioneering work in the study of medieval German literature. Those ancient Swabian texts, like the parchment of Cleopatra's letters, were also—and this time, truthfully—said to have come from Goldast's personal library. Despite his frequent encounters with poverty, he maintained an impressive and well-rounded collection, which he had augmented greatly by looting the civic library at St. Gallen in Switzerland, when he was brought to the Swiss city to draw up an inventory of its holdings.[30] But the manuscript behind the 1606 Frankfurt edition of *Letters* has never been found, any more than the printed Paduan edition, or the 1596 edition of Caspar Schoppe's commentary on the *Priapeia*—those texts emerged for the first time in print, between the same set of covers, from Frankfurt's Richter press in 1606. But, like the fictitious letter supposedly drafted by Caspar Schoppe from Ingolstadt in 1596, the story told by the fictitious printer of Padua was a tantalizing one, beginning with the word he uses to describe Goldast's library: *festivus* ("merry," "cheerful"). And amid the printer's countless protestations that the letters he publishes may be spurious, the most distracted reader cannot avoid being alerted that all may not be quite right in the merry Goldast-Bibliothek:[31]

> I have presented to you, most humane Reader, the testimony of a parchment codex, a copy of which that noble and illustrious man, Melchior Haiminsfeld Goldast made from his merry library, stocked with every kind of book, when he stayed here for a while. Now both the elegance of its script and the parchment itself attest to its age, but whether [the letters] are genuine offspring of those whose names they bear before them or are changelings planted by others seems to be a question. Certainly, when I consider the order and syntax of the language, which stands no closer to the eloquence of Cicero than the earth does to heaven, they seem not to be [genuine], but rather [the work] of someone from a subsequent century, who was not even entirely versed in Latin. I make this conjecture on the basis of the correspondence itself. . . .
>
> Still, although they may be by fictitious authors, I have learned by schooling at home that they nonetheless help greatly to understand certain passages in the ancient writers: Petronius, Martial, and others. As for the remedies, these are reliable beyond doubt, or at least their prescriptions are sufficient to testify on their

own behalf. Neither have they lost their utility in the present age for subduing the lust of corrupt women, which is the cause of miscarriage for some, and sterility for many. And not a few men are to be found who are bound by spells or tainted by poison, or, if I may use lawyer's terms, are cursed or unlucky; for them, a work like this may be helpful in their therapy. I wanted to say this so that you would be made aware. Farewell, Reader, and user—if you do so honorably—bear in mind that obscenity is hateful to God and abominable to the Angels.

QUEEN CLEOPATRA AS AUTHOR OF A MEDICAL TEXT?

The preface by the "Paduan printer" gives an excellent summary of recent scholarly work, in German-speaking Europe especially, on ancient medicine. As the "printer" (that is, Goldast) was well aware, Soranus of Ephesus was credited in antiquity with more than twenty books, of which only one is still preserved, the *Gynaecia* (*Gynecology*).[32] The name of Cleopatra likewise has been associated with two surviving ancient medical texts. One of them largely concerns the preparation of cosmetics, and was written not by the Egyptian queen, but by one of the many commoners named Cleopatra (the name means "Illustrious Father" or "of illustrious lineage") who populated the Greek-speaking world. The author Cleopatra was a female physician who lived during Roman Imperial times; women doctors were a familiar sight in the ancient world in every branch of medical practice, and several of them also left written treatises, in which the preparation of cosmetics is a standard feature.[33]

The other surviving treatise, however, was attributed to Cleopatra, Queen of Egypt, and this is the text to which the "Paduan printer" refers in the bibliographic section of his preface:[34]

Certainly there have been those who believe that the authors of these letters lived in a later age. . . . Hence there exists some other person, who with no less audacity would delete the book On the diseases and Cures of Women [written] in the name of this same Cleopatra the Queen, whom those same two I mentioned, Wolf and Spach, published. And certainly the insatiable libido of Cleopatra is proclaimed by ancient writers, which no one, in truth, has expressed more clearly and evidently than this Antony of ours. Whether in his own words or in those of some ancient writer who is now lost to us is uncertain. But to us, indeed, these letters, which come to us through the hands of many, are no less worthy than either that book of Cleopatra's published by those men who are sound of judgment and authority, or indeed the Introduction to the Art of Healing by Soranus himself.

This treatise *On the Diseases and Cures of Women* was originally published in antiquity under the name of Metrodora, a female doctor who wrote in Greek sometime between the second and fourth centuries of the Christian era.[35] The

Greek text as preserved deals with a whole range of pathologies, embracing every area of medical practice except obstetrics and surgery, and does so by combining scholarly preparation with clinical experience. As a result, this highly original book was translated into Latin, most probably between the third and fifth centuries, and excerpted repeatedly by later authors.[36] In one of her bibliographic references, Metrodora cites a "Berenice called Cleopatra" and this datum seems eventually to have inspired some medieval scribes to circulate the Latin translation of Metrodora or its excerpts under this more glamorous ancient name. It was thus that translated excerpts from Metrodora came to be edited and published under the name of Cleopatra by Caspar Wolf in 1566 and republished by Israel Spach in 1597—as the Paduan printer reminds his readers, and it was presumably in this state that Melchior Goldast first encountered them.[37] Goldast would have found Metrodora/Cleopatra's work, and the compendia in which it appears, a useful source for his own study of Ovid's *Ars Amatoria*; it deals, as mentioned, with pathology, but also with recipes to restore the appearance of virginity, aids to conception, cures for sterility, contraceptives, aphrodisiacs, tests for fertility and virginity, and advice about what to do "when a woman itches so that she seems to need a man."[38] In Wolf's 1566 edition, moreover, Metrodora's treatise, duly attributed to Cleopatra, appeared together with several other ancient gynecological treatises, including an ancient epitome (by Moschion) of that very *Gynaecia* written by none other than Soranus of Ephesus.[39]

SCHOLARLY, EPIGRAPHICAL, AND EROTIC FANTASIES

Still, Goldast couched his forgery in two more layers of introductory material before offering it to his readers. First, he quoted a letter by the fifteenth-century Italian humanist Francesco Filelfo "in which he recalls a certain codex in which these letters seem to have been contained."[40] In fact, the letter proves nothing of the sort, for it only states that Filelfo has read one of the medical texts that must underlie the forgery, presumably the very medical work attributed to Cleopatra that may have inspired Goldast to create his erotic epistolary novella in the first place. Filelfo writes (and actually did write—the letter is genuine):[41]

> I recall that when you were in Milan I saw at your home some very ancient manuscript that contains the writings of several Physicians, like Cornelius Celsus, and both Soranuses,[42] and of Apuleius, and Democritus, and also some women.

Only after this elaborate groundwork does Goldast present the contents of his own manuscript. He gives its texts with a copiously footnoted critical apparatus, as if he had needed to correct the original document from which he worked, changing "Saphocles" to "Sophocles," "porifice" to "orifice" and so on, in imitation of true philologists. First, he cites an exchange of letters between the Byzantine Emperor Heraclius (610–41), "Parthicus, Persicus, et Babylonicus, Triumphator semper Augustus" and the wise philosopher Sophocles:[43]

> As I was returning from the Persian War . . . and a great victory was gained by the grace of Christ, I decided to stop in Alexandria. . . . And as I stayed there for a few days, it pleased me to open some tombs of the ancient Kings. Likewise the tomb was opened of Cleopatra, that most famous Queen, who held sway with Antony over almost the entire East: and her body, placed there next to Antony and embalmed with spices, had remained intact up to our own time over one hundred twenty-five Olympiads. At the Queen's head a book was found, inscribed in unknown characters on bronze tablets, which was brought to us: and there was no doubt that it must contain something of great usefulness, because it had been laid so carefully at the head of so great of Queen.

After the bronze tablets proved illegible to all the sages of Alexandria, Heraclius finally remembered his old friend Sophocles, and sent him transcripts of the tablets in their peculiar script. As Sophocles attests, "by some secrets of our art" their contents were revealed to him. The philosopher could barely contain his vicarious excitement when he wrote back to his sovereign:[44]

> First of all, I think you the happiest of men, for in your time a secret hidden many centuries before has been revealed, more priceless than all your gold. . . . I warn you to keep it carefully hidden, and let it never emerge in public.

At last, after these three sets of preambles from three different eras, the *Letters* get down to the business with which we began. The missives themselves are comparatively brief. After recounting Cleopatra's exploit in the brothel, Antony reports that he has been told that there are women for whom the lack of sex for any more than thirteen days can be fatal, and that Cleopatra is one of these women. In reply, of course, Soranus supplies his remedies of milk of wild fig and root of spurge-laurel. A cooler Cleopatra writes her thank-you note, Soranus replies with rules for hot and cold diets and recipes for catnip poultices, and all is right with Antony and Cleopatra until the Battle of Actium brings stern young Octavian and ultimate defeat onto the scene. But that tragic denouement Goldast would leave to Plutarch and (soon) to Shakespeare.

A CLOAK OF PLAUSIBILITY FOR THE SPURIOUS LETTERS

The cast of characters for this exchange was drawn plausibly enough from Goldast's reading—from the medical writers to the Byzantine writer John Tzetzes, who asserted in the twelfth century, in the teeth of evidence placing the good doctor generations later, that Quintus Soranus had been Cleopatra's personal physician.[45] Cleopatra's position in the history of seductive womanhood, meanwhile, could be traced back to the *Odyssey*'s clever enchantress, Circe, whose potions turned the shipmates of Odysseus into animals, but Goldast seems to have drawn the particulars of his characterization of the queen from the Roman satirist Juvenal's attacks on the dissolute Empress Messalina,[46]

> Look at those who rival the gods; hear what Claudius
> Bore. When his wife sensed that he was asleep . . .
> She hid her black hair under a blonde hood
> And entered the hot brothel . . .
> Then naked, with gilded nipples
> She prostituted herself under the false name of "Foxy" . . .

For all that, the aphrodisiacs that Quintus Soranus suggests to his illustrious clients are remarkably tame concoctions: Goldast could have drawn on far more lurid compounds from his medical texts than the green salad, pepper, radishes, catnip, and spurge-laurel that "Soranus" actually recommends in these spurious letters; indeed, only the ointment from the Temple of Venus on the island of Chios has the least aura of exoticism. Instead, the garden-variety simples and the navel-to-knee poultice are comical enough to suggest that they added to Goldast's merriment as he whittled away at Caspar Schoppe's reputation from the sanctum of his merry library.

THE FORGER GOLDAST'S SUCCESS

The production of forgeries and anonymous pamphlets reached nearly industrial dimensions in the sixteenth and seventeenth centuries, the result of an insatiable— and highly fruitful—search for the remnants of ancient literature, but also of a familiarity with that literature that allowed a good deal of room for play, either lighthearted or vicious, or both, as in the case of Melchior Goldast's erotic publication of 1606. Furthermore, as the Church, particularly but not exclusively in Catholic countries, attempted to curtail freedom of the press, writers reacted by assuming fictitious identities. But few have been as diabolically effective as Melchior Goldast in his manipulation of the reputation of his erstwhile friend, Caspar Schoppe. There is not a library in the world whose catalog fails to attribute the 1606 Nuremberg commentary on the *Priapeia* to Schoppe, and Schoppe alone. As Horace, a younger contemporary of Cleopatra, would one day remark, "Life is short, art long." The dictum holds as well for the forger's as for the poet's muse.

NOTES

1. My thanks to Margaret Miles, Holt Parker, and Anthony Grafton, and to the Department of Special Collections at the Getty Research Institute, Los Angeles, California.

2. See David Bevington, ed., *The Complete Works of William Shakespeare*, 4th ed., (1997): 1293.

3. *Priapeia Sive Diversorum Poetarum In Priapum Lusus / illustrati Commentariis Gasperis Schoppii Franci, L. Apuleii Madaurensis Anechomenos / ab eodem [Gaspere Schoppio] illustratus. Heraclii Imperatoris, Sophoclis Sophistae, C. Antonii, Q. Sorani, & Cleopatrae Reginae Epistolae, De propudiosa Cleopatrae Reginae libidine. Francoforti, In Officina Typographica Wolffgangi Richteri, Sumptibus Conradi Nebenii, 1506 [i.e., 1606].*

4. *Heraclii Imperatoris, Sophoclis Sophistae, C. Antonii, Q. Sorani, & Cleopatrae Reginae Epistolae, De propudiosa Cleopatrae Reginae libidine*; also known as *De Priapismo*. Because the work is very short and appears in a number of editions, citations appear without page numbers, but rather refer to the correspondents. Antony to Soranus: "Amore Cleopatrae comprehensus atque formae ipsius supra modum pulchritudine delectatus, ultra quam oporteret virilem animum, ejus blanditiis delinitus, tamen ei de maritali freno relaxavi, quod me contempto legumque timore, adulterio se commaculaverit. Nec hoc mediocriter, sed animo postposita muliebri verecundia ad tantam impatientiam flagitii prorupit, quod sub una nocte sumpto cucullo in lupanari prostibulo centum et sex virorum concubitus pertulit. In tantum enim, ut professa est, in tentigine rigidae vulvae erat accensa, quod a lupanari quidem, sed non satiata recessit, et licet occultissime actum esset, me tamen non latuit. Tandemque hujus nefariae offensae ab ea sub interminatione vitae sciscitatus, impatientiam gemini caloris et fervorem inveni. Quod per quosdam Philosophicae artis peritos verum esse deprehendens, qui dicunt quarumdam mulierum tam ferventem esse naturam, ut si sine veretro pene assiduo et continuo virili amplexu infra tertium decimum expertes fuerint, nec vivere quidem possint . . ."

5. For this detail and its similarity to Juvenal's sixth satire, see below.

6. Soranus to Antony: ". . . in templo Veneris edoctus in Chio insula inveni librum continentem modum et vim hujus veri unguenti, quod tibi mitto . . . Vis sane hius unguenti talis est, per quod unaquaeque mulier ad amorem illius viri, qui cum ea concubuerit, ita attrahitur, ut omnium amoris obliviscatur."

7. Soranus to Antony: "Quod si non habes per naturam, debes habere per medicinas."

8. Cleopatra to Soranus: "Quantas gratiarum actiones magnitudini bonitatis debitrix sim, testis est conscientia mea, quae manifeste sentit a quanto periculo quantaque infamia tua sapientia liberata sim. Testis etenim est Antonius, quem te nunc operante unicum diligo." Testis, as often in Latin humor, is not an innocent word here.

9. See Amy Richlin, *The Garden of Priapus: Sexuality and Aggression in Roman Humor* (1983).

10. These letters were printed at the end of Schoppe's *Scaliger Hypobolimaeus* of 1607 (see following note); his admission that he wrote on the *Priapeia* is also contained in that nine-hundred-page diatribe. See Frank-Rutger Hausmann, "Kaspar Schoppe, Joseph Justus Scaliger und die Carmina Priapeia oder wie man mit Büchern Rufmord betriebt," in Kaspar Elm, Eberhard Gönner, and Eugen Hillenbrand, eds., *Landesgeschichte und Geistesgeschichte: Festschrift für Otto Herdina zum 65. Geburtstag* (1977): 382–95.

11. Gaspar Schoppe, *Gasp. Scioppii Scaliger Hypobolimaevs, hoc est: Elenchvs epistolae Iosephi Bvrdonis Psevdoscaligeri De vetustate et splendore gentis Scaligerae* (1607): 106.

12. Anne A. Baade, *Melchior Goldast von Haiminsfeld: Collector, Commentator, and Editor* (1992): 34.

13. Baade (1992): 34, with a presumable typographical error (*duplica*) in *De duplici concordia literarum et Religionis.*

14. See Luigi Firpo, *Il processo di Giordano Bruno* (1993): 348–55.

15. This was Vicente Nogueira, a Portuguese scholar who worked in Rome as a spy first for the Portuguese secessionists under Spanish rule and then, after Portuguese independence in 1640, for King João IV. Nogueira is writing very late in Schoppe's life and admits never having known him, but in general Nogueira is a shrewd judge of character: Biblioteca Apostolica Vaticana, MS Barb. Lat. 6472 32v, 16 July 1639: "tutti i suoi scritti paiono sanguinarii e niente hanno del spirito di Iesu cioe di

mansuetudine modestia humilta e temperanza. E pur tanto farisaico che si vanta d' esser uso stoico, non magnando carne ne bebendo vino portando cilicio e dormendo in terra [33r] et alia istiusmodi insuma io l'ho per forse Catholico pur cattivo e di termini basse."

16. Ed. of Justus Lipsius, 1547–1606, and Thomas Stapleton, 1535–98: *Admiranda et vere admiranda, siue, de magnitudine et urbis et ecclesiae Romanae / auctoribus Iusto Lipsio & Thoma Stapletono; curante Gasare. Schoppio . . . ; coniunctim nunc primum editi.: [Tertia editio correctior auctiorque]: Romae: ex bibliotheca Bartholomaei Grassi, apud Nicolaum Mutium,* 1600.

17. Schoppe's *Verisimilium libri quatuor* (1596) contains commentary on Petronius; it should be noted that John Edwin Sandys, *A History of Classical Scholarship* (1908): 362–63, reports that this work is largely plagiarized. Schoppe's Apuleius commentary appears in the same volume as "his" *Priapeia* and the letters of Antony, Cleopatra, and Soranus; see note 3 above.

18. Baade (1992): 37.

19. Baade (1992): 37: "non desperare futurum ut fato aliquando fratris utatur et sublime potius quam humi putrescat."

20. So Hausmann (1977): 394.

21. Melchior Goldast, ed., *Ovidii Nasonis Pelignensis Erotica et amatoria opuscula : de amoribus, arte, et modis amandi, & qua ratione quis amoris compos fieri debeat . . . : cum altis quibusdam ejusdem argumenti libellu., qui per fucum in Ocidianas inscriptiones transierunt, quorum auctores versa pagina exhibet . . . Francoforti: Richerus; Kopffius,* 1610.

22. Baade (1992): 37–38.

23. Cited in Pierre Bayle, *Dictionnaire Historique et Critique* (1740) 4: 173: "Scripsi fateor commentarium in Priapeia, sed septenum denum annorum puer, sed in haereticorum scholis institutus, sed exemplo tuo invitatus."

24. *Priapeia, sive Diversorum Poetarum in Priapum Lusus, Illustrati Commentariis Gasperis Schoppii, Franci, L. Apuleii Madaurensis, Ab eodem illustratus, Heraclii Imperatoris, Sophoclis Sophistae, C. (sic) Antonii, Q. Sorani, et Cleopatrae Reginae Epistolae De propudiosa Cleopatrae Reginae libidine, Huic editioni accedunt Josephi Scaligeri in Priapeia Commentaii, ac Friderici Linden-Bruch in eadem Notae.* Padua, Apud Gerhardum Nicolaum V. Sub signo Angeli Aurati, 1644, p. *2 verso:

"Ad hanc enim faciem putare mecum coepi. Cum carmina haec reipublicae, qua eruditione, qua virtutibus juvandis, commovere possint, exterminanda non videri. De eruditione heic non necesse habeo dicere, quando ea, ex his ipsis Commentariis, et Indice nostro, a quovis mediocriter literato intelligi potest. Habent, quod petant hinc Medici; ut verba quibus partes humani corporis minus severas commode et verecunde appellare possint; et alia nonnulla, a nobis in Commentariis observata. Habent Jureconsulti, ad quos suo quodam iure verborum significatio pertinet. Et quod mireris haberent denique, quod sibi cognitu sit necessarium, Theologi. Quo enim modo de horrendis ethnicorum sceleribus, de paedicatione, quam Sodomian vocamus, vere et certo loqui, eamque detestari poterunt, nisi eam ex scriptis illorum cognoverint? Sed qui verbis opus est? Cum carminum horum eruditio, non tam testimonio, quam obscoenitas venia, indigere videatur . . . Quis ergo Priapeia virtutibus juvandis, et modo non necessaria esse, negare ausit?"

25. For the meaning of *paedicare*, see Holt Parker, "The Teratogenic Grid," in Judith P. Hallett and Marilyn B. Skinner, eds., *Roman Sexualities* (1997): 47–65.

26. *Priapeia,* Poem XV. "Vernis passeribus: Omnia verno tempore in Venerem sunt proniora, maxime vero omnium passere. Cum Ingolstadii agerem vidi e regione musaei mei passerem coitum vicies repetentem, et inde adeo ad languorem datum, ut evolaturus in terram decideret." The sparrow is a well-known erotic symbol in Augustan poetry.

27. This is the conclusion of the erudite Hausmann (1977): 386, 389–95.

28. Holt Parker notes in a private communication of 2000 that a particularly trenchant "exam-

ple of damning with attributed porn[ography] is the case of Luisa Sigea of Toledo (ca. 1522–ca. 1560) whose letter of 1546 to Pope Paul III, written in Latin, Greek, Hebrew, 'Chaldaean' (i.e., Syriac), and Arabic made her the wonder of the age. But everyone knows her as the 'authoress' of the Satyra Sotadica, actually composed by the phenomenally learned Nicolas Chorier . . . (*Nicolas Chorier, Aloisiae Sigeae Toletanae Satyra Sotadica de Arcanis Amoris et Veneris sive Joannis Meurii Elegentiae Latini Sermonis*, 1660)." A new edition with commentary by Holt Parker is forthcoming.

29. Baade (1992): 37: "One assumes that these letters 'taken' from Goldast's library, to which the Scioppius Priapeia commentary was added, were a product of Goldast's imagination and humor."

30. *Svevicarum Rerm Scriptores Aliquot Veteres: Partim Primum Editi, partim emendatius atq[ue] auctius, In quibus Svevorum Origo, Migratio, Regna, Principes, bella, foedera, religiones, monasteria, Civitates, Comitatus . . . memoriae mandantur . . . / Ex Bibliotheca & recensione Melchioris Haiminsfeldii Goldasti. Francoforti: In Officina Wolfgangi Richteri, Impensis Conradi Nebenii, 1605.*

31. "Typographus Lectori Benevolo S.D. Praesentavi tibi, Lector humanissime, fidem membranei codicis, cujus mihi copiam ex festiva sua Bibliotheca et omnis generis librorum referta fecit vir nobilis et clarissimus Melchio Haminesfeldius Goldastus, cum hic aliquandiu subsisteret. Ejus autem vetustatem tum characterum elegantia, tum ipsa membrana satis commendat. An vero isporum, quorum nomina prae se ferunt, genuini partus sint, an ab aliis suppositi, quaestionis esse videtur. Equidem dum orationis filum et contextum considero, qui nonpropius a venustate Ciceroniani aevi abire quam coelum terra potest, videntur nonesse, sed unius cujusdam multis saeculis posterioris, qui ne Latine quidem admodum doctus erat . . . Nam fictitiorum licet sint auctorum, multum tamen facere ad veterum quorundam loca intelligenda, Petronii Arbitri, Martialis, et aliorum, domi doctus didici. Quod autem ad remedia attinet, certa et indubitate esse, vel ipsa eorum praescripta materies argumento esse potest. Nec perdidere usum suum hodie ad vitiosam mulierum tentiginem sedandam, quae nonnullis solet esse abortus, plerisque sterilitatis causa. Sed et viri non pauci reperiuntur fascinati et venficio tacti, sive, ut Jurisconsultorum vermib utar, maleficiati et sotilegiati, quibus persanandis remedio hujuscemodi opus. Haec volui nescius ne esses. Vale, lector, et utitor, sed more modoque honesto; obscoenitatem Deo invisam, Angelis cogita abominabilem."

32. See Ann Ellis Hanson and M.H. Green, "Soranus of Ephesus: Methodicorum princeps," in Wolfgang Haase, ed., *Aufstieg und Niedergang der Römischen Welt* II.37.2 (1994): 968–1075.

33. See Holt N. Parker, "Women Doctors in Greece, Rome, and the Byzantine Empire," in Lilian R. Furst, ed., *Women Healers and Physicians: Climbing a Long Hill* (1997): 131–50.

34. Preface to *Epistolae*: 118: "Quippe qui videntur posteriores harum epistolarum auctores fuisse. Ait porro Soranus, in quibus poteris addiscere etc. Unde exstitit alius quispiam, qui non minori audacia librum de vitiis et curatione mulierum hujus ipsius Cleopatrae Reginae nomine proscriberet, quem iidem illi, quos dixi, Wolfius et Spachius edidere. Et sane decantata est ab antiquis scriptoribus insatiabilis Cleopatrae libido, quam vero nemo clarius et evidentius expressit isto nostro Antonio. Ex se ne an veteri quopiam scriptore qui nobis perierit, incertum. Nobis quidem hae epistolae non minus dignae visae, quae ad plurium manus perveniant, quam vel ille Cleopatrae liber ab eis viris editus qui et judicio valent et auctoritate; aut etiam ipsius Sorani Isagoge in artem medendi."

35. Parker, "Women Doctors" (1997): 138: "We can date the text only in the most general way to the span of the second to fourth centuries A.D. plus or minus a century on either side."

36. Holt N. Parker, *Metrodora: The Gynecology: The Earliest Surviving Work by a Woman Doctor and Other Works from the Florentine Manuscript* (forthcoming).

37. Caspar Wolf, ed., *Gynaecorum, Hoc Est, De mulierum Tum Aliis, Tum gravidarum, Parientium & Puerperarum affectibus & morbis, Libri veterum ac recentiorum aliquot, partim nunc primum editi, partim multo quam antea* (1566); reprinted (1586–88) as *Gynaeciorum Sive de mulierum*

affectibus commentarii Graecorum, Latinorum, barbarorum, iam olim et nunc recens editorum: in tres tomos digesti et necessariis passim imaginibus illustrati; Israel Spach, ed., *Gynaeciorum sive de mulierum tum communibus, tum gravidarum, parientium, et puerperarum Affectibus & Morbis, libri Graecorum, Arabum, Latinorum veterum et recentium quotquot extant, partim nunc primum editi, partim vero denuo recogniti, emendati, necessarijs Imaginibus exornati, & optimorum Scriptorum autoritatibus illustrati, Opera & studio Israelis Spachii . . . Autorum catalogum post praefationem inuenire licet. Additi sunt etiam Indices Capitum, Rerum ac Verborum in his memorabilium locupletissimi & fidelissimi* (1597).

38. The solution to the latter problem is for a widow to "throw her hand in, and she will have relief" (manum iniiciat, et levius habebit). For virgins "make a likeness of the rod of wax, nitre, and cardamom of a size appropriate to her age . . . and she will be relieved of the problem." (Fac illi similitudinem virgae naturalis de cera, et nitro, et cardamomo, secundum aetatis eius magnitudinem . . . et subiice . . . et vitium carebit.) Caspar Wolf, *Harmonia Gynaeciorum sive de Mulierum Affectibus Commentarii* (1586): 75–76. For such wax likenesses used as votive offerings in antiquity, see Ian Jenkins and Kim Sloan, *Vases and Volcanoes: Sir William Hamilton and His Collection* (1996): 238–39. My thanks to Holt Parker for the first reference and to Margaret Miles for the last.

39. *Moschionos peri gynaikeion pathon = id est, Moschionis medici Graeci de morbis muliebribus liber unus; cum Conradi Gesneri viri clarissimi scholijs & emendationibus / Nunc primum ed. opera ac studio Caspari Uuolphii Tigurini medici* (1566).

40. "Paduan printer," prefatory letter: "cuiusdam codicis meminit quo comprehensae videntur fuisse et haec epistolae."

41. Francesco Filelfo, prefatory letter: "Memini cum nuper esses Mediolani, vidisse apud te vetustissimum quendam codicem, qui Medicorum plurium scripta complecteretur, ut Corn. Celsi, et utriusque Sorani, et Apulei, et Democriti, et quarundam etiam mulierum."

42. The tradition that there were two physicians named Soranus is now known from the Byzantine dictionary known as the Suda; it may be earlier in date; see Hanson and Green (1994): 986–87.

43. Heraclius to Sophocles: "Remeanti mihi a Persico bello . . . et insigni victoria per Christi gratiam sumpta est, visum est, ut Alexandriam contenderem . . . Ubi dum per aliquot dies permanerem, placuit ut quaedam sepulchra veterum Regum aperientur . . . Itemque apertum est Cleopatrae sepulchrum illius formosissimae Reginae, quae cum Antonio imperium totius penè Orientis tenuerat: ubi et corpus eius juxta Antonium collocatum aromatibus conditum illaesum usque ad nostra tempora per centum viginti quinque Olympiades permanserat. Ad cuius Reginae caput inventus liber est per ignotos characteres in aeneis tabulis inscriptis, nobisque delatus: de quo dubium non erat, quin in eo aliquid magnae utilitatis contineretur, quod tanta in eo aliquid magnae utilitatis contineretur, quod tanta diligentia ad caput tantae Reginae reconditus iaceret."

44. Sophocles to Heraclius: "per quaedam secreta artis nostrae revelatae." "In primis quidem felicissimum te hominem esse censeo, cuius temporibus revelatum arcanum multis ante seculis absconsum, omnique tuo auro pretiosius . . . Quod moneo diligenter recondi facias, nec umquam procedat in publicum."

45. Hanson and Green (1994): 986–87.

46. "Lycisca" literally means "Little Wolf" in Juvenal 6.115–32:

respice riuales diuorum, Claudius audi
quae tulerit. dormire uirum cum senserat uxor,
ausa Palatino et tegetem praeferre cubili
sumere nocturnos meretrix Augusta cucullos
linquebat comite ancilla non amplius una.
sed nigrum flauo crinem abscondente galero
intrauit calidum ueteri centone lupanar

et cellam uacuam atque suam; tunc nuda papillis
prostitit auratis titulum mentita Lyciscae
ostenditque tuum, generose Britannice, uentrem.
excepit blanda intrantis atque aera poposcit.
[continueque iacens cunctorum absorbuit ictus.]
mox lenone suas iam dimittente puellas
tristis abit, et quod potuit tamen ultima cellam
clausit, adhuc ardens rigidae tentigine uoluae,
et lassata uiris necdum satiata recessit,
obscurisque genis turpis fumoque lucernae
foeda lupanaris tulit ad puluinar odorem.

7

HRH Cleopatra

The Last of the Ptolemies and the Egyptian Paintings of Sir Lawrence Alma-Tadema

Margaret Mary DeMaria Smith

ALMA-TADEMA'S INTEREST IN ANTIQUITY

Because ancient Greek and Roman subjects make up the majority of the four hundred and eight paintings produced and numbered by Sir Lawrence Alma-Tadema, he has long been known as the "painter of the Victorian vision of the ancient world."[1] Only twenty-six of his paintings are linked to Egypt, most of them from early in the artist's career, when Egyptian topics were of special interest to him.[2] Vern Swanson estimates that Egyptian themes constitute approximately 20 to 30 percent of Alma-Tadema's work from the 1860s and 1870s.[3] The artist began by painting scenes of life in the Egypt of the Pharaohs, establishing his artistic reputation with two of these studies: *Pastimes in Ancient Egypt, 3000 years ago* (1863) and *The Death of the Firstborn* (1872).[4] So fond was the artist of the latter painting that he did not accept any offers to buy it and treated it as a family heirloom.[5] He kept the work in his studio behind a curtain that he would open dramatically for appreciative guests who attended his weekly "at home," a combination open house and one-artist exhibition.[6] He not only favored his Egyptian paintings, but continued to feature Egyptian historical themes in his work until the end of his life, despite the greater popularity of his other works. Within the larger framework of his Egyptian paintings, Alma-Tadema produced a series of portraits of Cleopatra from 1859 to 1883. These present a curious combination of Hellenistic and Victorian monarch that reflects both his respect for legendary figures from the past and his belief that human beings had not changed much over the intervening centuries.

Alma-Tadema's Egyptian paintings generally look different from his works on ancient Greek and Roman themes. He used a darker palette and softer lighting; often, their subjects are intensely emotional, as in his paintings about mourning in ancient Egypt. Although some of the subjects that Alma-Tadema depicted are also commonly seen in the work of nineteenth-century Orientalist painters, Alma-Tadema often treats his Egyptian subjects in a manner that does not appear to be Orientalizing. Indeed, he was not an adherent of the French Orientalist school. Perhaps uniquely in the Victorian period, Alma-Tadema followed no particular school of painting. He was neither a neoclassicist, nor a strict néo-Grèc, nor a pre-Raphaelite, nor a genre painter. Although critics can identify elements of these different schools in his work, Alma-Tadema carved out his own niche with his attention to detail, technical expertise, and defiance of conventional rules of composition that few artists dared rival.[7] For all of Alma-Tadema's distinctive qualities as a painter, however, he was a creature of his time and his paintings participate in the Egyptomania and perhaps even the "Orientalism," as defined by Edward Said, of the nineteenth century. This essay examines some of Alma-Tadema's paintings on Egyptian themes to place them in the cultural and artistic context of nineteenth-century Victorian England, where Alma-Tadema lived for over half of his life.

EGYPTOMANIA AND ORIENTALISM IN EUROPE

The Egyptian paintings of Alma-Tadema participate in the shifting social, cultural, and artistic trends of nineteenth-century Europe. Egypt had seized European popular imagination after Napoleon's conquest of North Africa, and deeper interest was prompted by the French artistic documentation of sites, temples, and statuary. Archaeological excavations and other enterprises brought Egyptian artifacts to the museums of Europe where the public marveled at them and artists made their own sketches. Throughout the nineteenth century, travel to Egypt became gradually easier, until that country became a regular stop in Cook's tours.[8] This allowed artists and wealthy tourists to see the archaeological sites of Egypt firsthand. Tourism, in turn, inspired the public demand for things Egyptian, especially picture books, travel diaries, lithographs, and paintings. This wave of Egyptomania arose at the beginning of the nineteenth century and waned, but it had not disappeared altogether by the end of the century. Alma-Tadema made his mark in the art world when European interest in Egypt was near its peak; he found his rewarding place as a painter of ancient Greek and Roman life just when Victorian interest in Egypt was beginning to shift to the Classical past. Because his paintings engaged and responded to the demands of popular culture, they are effective mirrors of nineteenth-century Egyptomania.

Any discussion of nineteenth-century European paintings of Egypt, especially those featuring Cleopatra, must consider the analytical framework of Edward

Said's Orientalism.[9] In recent decades it has become customary for scholars studying any facet of Mediterranean history to take into account the critical theory of Orientalism when evaluating any cultural artifact produced by a colonialist power. A reassessment of the impact of Said's theory of Orientalism, however, calls for careful application of the theory and discusses the limits of the paradigm.[10] According to Said, there are no passive reflections of Orientalism. Theoretically, all nineteenth-century artists were potentially active participants in the extension of French and British hegemony over Egypt. Said defines Orientalism as "a way of coming to terms with the Orient that is based on the Orient's special place in European Western experience."[11] *Orientalism*, as Said uses the word, thus denotes the generation of ideas of cultural hegemony that distinguish Europeans as being different from and superior to "Orientals." Said cautions his readers, however, that Orientalist ideas need not be "false," based on myths or lies; in fact, in his view Orientalism is made stronger and more complex as a result of scholarly pursuits, which only seem to add details to the already imaginary picture of the culture labeled as foreign.

With Egyptology as an example of this power relationship, Said points to Napoleon's invasion of Egypt that wove together military and cultural objectives to assert French power in the region and "to put Egypt before Europe, in a sense to stage its antiquity, its wealth of associations, cultural importance, and unique aura for a European audience."[12] He notes this aura of cultural importance in the manner of illustration in *Description de l'Egypte*, a monumental publication of material gathered by Napoleon's *savants* in Egypt as part of the French campaign and a major source of inspiration for the production of Egyptian-style items ("Egyptomania") throughout the nineteenth century.[13] According to Said, the text reconstructs Egyptian architecture in its prime, which in turn creates a "projective grandeur":

> I say "projective" because as you leaf through the *Description* you know that what you are looking at are drawings, diagrams, paintings of dusty, decrepit, and neglected pharaonic sites, looking ideal and splendid as if there were no modern Egyptians but only European spectators.[14]

It should be noted (*pace* Said) that most early-nineteenth-century views of Egypt, including those in the book he criticizes, do include modern Egyptians as well as neglected, half-buried ruins. Nonetheless, for Said, these reconstructions elide modern Egypt in favor of revealing an idealized ancient Egypt made available by print in France and Europe at large; as a by-product, the volumes of the *Description* provided a premise justifying French protection as a means of preserving and studying the ancient remains.

There seems to be no escape from Said's charge of orientalizing since one need not consciously create or impose a political agenda to be thus charged, but simply participate in the cultural dialogues generated by colonialist hegemony. According to Said's theory of Orientalism, to be an Egyptologist, a writer of Egyptian stories, or a painter of Egyptian subjects implicates one in the production of ideas that justify domination of Egypt by French and then British colonial powers. Storytellers, artists, and archaeologists are equally implicated, according to Said, in the generation of an ideal Egypt that must be recovered by Europe.

The theory of Orientalism collapses all cultural production into one pretext for the extension of European power over Asia and Africa, and as a summary judgment is problematic because its emphasis on one overarching cultural vantage point limits our view of the detailed historical and cultural contexts of a work of art. In *Culture and Imperialism*, Said admits that it is difficult to balance the particular and the general when tracing cultural interactions.[15] While the global mapping of cultural affiliations makes Said's concept of Orientalism an effective tool of general cultural critique, the difficulty of balancing the particular and the general, and the uniqueness of art while setting it into a global context of empire, frequently reduces discussions of nineteenth-century art to the level of denigration or apology.

Said's theory of Orientalism has sparked ongoing scholarly conversations and stimulated new forms of analysis of historical periods and genres within colonial art.[16] J. MacKenzie argues that Orientalism is too confining a theory to be useful in analyzing art: "In arguing this way [from the theoretical point of view of Said's Orientalism], art historians ... have narrowed and restricted the possible readings of paintings and other visual forms in extraordinarily limiting ways."[17] MacKenzie points out the gap between the artist's intended meaning and the audience's understanding of the work, and the resulting difference between an interpretation made by a late-twentieth- [or early-twenty-first-] century audience and that of a nineteenth-century audience, and notes that contextualization of a work of art is key to understanding it, since the message we read may differ from the one intended by the artist.[18] MacKenzie reminds us that imperial expansion is only one aspect of the Victorian age, and that "meaning" in art is decidedly elusive and cannot be approximated in terms of only one cultural variable. Here I shall first set the nineteenth-century context of Sir Lawrence Alma-Tadema and his art so as to avoid the reductive impulse of Orientalism's critique.[19]

EARLY INFLUENCES ON THE CAREER
OF ALMA-TADEMA

The paintings of Sir Lawrence Alma-Tadema are as complex as the eclectic times in which he lived, hence the difficulty for critics in placing his work within the dominant artistic movements of the age.[20] He was born in 1836 in Holland and received his artistic education at the Antwerp Academy of fine arts in Belgium beginning in 1852. The Antwerp Academy, at that time, specialized in teaching the techniques of historical narrative painting.[21] After he began his career in Belgium under the influence of the European art scene, Alma-Tadema moved to London in 1870 where he took British citizenship in the early 1870s and spent the rest of his career, now a Victorian gentleman. We can trace the impetus for his Egyptian paintings in the larger context of European interest in Egypt.

Paintings featuring ancient Egyptian subjects were popular in Europe and Great Britain throughout the nineteenth century, but especially so in the first half of the century. In literary circles poets such as Keats and Shelley were fascinated with the desolation of Egypt and the impressive and romantic drama of the disappearance of a once-dominant dynastic culture.[22] The paintings of the early nineteenth century have been designated "Egyptian Capriccio" because artists relied more on literary references in texts and their imagination than on archaeological evidence. The Paris Salon and the judges of the Rome Prize drove the production of paintings on Egyptian themes; their judgments in favor of such paintings reflect a general public demand for Egyptian designs of all types. In the 1820s scenes of ancient life were set among the subjects to be judged, then in the 1830s the subjects for the Rome Prize were to be taken from the Bible, an indication of the increasing importance of church art for academically trained artists.[23] By the 1840s, ancient historical subjects were again among those set for competition. MacKenzie observes that the organizers of exhibitions in the nineteenth century, where Orientalist paintings were displayed, seem obsessed with eastern architecture and crafts.[24] Young artists of the mid-nineteenth-century, among them Alma-Tadema, who were looking to establish themselves by means of official recognition, had to be able to submit paintings of ancient themes taken from Egyptian, Greek, Roman, or biblical subject matter. In order to compete, it probably helped to prepare at least one of each.

During the early part of the nineteenth century, French artists such as the néo-Grècs were concentrating on Greek and Roman antique scenes, while other French artists painted Egyptian themes. British artists also painted Egyptian scenes in response to continental European interests and to their own home-bred demand for such subjects. Although Alma-Tadema did not make his first trip to England until 1862, his Egyptian paintings bear comparison with those painted by his contemporaries in Great Britain.[25] One reason Alma-Tadema moved to Britain is surely that his artistic sensibility and style (even with continental training) found much in common with English painters of his generation.

After Nelson's defeat of the French navy in Egypt and the ensuing Treaty of Alexandria brought Egyptian artifacts into English possession, popular tastes in Great Britain immediately demanded Egyptian themes in painting and design.[26] Travel to Egypt was difficult and dangerous. Lord Byron, attracted by the remoteness of Egypt and intrigued by the possibility of studying the country and its ancient monuments in person, tried to arrange several expeditions to Egypt, but each failed.[27] Since direct observation of Egypt was nearly impossible, British artists had to be contented with studying artifacts that arrived at the British Museum and with the illustrations in the volumes of *Description de l'Egypte*. Alma-Tadema's immediate British predecessors included J.M.W. Turner, John Martin, David Roberts, and Benjamin Haydon, who painted successful Egyptian capriccios that featured small-scale humans pitted against nature and acts of God.[28] Like the Romantic poets, Haydon focuses on the sadness evoked by Egypt, its exotic architecture, and the biblical story of the death of Pharaoh's son. Haydon, like his successor Alma-Tadema, worked hard to capture as many accurate details of the monuments as possible by making preparatory sketches, visiting the British Museum, and consulting publications.

ANTIQUARIAN SPIRIT IN EGYPTIAN SCENES

The popularity of the work of Haydon's contemporary David Roberts lasted well into the 1850s and spans the period when public taste shifted from Egyptian capriccios to paintings with greater archaeological accuracy. By the late 1830s, artists such as Roberts and other tourists could now travel to Egypt with greater ease, and this new access became the driving force behind the new expectations.[29] England's empire had expanded and required safer means of transport to India for bureaucrats and military personnel. The British found in the Overland Route an alternative to the exhausting, dangerous, and time-consuming sail around the Cape of Good Hope.[30] Now a wider public could tour Alexandria and inland Egypt while on holiday and they wrote informative letters home. The late 1830s saw the publication of J.G. Wilkinson's *Manners and Customs of the Ancient Egyptians*, a work eagerly received by the general public and artists alike. After more direct exposure to Egypt, public taste in art changed, and realistic views became more attractive than imaginative ones.[31]

Roberts responded to this antiquarian trend in Egyptomania by attempting to represent ancient Egypt as faithfully as possible in his paintings, first by consulting available texts and the artifacts in the British Museum, and then by travel to Egypt. He declared himself the first English artist to travel to Egypt (actually, he was the first professional British artist to go without outside funding), and when he arrived in Egypt in December 1838, he patriotically observed that the French had not done justice to it. Roberts then set about the work of "doing justice" to his chosen subject: the result is a multi-volume compilation of his sketches of ancient and modern Egyptian scenes, including Islamic design and architecture, titled *The Holy Land, Egypt, and Nubia*. Roberts' work, especially on ancient and modern Egyptian life, was well received. Among his paintings with ancient subjects were all ten biblical plagues on Egypt, including his *Death of the Firstborn*, and *The Departure of the Israelites*. B. Llewellyn attributes Roberts' popularity to his ability to capture in his paintings the three aspects of Egypt that were uppermost in the Victorian popular imagination: Egyptian antiquities, Egypt's association with the Bible, and the exotic image of Egypt found in *Arabian Nights*.[32] These were the antecedents to the repertoire developed by Alma-Tadema.

FINDING THE PRESENT IN THE PAST

Depictions of Egypt made during the Victorian age often draw on common human experiences and celebrate cultural and historical parallels. MacKenzie comments that the Victorian artists evidently sought common ground with the people featured in depictions of ancient Egypt: they "projected on to the East not only the fantasies and fears of the West, but also the aspirations, received values and wished-for freedoms. Paradoxically, they often sought to portray not the strikingly different, but the oddly familiar."[33] Love of the theater also affected Victorian artistic tastes, so that the art-buying public appreciated representations of striking incidents, picturesque costumes, figures with beautiful forms, and dazzling or lustrous color.[34] This Victorian audience wanted illustrations of common human realities dramatically recalled in ancient settings.

This humanist drive to seek common experiences across cultural divides informs the nineteenth-century literary and artistic focus on the perceived "desolation" of Egypt. The sheer size of the monuments and temples punctuating the sweeping Egyptian landscape was matched only by their emptiness. The inescapable conclusion that a complex and dominant civilization once thrived along the river banks, built marvelous feats of architecture, left monumental writing in hieroglyphics and signs of a rich material culture, and then disappeared completely, impressed the Europeans who were themselves empire builders. They saw their own mortality in the rise and disappearance of this great ancient culture, and felt united with the Egyptians in a common bond of impermanence. Shelley's famous poem "Ozymandias" captures this idea of fleeting accomplishment (lines 9–11):

> . . . And on the pedestal, these words appear:
> My name is Ozymandias, King of Kings,
> Look on my Works, ye Mighty, and despair!
> Nothing beside remains. Round the decay
> Of that colossal Wreck, boundless and bare
> The lone and level sands stretch far away.[35]

EGYPT AS A LOCUS OF BIBLICAL AND
MODERN EVENTS

Biblical scenes set in Egypt found a positive reception in Victorian audiences. William Müller, David Wilkie, and Thomas Seddon became well known for their renderings of biblical scenes, popular because they evoked a shared sense of iden-

tity and even continuity with Egypt.[36] Victorians were preoccupied with evan-
gelizing the growing numbers of non-Christians within the British Empire with
an increasingly fervent missionary spirit. Many credited Sir (Dr.) Livingstone
with bringing civilization, Christianity, and commerce to Africa through his
primary project of discovering trade routes. His memoir, *Missionary Travels and
Researches in South Africa*, struck a resonant chord with the general public and
became a best seller.[37] The promotion of Christianity, with its ties to the Egyptian
past and African present, was a priority for Victorians and stimulated the public
taste for biblical themes in art.

The Victorian art public was also interested in modern Egypt, perhaps out
of nostalgia for a presumably simpler past. Artists such as Carl Haag and John
Frederick Lewis painted popular scenes of daily life in Egypt, popular largely
because they depicted people "unspoiled by Western affectations."[38] These artists worked from their own sketches made while traveling, from photographs,
and even employed as models Egyptians living in London. E. W. Lane published
Manners and Customs of Modern Egypt in 1837, as popular with Victorian readers
and artists as Wilkinson's work on ancient Egypt would prove to be when released
in 1838.[39] Yet as British power extended in the region, the military encountered
Egyptian resistance. These realities contrasted with the romantic myth-making
of the Victorian public. In 1875, British Prime Minister Disraeli arranged for the
government to purchase a 44 percent interest in the Suez Canal for four million
pounds, taking advantage of Egypt's delinquent debts to European creditors.[40]
The British occupied Egypt without formally annexing it; they nostalgically
looked for unspoiled Egyptiana, while taking a romantic Egyptian identity onto
themselves.[41] In this, Said's label of Orientalism seems appropriate. Nonetheless,
Victorian interest in Egyptians both past and present, as real people who share
a common ground of humanity, was genuine. And while the material fact of
Egypt influenced European demand for paintings, at the same time the duality of
power noted by colonial theorists was at work when British bureaucrats adopted
Egyptian fashion to celebrate Christmas at the Great Pyramid, becoming faux
Egyptians in their own popular imaginings.

ALMA-TADEMA'S EGYPTIAN PAINTINGS

These cultural trends find expression in Alma-Tadema's Egyptian paintings: in
a list of some of his Egyptian titles (see Appendix), biblical themes and daily life
are well represented. *The Sad Father* (1859)[42] and *Death of the Firstborn* (1872) both
depict the outcome of the tenth plague on Egypt as told in Exodus 12:29, a subject
that clearly would have appealed to biblical tastes. But the topic also refers to a
universal phenomenon of the time, the death of a beloved child. In an era before
antibiotics and modern medical interventions, the death of a child was a sor-

row that Alma-Tadema and many other Victorians endured.[43] The two paintings reflect the sense of imperial impotence in the face of protecting children from death; no matter how powerful the king, he cannot defeat death. The Sad Father appears to serve as an early study for Death of the Firstborn, the painting that won a Gold Medal at the Paris Exposition of 1878.[44] The drama and pathos of a bereft father cradling the lifeless body of his young son in his arms would have appealed to the theatrical sensibilities of the Victorian audience. The dark color palette in both paintings heightens the sense of drama and allows a chiaroscuro spotlight on the pieta-like composition of the central figures.[45] The intimate indoor setting, a contrast to the popular paintings of monuments in landscapes by David Roberts, allows a shift of focus in the drive for accuracy. In Death of the Firstborn, Alma-Tadema uses his research for the richly detailed set that includes mourners, tables, wall decoration, hieroglyphs, jewelry, and a prayer stele. The accuracy of these details has won critical praise for Alma-Tadema: critic Maarten Raven, for example, commented favorably on Alma-Tadema's use of detail to set the painting in the time of Ramses II, when nineteenth-century scholars believed the tenth plague took place.[46] During Alma-Tadema's lifetime, Egyptologist Georg Ebers praised Death of the Firstborn for its archaeological accuracy.[47] The two paintings capture the Victorian humanistic interest in the ancient Egyptians as people and the Victorian taste for accurate, detailed setting.

Pastimes in Ancient Egypt: 3,000 Years Ago (1863), An Egyptian in His Doorway (1865), and An Egyptian Game (1865) are all based on subjects from ancient Egyptian daily life, yet contain modern elements. Although An Egyptian in His Doorway is set in the Roman period, the man himself could have been painted from one of Alma-Tadema's many photographs of modern Egypt and Egyptians. Alma-Tadema maintained an extensive collection of photographs of Egypt and Pompeii from which he worked.[48] He believed that photography was a great boon to the painter: "I am convinced that the camera has had a most healthful and useful influence upon art. It is of the greatest use to painters."[49] The Egyptian appearance of the subjects at rest and play in these paintings indicates that Alma-Tadema either hired Egyptian models or copied photographs or drawings. Alma-Tadema maintained a substantial private reference library of sources on Egypt.[50] His attention to detail was hailed as impeccable, and Pastimes won a Gold Medal at the Paris Salon in 1864.[51] These depictions of Egyptians at play depart from any Christianizing theme and instead address human curiosity about what another culture did for diversion.

An Egyptian Game (1865) shows three people playing a board game in a setting whose architecture, clothes, jewelry, and furniture are taken from archaeological drawings and artifacts. An interesting detail about the history of this painting is that it was originally published under the anachronistic title The Egyptian Chess Players.[52] A common subject for social realist paintings of middle-class

Victorians shows them enjoying parlor games, frequently cards and chess.[53] The game in Alma-Tadema's painting is not chess but its confusion with the popular Victorian leisure pursuit shows that both the artist and the audience expect parallels rather than differences in this archaeologically accurate Egyptian scene.

Like *The Sad Father* and *Death of the Firstborn*, *The Egyptian Widow in the Time of Diocletian* (1872) focuses on the pathos of the death of a loved one, again reflecting a Victorian search for points of contact with the ancient culture. We may surmise that the death in 1869 of his beloved first wife Pauline spurred Alma-Tadema to depict Egyptian mourning for a spouse as experienced by a nameless Egyptian woman rather than a famous Pharaoh. Yet in spite of its accuracy of funerary detail, taken from the funerary artifacts on display at the British Museum and Wilkinson's *Manners and Customs of the Ancient Egyptians*, this painting approaches the Egyptian capriccio.[54] The temple courtyard in the background, with columns, sphinx, and statue, may even recall the Egyptian Court at the Crystal Palace, as though Alma-Tadema were displaying his work in a gallery within a gallery.[55] *The Egyptian Widow* illustrates the shift in taste of the Victorian art-buying public, since the painting was still unsold eight years later in 1880. In addition, Barrow surmises that the respectful but tepid reviews by art critics (who both reflect public taste and act as its arbiters) may have turned Alma-Tadema away from Egyptian themes.[56] People came to prefer Alma-Tadema's Greek and Roman paintings over the Egyptian. Despite the public's changed preference, the artist maintained his interest in Egypt, and painted more on that theme, including four pictures of Cleopatra.

ALMA-TADEMA'S PAINTINGS OF CLEOPATRA

Alma-Tadema's portraits of Cleopatra reflect the artist's work at different points in his career. His early painting of Cleopatra (1859) showed her at the moment of her death, a moment of high drama typical of genre painting. Three later portraits of Cleopatra depict a Hellenized monarch, calm in her repose, demure, yet seductive; she is not just a Ptolemy but, rather, Ptolemaic-queen-as-Victorian-lady. In the theatrical *The Meeting of Anthony and Cleopatra: 41 B.C.* (1883), the third and last painting in the portrait series, the queen is surrounded by the iconography of her reign yet she is arranged no differently than the wealthy patrons in Alma-Tadema's many private portraits (Fig. 15). Richard Jenkyns calls this sort of portrait "Victorians in fancy dress," and notes that Sir Lawrence was often seen at parties *in togata*.[57] However eccentric this may seem, it reflects Alma-Tadema's humanist belief that people are more alike than different, a philosophy illustrated throughout the body of his work. Alma-Tadema highlights that connection between the Hellenistic queen and his Victorian audience.

The Dying Cleopatra (1859) was a study of the Egyptian queen that he painted

FIGURE 15. *Anthony and Cleopatra* by Sir Lawrence Alma-Tadema. The Bridgeman Art Library/Getty Images.

early in his career and destroyed, perhaps without exhibiting it.[58] Its image survives in an old photograph in which it appears to be somewhat unfinished. *The Dying Cleopatra*, *The Sad Father*, and the later *Death of the Firstborn* (1872) focus on lamentation as a reaction to death: intense mourning at the sight of the dead beloved is the source of drama in these paintings. In *The Sad Father*, we see the mother's mourning face pressed against the cheek of her dead son while Pharaoh holds the boy's body. In spite of the title, Pharaoh's face is not apparent owing to the fact that the painting was later cut down.[59] The composition of *Death of the Firstborn* is similar to the earlier study: Pharaoh sits, staring in stunned silence; the child's mother has thrown herself across the child in the father's lap, her arms around her son. Both are suspended in attitudes of deep parental grief and surrounded by priests already beginning the funerary prayers.

The Dying Cleopatra, which is also a study in grief, depicts her trusted servants, Iras and Charmian, as they mourn Cleopatra's death. Their mourning is no less important than the death of their mistress, and their grieving postures are evident in the faded photograph. The form of Cleopatra was undraped and details seem sketchy given the washed-out appearance of the photograph. There is little to say about this Cleopatra except that she echoes Titian's *Venus of Urbino* (ca.

1538) or anticipates, in form at least, Manet's *Olympia* (1863). One of the attendants appears to be bare-breasted. Since Alma-Tadema rarely exhibited nude female figures, and since other painters of his time painted nude figures then added the clothes, it seems likely that this Cleopatra would later have been clothed or draped in some fashion.[60] However, it is also likely that the artist, still early in his career, was attempting to demonstrate his technical skill with the nude, imitating old masters, or echoing the "dying Cleopatras" of other artists. We do not know why Alma-Tadema destroyed it but the upper portion of the painting shows his interest in the study of demonstrative mourning—the silent wails of Iras and Charmian.

His early vision of Cleopatra remains indistinct, but the three paintings that comprise the studies for and final edition of *The Meeting of Anthony and Cleopatra: 41 B.C.*, give Cleopatra a very human face. Scholars generally agree that *The Meeting of Anthony and Cleopatra: 41 B.C.* recreates the first meeting at Tarsus between the Roman general and the Queen of Egypt as described by Enobarbus in act 2, scene 2 of Shakespeare's *Antony and Cleopatra*. (The title of the painting is usually shortened to reflect that correspondence to *Antony and Cleopatra*.)In a preserved letter to Georg Ebers, however, Alma-Tadema indicates that he had a subsequent meeting (at Alexandria rather than Tarsus) in mind as the subject of the nearly finished painting.[61] The issues of dependency on texts (or inspiration from them), and historical accuracy has affected modern assessments of Alma-Tadema's work, and deserves closer scrutiny here.

The case for connecting the painting to Shakespeare's play is based on the popularity of the play and its subject matter in the 1880s, and a perceived correlation between Shakespeare's text and some details of Cleopatra's barge in the painting.[62] In this dramatic flashback, which takes place after the play firmly establishes the affair between Antony and Cleopatra, Enobarbus tells of the first meeting on the River Cydnus at Tarsus in Cilicia (*Antony and Cleopatra* 2.2.191–201):

> The barge she sat in, like a burnish'd throne,
> Burn'd on the water. The poop was beaten gold,
> Purple the sails, and so perfumed that
> The winds were love-sick with them; the oars were silver,
> Which to the tune of flutes kept stroke, and made
> The water which they beat to follow faster,
> As amorous of their strokes. For her own person,
> It beggar'd all description: she did lie
> In her pavilion—cloth of gold, of tissue—
> O'er-picturing that Venus where we see
> The fancy outwork nature.

Alma-Tadema's painting contains some of the elements mentioned here: a pavilion with gold drapery, the perfumes, a flute, and the reclining queen herself.

This link between the painting and Shakespeare's play, when viewed in the context of the erotic consequences of Cleopatra and Antony's encounter on the barge, has raised concerns about historical accuracy and whether this painting is a capriccio, since it is known to be intended as a meeting in Alexandria, not Tarsus. Barrow observes that *The Meeting of Anthony and Cleopatra: 41 B.C.* "although a Romano-Egyptian history painting, does not look to an ancient source."[63] Her analysis captures the immediate social and historical contexts of Alma-Tadema's painting: the popularity of the play and its principals during the late Victorian era. Nonetheless, *The Meeting of Anthony and Cleopatra: 41 B.C.* does have an ancient foundation that is both mediated and masked by Shakespeare's text. Plutarch's *Life of Antony* provides firm grounding in Hellenistic antiquity for both Shakespeare and, in turn, Alma-Tadema. Literary scholars have established that Shakespeare consulted North's translation of Plutarch's *Lives* for source material about the ancient Romans and Greeks. The description that Enobarbus provides in the speech excerpted above and throughout the scene takes as its source Plutarch's description of the first meeting of Antony and Cleopatra (*Life of Antony* 26):

> Therefore when she was sent unto by divers letters, both from Antonius him selfe, and also from his frendes, she made so light of it, and mocked Antonius so much, that she disdained to set forward otherwise but to take her barge in the river of Cydnus, the poope whereof was of gold, the sailes of purple, and the owers of silver, which kept stroke in rowing after the sounde of the musicke of flutes, howboyes, citherns, viols, and such other instruments as they played upon in the barge. And now for the person of her selfe: she was layed under a pavilion of cloth of gold of tissue, appareled and attired like the goddesse Venus, commonly drawen in picture . . . [64]

Not only does this passage demonstrate Shakespeare's faithful transmission of the text, but also a comparison of North's text and the original Greek, in turn, indicates that North's edition is faithful to Plutarch's description of Cleopatra's boat.[65] The accuracy of the historical foundation is enhanced by Plutarch's own use of eyewitness testimony for his *Life of Antony*.[66] Furthermore, since Alma-Tadema consulted Plutarch directly as a source for other paintings it is just as likely that he did so in this case as well.[67]

Yet Alma-Tadema's letter to George Ebers clearly states that the meeting depicted is at Alexandria, not Tarsus. The chosen title pinpoints the exact year (in which both meetings, the first at Tarsus and the second at Alexandria) took place and indicates the artist's knowledge of the accurate historical sequence of events. Shakespeare, writing neither history nor biography, breaks up the chronology for dramatic effect: the play begins at Alexandria when the affair between Antony and Cleopatra is well established, then presents the events at Tarsus as a dramatic flashback. Thus, *The Meeting of Anthony and Cleopatra: 41 B.C.* has a definite, if understated, foundation in ancient source material.

Alma-Tadema's statement that the setting was Alexandria not Tarsus, made while the painting was still in production, does not run counter to the artist's usual high standards for historical accuracy. Even though there are some details drawn from the famous passages in Shakespeare and Plutarch about the meeting at Tarsus, the painting also departs from them appropriately. Most strikingly, the bright (Alexandrian) sunlight of the painting is a stark contrast to the evening setting of the first meeting in Tarsus. Both Plutarch (and Shakespeare's Enobarbus) report that Antony arrives at Cleopatra's barge after she refuses his invitation to supper but requests in turn that he dine with her (*Life of Antony* 26.3–4 ; *Antony and Cleopatra* 2.2.219–26). Plutarch intimates that the meeting took place in the evening when Cleopatra added to the dramatic effect of her craft by putting on a light show for her guest (*Life of Antony* 26.4.5–9).

Moreover we see Cleopatra in a small barge (clearly not large enough for a dinner-party), evidently meeting Antony just outside the harbor of Alexandria, with no land in sight. Four large Roman warships loom in the background. Cleopatra has made the Romans come to her. Alma-Tadema believed that literature ought to serve art but not the reverse.[68] By changing the setting and time of day but keeping some historical details of Cleopatra's barge for this smaller version, Alma-Tadema went beyond illustration or set-design to attach his own creative vision to the scene.

In this setting, Alma-Tadema presents Cleopatra not merely as the object of Antony's romantic attention, but also as a queen, one who is politically adept and powerful—thus complicating and challenging popular Victorian views of the queen as a seductress. While Cleopatra reclines on her throne and gives the appearance of an Egyptian monarch surrounded by symbols of state and conspicuous wealth, the Roman craft pulls alongside the barge. Framed by the open curtains of the barge's pavilion, Antony and his companion look in at Cleopatra. Antony is frozen in a half-standing position, has a distinctly anxious look on his face that portends a potential clash of powers. By 41 B.C., Cleopatra was already involved in Roman power politics, having endorsed Julius Caesar as well as having given birth to their son, Caesarion. While at Tarsus Antony had initially summoned Cleopatra to account for her support of Cassius in the Roman civil war that followed Caesar's assassination (Plutarch, *Life of Antony* 25.1), a clear attempt by the Queen to influence the balance of power at Rome. Cleopatra refused to concede to any of Antony's commands or invitations to dinner and countered with a display of wealth that left Antony sitting alone in the town square while all the townspeople gawked at her barge (26.1–3). The story implies that even at the start of their relationship, Cleopatra had a strong will and was better at manipulating the symbols of state. She left Antony with no choice but to meet her on her own terms. The triremes may loom threateningly but the center of power is not with the Roman general, but with the queen who reclines in her stately barge.

Cleopatra sits in a relaxed posture on a throne decorated with baboon heads, symbols of the god Thoth. She holds the pharaonic crook and a flail as symbols of her queenly authority. An authentic Egyptian cartouche on the side of the boat translates as "Mistress of Two Lands, Cleo."[69] The gold draperies of the barge, the servants, the perfume pipes all echo Plutarch and Shakespeare. Yet the woman on the throne in no other way resembles pharaonic portraits: she wears a serpent-style headband but no headdress, collar, wig, or Egyptianizing makeup. Her figure is almost entirely draped; her Greek-style peplos covers her from her shoulders to her feet and the material appears diaphanous but only slightly revealing, with a leopard pelt over her breasts and one shoulder. Her gaze is not seductively engaging Antony as one might expect given her popularized ethos, rather she glances sideways, perhaps at the viewer, while her servant (Iras or Charmian?) is looking at Antony and appears to be reporting observations to the queen. The Cleopatra of this portrait is a Hellenistic queen, like the portrait busts of Ptolemaic women in the British Museum, but in an Egyptian context. In many ways she resembles portraits of wealthy women painted by Reynolds or Alma-Tadema himself. This Cleopatra is both ancient and modern, making her a Cleopatra of the Victorian age.

Other associations viewers could bring to this painting include the long repertoire in Western art (going back to antiquity, including images in Pompeii that Alma-Tadema might have seen) of Venus and Mars, also hinted in Plutarch's original description of the meeting at Tarsus. The Alexandrian vantage is given to the viewer, with the Egyptian queen venturing out to receive war from the open sea in the form of Antony and his ships. Cleopatra's barge is covered with soft fabrics; there is music and perfumes, and flower-garlands frame the scene. But Antony's barge is covered in bronze, and his companion and the oarsmen are all helmeted, with a silver shield reflecting the gold of the Egyptian drapery. Here it is setting and content that remind us of the long tradition in art of Venus and Mars together, rather than the overt sexuality in so many other nineteenth-century paintings of Cleopatra, often shown by herself or with a few attendants.[70]

Two preliminary studies for Cleopatra (1875 and 1877) provide evidence for the model Alma-Tadema used. Alma-Tadema's friend Helen Zimmern claimed that the model for Cleopatra was a portrait bust of her own mother Bernice, and since Alma-Tadema often worked with living models, often wealthy patrons, some scholars support this claim.[71] Other scholars point out, however, that the model was either a bust of Queen Berenike, Cleopatra's mother,[72] or a portrait bust of Cleopatra VII found in the British Museum,[73] in keeping with Alma-Tadema's scrupulous attention to authenticity of detail.

CLEOPATRA AS MONARCH AND GODDESS

During the 1880s in London, plays featuring Marc Antony and/or Cleopatra became fashionable. Sarah Bernhardt, when portraying Cleopatra, wore a ring that she said once belonged to the Queen of Egypt. Lily Langtry, who also played Cleopatra, was called "Cleopatra" by Max Beerbohm because of her many admirers.[74] Although the theater-going public of the late Victorian era had a fondness for plays about Cleopatra, they did not always approve of each performer's interpretation. When the great Sarah Bernhardt played Cleopatra, audiences were shocked by the intensity of the emotion she displayed in reaction to Antony's death. A woman was said to have remarked after one particularly emotional performance that Cleopatra's home-life was indeed very different from that of England's own queen, Victoria.[75]

One year prior to painting *The Meeting of Anthony and Cleopatra: 41 B.C.*, Alma-Tadema had completed a portrait of the great Shakespearean actor, Ludwig Barnay, in costume for his role of Marc Antony in Shakespeare's *Julius Caesar*. Alma-Tadema loved the theater and designed sets and costumes for several stage productions.[76] Alma-Tadema's theatrical interests, eclecticism, and taste for the less obvious subject led him to the inspired choice of the moment of anticipation just before Cleopatra and Antony meet. Alma-Tadema's Cleopatra is composed and confident in all her powers. She does not make obeisance to Antony; rather, she surrounds herself with the icons of her power, and sits in a beautiful, flowing dress as Victorian ladies often do in their own portraits. In these details, she is the picture of a monarch of whom the Victorians could approve: a lady who knows how to dress and present herself appropriately for any occasion.[77] *The Meeting of Anthony and Cleopatra: 41 B.C.* offers a stage setting for the queen's composure, with no hint of Sarah Bernhardt's emotive interpretation of Cleopatra.

Artistic images of Cleopatra, the last of the Ptolemaic rulers of ancient Egypt, were once again held up as a mirror to a female monarch. Writers and artists of both the Elizabethan and Victorian periods explored the nature of government by a queen, and looked to the past for parallel examples and contrasts in fashioning an appropriate image of a female ruler. Cleopatra was a natural vehicle for artistic philosophizing about the nature of monarchy ruled by a queen. Such comparison was to the modern queen's advantage. Under the rule of both Elizabeth I and Victoria, the British empire thrived. Like Cleopatra, the modern queens were intelligent and talented monarchs. Yet both Elizabeth I and Victoria took care to present their personal lives in a manner pleasing to their subjects, and in so doing they put distance between themselves and Cleopatra's more complicated personal life. Elizabeth I portrayed herself as the bride of her people, while Victoria set herself before her people as the chaste wife and after the death of Albert, as the *univira* in perpetual, dignified mourning.[78] Therefore in both the Elizabethan and

FIGURE 16. *Study of Columns at Philae* by Sir Lawrence Alma-Tadema. Victoria and Albert Museum, London. Photo credit Victoria and Albert Museum/Art Resource, NY.

Victorian periods, Cleopatra appealed to the popular imagination: her strengths underscored those of the current monarch, her weaknesses—as perceived by the later ages through Roman texts—enhanced the reigning monarch's own projected image of personal stability as defined by the age.

Alma-Tadema contemplated the image of Cleopatra until the end of his life. She is the subject of one of his last six paintings; although incomplete, he worked on it during the last months of his life in 1912. The subject, *Cleopatra at the Temple of Isis at Philae*, was inspired by his trip to Egypt in 1902; he might have started it as early as his return but neglected it until 1912.[79] Only the capitals of the columns are finished in any detail, in the preserved *Study of Columns at Philae* (Fig. 16). Figures are sketched at the base of the columns and may be priests and musicians. The painting was intended to show Cleopatra visiting Philae but her figure is not apparent.[80] A hazy figure appears mid-ground in the painting that could be construed as a seated Cleopatra or perhaps a statue of Isis. Thus any interpretation is speculative and inconclusive. Yet the title indicates that the painting was meant to show Cleopatra's affiliation with Isis: a fitting symbol of Cleopatra, in view of her historical association with the goddess.[81] In the end Alma-Tadema's final Cleopatra is as enigmatic as her historical counterpart.

Alma-Tadema's meditations on the life of Cleopatra run throughout his work. She inspired one of his first two Egyptian paintings, and she was among his last subjects. He focused on the drama of Cleopatra's life in its ancient Egyptian context: the personal meaning of her death for her household, her image as the last Egyptian monarch at the peak of her power, and finally, her role as a living goddess. This final depiction of Cleopatra in her religious aspect in the Temple of Isis would have shown her in a role least sensationalized in the Victorian period but especially promoted by Cleopatra herself. As a body of work, Alma-Tadema's Egyptian-themed paintings show him to be responsive to his public over several decades and a participant in British cultural expectations after Egypt became more accessible. At the same time, he was deeply interested in exploring for himself the most significant events of Cleopatra's brilliant life.

APPENDIX:
SELECT CATALOG OF WORKS ON EGYPTIAN THEMES
BY SIR LAWRENCE ALMA-TADEMA

1859   *The Sad Father* (*The Death of the Firstborn*, first version), Johannesburg Art Gallery, South Africa

   The Dying Cleopatra, unfinished/destroyed by artist

1863   *Pastimes in Ancient Egypt: 3,000 Years Ago*, Harris Museum and Art Gallery, Preston, England

1865   *Egyptian Chess Players*, location unknown

   An Egyptian in his Doorway, location unknown

   An Egyptian in his Doorway in Memphis, private collection

1867   *Egyptians 3,000 Years Ago*, unfinished, Auckland City Art Gallery, New Zealand

   The Mummy in the Roman Period (*Egyptians Lamenting Their Dead*), location unknown

1868   *Egyptian Game*, watercolor, location unknown

1869   *The Grand Chamberlain to His Majesty King Sesostris the Great*, location unknown

1870   *The Juggler*, location unknown

1872   *An Egyptian Widow in the Time of Diocletian*, Rijksmuseum, Amsterdam

        The Death of the Firstborn, second version, Rijksmuseum, Amsterdam

1874   *Joseph, Overseer of Pharaoh's Granaries*, location unknown

1875   *Cleopatra*, first version, Art Gallery of New South Wales, Melbourne, Australia

1877   *Cleopatra*, second version, Auckland City Art Gallery, New Zealand

1883   *The Meeting of Anthony and Cleopatra: 41 B.C.*, location unknown

1901   *The Death of the Firstborn*, drawing for Bible illustration, location unknown

1904   *The Finding of Moses*, private collection

1912   *Cleopatra at the Temple of Isis at Philae*, Victoria and Albert Museum, London

NOTES

1. A phrase used by V.G. Swanson, *Alma-Tadema: The Painter of the Victorian Vision of the Ancient World* (1977). Thanks to Margie Miles for her infectious enthusiasm, incisive observations, and unflagging encouragement.

2. Swanson (1977): 13. The paintings are listed in the Appendix of the present essay.

3. V.G. Swanson, *The Biography and Catalogue Raisonné of the Paintings of Sir Lawrence Alma-Tadema* (1990): 165.

4. Zimmern reports that Alma-Tadema felt that the study and portrayal of life in ancient Egypt was the natural place to begin the second phase of his career: H. Zimmern, *Sir Lawrence Alma-Tadema, R.A.* (1902): 22–23.

5. Zimmern (1902): 24.

6. T. Meedendorp and L. Pijl, "28: *The Death of the Firstborn*," in E. Becker et al., eds., *Sir Lawrence Alma-Tadema* (1997): 172.

7. R. Jenkyns, "Hellenism in Victorian Painting," in G.W. Clarke, ed., *Rediscovering Hellenism: The Hellenic Inheritance and the English Imagination* (1989): 105–6.

8. J. Premble, *The Mediterranean Passion: Victorians and Edwardians in the South* (1987): xi.

9. E.W. Said, *Orientalism: Western Concepts of the Orient* (1978): 12.

10. A.J. Rotter, K.E. Fleming, and K. Biddick, "Review Essays: Orientalism Twenty Years On," *American Historical Review* (2000): 1204–49.

11. Said (1978): 1–7.

12. E.W. Said, *Culture and Imperialism* (1994): 118.

13. For discussion of the cultural significance and impact of the publication, see J.S. Curl, *Egyptomania: The Egyptian Revival: A Recurring Theme in the History of Taste* (1994): 131–32, and M. Jasanoff, *Edge of Empire: Lives, Culture, and Conquest in the East, 1750–1850* (2005): 222–23.

14. Said (1994): 118.

15. "It is difficult to connect these different realms, to show involvements of culture with expanding empires, to make observations about art that preserves its unique endowments and at the same time map its affiliations, but, I submit we must attempt this, and set the art in the global, earthly context," says Said (1994): 7.

16. One such recent work is a compilation of essays edited by J.F. Codell and D.S. Macleod,

Orientalism Transposed: The Impact of the Colonies on British Culture (1998). The essays in this text establish the existence of a two-way dynamic of cultural power that existed between the British imperialists and their subject colonies in India and Egypt. One of the major purposes of their book is to demonstrate the ways in which colonial subjects co-opted and used the art and language of the dominant culture to achieve their own goal of subverting imperial power. See also Jasanoff (2005).

17. J. M. MacKenzie, *Orientalism: History, Theory, and the Arts* (1995): xiii.

18. MacKenzie (1995): xvii.

19. For excellent discussion and additional support for MacKenzie's position on contextualization, see J. Elsner, "From the Pyramids to Pausanias and Piglet: Monuments, Travel, and Writing," in S. Goldhill and R. Osborne, eds., *Art and Text in Greek Culture* (1994): 224–54. For a careful study of cultural engagements earlier in the nineteenth century that clearly went both ways, Jasanoff (2005).

20. Discussion in Becker et al. (1997).

21. Swanson (1977): 9. See also T. Meedendorp and L. Pijl, "Alma-Tadema's Artistic Training: Critics on the Continent 1852–1870," in E. Becker et al. (1997): 22–24.

22. P. Conner, "Egypt and the Romantic Imagination," in P. Conner, ed., *The Inspiration of Egypt: Its Influence on British Artists, Travellers, and Designers, 1700–1900* (1983): 75–77.

23. Jon Whiteley, "Alma-Tadema and the néo-Grècs," in Becker (1997): 71–72.

24. MacKenzie (1995): 62.

25. Swanson (1977): 12.

26. Curl (1994): 117.

27. Conner, "Egypt and the Romantic Imagination" (1983): 76.

28. For example Turner's *The Fifth Plague of Egypt* (1800) depicts a cataclysmic hailstorm in a landscape with a pyramid and an aqueduct. John Martin, known for eclectic architectural groupings, painted *The Seventh Plague* (1823) featuring a large complex of temples but small human figures. Benjamin Haydon's *Pharaoh Dismissing Moses at Dead of Night, on Finding His Firstborn Dead at the Passover* (1826) is most noted for its architectural setting and pathos; these artists and their Egyptian work are discussed by Conner, "Egypt and the Romantic Imagination" (1983): 78–79, 81–82.

29. For an excellent discussion of the development of the Grand Tour and European tourist travel to Egypt in the nineteenth century, see J. Premble (1987): 15–110.

30. P. Conner, "The British in Egypt," in P. Conner, ed., *The Inspiration of Egypt: Its Influence on British Artists, Travellers, and Designers* (1983): 145–48.

31. B. Llewellyn, "The Victorian Vision of Egypt," in P. Conner, ed., *The Inspiration of Egypt: Its Influence on British Artists, Travellers, and Designers* (1983): 115.

32. Llewyllyn (1983): 115–18.

33. MacKenzie (1995): 55.

34. Llewellyn (1983): 118.

35. Percy Bysshe Shelley, "Ozymandias," in D. Perkins, ed., *English Romantic Writers* (1967): 971.

36. Llewellyn (1983): 117.

37. J. Phillips and P. Phillips, *Victorians at Home and Away* (1978): 73.

38. Llewellyn (1983): 118.

39. Llewellyn (1983: 118) credits Lane's work with helping to "dispel the vague image of 'the Orient' as a picturesque, perfumed, pagan, fantasy world."

40. Conner, "The British in Egypt" (1983): 148–49.

41. Victorian ambivalence toward Egypt is well represented in the pageantry of the Christmas celebrations the British held at Giza: dressed in native Egyptian costumes, they drank mulled claret at the Great Pyramid, an episode noted by Conner, "The British in Egypt" (1983): 149–50.

42. Also called *Death of the Firstborn*, first version.

43. The humanistic interest in the death of a firstborn son was also an intensely personal one for Alma-Tadema, because his own first child, a son, died of smallpox shortly after his birth in 1864. Swanson (1990): 29.

44. Swanson (1977): 23.

45. Swanson (1977: 43) notes that the dark color palette also reflects Alma-Tadema's use of color early in his career.

46. Meedendorp and Pijl, "28: *The Death of the Firstborn*" (1997): 172–73.

47. Meedendorp and Pijl, "28: *The Death of the Firstborn*" (1997): 173.

48. U. Pohlmann, "Alma-Tadema and Photography," in E. Becker et al. (1997): 113, 118.

49. B. Denvir, *The Late Victorians: Art, Design, and Society 1852–1910* (1986): 89.

50. R. J. Barrow, *Lawrence Alma-Tadema* (2001): 23, 66–68.

51. Curl (1994): 204; Swanson (1990), 131–32.

52. T. Meedendorp and L. Pijl, "8: *An Egyptian Game*," in E. Becker et al. (1997): 140.

53. G.-N. Anderson and J. Wright, *The Pursuit of Leisure: Victorian Depictions of Pastimes* (1997): 8–9 and 67–70.

54. Because Alma-Tadema follows Wilkinson's drawings so faithfully, he paints a harp upside-down—as it was drawn by Wilkinson—while the anachronistic details of the floor design and the door seem to be fabrications from Alma-Tadema's imagination, as noted by Meedendorp and Pijl, "27: *An Egyptian Widow in the Time of Diocletian*," in E. Becker et al. (1997): 170–71.

55. J.-M. Humbert, "333: *An Egyptian Widow*," in J.-M. Humbert et al., eds., *Egyptomania: Egypt in Western Art 1730–1930* (1994): 488.

56. Barrow (2001): 68.

57. Jenkyns (1989): 106–7.

58. Swanson (1990): 125.

59. Swanson (1990): 126.

60. Jenkyns (1989): 97, 109.

61. Swanson lists the setting as Alexandria; nonetheless the Shakespearean connection has dominated the scholarly discussion. Alma-Tadema wrote to Ebers in November 1882: "The picture that troubles me most just now is still Cleopatra and Anthony that is their meeting in Alexandria water for the first time after Tarsus, both in boats and the Roman trireme in the background besides blue sky and sea, I hope to have it finished by the end of the month." Cited in Swanson (1990): 219.

62. Swanson (1990): 219; Barrow (2001): 114.

63. Barrow (2001): 114.

64. Trans. Thomas North, *Plutarch* (1579). M. R. Ridley, ed., *The Arden Edition of the Works of William Shakespeare: Antony and Cleopatra* (1991): 246.

65. Trans. B. Perrin (Cambridge, Mass. 1988): "Though she received many letters from both Antony himself and from his friends, she so despised and laughed the man to scorn as to sail up the river Cydnus in a barge with gilded poop, its sails spread purple, its rowers urging it on with silver oars to the sound of the flutes blended with pipes and lutes. She herself reclined beneath a canopy spangled with gold, adorned like Venus in a painting . . ." (Plutarch, *Life of Antony* 26.1).

66. A family friend, Philotas was a physician in training in Alexandria at the time of Antony's stay there in the winter of 41–40 B.C. and provided firsthand information gained from inside the household of Antony's eldest son (Plutarch, *Life of Antony* 28). Philotas is likely among the sources that Plutarch used for the Tarsus meeting as well.

67. E. Prettejohn, "13: *Phidias Showing the Frieze of the Parthenon to His Friends*," in E. Becker et al. (1997): 146, and R. Barrow, "68: *The Women of Amphissa*," in E. Becker et al., eds. (1997): 232.

68. Swanson (1977): 45.

69. Swanson (1990): 219–20.

70. *Pace* Barrow (2001: 116), who sees this painting as an "eroticized construction of the east," citing languorous, nude or semi-nude versions as comparisons.

71. Swanson (1990): 220.

72. R. Ash, *Sir Lawrence Alma-Tadema* (1990): pl. 13.

73. Swanson (1990): 182.

74. L. Hughes-Hallett, *Cleopatra: Histories, Dreams, and Distortions* (1990): 280.

75. N. Vance, *The Victorians and Ancient Rome* (1997): 199.

76. Swanson (1990): 73–83.

77. S. P. Casteras, *Images of Victorian Womanhood in English Art* (1987): 70–73.

78. M. Homans, *Royal Representations: Queen Victoria and British Culture, 1837–1876* (1998): 4, 58–59, 172–74.

79. Swanson (1990): 275.

80. Swanson (1990): 275 with figure 433.

81. See Sarolta Takács' essay in this volume.

8

Glamour Girls

Cleomania in Mass Culture

Maria Wyke and Dominic Montserrat[†]

While Elizabeth Taylor was in Rome shooting the spectacular Hollywood epic *Cleopatra*, women's magazines began to advise their readers how to create "a new Egyptian look" whose models were Nefertiti and Cleopatra, Egypt's two most iconic queens.[1] An article in *Look* magazine for 27 February 1962 predicted:

> Superimpose two such famous glamour girls as Elizabeth Taylor and Cleopatra, and you are in for a beauty boom. In her role as Egypt's seductive queen, actress Taylor's exotic eye makeup, diverse hair styles (devised with 30 wigs), magnificent jewels and gowns are bound to inspire a new Egyptian look every bit as sweeping as the recent tousled B.B. and pale-lipped Italian looks.

Alongside a glamour photograph of two models, the text indicates what the staff has done to give them "the new Egyptian look reminiscent of the regal, exotic beauties seen on ancient bas-reliefs": eyes lined with kohl to cultivate a sensuous, catlike look; mouths boldly painted to create the illusion of a full lower lip; eyebrows heavily outlined in black; Nile-green eye shadow, henna-colored powder, and a Cleopatra coif applied to the blonde; white shadow, very pale powder, and a high-rising Nefertiti hairstyle applied to the brunette; the necks of both decorated with elaborate beaded collars made out of costume jewelry.[2] The following page instructs the magazine's readers "How to change American girls into Egyptian beauties—with new hairdos," while the article's final page shows "a Liz Taylor look-alike" successfully kitted out for the evening in the Cleopatra look.[3]

This essay explores the most personalized and intimate technology of Egyptomania that has been widely disseminated and even inscribed on the bodies of modern women. Starting in the nineteenth century, we trace a range of female

[†]Deceased 23 September 2004

identifications with Cleopatra and analyze their widespread solicitation in the mass culture of that century and the one that follows. Like the faces of Cleopatra and Nefertiti projected onto those of modern "American girls," these identifications cross boundaries between past and present made fluid and porous by the familiarity of Egyptian culture and its domestication in popular media. If the American girl becomes the Egyptian beauty, the Egyptian beauty also becomes the American girl. We argue that the thoroughly modern Cleopatras of the Hollywood film stars Theda Bara and Claudette Colbert can be seen as the predictable outcome of many years of such essentialist appropriations of Cleopatra to create star personae. We place these modern embodiments of Cleopatra in their historical contexts, asking what knowledge of Egypt is deployed to shape them and what conceptions of gender and sexuality they parade.[4]

VICTORIAN CLEOPATRAS

Victorian England conveniently provides exemplars of the two popular traditions of Cleopatra that were in place by the beginning of the twentieth century. For the Victorians, the name Cleopatra was a signifier for Egypt itself, a transhistorical signifier that marked *any* Egyptian cultural material, of whatever period, as Egyptian. The name "Cleopatra's Needle," was applied to the obelisk brought from Alexandria to London in 1870, to enormous media attention. The obelisk itself was carved during the reign of Thutmose III, more than 1,400 years before Cleopatra was born. But a huge range of Cleopatras was available to the Victorian Londoners who walked past the newly erected obelisk on the Thames Embankment, a range that reflected the high profile of Egypt in the media of the time. Political events connected with imperialist government, such as the opening of the Suez Canal in 1870 and the establishment of the British Protectorate in Egypt in 1882, reminded people that in antiquity Egypt itself had ruled a great empire, and that Cleopatra, the Eastern opponent of the West, had been its last queen before she was vanquished by Rome. They would have been able to go to the theater and see plays about her: not only Shakespeare's canonical *Antony and Cleopatra*, but also burlesques that used the Cleopatra story to satirize contemporary culture and mores, and new treatments by Victorien Sardou and George Bernard Shaw. There was also a proliferation of novels and other fictional treatments that reinforced the connection of Cleopatra with unbridled Eastern sensuality and mystic knowledge, especially those of H. Rider Haggard (1889) and Théophile Gautier (1894). Rider Haggard's influential *Cleopatra* had been serialized in an illustrated literary magazine before it was published as a book, and its elaborate illustrations (by different artists) created a diversity of images of the Egyptian queen. But there were more sober and historically accurate novels, too, such as Georg Ebers' successful *Cleopatra* of 1894, the only version ever to be written by a professional Egyptologist (Ebers was professor of Egyptology at Leipzig). Finally, people were able to bring Cleopatra into their own homes via a variety of objects that ran the gamut from expensive to humble; from an elaborate enameled oil lamp in the shape of Cleopatra's Needle or a framed lithograph of Sir Lawrence Alma-Tadema's painting of Cleopatra, down to cigarette paper with an image of Cleopatra based on an ancient relief, or postcards of the actress Lillie Langtry in pseudo-Egyptian costume as Cleopatra (Fig. 17). Visions of Cleopatra, in short, were commodities available to almost everyone. Her image, multiply reproduced by modern technology, could be collected and pasted into an album like a family snapshot.

An anecdote often retold about Victorian notions of Cleopatra concerns Sarah Bernhardt's performance in the title role of Sardou's play *Cléopâtre* in London. After watching Bernhardt's erotic contortions, a member of the audience is supposed to have remarked how unlike this was to the home life of "our own dear Queen." Apropos of this, Lucy Hughes-Hallett has commented that this almost certainly apocryphal remark "hints that Cleopatra's attraction lies precisely in her unlikeness, in her embodiment of everything that Victorian England . . . denied."[5] Thus Sarah Bernhardt, to enhance her exotic persona offstage, claimed that the snakes she used on stage in the death scene were live and kept in her house, adorned with jewels.[6] While this use of Cleopatra has been studied, little attention has been paid to the process whereby Cleopatra, and Egypt itself, were also domesticated and rendered everyday. Tamed and domesticated images of Cleopatra were available as commodities in the Victorian home; these need to be seen in terms of the more general presentation of ancient Egypt in popular media at this time. As well as being a place of mystery, magic, and spectacle, Egypt was at the same time the birthplace of Western monotheism and the cradle of Western culture. It was a place where "the utter absence of the social affections, which so painfully characterizes the pictures of the life of man at all other epochs, . . . is greatly mitigated."[7] "The social affections" and domesticity were important foci of late-nineteenth- and early-twentieth-century ideas about Egypt in England, abetted by popular redactions of archaeological expeditions to Egyptian settlement sites in guide books for tourists, general works on Egyptian history, and even magazines that were acceptable reading for sabbatarian households who observed Sunday as a day of complete rest. Ancient Egyptian houses were compared to modern ones, and shops to those in London, even down to "by royal appointment" signs fixed outside.[8] This blurring of the boundaries between past and present, between Egypt and England, sets up the possibility for identifications with Cleopatra unmediated by temporal and cultural difference. A minimum of cultural adjustment is required in order to identify with Cleopatra, because she inhabits an ancient world so closely related to the contemporary.

This tendency can perhaps be seen best in Victorian stage burlesques of the Cleopatra story. As performance pieces that included many of the same mise-

FIGURE 17. Cigarette paper (1912).
Private collection of D. Montserrat.
Photo by Dominic Montserrat.

en-scènes as early films, burlesques are a useful place to investigate the cultural antecedents of filmic Cleopatras; also, their part in the development of the Cleopatra myth has received almost no attention. Burlesque was a theatrical form that combined political and social satire, broad (sometimes bawdy) comedy with spectacular sets and costumes, music and dance numbers. Often they took caricatures of famous literary texts as their point of departure, and Cleopatra's story was obviously ripe for appropriation by the genre. The titles of some of the Victorian burlesques give a sense of the way they conflate ancient and modern, thus allowing for the possibility of audience identification: *A Grand, New and Original Burlesque Entitled Antony and Cleopatra, or, His-tory and Her-story in a modern Nilo-metre* (1866); *Antony & Cleopatra: A Classical, Historical, Musical, Mock-Tragical Burlesque* (1870); *Antony and Cleopatra Married and Settled* (1885); *Miss Cleopatra: A Farce* (1891). At the center of all these burlesques lies the humorous projection of the luxury and grandeur that was Cleopatra's Egypt onto modern domestic life and manners. One episode in James Draper's *Antony & Cleopatra: A Classical, Historical, Musical, Mock-Tragical Burlesque* has a maid doing the dusting—but "with a silver-handled dusting brush and gold-embroidered dusting cloth."

As an illustration of the relationship between Cleopatra, modern women, and commodity culture, one of the most interesting burlesques is Francis Cowley Burnand's *Antony and Cleopatra, or, His-tory and Her-story in a modern Nilo-metre*, first performed at the Theatre Royal, Haymarket, London, on 21 November 1866. Burnand (1836–1917) was a prolific man of letters: the author of many burlesques satirizing classical themes (one of them titled *Sappho, or, Look Before You Leap*), he was also an editor of the satirical magazine *Punch*, and was later knighted. His *Antony and Cleopatra* illustrates the filtering-down of a variety of sources about Egypt, combining references from Plutarch and Shakespeare with punning references to contemporary archaeologists, such as Sir Austin Henry Layard. In the burlesque Burnand demotes Antony from a world statesman to a tourist trying to learn a foreign language by staying with a local family. He is first encountered sipping chocolate and trying to learn hieroglyphs out of a book:

I at the language each day take a spell,
And I'm progressing moderately well;
The folks are very right, I find, in saying
That there is nothing that can equal staying
In a nice native family such as this is
To learn a language—teaching from the Missis.

In spite of the familiar picture this evokes, the stage directions show that the set was anything but domestic and homely: "Sphinxes support the roof. Steps lead up to a terrace at the back. Beyond the terrace is water. The palace is full of exotics."

Cleopatra then enters "in an elegant pony-carriage, two little grooms sitting behind" with her son Caesarion, whom she repeatedly scolds like any harassed mother. She is in need of a restorative drink, and Burnand brings Plutarch's famous story of the pearl dissolved in wine right up to date:

CLEOPATRA: I'll feel a little better when I've quaffed
            My new invented drink.
CHARMIAN: A pearl dissolved in wine.
(Cleopatra takes off pearl and puts it in cup)
CLEOPATRA: Yes. Fill up, girl.
            Moderns will call this drink: The early Purl.

Purl was a mixture of hot beer and gin, reputed in nineteenth-century England to cure hangovers and as a general morning pick-me-up. Elsewhere in Burnand's burlesque, Cleopatra is associated with other modern drinks: mint juleps and gin-slings are consumed "in the American fashion," and Cleopatra's beauty is compared to the effervescence of ginger beer, a novelty in the 1860s, when advances in bottling technology stopped it from going flat. Burnand's Cleopatra is, in fact, poised at the limits of the technologies of the day, including, significantly, cosmetic ones:

> ANTONY: Why, it's very strange,
> But in your hair, don't I observe some change?
> I know it is a little rude to stare.
> CLEOPATRA: The fashion, Antony. I've bleached my hair.
> 'Tis dyed. The fact, before them [i.e., the slaves] don't remark.
> ANTONY: You've made it light, and wish to *keep it dark.*

As permanently fizzy as the new ginger beer, her dark hair dyed blonde with one of the new patent bleaches, Burnand's Cleopatra is a Cleopatra transposed from the East to the West and made into a modern northern European. Yet at the same time she is still the familiar siren from the unknowable East, as in the scene where she flies into a rage with Antony, who is paying too much attention to studying Egyptian language and not enough to her:

> Put down that book, your brains are getting muddy.
> D'you want Egyptian characters to study?
> For if Egyptian character you need,
> Here's one you'll find mighty hard to read.
> I change from fair into a storm terrific—
> In fact, I'm an Egyptian hieroglyphic.
> Make a shot at my meaning. You've an eye for me.
> Riddle me, riddle-me-ree, you can't decipher me.

Burnand's polysemic interpretation of Cleopatra prefigures many of her filmic incarnations in some significant ways, especially in its combination of the spectacular with the mundane and the extraordinary with the quotidian. What is striking, in the context of late-nineteenth-century receptions of Cleopatra, is that two distinct versions of her were available. The first and most familiar is the projection of Cleopatra's image to exoticize the modern woman, as exemplified by Bernhardt. The second, less familiar, is the rendering of Cleopatra as everyday by her incorporation into contemporary commodity culture, as the burlesques show. The following examination of a series of Cleopatra films reveals that while early cinema picked up on the first aspect of this tradition, in the cinema of the 1930s and later both aspects were in simultaneous operation.

THE VAMPIRE QUEEN:
THEDA BARA AS CLEOPATRA (1917)

A publicity blurb released by the Fox Film Corporation in October 1917 to coin-cide with the opening of its spectacular epic *Cleopatra* asked moviegoers por-tentously: "What will be your verdict after you see Theda Bara's portrayal of the passions and pageants of Egypt's vampire queen?"[9] Both film (now sadly lost) and marketing framed the cinematic representation of the Ptolemaic ruler as a prom-ised authentication of the star image long since established for the American actress. According to film historians, no discursive apparatus existed before 1907 for the production of film stars. By 1914, however, a star system was in place as knowledge concerning the picture-players was expanded and transformed to not only include their acting skills and their personality as constituted across their films, but also address questions about their extra-cinematic existence.[10] Bara was the first American film actress to have a star image manufactured for her by studio press agents, and this image was heavily invested in nineteenth-century Orientalist constructions of Egypt (Fig. 18).[11]

As an industrial marketing device to create and organize audiences for its films, the Fox studio invented an alluring past and an exotic, occult lifestyle for the Cincinnati-born actress. Theodosia Goodman was to star in almost forty of their films from 1915 to 1919, largely in the role of a modern "vamp" or home-breaker who takes pleasure in ruthlessly seducing men, and abandons them, once drained of their fortunes and their will to live, and she was placed under contract both to play and seemingly be the part. Press releases fed to newspapers and fan magazines claimed fantastically that the star had been born at an Egyptian oasis in the shadow of the Sphinx and had sucked the venom of serpents as an infant. Her stage name, they noted, was an anagram of "Arab death." Her home in Los Angeles (to which she moved in mid-1917) was reportedly furnished in "Early Vampire" ottomans, rugs, and beaded curtains, and reeked with musk. In the presence of the press she would stroke a snake and speak of her attachment to a statue of Amun-Ra. She was not to be seen outdoors in daylight. More spe-cifically, in anticipation of the release of *Cleopatra*, Fox suggested that Bara had received a tribute in hieroglyphs from a reincarnated servant of Cleopatra, then posed her in a museum gazing reflectively at "her own" mummified remains, and quoted their star as proclaiming:

> I know that I am a reincarnation of Cleopatra. It is not a mere theory in my mind. I have positive knowledge that such is the case. I live Cleopatra, I breathe Cleopatra, I *am* Cleopatra.[12]

Drawing on nineteenth-century fantasies of Egypt, the Fox studio dressed its star in the aesthetics of occult ritual, despotic power, a dripping and languid sexuality, and perverse death.[13]

FIGURE 18. Bara's Cleopatra. 1917: Promotional portrait of American actor Theda Bara (1885–1955) wearing an Egyptian headdress and breast plates with a snake design for director J. Gordon Edwards' film, *Cleopatra*. Photo by Hulton Archive/Getty Images.

Star images are marketing devices in the economy of the film industry, but they are also cultural commodities or discursive sites for the exploration of threatened social values.[14] The particular star image of the vamp (so popular in the 1910s) has been interpreted as an index of the struggle at the beginning of the twentieth century to define appropriate genders and sexualities for an America that, faced with the growth of immigration, feminism, and a multicultural urban life, could no longer sustain a picture of itself as an agrarian, small-town, Anglo-Saxon republic of domesticated wives and puritan husbands. The vamp and her foolish victims played out fears concerning man's frailty in relation to sexuality, and woman's potential power, projected onto Orientalism's Other.[15] The perceived problem of female self-gratification is clothed in the antiquity and occult mystery of Egypt, and the modern woman of the 1910s reassuringly figured as a social hieroglyph, her desires an eternal riddle as indecipherable as the Sphinx.[16] Thus according to surviving descriptions of the opening sequence of *Cleopatra*, after a long shot of the "desert wastes" of Ventura County, the camera races toward the studio-produced pyramids and next the Sphinx, which then dissolves into the features of Theda Bara (as Cleopatra) suddenly opening her eyes.

The Orient of Fox's *Cleopatra* provides an imaginative field of free play for a shamelessly paranoid, hyperbolic elaboration of American traumas about gender, sexuality, ethnicity, and race,[17] set safely in a distant elsewhere and elsewhen that offers the historical guarantee of woman's ultimate subjugation. In a film that, according to Fox publicity, generally cast Mexicans as Egyptians, "fair-haired Americans" as Romans, and "real negroes" as slaves,[18] Cleopatra is shaped as an alarmingly literal version of the twentieth century's metaphoric vamp. Drawing on the nineteenth-century "man killer" fantasies of Rider Haggard and Victorien Sardou (as well as the more customary Plutarch and Shakespeare), the film's narrative drive displays no fewer than three examples of transgressive female sexuality.[19] For sandwiched between the expected seductions of Julius Caesar and Marc Antony is that of the fictional Pharon who steals from the tombs of his ancestors, the Pharaohs, in order to please his demanding mistress. In an earlier draft of the scenario, still preserved in the archives of the University of Southern California, explicit instructions are given that Cleopatra's love scenes "should be as strong and 'Oriental' as will be allowed. Cleopatra when she did love must have been a 'bear.'"[20]

Driving an Orientalist narrative of a deadly but seductive Egypt, Cleopatra provides seemingly historical justification for a cinematic parade of aggressive female sexuality and a spectacle of erotic excess. Alongside claims that the production cost over half a million dollars, the Fox pressbooks illustrated and dwelt lovingly on the numerous exotic costumes in which Theda Bara could be viewed seducing her on- (and off-) screen admirers:

> It was an age of barbaric splendor in everything, and with all the ruby and sapphire mines of the East to call upon, a Queen went robed in brilliance. There is one filmy robe of gold tissue, and with it are worn a perfect outfit of pearls and rubies which are so remarkable a specimen of jeweler's art that they must be seen to be believed. The headpiece of massed pearls with its great cabochon rubies inset in it, matched by the great ruby star worn at the breast, must be seen to be realized.[21]

The accompanying photograph displays Theda Bara so costumed, seated majestically so as to look back and down at the humbled viewer of her jeweled splendors.[22] The star image, film, and marketing that encourage the identification of Theda Bara with Cleopatra can all be read as conforming to the structures of an Orientalist cinema that creates a "colonialist imaginary" and solicits a "gendered Western gaze." The spectator is constituted as a Western traveler who is being initiated into the barbaric splendors of an unknown culture, their gendered male gaze drawn to an East embodied as a mysterious but alluring woman.[23]

In contrast with later studio descriptions of the costumes paraded in "Cleopatra" films, the Fox pressbooks do not offer details of jeweler and fabric in terms that a woman could or would attempt to reproduce in her life outside the cinema. They do not solicit from women audiences their own practical identification with the star-as-Cleopatra. Instead the studio press agents fed to fan magazines representative "examples" of audience responses to Bara's image as Oriental vamp. In *Picture-Play Magazine* for 15 February 1916, for example, an article supposedly written by the star herself talks of letters of abuse received from angry women and letters of love from desirous men. One of the latter, writing all the way from Australia, is said to have declared:

> I have gone insane over dreams of you, my Egyptian queen, soul of my soul! Without you, life is but a void, and earth a desert drear. Come to my arms, oh, Cleopatra; my heart is burning for you! I want you. I want you!

Yet the same *Picture-Play* article also clearly acknowledges that any identification of Bara with a vamping Cleopatra is but an entertaining charade. Bara professes herself amused by letters that suggest some spectators have been duped by her star image. The photographs that illustrate Bara's account of her birth in the desert sands of Egypt and her subsequently strange life carry captions such as "Theda Bara's greatest ambition away from the screen is to live down her film reputation—and look as unlike a vampire as possible." The largely female readership of the magazine is drawn into a community of women utterly aware of the film industry's machinations. They understand that Theda Bara's brand of femininity is performative and therefore, if anything, more appealing. Divested of any real dangers, it offers a momentary escape from the domestic constraints of the 1910s into an Orient figured (both on and off screen) as home to a woman of power and sexual passion.[24] Too extraordinary to be imitable, Theda Bara's performance of *Cleopatra* was the biggest American box-office success of 1917. The most advertised, written-about, and talked-about film of the year formed part of an early-twentieth-century Cleomania that concerned spectator desire but only star identification.

GO CLEOPATRA!:
CLAUDETTE COLBERT AS CLEOPATRA (1934)

In sharp contrast, a press sheet released by Paramount around November 1934 (and designed to aid exhibitors in selling to British audiences the Hollywood studio's new release *Cleopatra*) carried the dramatic headline "Season's Styles Go 'Cleopatra'! From Head to Toe Fashionable Ladies Emulate Egypt's Queen." Below examples of "Egyptian" styles inspired by Paramount's film, exhibitors were also conveniently supplied with a sample article for placement in national newspapers and women's magazines:

"Cleopatra" has gone to the ladies' heads! And to their feet—and into almost every article of apparel, judging by the growing vogue of "Cleopatra" styles, following the release of the Paramount picture of that name, which comes _____ to the _____ Theatre. Directed by Cecil B. DeMille, it features Claudette Colbert, Warren William and Henry Wilcoxon.

A few of the highlights of the "Cleopatra" vogue are illustrated here in the two dresses designed by Travis Banton for Miss Colbert, and the "Cleopatra" hat and coiffure, the marked influence of Egyptian style and designs is evident in the sandals, jewelry and buckles selected to illustrate the new season's offerings.[25]

Elsewhere in the studio's publicity, British exhibitors were notified that Selfridge's department store had brought out a special "Cleopatra" hat that had been posed on a wax model of Colbert-as-Cleopatra and displayed in a dedicated window of its Oxford Street store in London, while Dolcis had brought out a special sandal for evening dress wear and, for the duration of the film's run, was displaying it and other "Cleopatra models" in all its shoe shops throughout Great Britain. Similarly the manufacturers of Lux soap and Marcovitch Egyptian cigarettes were running special advertising campaigns that used stills of the star of *Cleopatra* and thereby tied up their products with the glamour of Hollywood's Egypt. It would be a different and more difficult project to establish whether these tactics did indeed generate a genuine Cleopatran vogue or sell more soap and cigarettes, but proof that they were actually deployed is much easier to find. Another Paramount campaign book, for example, illustrates its suggestions for selling the film with photographs of those shop windows of R.H. Macy & Co. (the smart New York department store) that had been given over to "Cleopatra" gowns and shoes, or "Egyptian" backgammon sets, and to copies of newspaper advertisements for "Jewel-Studded Cleopatra Sandals" or the evening dresses worn by Colbert as the "Queen of Glamour." By 1934 Cleopatra and her Egypt had been commodified as a glamorous fashion-style that was now widely available for purchase in all good department stores.

The bond between the Hollywood film industry and the institution of the department store was at its most intimate in the 1930s. Film historians generally place the director DeMille at the point of origin of this process whereby a department store aesthetic entered American cinema. During the course of the 1910s and 1920s, DeMille perfected a technique for turning the film frame into a living display window occupied by marvelous mannequins. His stylish sex comedies regularly showcased modern fashions, furnishings, accessories, and cosmetics in fetishized form as commodities. In numerous bathroom and bedroom scenes, DeMille's glamorous heroines ostentatiously put products to use in an appeal to middle-class female spectators with disposable incomes. His chic sets and costumes in which love affairs were played out received such strong and attractive visual emphasis that they set American consumer trends.[26] By the 1930s, as women became its core audience, the Hollywood film industry gave female stars a central role both on- and off-screen in differentiating its mass production of films, and in glamorizing commodities and activating their consumption.[27] With the advent of the technology of sound, and in the era of the Depression, such stars had also become less divine and extraordinary in status and appearance, their screen characters more commonly motivated by a credible psychology than by occult possession. Stars continued to be special but now combined the exceptional with the ordinary and the everyday.[28] Claudette Colbert, the Paramount star whose function was to display and endorse a Cleopatran vogue, was among the top five female box-office draws of the early 1930s (and by 1938 Hollywood's highest earner). Her star image was that of a modern American woman who was sleek, sophisticated, witty, resourceful, and chic. Immediately prior to the production of *Cleopatra*, that image had been reinforced by the extraordinary success of her contemporary role as an American heiress in *It Happened One Night*.[29] How then could Cleopatra and ancient Egypt be drawn into the economy of a film industry committed to an aesthetics of commodity display, dominated by modern star images, and driven by a desire to encourage among female spectators the purchase of star-inspired products?

TUTMANIA AND NEFERTITIANA

As part of the nineteenth century's colonialist project to claim territories and subjects by their visual reproduction and display, ancient Egypt had already been reified and turned into a spectacle of material abundance in exhibitions in museums and world's fairs, in magic lantern shows, panoramas, dioramas, photography and documentary footage.[30] More recently, the discovery of Tutankhamen's tomb and the widespread and persistent dissemination of details of its contents in the mass media (from the famous first report in the *Times* on 30 November 1922 into the early 1930s) gave impetus to the mass production and consumption of Nilotic designs, from ashtrays to ocean liners, from evening gowns to pseudo-Egyptian cinemas. Already in April 1923, American *Vogue* carried the headline "The Mode Has a Rendezvous by the Nile" and predicted that New York fashions would soon be gripped by a taste for the Egyptian.[31] While Tutmania gave modern mass-produced objects a sheen of luxury, exoticism, and exclusivity, Egypt could also be clothed in the ordinary, the everyday, and the accessible. It was precisely this combination of resonances that made Egypt so marketable in British and American mass culture in the 1920s and 1930s. Tutankhamen and Cleopatra were by no means the only ancient Egyptian celebrities on offer to the public. The rediscovery by British archaeologists of the ruins of el-Amarna, the city of the pharaoh Akhenaten and his wife Nefertiti, received unprecedented coverage in magazines and papers on both sides of the Atlantic, such as the

Illustrated London News and the *National Geographic* for the duration of the expedition (1921–36). This coverage enabled Akhenaten and Nefertiti to join the pantheon of Egyptian stars, having the required star combination of the ordinary and accessible with the extraordinary and inaccessible.

The archaeological rediscovery of el-Amarna was an important moment in Western appropriations of Egypt. It was the first time that the houses of "real" ancient Egyptians had been revealed—Amarna's unique archaeology, with many houses but few tombs, enabled its excavators to show the public the homes and workplaces of ancient Egypt's ordinary people. The articles accompanying their photographs, all written by the archaeologists themselves, explicitly encouraged the reader/viewer to identify with the ancient inhabitants of el-Amarna, a city that was associated with daily life, knowableness, and bourgeois comforts. In the *Illustrated London News* of 6 August 1921, the byline was "Home Life in Egypt 3000 years ago," and a double-page spread featured a photograph captioned "A convenience as much demanded in Ancient Egypt as modern London: a bath-room of 1350 B.C., the bath being a limestone slab with a raised edge and runnel." The difference between the excavations at el-Amarna and the clearing of Tutankhamen's tomb were discussed in the popular press. An article in the large-circulation British newspaper the *Daily Chronicle* (18 June 1923) made this clear. Praising the fact that the publicity surrounding Tutankhamen's tomb had raised money for the dig at el-Amarna to resume, it went on to say:

> This work promises far more interesting results than any so far yielded up at Luxor. Whatever may be thought of the artistic value of the discoveries in the tomb of Tutankhamun, there can be no doubt that the accumulation of such a vast hoard of property in a temple of the dead made a rather unpleasant appeal to the materialistic side of our nature. Investigators at Tell el-Amarna will not be digging among the houses of the dead, but will seek for knowledge among dwellings that were once inhabited by the living.

As well as being associated with daily life, el-Amarna was also associated with glamour and beauty via Egypt's other most iconic queen, Nefertiti. El-Amarna was the findspot of the famous bust of Nefertiti (now in Berlin), the exemplar for the brunette model's swept-up coiffure in the magazine article with which we began. Women had begun to identify with Nefertiti's beauty well before the 1960s, however. She was a popular guise for American women to assume at fancy-dress parties in the 1920s and 1930s.[32] Nefertiti appeared as the cover girl for the *National Geographic* and the *Illustrated London News*. In the latter she is dubbed "The Loveliest Woman of Antiquity? A Rival to Helen of Troy" (13 December 1924) and "Ancient Egypt's Queen of Beauty" (6 May 1933): like a Hollywood star, her celebrity is such that her image needs no identification. Even though dead for over three thousand years, Nefertiti in the 1930s was the focus for a type of

FIGURE 19. *Cleopatra*. 1934: Claudette Colbert (Lily Chauchoin, 1903–96), as she appears in the title role of Cecil B. DeMille's *Cleopatra*. Costume designed by Travis Banton. Photo by Hulton Archive/Getty Images.

journalism increasingly reliant on photographs and fascination with celebrity that is also associated with film stars. Apart from her beauty, Nefertiti's modernity was augmented by the garments of her and her daughters in sculpture from el-Amarna. They wear floating, figure-hugging dresses, similar to the clinging, bias-cut clothes that would be worn by Colbert as Cleopatra.

Given this range of Egypts made available by popularized archaeology in the 1920s and 1930s, it was unsurprising that by the mid-1920s American women were shopping in emporia laden with examples of an Egypt simultaneously commodified and domesticated.[33] Consequently the spectacular art deco sets of DeMille's *Cleopatra*, awash with feathers, fans, pearls, and leopard skins, evoked the Orientalist aesthetic of the department store, while Travis Banton's designs for Cleopatra's costumes (elegantly understated, cut on the bias, in soft, smooth fabrics that clung to the contours of Colbert's slim body) could appear to be simultaneously of an Other and of this world (Fig. 19).

The narrative of Cleopatra's relations with Rome could also be adapted very easily to suit the commercial concerns of the Hollywood film industry. For, in her Western tradition, this Ptolemaic ruler was already the supreme historical embodiment of Woman engineered as seductive spectacle—a queen unraveled from a rug for the pleasure of Caesar, a Venus riding on her barge to capture Antony. The union in her person of a seductive sexuality with political power gave Cleopatra special modern currency. Her screen characterization in DeMille's film could incorporate a flattering recognition of the growing economic and sexual independence that American women had been achieving since they won the vote in 1920.[34] At a time when Hollywood was attempting to prove the respectability of cinema and regulate its content in the face of considerable municipal and state censorship,[35] DeMille was able to justify the production of another suggestive sex comedy by putting it in fancy dress and calling it high art. A study guide distributed to schools on the treatment of history in *Cleopatra* claimed for the film the accuracy of a Plutarchian biography and the cultural prestige of a Shakespearean or Shavian drama, but reviewers remarked (often unhappily) upon the privileging of the present that seemed to undercut all such claims: "all the early Romans and Egyptians seem so definitely like modern Americans, all ready for the costume ball" (*New York Herald Tribune*, 17 August 1934). Thus it was not difficult for Claudette Colbert, in keeping with her star image and aided by the modernity of the film's dialogue, to play Cleopatra as a sassy, easy-going, glamour girl who finds herself on a journey between public responsibility and romantic love, nor for female spectators of the thirties to consume her as deserving of imitation.

CLEOMANIA FOR SALE

Hollywood pressbooks of the 1930s included articles on the costumes and cosmetics of female stars, suitable for reprinting in women's magazines, that were designed to encourage a *practical*, not just a fantastical, identification between women audiences and the character who appeared on the screen.[36] From 1930 the Modern Merchandising Bureau, acting as a middleman between studios and retailers, regularly adapted screen fashions for promotion in an international mass market. Reproduced in the Paramount pressbook, the Bureau's suggested copy in connection with the costumes designed by Travis Banton for *Cleopatra* declares:

They are lavish, glamorous gowns with authentic details in jewels and trimming. From these we have made exciting adaptations in evening gowns and accessories. Our copies have all the allure of the original with exotic edges rubbed down and subdued into fashions that are definitely 1934 and wearable.

The press books for the 1930s *Cleopatra* provide vivid evidence of how Hollywood's Egypt was brought out of the film frame and the cinema and, after slight adjustments, transferred to retail outlets throughout the United States and abroad in order to encourage a very personal (and purchasable) Cleomania.

Such marketing strategies have been condemned by some feminist film historians as examples of how Hollywood cinema's commodity logic was designed to deflect women's dissatisfaction with their social conditions onto an intensified concern with their bodies and an overriding interest in romance.[37] Other feminist theorizations of the relationship between the female spectacle and the female spectatorship of Hollywood cinema have considered how women moviegoers actually (and actively) responded to the invitation to purchase an apparently traditional feminine identity.[38] On this basis, contradictions have been explored between the narrative drives and the visual styles of films directed at women. Although the narratives of Hollywood cinema often closed with a last-gasp reassertion of male dominance (in DeMille's film, Cleopatra eventually gives up politics and patriotism and submits to personal love for a newly virile Antony), their visual discourses of clothing and cosmetics often transcended such conventional narrative structures and frequently paraded before spectators a vision of femininity as masquerade, that is as a mask or dress that must be worn to hide female strength from anxious males. Thus, although DeMille's *Cleopatra* closes with the apparent submission of the queen to tragic romance, Colbert-as-Cleopatra acknowledges in the film that the paraphernalia of her glamorous femininity are designed to seduce Roman statesmen to her political ambitions. In an amusing double-bluff, she even talks to a foolish Antony explicitly of the plans she had had to dazzle him, at the very moment that she proves their usefulness. If we had access to the recollections of those female moviegoers who might once have bought and worn Cleopatra sandals, gowns, hair curlers, and hats, who washed with Lux soap or smoked Egyptian cigarettes, it is just possible that they too may have thought of these rituals of femininity as cunning acts of public empowerment. The reviewer of the *New York Herald Tribune* may have caught a glimpse of just such a response to *Cleopatra* when he wrote with clear irritation of its double romance: "In each case the conquering Roman is determined to break the will and the spirit of the Egyptian woman only to find that her wiles are just a bit too much for him."

LIZPATRA: ELIZABETH TAYLOR AS CLEOPATRA (1963)

Western representations of ancient Egypt have their own history and their own national specificities. Although American cinematic visions of that past often appropriated the structures of Orientalist discourse, until the 1950s (unlike France or Great Britain) the United States had no concrete colonial or political connection with Egypt. Once the United States took on its new postwar imperial role and became heavily invested in the Middle East, present political concerns came to the surface of Hollywood's ancient histories.[39] Thus desires for an Arab-Israeli settlement enter the epic film *Ben-Hur* (1959) in the shape of an amenable sheik who offers support to the film's fictional Jewish hero. Given American concerns about the presidency of Gamal Abdel Nasser and his vision of an Arab nationalism for Egypt, it is no surprise that the *Cleopatra* released by 20th Century Fox in 1963 constructs the political vision of Egypt's earlier leader in less problematic, utterly Western terms. In the first half of the film, before the tomb of Alexander, Cleopatra talks to Julius Caesar of her desire for one world, one nation, one people living in peace. In an early draft of the screenplay, the director Joseph L. Mankiewicz described this Cleopatra as "an early-day Kennedy,"[40] but in response, a newspaper review at the time of the film's release derided her as "a World Federalist at heart,"[41] while ten years later a film historian observed her to be "a kind of Eleanor Roosevelt captivated by the ideal of one-world unity."[42] Most commentators on the film have also observed that its attempt at a contemporary political resonance is both fragmentary and fragile, because the film was radically cut before and after its release, and because whatever political narrative it possessed was utterly swamped by the star image of the film's true protagonist, Elizabeth Taylor.

In her previous screen roles Taylor's ambitions had never exceeded those of romance, nor could her stardom carry a performance of international statecraft.[43] During the 1950s, the narrative and visual style of Marilyn Monroe's films and the extra-cinematic discourses about her (such as film reviews, studio promotions, and mass media publicity) gave that film star a popularity that became an intertext in discourses of female sexuality and even figured in the publication of Alfred Kinsey's reports on sexual behavior and the launch of *Playboy* magazine.[44] By the beginning of the 1960s, however, Elizabeth Taylor's star image had become a common reference point more specifically for discourses of adultery. The high-class prostitute she played in *Butterfield 8* (1960) bore a significant resemblance to the free-living and free-loving playgirl articulated each month in *Playboy* magazine, while the screen character's self-indulgence and freedom from moral constraints appeared to match the manners of the actress herself who was by now notorious for her extramarital affairs and for apparently breaking up the ideal marriage of Debbie Reynolds.[45] Taylor's star status as a serial adulteress was radically reinforced early in 1962, when rumors of an on-set affair with Richard Burton, one of her co-stars in *Cleopatra*, drew uninvited publicity and within a matter of months had grown into an international sex scandal condemned by both members of Congress and the Vatican. According to a recent resume of the events in *Vanity Fair*, "When Liz Met Dick," the celebrity scandal was taken up so intensely in the popular press that on front pages worldwide it soon superseded news of John Glenn's orbiting of the earth or details of the U.S.-Soviet tensions that by year's end would lead to the Cuban missile crisis.[46] The sex scandal had a significant impact on the production and reception of *Cleopatra* and on the formation of a new superstar image for Taylor as "Lizpatra."[47]

Ultimately almost three years passed between initial shooting for *Cleopatra* (begun in October 1960) and its premiere in June 1963.[48] At the start of 1962, the studio publicity that was fed into magazines like *Look* and *Vogue* attempted to pre-sell interest in the troubled film by twinning Taylor and Cleopatra as two legendary glamour girls who both enjoyed a fabulously luxurious lifestyle. But, at the very same time, the Taylor/Cleopatra link was being taken out of the hands of the studio and redirected to signify not glamour and luxury but wastefulness and adultery. In February 1962, for example, *The Perry Como Show* ran a comic sketch in which a slave going by the name of Taylor's husband kept getting in Marc Antony's way. The opportunities provided by both the shooting of the film and the rhetoric of studio promotions to trope the affair in terms of Cleopatran high farce were too splendid to miss, and in the excitable gossip of newspapers, magazines, and television shows the Ptolemaic queen was reconfigured exactly to match Elizabeth Taylor as a classic Other Woman.[49] This Cleomania, unlike that concerning Theda Bara, operated outside the control of the Hollywood studio. Its apparent escape from the star image 20th Century Fox had attempted to promote made it seem more authentic and, therefore, more like a privileged glimpse of a real Lizpatra.[50]

Stars are cast in Hollywood's histories not as characters but in character and thus they people the represented past with the present, while extracinematic discourses about them and about the moment of film production further extend the temporality of the time represented into the here-and-now.[51] In the same year as the release of the film *Cleopatra*, two insider accounts of its production were published and widely sold. *My Life with Cleopatra* written (with the aid of the reporter Joe Hyams) by Walter Wanger, himself the producer, and *The Cleopatra Papers: A Private Correspondence* written by two studio publicists, Jack Brodsky and Nathan Weiss, both worked to suggest that the discourses of film-star adultery had infected the film-making process itself, in particular the overnight revisions of the script by Mankiewicz and its performance by the two stars. For example, in a vivid diary-format Wanger recalls what happened on 5 March 1962:

Today we filmed the bath scene [. . .]
Cleopatra comes in to see Antony, who is in the bath [. . .] They commence a beautiful love scene.

JLM's [Mankiewicz's] dialogue is right out of real life, with Cleopatra telling how she will feel if Antony leaves her. "Love can stab the heart," she says.

It was hard to tell whether Liz and Burton were reading lines or living the parts.[52]

Wanger's biographer notes that his account of events (published before the film opened) is full of petty deceptions designed to help publicize the much-criticized film and its much-maligned star. Given the immense public fascination with the adultery, the producer took up the trope of a Cleopatran romance in order to suggest that cinemagoers could now see that notorious adultery played out before their eyes in Technicolor and on wide screen.[53] Similarly, to coincide with the month in which *Cleopatra* was finally released, 20th Century Fox cooperated in the reprint of a novel about Cleopatra by Carlo Maria Franzero that was illustrated with stills from the film and production photographs showing Taylor-as-Cleopatra *between* takes, as if Taylor had lived Cleopatra off-set as well as on (Fig. 20).[54]

Reviewers certainly read Elizabeth Taylor's performance of the title role as utterly of the present. In a blistering critique, the *New York Herald Tribune* of 13 June 1963 said of Taylor that "out of royal regalia, en negligee or au naturel she gives the impression that she is really carrying on in one of Miami Beach's more exotic resorts rather than inhabiting a palace in ancient Alexandria or even a villa in Rome." For this critic, even the elaborate detail of the sets did not help to place the performances in the past of ancient Egypt: "Even in their most dramatic moment, when Cleopatra and Antony are slapping each other around in her tomb, one's immediate image is of Miss Taylor and Mr. Burton having it out in the Egyptian Wing of the Metropolitan Museum." Interestingly, for our purposes, the critic also scoffs at the "orgy" that takes place on Cleopatra's barge:

skimpy—and not helped one bit by having one of the dancing girls decked out as a double for Cleopatra. We should not be reminded that other girls can look just like Elizabeth Taylor, particularly when she is trying to portray the Queen of Queens.

In her effort to deride the film, the critic clearly missed the full significance of this sequence, which closes with Antony angrily abandoning the fake queen he has just kissed in order to track down the real one in her boudoir. Here, we would argue, is made visible the outcome of the film's opportunistic promotional strategies.[55] By placing so much emphasis on Taylor's new superstar image as Lizpatra, the studio solicited from spectators a hermeneutic reading of Cleopatra's representation on screen, that is an interpretation directed at the discovery of a "real" Lizpatra lying behind the screen performance.[56] The attempt to solicit a Cleopatra look for "other girls" is abandoned, recognized as fake, as a matter of superficial

FIGURE 20. Set of *Cleopatra*. Film actors Richard Burton (1925–84) and Elizabeth Taylor on the set of *Cleopatra*. Photo by Ron Gerelli/Getty Images.

appearance, while the film itself invites us instead to track down the only woman who can now truly embody the Egyptian queen.

NOTES

1. Dominic Montserrat died a while after the completion of this essay and before we could initiate a planned monograph together on antiquity in popular culture. I would like to acknowledge here what a great privilege and, more importantly, pleasure it was to have worked with him however briefly.

2. Illustrated in Wyke (2002): 280, fig. 8.1.

3. Cf. an earlier article in *Vogue* for 15 January 1962, which focuses rather more on the supposed

Cleopatran lifestyle of Elizabeth Taylor but also talks in terms of "a new Cleopatra complex" in fashions, hairstyles, and cosmetics. Our thanks are due to Peter Kramer for the very welcome advice he gave on recent literature concerning film stardom and commodity tie-ins.

4. For a broad survey of the reception and appropriation of Cleopatra from antiquity to the present, see L. Hughes-Hallett, *Cleopatra: Histories, Dreams and Distortions* (1990). For a close reading of some specific examples, see M. Hamer, *Signs of Cleopatra: History, Politics, Representation* (1993). On Cleopatra and cinema see Maria Wyke, *Projecting the Past: Ancient Rome, Cinema and History* (1997): 73–109. Some parts of the material in this essay (without the imput of Dominic Montserrat) also have been published in Maria Wyke, *The Roman Mistress: Ancient and Modern Representations* (2002): 244–320.

5. Hughes-Hallett (1993): 258. See also Smith's paper in this volume.

6. Hughes-Hallett (1993): 346–48.

7. W. Osburn, *The Monumental History of Egypt as Recorded on the Ruins of Her Temples, Palaces and Tombs* (1854): 333.

8. D. Montserrat, *Akhenaten: History, Fantasy, Representation* (2000): 55–94.

9. Quoted in F. N. Magill, *Magill's Survey of Cinema: Silent Films*[1] (1982): 322. Cf. the very favorable verdict on *Cleopatra* in *Moving Picture World* for 3 November 1917, which reproduces the studio description of Theda Bara as acting "the Egyptian vampire."

10. See esp. R. de Cordova, *Picture Personalities: The Emergence of the Star System in America* (1990).

11. That is, in Edward Said's terms, the imaginative geography of colonialist discourses, for which see *Orientalism* (1978).

12. Quoted in E. Golden, *Vamp: The Rise and Fall of Theda Bara* (1996): 130. For other accounts of Theda Bara's star image, see also J. R. Parish, *The Fox Girls* (1971): 17–47; D. Bodeen, *From Hollywood: The Careers of 15 Great American Stars* (1976): 13–28; R. Genini, *Theda Bara: A Biography of the Silent Screen Vamp* (1996).

13. For a convenient summary of nineteenth-century fantasies of Egypt, see L. Meskell, "Consuming Bodies: Cultural Fantasies of Ancient Egypt," *Body and Society* 4.1 (1998): 64–67. For a more detailed treatment of visual realizations of Cleopatra see J.-M. Humbert, M. Pantazzi, and C. Ziegler, eds., *Egyptomania: Egypt in Western Art 1730–1930* (1994): 552–81 and H. De Meulenaere, *Ancient Egypt in Nineteenth Century Painting* (1992).

14. For theories of film stardom, see esp. R. Dyer, *Stars*[2] (1998); and C. Gledhill, ed., *Stardom: Industry of Desire* (1991).

15. On cinema's vamps, see S. Higashi, *Virgins, Vamps, and Flappers: The American Silent Movie Heroine* (1978): 55–78; and J. Staiger, *Bad Women: Regulating Sexuality in Early American Cinema* (1995): 147–62.

16. A. Lant, "The Curse of the Pharaoh, or How Cinema Contracted Egyptomania," *October* 59 (1992): 109–10.

17. We here adapt Peter Wollen's description of the functions of the Orient in early-twentieth-century visual arts including the scenography of dance, "Fashion/Orientalism/The Body," *New Formations* 1 (1987): 17. For a feminist and postcolonial cultural critique of Orientalism in cinema, see E. Shohat, "Gender and Culture of Empire: Toward a Feminist Ethnography of the Cinema," *Quarterly Review of Film & Video* 13 (1991): 45–84; and M. Bernstein and G. Studlar, eds., *Visions of the East: Orientalism in Film* (1997), in which the 1991 article by Shohat is also reproduced.

18. Cited from the pressbook produced for the British release of the film that can be found in the Special Collections of the British Film Institute.

19. For nineteenth-century depictions of Cleopatra as a man killer, see Hughes-Hallett (1990): 281–311.

20. USC Film and Television Archive, 20th Century Fox Collection, Box 41, Item 1464.

21. See note 12.

22. Illustrated in Wyke (2002): 276, fig. 7.5.

23. See esp. Shohat (1991).

24. As argued by G. Studlar in "'Out-Salomeing Salome': Dance, the New Woman, and Fan Magazine Orientalism" in Bernstein and Studlar (1997): esp. 115–19.

25. Several such campaign books for *Cleopatra* (1934) can be viewed in the Special Collections of the British Film Institute.

26. The first history of the relationship between the Hollywood film industry and department store fashions is that of C. Eckert, "The Carole Lombard in Macy's Window," *Quarterly Review of Film Studies* 3.1 (1978): 1–21. His famous article has been followed by numerous other studies, such as J. Allen, "The film Viewer as Consumer," *Quarterly Review of Film Studies* 5.4 (1980): 481–99; M. A. Doane, "The Economy of Desire: The Commodity Form in/of the Cinema," *Quarterly Review of Film and Video* 11 (1989): 23–33; J. Gaines, "The Queen Christina Tie-ups: Convergence of Show Window and Screen," *Quarterly Review of Film and Video* 11 (1989): 35–60; C. C. Herzog and J. M. Gaines, "'Puffed Sleeves Before Tea-Time': Joan Crawford, Adrian and Women Audiences," in Gledhill (1991): 74–91. On DeMille in particular, see also S. Higashi, *Cecil B. DeMille and American Culture: The Silent Era* (1994): 2–4 and 142–78.

27. On the importance of the star system in 1930s Hollywood, see T. Balio, ed., *Grand Design: Hollywood as a Modern Business Enterprise 1930–1939* (1993): 143–77.

28. Dyer (1998): 21–23.

29. J. R. Parish, *The Paramount Pretties* (1972): 92–141; W. K. Everson, *Claudette Colbert* (1976); Balio (1993): 149–50; Hamer (1993): 120–21.

30. Lant (1992): 91–98; Higashi (1994): 154.

31. C. Frayling, *The Face of Tutankhamun* (1992): 10–28. Cf. J. S. Curl, *Egyptomania: The Egyptian Revival: A Recurring Theme in the History of Taste* (1994): 211–20.

32. See G. Stark and E. C. Rayne, *El Delirio: The Santa Fe World of Elizabeth White* (1998).

33. Higashi (1994): 90–92.

34. Hamer (1993): 104–34.

35. R. Maltby, "The Production Code and the Hays Office," in Balio (1993): 37–72.

36. See esp. Herzog and Gaines (1991).

37. Eg. Doane (1989): 26–27, and Gaines (1989): 49–50. For *Cleopatra* specifically, see Hamer (1993): 121–24 and 132–34.

38. See, for example, J. Stacey, *Star Gazing: Hollywood Cinema and Female Spectatorship* (1994), and S. Bruzzi, *Undressing Cinema: Clothing and Identity in the Movies* (1997).

39. Said (1978) and "Egyptian Rites," *Village Voice* August 1983 (reprinted in Frayling [1992]: 276–85).

40. USC Film and Television Archive, 20th Century Fox collection 5042.17. The item is dated 1961.

41. *New York Herald Tribune*, 13 June 1963.

42. F. Hirsch, *Elizabeth Taylor* (1973): 101.

43. For Elizabeth Taylor as film star, see esp. Hirsch (1973); A. Walker, *The Celluloid Sacrifice: Aspects of Sex in the Movies* (1966): 131–45; A. Walker, *Elizabeth* (1990).

44. R. Dyer, *Heavenly Bodies: Film Stars and Society* (1986): 27–42.

45. Walker (1990): 221–22. Cf. M. Bernstein, *Walter Wanger: Hollywood Independent* (1994): 351.

46. *Vanity Fair* no. 452, April 1998. Cf. Bernstein (1994): 368–69.

47. "Lizpatra" is used by Dwight MacDonald in *Esquire*, February.1965, to describe Taylor's performance of Cleopatra.

48. Full details of the film's troubled production history can be found in Bernstein (1994).

49. For discussion of the *Vogue* piece published on 15 January 1962 and salacious press links made between Cleopatra and Taylor, see Wyke (1997): 101–4, (2002): 307–15. Cf. Hughes-Hallett (1990): 348–50 and 357–60.

50. See Dyer (1986): 61 on the apparent credibility of uninvited publicity concerning star scandals.

51. V. Sobchack, "'Surge and Splendor': A Phenomenology of the Hollywood Historical Epic," *Representations* 29 (1990): 35–36.

52. W. Wanger, *My Life with Cleopatra* (1963): 134. See also Wyke (1997): 103–5, (2002): 311–13.

53. Bernstein (1994): 375–80.

54. See for example the British reprint of C. M. Franzero, *Cleopatra Queen of Egypt* (1963), dated June 1963.

55. According to Bernstein (1994): 372–73, after the promotion of hairstyles and costumes in *Look, Vogue,* and *Life* early in 1962, Wanger continued to suggest merchandising ideas to sell in connection with *Cleopatra,* but they were all dismissed by the studio.

56. For the concept of the hermeneutic reading of the performance of stars on screen, see de Cordova (1990): 112–13.

9

Every Man's Cleopatra

Giuseppe Pucci

The title of this essay, borrowed from John Dryden's *All for Love* (4.299), should suffice to explain my intention: I am concerned less with the historical Cleopatra than with the many Cleopatras different epochs have created to embody their own fantasies and desires. Leaving aside for the moment ancient Latin and Greek authors, my story could begin appropriately with Françoise de Foix, the mistress of Francis I of France, who demanded in 1519 the first modern translation of Plutarch's *Life of Antony*, hoping to learn from an unsurpassed model in Françoise's line of business. From Jodelle's *Cleopâtre Captive* (1552) to Margaret George's *The Memoirs of Cleopatra* (1997), at least two hundred plays and novels, forty-five operas, five ballets, and forty-three movies have been inspired by the Queen of Egypt.[1] As for paintings and statues, A. Pigler records no fewer than 230 works in the seventeenth and eighteenth centuries alone.[2] No one, to my knowledge, has attempted to compile an exhaustive list, but were one were to do so, the numbers I have given above would increase dramatically. Few other historical characters have been significant to so many generations and different cultures.[3] In fact, we are dealing with a myth, and it is the creation and transformation of this myth that I wish to examine. The origin of Cleopatra's myth dates back to Cleopatra herself.

LIFE PROJECTED INTO MYTH

According to Thomas Mann, who wrote a penetrating essay on this topic, Cleopatra is a perfect example of a life intentionally projected into myth.[4] Mann notes that Cleopatra's self-identification with Isis-Aphrodite is not only recorded fact, found in Plutarch and elucidated by Bachofen, but also the real content of her subjective existence. In other words, she really lived her mythical role. In Plutarch's famous depiction of the rendezvous with Antony on the barge on the river Cydnus (*Life of Antony* 26), Cleopatra is said to have attired herself "like the goddess Venus commonly drawn in pictures," whereas "on either hand of her pretty fair boys [were] apparelled as painters do set forth god Cupid." This mythical identification was revived by Shakespeare, who clearly equates Cleopatra with Venus—and Antony with Mars—in the well-known scene where Cleopatra delights in recalling how she had dressed Antony in her clothes, while herself strapping on his "sword Philippan."

Shakespeare added a relevant detail: in the original myth Mars and Venus undress, whereas in his play Antony and Cleopatra cross-dress; but in fact Cleopatra has been associated with the confusion of genders since her own lifetime. In Augustan propaganda she was identified with Omphale and accused of feminizing Antony, who was likened, by both himself and his enemies, to Heracles. To exploit Heracles' affair with Omphale as a criticism of Antony must have seemed obvious. As Omphale divested Heracles of his club and lion's skin, so Cleopatra reportedly disarmed Antony and made him her playmate (Plutarch, *Life of Antony* 90.4).[5] Shakespeare's Cleopatra similarly dresses Antony in her tiaras and mantles and appropriates the token of his manhood (an obvious phallic symbol), the sword.[6] The power to emasculate a valiant warrior is an important component of Cleopatra's myth. In an early nineteenth-century cartoon by James Gillray (Fig. 21), Sir William Hamilton, the British envoy to Naples and a famous antiquarian, contemplates his art collection, which includes a pair of portraits labeled *Cleopatra* and *Antony* that actually depict Hamilton's wife, Emma, and her lover, Nelson.[7] Although the satire is directed in the first place at the cheated husband, it also included Nelson, for putting the honor of the British in the hands of a woman of ill repute.[8]

It is worth stressing that in antiquity the change of sexual roles was regarded as typical of Egypt (and of the Orient). Herodotus, in describing that country, points out the antitheses between its customs and those of Greece (Hdt. 2.35). In Egypt women go to the market and trade; men live at home and weave. Women urinate standing, men, squatting. Cleopatra exemplifies the reversal of roles and customs (as do males of the Ptolemaic dynasty). We are told by Plutarch (*Life of Antony* 29.2) that she played dice, drank, hunted with her companion, even attended his military exercises and followed him in war. If we refer to the model of the Roman matrona, Cleopatra is a clear example of reversed femininity.[9] Thus she could easily become for the Romans an abhorrent and terrifying figure, a *monstrum* for Horace and an Erinys for Lucan, that is, an icon of female potency and castration.[10]

A COGNOCENTI contemplating ỹ Beauties of ỹ Antique.

FIGURE 21. *A Cognocenti Contemplating ye Beauties of ye Antique* by James Gillray, published 1801. British Cartoon Prints Collection, Library of Congress. Photo Library of Congress, LC-USZC4-8796.

On her first encounter with Caesar, when Cleopatra supposedly comes out of the carpet, she appears to him, in Plutarch's words, as *lamyrá* (*Life of Caesar* 49.3). Although *lamyrá* can be translated as "impudent," or "coquettish," nevertheless the term has a sinister overtone, being connected with the *Lamyai*, the vampire-like monsters. The frightening glamour of Cleopatra is caught in a *fin-de-siècle* painting by Adolphe Cossard that represents Cleopatra as a dark, weird creature, whose eyes mesmerize the beholder and whose lips are likely to part any moment and expose two sharp canines.

A BIFURCATED IMAGE

In fact, there are at least two Cleopatras. One is a heroine whose tragic loves and death deserve admiration and pity; the other is a monster, a temptress that ruins all men who fall for her. She can be associated with two other temptresses who cause men's ruin, Eve and Pandora. In the famous painting by Jean Cousin (ca. 1490–1560), *Eva Prima Pandora* (Fig. 22), the Egyptian queen is not included explicitly, but, on a closer examination, the serpent clasping the left arm of the figure appears quite different from the usual diabolic serpent of Eve.[11] Moreover, another serpent lurks on the ground, near the jar. Two serpents are definitely too many for Eve, and are problematic for Pandora too. We should expect them to come out of the Pandora's jar of evil, after she opens it, but the only open jar is the just-noted. The one obstructed by Pandora's hand is thus the jar of good, and this does not make sense. It only makes sense if a third fatal woman is meant here—Cleopatra. Panofsky believed that the city represented in the background was Rome.[12] But Rome is not on the sea. Nobody, as far as I know, has remarked that the main building that overlooks the sea seems to be an ancient lighthouse: in my opinion it is Alexandria's lighthouse, which would strengthen the allusion to Cleopatra.

We may wonder whether, by hinting at Cleopatra, Cousin was not aiming at the *femme fatale* of that epoch, Diane de Poitiers, the favorite of Henry II. Yet the Renaissance temptress was only the present avatar of a cliché coming down from antiquity. In the fourth century A.D. the Latin historian Sextus Aurelius Victor wrote of Cleopatra: "She was so lustful that she often prostituted herself, and so beautiful that many men paid with their lives for a night with her."[13] The latter statement was destined to ignite morbid fantasies in the Romantic era, but meanwhile Dante had placed Cleopatra in the second circle of his *Inferno* (5.63), characterizing her by the epithet *lussuriosa* (lustful), and Boccaccio, in *de claris mulieribus*, had depicted her as a woman "known throughout the world for her greed, cruelty and lustfulness." Again, I believe, the origin of this myth dates back to Cleopatra's time. Plutarch (*Life of Antony* 27.3–4) states that her beauty was not unmatchable, but that the sound of her voice enchanted. It gave pleasure (*hedoné*). One thinks of certain mythical characters that take advantage of their voice to detain mortal heroes far from their human routes, such as Calypso, or to destroy them, such as Circe or the Sirens. Moreover, according to Plutarch, the queen used her tongue "as a multichord instrument," through which she attained an extraordinary *pithanótes* (force of persuasion). That ability of hers appeared to be superhuman, so astounding that it bordered on witchcraft.

The queen could transform her physical aspect as well. She was said to be an expert in make-up and capable of losing weight at will in order to deceive Antony.

FIGURE 22. *Eva Prima Pandora* by Jean Cousin the Elder. Louvre, Paris. Photo credit Erich Lessing/Art Resource, NY.

Cleopatra is protean, and Proteus dwelt in Egypt.[14] The fascination for Egypt and the mysterious Orient climaxed in the Romantic era. Imperialistic conquests fueled the desire for the exotic, and the East was perceived as a sensuous woman, to be penetrated and possessed by a Western male lover, whether conqueror, scholar, or tourist.[15] And if the Orient is female, Cleopatra is the Orient. In representations of this period just as in those produced in her own lifetime, the discourses of politics and eroticism overlap.[16]

NINETEENTH-CENTURY CLEOPATRAS AT LEISURE

Nineteenth-century Cleopatras wear gorgeous robes, their thrones flaunt solid gold sphinxes and are draped with leopard skins.[17] They are a spectacle meant to entice the desire of the male beholder facing the picture. In a painting by Jean-Léon Gérôme (1824–1904), *Cleopatra Before Caesar,* in which Cleopatra steps out of a carpet in front of Julius Caesar, who is seated behind a desk, and other male on-lookers, the basic situation—it has been rightly remarked—is that of a brothel.[18] Egypt had a reputation as a garden of sexual delights, and Cleopatra epitomizes all these sexual fantasies. Even today, the expression "Cleopatra's grip"

FIGURE 23. *Death of Cleopatra* (1875–76) by Hans Makart. Neue Galerie, Museumslandschaft Hessen Kassel, Kassel. Photo credit Bildarchiv Preussischer Kulturbesitz/Art Resource, NY.

indicates a particular sexual skill that some women are credited with (including Wallis Simpson, the late Duchess of Windsor).[19]

The Roman preconceptions against the Queen's dissolute court already had a long life. At a London performance of Victorien Sardou's *Cléopâtre*, in which Sarah Bernhardt played the title role, one theatergoer supposedly commented: "How unlike—how so unlike—the home life of our own dear Queen!" The purported remark, while expressing the sense of moral superiority of Victorian England, also reveals that Cleopatra fascinated in that she embodied everything that Western bourgeoisie affected to abhor.[20]

Placed before a contemporary painting of Cleopatra, Lucy Snowe, the heroine of Charlotte Brontë's *Villette* (1853), comments: "She lay half-reclined on a couch: why, it would be difficult to say. . . . She had no business to lounge away the noon on a sofa. She ought likewise to have worn decent garments . . . which was not the case." And Monsieur Paul, her fiancé-to-be, cannot help exclaiming: "How dare you . . . sit coolly down, with the self-possession of a garçon, and look at *that* picture?"[21]

For the nineteenth century, however, Cleopatra is more than a royal cocotte. Embroidering upon Aurelius Victor's sentence, Pushkin in 1837 made of her the *femme fatale* par excellence. In the *Egyptian Nights* he imagines Cleopatra making, in the course of a feast, her fearful announcement: "My love is for sale. Who dares to barter his life against one night of mine?" Three volunteers step forward. The choice falls upon a nameless boy, who meets his death without regrets. Pushkin's text was enormously influential. One year later Théophile Gautier, who in *Mademoiselle de Maupin* had already described how Cleopatra had each of her lovers killed after one night of love, published *Une nuit de Cléopâtre*, the story of the young lion-hunter Meiamun who offers himself like a sacrificial lamb to the cruel queen. Many subsequent authors, including de Girardin, Sardou, Cantel, and Rider Haggard, make their Cleopatras impassively take the life of an innocent young devotee enchanted by her beauty. To love Cleopatra is a pleasure mixed with pain, and potentially fatal. Swinburne, whose taste for flagellation is well known, not surprisingly adored his Cleopatra.

Like all *belles dames sans merci*, Cleopatra does not feel any compassion.[22] The *Serpent of Old Nile*—like all the reptilian females who haunt folklore and mythology—is fatal to the man who loves her. In literary and pictorial works, she enjoys poisoning slaves, as we see in Alexandre Cabanel's famous scenario, and having her lovers killed, but all that does not prevent her from suffering from boredom. "Cleopatra is bored," we read in de Girardin, "the world is in danger!" Oppressed by *ennui*, painted Cleopatras appear in a state of languishing torpor. Alma-Tadema's *Antony and Cleopatra* (see Fig. 15) does not even turn her head to salute Antony. Actresses who played her, from Sarah Bernhardt to Theda Bara, used to be photographed on *chaises longues*.[23]

We have already stressed how deeply rooted was the association of Egyptian women with sexual expertise. By contrast, in the nineteenth century African black women were associated with uncontrolled, animal-like lust. This opposition is generally reflected in contemporary painting. In Hans Makart's *Death of Cleopatra* (Fig. 23) the juxtaposition of colors in the queen and her maids emphasizes the antithesis of decadent eroticism and savagery (one of the servants also has tattoos or body painting). Even the Cleopatra created in 1876 by the African-American sculptor, Edmonia Lewis, despite the artist's standing against the exploitation of the non-white female body, has nothing of the African racial type (Fig. 24).[24] To give Cleopatra a white complexion is quite correct, given her Macedonian descent. In literature, however, Cleopatra's racial features are more ambiguous.[25] Curiously enough, the Cleopatra created in our days by René Goscinny and Albert Uderzo (in one of the *Astérix* series) shows a light brownish complexion, along with a nose doubtless reminiscent of Pascal's dictum.[26]

FIGURE 24. *The Death of Cleopatra* (1876) by Edmonia
Lewis. Gift of the Historical Society of Forest Park,
Illinois. Smithsonian American Art Museum,
Washington, D.C. Photo credit Smithsonian American
Art Museum, Washington, D.C./Art Resource, NY.

THE TRAGIC, BUT STILL THREATENING, CLEOPATRA

I stated above that there are two Cleopatras: one is a dangerous and potentially
destructive lover, the other an ill-fated, self-destructive woman. Yet even in the
tragic conclusion of her life, Cleopatra is sexually appealing. We do not have any
unquestionable ancient representations of Cleopatra's suicide.[27] A statue of the
queen committing suicide was paraded by Augustus in his triumph (Plutarch,
Life of Antony 86.6), but we have no idea what it looked like. However, some years
ago an archaeologist remarked that a small snake appears on the right breast of
an ancient statue in the Vatican Museum, representing a feminine figure draped
in a mantle with the typical Isiac knot.[28] If the statue portrays the suicide of

Cleopatra dressed as Isis, it would prove that in antiquity the iconography of that event did not diverge from the literary tradition, at least as far as her dress is concerned, since ancient sources clearly state that the Egyptian queen dressed herself for death, putting on her crown and all her royal robes. As for the asp, on the contrary, all classical authors—with the only relevant exception of Galen—have it biting the arm, not the breast, while modern artists almost invariably prefer the titillating image of Cleopatra's nude torso exposed to the poisonous fangs of the serpent (whose phallic meaning hardly needs to be stressed).[29]

In some paintings she sprawls in a quasi-erotic abandon. In others the spasms of the agony become similar to a sexual orgasm, reminiscent of Bernini's ecstatic Saints. These Cleopatras are unequivocally erotic objects, yet the sleep of death that makes them motionless puts their scary sexuality at last under control. The Cleopatra by Artemisia Gentileschi (1593–ca. 1656) assumes the position that in classical art is typical of the sleeping figures, with an arm bent over the head. Obviously, Artemisia was influenced by the famous *Sleeping Ariadne* of the Vatican museum (see Fig. 14), long believed to be a dying Cleopatra because of the serpent on her arm bracelet.[30] In the second half of the nineteenth century, the "sleeping beauty" became an almost obsessive subject for some British painters, in particular Edward Burne-Jones (1833–98). It has been argued that Victorian artists used the unconsciousness of their subjects as a means to make acceptable the intense eroticism of the recumbent female body.[31]

The gesture of the arm bent over or behind the head is of particular interest. The Vatican *Sleeping Ariadne* (see Fig. 14), a model for countless artists (from Titian to Schiele), was included by Aby Warburg in his atlas *Mnemosyne*, among other figures that, in his view, symbolize passivity.[32] In Warburg's vocabulary, it is a *pathosformel*. Now, Warburg's *pathosformeln* are powerful and meaningful because they incorporate, at least potentially, their opposite valency. Thus the unconscious inertia implies a sexual offer (Ariadne herself is soon to be aroused by Dionysos' caresses). All *pathosformeln* originate from the need to delimit and control an ancestral terror—in this case the fear of the male to be phagocytized by the female's sex. The passivity of the naked, recumbent Cleopatra exorcises such a fear in the male viewer.

CINEMATIC CLEOPATRAS

No discourse about Cleopatra's fortune in modern times may leave out of consideration the cinematic versions. Cinema appropriated Cleopatra since its infancy.[33] As early as 1899 Georges Méliès made in France *Cléopâtre*, while in the United States Charles Kent made an *Antony and Cleopatra* (1908), followed by the Italian *Marcantonio e Cleopatra* (1913) directed by Enrico Guazzoni. In the latter, released after the war Italy had fought in 1911–12 against Turkey for the

FIGURE 25. Costumed visitors in Las Vegas, ca. 1998.
Photo by Giuseppe Pucci.

Tripolitania, Cleopatra embodied the cruel Orient that dares to defy Rome, while Antony, after his suicide, is unexpectedly forgiven by Octavian!

In 1917 Fox Studios produced a *Cleopatra*, using the plot of Rider Haggard's novel. It starred Theda Bara, the actress for whom the word *vamp* was coined (see Fig. 18). She was the daughter of a Jewish tailor from Cincinnati, but the press agents made her out to have been born in Egypt, to an Italian artist and an Arabian princess. As an infant—so ran the preposterous biography—she had sucked, not milk, but the venom of serpents, and her name was the anagram of "Arab Death." Thus, while reviving the literary *femme fatale*, cinema provided a historical ancestor for the contemporary Mata Hari, and a paradigm of sexual power combined with luxury.

The *Cleopatra* shot in 1934 by DeMille offers a subtler interpretation of the character. Claudette Colbert was undoubtedly the sexiest Cleopatra of modern time (see Fig. 19), yet in this movie she conquers Antony primarily by means of her brain. Colbert excelled in the representation of the emancipated woman of the '30s. Her Cleopatra is in a sense the avatar of Rider Haggard's Cleopatra, who scorned the hero's honorable proposal: "Marriage! *I* to marry! *I* to forget freedom and court the worst slavery of our sex!" While Mankiewicz's *Cleopatra* (1963), based on the novel by Carlo Maria Franzero, might be regarded as an attempt to do justice to the historical Cleopatra's acumen, other screen Cleopatras have no such concerns. *Totò e Cleopatra*, the Italian movie released in the same year, is a comic parody, tailor-made for the great Neapolitan comedian Totò. In 1954 the Italian *Due notti con Cleopatra* was issued, a farce starring a young, provocative Sophia Loren; later on, in 1964, the British *Carry on Cleo* would trespass on the slapstick. Other *pepla* are not worth mentioning. But Cleopatra has taken her revenge. Not long ago a thirty-million-dollar TV movie was shot in Morocco, in which the fatal queen of Egypt assumes the attractive appearance of the Chilean actress Leonor Varela to accompany us through the new millennium.[34] Meanwhile, if you cannot resist seeing our idol, go to Las Vegas: she is waiting for you at Caesars Palace (Fig. 25).

NOTES

1. I updated—by means of different dictionaries and reference books—the figures given by R. Calvat, "Cléopâtre de Virgile à Mankiewicz. Origine et évolution d'un mythe," *Bulletin de l'Arelam* 32 (1995): 43–57. For movies, particularly useful is "Chronologie du film historique à l'antique" published by H. Dumont in issue 89 (1988): 153 ff., of the magazine *CinémAction*, devoted to *Le péplum: l'Antiquité au Cinéma*.

2. A. Pigler, Barockthemen, *Eine Auswahl von Verzeichnissen zur Ikonographie des 17. und 18. Jahrhunderts* (1974) 2: 395 ff. See also S. Urbini, "Il mito di Cleopatra. Motivi ed esiti della sua rinnovata fortuna fra Rinascimento e Barocco," *Xenia Antiqua* 2 (1993): 181–222.

3. See the excellent book by Lucy Hughes-Hallett, *Cleopatra: Histories, Dreams and Distortions* (1990), to which this paper is much indebted.

4. T. Mann, *Nobiltà dello spirito e altri saggi*, trans. A. Londolfi (1999): 1396 ff.

5. It is possible that some Arretine cups preserve the iconography used in the Augustan period against Antony: see P. Zanker, *The Power of Images in the Age of Augustus* (1988): 57–60; N. Kampen, "Omphale and the Instability of Gender," in N.B. Kampen, ed., *Sexuality in Ancient Art* (1996): 233–46, esp. 235; V. Saladino, "Centauri *restrictis ad terga manibus*: un'ipotesi sul Torso Gaddi," in G. Capecchi, O. Paoletti, A.M. Esposito, and A. Romualdi, eds., *In memoria di Enrico Paribeni* (1998): 379–95, esp. 380. According to M. Della Corte, *Cleopatra, M. Antonio e Ottaviano nelle allegorie storico-umoristiche delle argenterie del tesoro di Boscoreale* (1951), echoes of the Augustan polemics against Antony and Cleopatra are also detectable in the silver cups of the Boscoreale treasure and in other cups from Pompeii.

6. See C. Davidson, "Antony and Cleopatra: Circe, Venus, and the Whore of Babylon," in H.R. Garvin, ed., *Shakespeare: Contemporary Critical Approaches* (1980): 31–55.

7. A. Solmi, *Lady Hamilton* (1982): 131 ff., reports that Hamilton himself, in order to receive Nelson in Naples after his victory at Aboukir in 1798, had a boat restyled as to recall Cleopatra's

barge, while his wife, who was aboard, was wearing a Greek tunic. Emma Lyons, before she married Hamilton, posed for George Romney as Cleopatra, and also as Phryne, the mistress and model of Praxiteles; these paintings were exhibited in London: Solmi (1982): 39 ff.

8. Although Nelson was widely hailed as the hero who defeated Bonaparte's navy at the Battle of the Nile, during his subsequent assignment from the Admiralty to protect the Kingdom of the Two Sicilies he became involved in a *ménage à trois* with the Hamiltons. Visitors to Naples and Palermo such as Lord and Lady Elgin wrote letters home with disapproving gossip about Nelson, and this gossip was eventually published (1799) in the *Times* newspaper without naming Nelson, but clearly referring to him as Marc Antony and Emma as Cleopatra; another private letter cited by Nelson's biographer Edgar Vincent refers to Nelson and Emma as "Antony and Moll Cleopatra." See Edgar Vincent, *Nelson, Love and Fame* (2003): 342–43, 376.

9. B. Zanini Quirini, "Le astuzie di Cleopatra," *Civiltà classica e cristiana* 10 (1989): 71–94.

10. The literary tradition is fully reported by F. Stählin, s.v. "Kleopatra" 20, RE 11.1 (1921): 750–81. Herodotus' use of inversions for his Egyptian ethnography is analyzed by P. Vasunia, *The Gift of the Nile: Hellenizing Egypt from Aeschylus to Alexander* (2001): 92–100.

11. J. Guillaume, "Cleopatra nova Pandora," *Gazette des Beaux-Arts* 80 (1972): 185–94.

12. D. and E. Panofsky, *Pandora's Box*[2] (1962): 55–57, 154–55.

13. *De viris illustribus* 86: Haec tantae libidinis fuit, ut saepe prostiterit, tantae pulchritudinis, ut multi noctem illius morte emerint.

14. See Zanini Quirini (1989).

15. Hughes-Hallett (1990): 259, reports, among other interesting anecdotes, Prosper Enfantin's statement at the eve of the opening of the Suez Canal, in 1833: "We shall carry out the act for which the world is waiting to proclaim that we are male!"

16. A medal commemorating Napoleon's expedition to Egypt in 1798 shows a Roman general unveiling the queen of Egypt (Hughes-Hallett, 1990: 258).

17. E.g., a painting by an unidentified Italian artist, published and discussed in V. Terraroli, "Pioggia di opale e di perle: itinerario iconografico fra temi e invenzioni degli orientalisti italiani," in R. Bossaglia, ed., *Gli orientalisti italiani, Cento anni di esotismo. 1830–1940* (1998): 39 ff.

18. Hughes-Hallett (1990): 268 and pl. 20.

19. Hughes-Hallett (1990): 371.

20. Hughes-Hallett (1990): 258.

21. This incident was inspired to Brontë by a picture by de Biefve that she had seen at the Brussels Salon in 1842: see G. Charlier, *Passages: Essais* (1947): 81–84. Actually, the picture did not represent Cleopatra, but an anonymous Oriental dancer: the two subjects merge in fact in the nineteenth-century imagination.

22. See M. Praz, *La carne, la morte e il diavolo nella letteratura romantica* (1948): esp. 213 ff. and, in general, B. Dijkstra, *Idols of Perversity* (1986).

23. Hughes-Hallett (1990): 269.

24. M. Richardson, "Edmonia Lewis' *The Death of Cleopatra: Myth and Identity*," *The International Review of African American Art* (1995) 2: 36–52.

25. Hughes-Hallett (1990): 253–54.

26. R. Goscinny, *Astérix et Cléopâtre* (Paris 1968), now available in 16 languages.

27. For a different opinion see M. Guarducci, "La 'morte di Cleopatra' nella catacomba della Via Latina," *Atti della Pontificia Accademia Romana di Archeologia*, ser. 3, vol. 37 (1964–65): 259–81. In a wall painting from the House of Joseph II in Pompeii (and in another version in the house Reg. I, insula X.), Olga Elia has recognized Cleopatra surrounded by the doctor, the peasant with the figs, the attendants, and a soldier that arrives too late: "La tradizione della morte di Cleopatra nella pit-

tura pompeiana," *Rendiconti dell'Accademia di Archeologia, Lettere e Belle Arti di Napoli* 30 (1956): 3–7. Her arguments and identifications are not fully convincing.

28. J.-C. Grenier, "Notes isiaques I," *Bollettino dei Musei e Gallerie Pontificie* 9 (1989): 10 ff. The statue is said to have come from Villa Hadriana.

29. F. Sbordone, "La morte di Cleopatra nei medici greci," *Rivista Indo-Greco-Italica* 14 (1930): esp. 14 ff. See also Robert Gurval's essay in this volume.

30. See S. McNally, "Ariadne and Others: Images of Sleep in Greek and Early Roman Art," *Classical Antiquity* 4 (1985): 152–92, and Brian Curran's essay in this volume.

31. For visual representations of passive female sexuality see A.R. Tintner, "The Sleeping Woman: A Victorian Fantasy," *The Pre-Raphaelite Review*[2] (1978): 12–26.

32. See the *Begleitmaterial zur Ausstellung "Aby M. Warburg. Mnemosyne"* edited by M. Koos, W. Pichler, W. Rappl, G. Swoboda (1996): pl. 4. In the same plate Warburg had included a relief with Rhea Silvia awaiting the embrace of the god Mars.

33. An excellent, accurate study of the cinematic Cleopatras is provided by M. Wyke, *Projecting the Past: Ancient Rome, Cinema and History* (1997): 73 ff. See also M. Hamer, *Signs of Cleopatra: History, Politics, Representations* (1993): 104 ff.

34. The movie, directed by F. Roddam and inspired to Margaret George's novel, was actually released in 1999.

Cleopatra

The Sphinx Revisited

Peter Green

I

Octavian trashed her statues, but a handful of coins survive
    to disconcert the romantic. If her nose
had only been shorter, said Pascal—but that profile's alive
    ·With determined character, its avatar Glenn Close

Or, better, Meryl Streep. Anyway, *there's no art*
    To find the mind's construction in the face:
she is what she was and did. Where should we start:
    Perhaps with the tricky question of genes and race.

incest, wealth, privilege, cumulatively compounded
    from three Macedonian centuries, not dilute
but distilled essence, royal arrogance only bounded
    by sun and Nile. So much, too, to refute:

a palimpsest of lies, taking off from the drunken whore
    of Augustan propaganda, all the way down
to De Mille and Elizabeth Taylor. Less is more,
    and in our drab world any head that wore a crown

can't escape myth and tinsel. Yet her sheer power,
    palpable as high voltage, still must take us aback,
rubbish our easy clichés. The last romantic flower
    of Alexandrian decadence? Ask the claque

This poem was originally published in *Arion* 14.1 (2006): 29–34.

of courtiers who fought her and lost. Ask the two men
    reforged by her white-hot ambition, in every scene
believing they called the shots, especially when
    (*also sprach* Antony) they "got into the Queen"—

yet promoting her dreams to the end, less masters than acolytes
    of a not-so-new Isis. Caesar lost his cloak
(and arguably much more) near the Pharos. Those festive nights
    showed Antony up as the hulking glutton and soak

for whom she'd designed her Alexandrian tableau
    on that same river where, with royal élan,
another royal myth, kin maybe, plunged in snow-
    chilled waters, and being, despite all the hype, a man,

caught a bad cold. But sauce for Caesar, smart gander,
    wouldn't do for goose Antony: a more vulgar bait
was right for this vulgar man, whose mimesis of Alexander
    tumbled into the fleshpots, and anyway came too late.

II
Was it all politics, then? Did Shakespeare get it wrong
    taking off from uxorious Plutarch? Did she clutch
at dominance only? No passion in all the wine and song?
    If it be love indeed, tell me how much.

How much, how little? Romantics at least must admit
    that her list of grand passions argues luck above
the norm: two dynastic winners—sex or true grit?
    The world well lost for, or acquired by, love?

For the rest, a blank dance-card. She got sensuous delight
    from literature (persona-freaks don't make
as much of this, I've often thought, as they might):
    which could explain Antony's over-the-top mistake

in removing from Pergamon's libraries every last one
    of their two hundred thousand rolls, as her personal gift:
a lavish literary gesture, guaranteed not only to stun
    the hungriest bookworm, but to leave large numbers of miffed

researchers in Asia. Where, pray, did Octavian find
    all his scurrilous pamphleteers? No sweat, go figure:
writers are always hungry, justice is blind,
    and the Lagids displayed a perennial taste for bigger

ships, statues or scandals. What was her private dream,
    her Ptolemaic hyperbole? *As surely as I*
shall yet dispense justice—justice? so it would seem—
    on Rome's Capital, she declared. To climb the sky

was classic Greek hubris, but Macedon had provided
    a template for godlike ambition. And what was Rome?
An overblown Sparta, a massively lopsided
    barrack-room empire, a seven-hilled myth of home

dreamed up by field-hands and jailbirds, a natural domain
    for the royal justice of Isis. But, tediously, first
there were legions and fleets to be conquered: her glorious reign
    gleamed out of reach still, a bubble. And then the bubble burst.

III
Si modo . . . To go chasing the might-have-beens
    Is labor lost. As Charmian said, she died well:
so many kings in her pedigree—not to mention queens
    with a taste for murder and godhead. Her exotic spell—

whatever feminists claim—*was* rooted in sex,
    but sex as a weapon of power, to make or break
in a high-rolling contest where the charmer's hex
    could ace any royal gambit. To have your political cake

and eat it too has always demanded skills
    beyond most male contenders. Today in our plastic
egalitarian age we forget it's the crown that kills:
    politics start in the ganglia, sex is dynastic—

as by instinct she knew from the egg. But brains and style
    counted for something too. Nine languages spoken,
but not, ironically, Latin, so that good Greek guile
    set the ground-rules for her lovers: that unbroken

diplomatic inheritance, polished, ground, refined
    to a pitiless lens on all man's frailty
by three centuries of the inbred, sceptred mind
    now moving, inexorably, towards entropy.

IV
    Her coins, few and teasing, stop short at the throat:
but what lay below? Lear's dark and sulphurous pit
    might do for Octavian or Hamlet: when the bloat
Antony paddled his fingers in that split

meadow of Aphrodite, the shock-waves brought
    Rome's legions out, and a struggling kingdom down:
the sun and moon she bore were a future fraught
    with bloody peril. The head that wore that crown

would lie uneasy indeed. *Beware the Ides of March*:
    after Caesar, what? An undignified scrambling retreat
To the city *by* Egypt, not *of* it. Her strongest Roman arch
    had proved a rainbow, her passport to the elite

world of Rome's power-brokers was out of date
    with no great hope of renewal, her son at risk.
She shook the dice, threw a Venus. To trust her fate
    to Antony meant long odds. Still, she had the fisc

and all that such treasure could purchase, which gave her an edge
    at the bargaining table. Yet however she might deploy it,
bait her carnal lure with gold, charm, wheedle, or hedge,
    when the time came to deliver, did she really enjoy it?

and if so, why? True achievers seldom distinguish
    between those fierce charges that fuel their upward drive:
all imperatives lead to fulfillment. Who'd relinquish
    ambition for sex when it takes both to stay alive,

much less in control, and doubly so for any
    woman, royal or not? She dared to bet her body
on the succession: in for a twice-spun penny,
    and Caesar at least was no overbred tom-noddy

but a dangerous mindfucker, wits against sharp wits,
    brushed, too, by the sacred disease, who played her game
with style and finesse; quick to throw double or quits
    on one roll of half-loaded dice, no praise, no blame.

V

Her great moment of witty self-devaluation—
    the package delivered in a rolled-up mat—
was a one-shot teenage joke, on a unique occasion
    and designed for a unique man. The joke would fall flat

if ever tried again, not least when loss and age
    had left their mark on Shaw's young skittish kitten
and sharpened her adult claws, tempered her rage
    at all courtiers: never shy, too often bitten.

Yet—how did she look at the first of her epiphanies,
     how much of a Ptolemy, when the dew was still on the rose
and the bud just unfolding? Breakfast at Tiffany's
     or Botticelli? What did Caesar make of the nose—

a family trait, too—or the rest of her? Was she short or tall,
     busty or sinuous? And in the end does it matter?
Sheldon and Kretschmer nod. Oh, Pascal said it all—
     but—*Would the world have changed had she been fatter?*

is a question that gives one pause. The worst mistake?
     To see only the public figure. No persona
stays onstage all twenty-four hours, is on the make
     nonstop. Enigmatic? Oh sure: she beats the Mona

Lisa at that game. Which is why we can't resist
     reinventing her in our own image. But the private face
is lost for ever, lost even the merest gist
     Of all she felt, thought, suffered. Oh, we can trace

policy, spot a hard bargain. But the heart eludes
     our searching: her childish dreams, her taste in wines,
her jokes, her favorite scents, her kitchen feuds,
     the losses that made her cry, portents and signs

that moved her. All we know is the queen,
     take her or leave her. A mystery. What it meant
is your guess or mine, for ever: what might have been
     had Actium gone her way, had she been sent

a luckier consort. In the end we avert our gaze
     from the torn breasts of her grief, after Rome's mighty
power had turned royal Isis, in those last sad days,
     to Auden's weeping anarchic Aphrodite.

BIBLIOGRAPHY

Alberti, L.B. 1998. *On the Art of Building in Ten Books*, ed. J. Rykwert, N. Leach, and R. Tavernor. Cambridge, Mass.

Albertini, Francesco. 1510. *Opusculum de mirabilibus novae et veteris urbis Romae*. Rome.

Aldrovandi, Ulisse. 1557. "Delle statue antiche che per tutta Roma in diversi luoghi, e case si veggono," in L. Mauro, *Le antichità della città di Rome breviussima raccolte da chiunque ne ha scritto*. Venice.

Alexander, W.H. 1944. "*Nunc Tempus Erat*: Horace, *Odes* 1.37.4," *Classical Journal* 39: 231–33.

Alföldi, A. 1954. "Isiskult und Umsturzbewegung im letzten Jahrhundert der römischen Republik," *Schweizerische Münzblätter* 5: 25–31.

Alföldy, G. 1989. "Die Krise des Imperium Romanum und die Religion Roms," *Religion und Gesellschaft in der römischen Kaiserzeit: Kölner Historische Abhandlung* 35: 53–102.

———. 1990. *Der Obelisk auf dem Petersplatz in Rom: Ein historisches Monument der Antike*. Heidelberg.

Allen, J. 1980. "The film viewer as consumer," *Quarterly Review of Film Studies* 5.4: 481–99.

Allen, M.J.B. 1990. "Marsilio Ficino, Hermes Trismegistus and the Corpus Hermeticum," in J. Henry and S. Hutton, eds., *New Perspectives on Renaissance Thought: Essays in the History of Science, Education and Philosophy in Memory of Charles B. Schmitt*. London: 38–47.

Amelung, W. 1903. *Die Sculpturen des Vaticanischen Museums*. 4 volumes. Berlin.

Anderson, G.-N., and J. Wright. 1997. *The Pursuit of Leisure: Victorian Depictions of Pastimes*. London.

Andreae, B., and K. Rhein, eds. 2006. *Kleopatra und die Caesaren*. Munich.

Arnold, D. 1999. *Temples of the Last Pharaohs*. New York and Oxford.

Ash, R. 1990. *Sir Lawrence Alma-Tadema*. New York.

Ashby, T. 1904. *Sixteenth-Century Drawings of Roman Buildings Attributed to Andreas Coner*. London.

Ashton, S.-A. 2000. "The Ptolemaic Influence on Egyptian Royal Sculpture," in A. McDonald and C. Riggs, eds., *Current Research in Egyptology 2000* (*BAR* International Series 909). Oxford: 1–10.

———. 2001. "Identifying the Egyptian-style Ptolemaic Queens," in S. Walker and P. Higgs, eds., *Cleopatra of Egypt: From History to Myth*: 148–55.

———. 2001. *Ptolemaic Royal Sculpture from Egypt: The Interaction between Greek and Egyptian Traditions*. (*BAR* International Series 923). Oxford.

———. 2003. "Cleopatra: Goddess, Ruler or Regent?" in S. Walker and S.-A. Ashton, eds., *Cleopatra Reassessed* (*BM Occasional Paper* 103). London: 25–30.

———. 2003. *The Last Queens of Egypt: Cleopatra's Royal House*. London.

———. 2004. *Roman Egyptomania: A Special Exhibition at the Fitzwilliam Museum, Cambridge, 24 September 2004–8 May, 2005*. London.

———. 2005. "The Use of the Double and Triple Uraeus in Royal Iconography," in A. Cooke and F. Simpson, eds., *Current Research in Egyptology 2000*. Oxford: 1–9.

———. 2008. *Cleopatra and Egypt*. Malden, Mass. and Oxford.

Assmann, J. 1991. *Stein u. Zeit*. Munich.

Auerbach, J. A. 1999. *The Great Exhibition of 1851: A Nation on Display*. New Haven and London.

Austin, M. M. 1981. *The Hellenistic World: Sources in Translation*. Cambridge.

Baade, A. A. 1992. *Melchior Goldast von Haiminsfeld: Collector, Commentator, and Editor*. New York.

Baldwin, B. 1964. "The Death of Cleopatra VII," *Journal of Egyptian Archaeology* 50: 181–82.

Balio, T., ed. 1993. *Grand Design: Hollywood as a Modern Business Enterprise 1930–1939* (*History of the American Cinema* 5). New York. Repr. Berkeley 1995.

Ballistreri, G. 1975. "Capodiferro, Evangelista Maddaleni (Maddalena) de', detto Fausto," *Dizionario biografico degli Italiani*, vol. 18. Rome: 621–25.

Balsdon, J. P. V. D. 1958. "The Ides of March," *Historia* 7: 80–94.

———. 1960. "Review of Volkmann, *Cleopatra*," *Classical Review* 10: 68–71.

Barberi, O. L., G. Parola, and M. P. Toti. 1995. *Le antichità egiziane di Roma imperiale*. Rome.

Barkan, L. 1991. "Rome's Other Population," *Raritan* 1.2: 66–81.

———. 1993. "The Beholder's Tale: Ancient Sculpture, Renaissance Narratives," *Representations* 44: 133–66.

———. 1999. *Unearthing the Past: Archaeology and Aesthetics in the Making of Renaissance Culture*. New Haven.

Barrow, R. J. 1997. "68: *The Women of Amphissa*," in E. Becker et al., eds., *Sir Lawrence Alma-Tadema*. New York: 232–34.

———. 2001. *Lawrence Alma-Tadema*. London.

Barton, C. 1993. *The Sorrows of the Ancient Romans: The Gladiator and the Monster*. Princeton.

Bastéa, E. 2000. *The Creation of Modern Athens: Planning the Myth*. New York.

Baxandall, M. 2003. "Jacopo Sadoleto's Laocoön," in M. Baxandall, *Words for Pictures: Seven Papers on Renaissance Art and Criticism*. New Haven and London: 98–116.

Bayle, P. 1740. *Dictionnaire Historique et Critique*. Amsterdam.

Becher, I. 1966. *Das Bild der Kleopatra in der griechischen und lateinischen Literatur*. Berlin.

Becker, E., E. Morris, E. Prettejohn, and J. Treuherz, eds. 1997. *Sir Lawrence Alma-Tadema*. New York.

Benne, S. 2001. *Marcus Antonius und Kleopatra VII: Machtausbau, herrscherliche Repräsentation und politische Konzeption*. Göttingen.

Benoist-Méchin, J. 1978. *Bonaparte en Égypte, ou le rêve inassouvi 1797–1801*. Paris.

Bentivoglio, E. 1992. "Bramante e il geroglifico di Viterbo," *Mitteilungen des Kunsthistorischen Instituts in Florenz* 16: 167–74.

Berlinerblau, J. 1999. *Heresy in the University: The Black Athena Controversy and the Responsibilities of American Intellectuals*. New Brunswick.

Bernal, M. 1987, 1981. *Black Athena: the Afrocentric Roots of Classical Civilization*. 2 volumes. New Brunswick, N.J.

———. 2001. *Black Athena Writes Back*. Durham and London.

Bernstein, M. 1994. *Walter Wanger: Hollywood Independent*. Berkeley.

Bernstein, M., and G. Studlar, eds. 1997. *Visions of the East: Orientalism in Film*. New Brunswick, N.J.

Bevan, E. 1927. *A History of Egypt under the Ptolemaic Dynasty*. London.

———. 1968. *The House of Ptolemy: A History of Egypt Under the Ptolemaic Dynasty*. Chicago.

Bevington, D., ed. 1997. *The Complete Works of William Shakespeare*.[4] New York.

Bianchi, R. S. 1980. "Not the Isis Knot," *Bulletin of the Egyptological Seminar* 2: 9–31.

———. 1988. "Pharaonic Art in Ptolemaic Egypt," in R. S. Bianchi, R. A. Fazzini, and J. Quaegebeur, eds., *Cleopatra's Egypt: Age of the Ptolemies*. Brooklyn: 55–80.

Bianchi, R. S., R. A. Fazzini, and J. Quaegebeur, eds. 1988. *Cleopatra's Egypt: Age of the Ptolemies*. Brooklyn.

Bicknell, P. J. 1977. "Caesar, Antony, Cleopatra, and Cyprus," *Latomus* 36: 325–42.

Bieber, M. 1961. *The Sculpture of the Hellenistic Age*. New York.

Bizzocchi, R. 1995. *Genealogie incredibili: Scritti di storia nell'Europa moderna*. Bologna.

Black, J. 1992. *The British Abroad: The Grand Tour in the Eighteenth Century*. New York.

Bloedow, E. 1963. *Beiträge zur Geschichte des Ptolemaeus XII*. Würzburg.

Boatwright, M. T. 1987. *Hadrian and the City of Rome*. Princeton.

Bober, P. P. 1977. "The 'Coryciana' and the Nymph Corycia," *Journal of the Warburg and Courtauld Institutes* 40: 223–39.

Bober, P. P., and R. Rubinstein. 1987. *Renaissance Artists and Antique Sculpture: A Handbook of Sources*.[2] London.

Bodeen, D. 1976. *From Hollywood: The Careers of 15 Great American Stars*. South Brunswick and New York.

Borsi, S. 1985. *Giuliano da Sangallo. I disegni di architettura e dell'antico*. Rome.

Bouché-Leclercq, A. 1904. *Histoire des Lagides*. 2 volumes. Paris.

Bowman, A. K. 1996. *Egypt After the Pharaohs, 332 B.C.–A.D. 642*. Berkeley and Los Angeles.

Bowman, A., A. Lintott, and P. Garnsey, eds. 1994. *Cambridge Ancient History*,[2] vol. 10. Cambridge.

Braund, D. 1984. *Rome and the Friendly King*. London.

Brenk, F. E., S.J. 1992. "Antony-Osiris, Cleopatra-Isis. The end of Plutarch's *Antony*," in P. Stadter, ed., *Plutarch and the Historical Tradition*. London and New York: 159–82.

Brett, A. B. 1937. "A New Cleopatra Tetradrachm of Ascalon," *American Journal of Archaeology* 41: 452–63.

Bricault, L., M. J. Versluys, and P. G. P. Meyboom, eds. 2007. *Nile into Tiber: Egypt in the Roman World. Proceedings of the IIIrd International Conference of Isis Studies, Leiden, May 11–14 2005 (Religions in the Greco-Roman World, 159)*. Leiden.

Broughton, T. R. S. 1952. *The Magistrates of the Roman Republic*. 3 volumes. New York.

Brown, D. 1986. "The Apollo Belvedere and the Garden of Giuliano della Rovere at SS. Apostoli," *Journal of the Warburg and Courtauld Institutes* 49: 235–38.

Brown, P. F. 1996. *Venice and Antiquity: The Venetian Sense of the Past*. New Haven and London.

Brummer, H. 1970. *The Statue Court in the Vatican Belvedere*. Stockholm.

———. 1998. "On the Julian Program of the Cortile delle Statue in the Vatican Belvedere," in M. Winner, B. Andreae, and C. Pietrangeli, eds., *Il cortile delle statue: der Statuenhof des Belvedere im Vatikan. Akten des Internationalen Kongresses zu Ehren von Richard Krautheimer, Rom, 21–23 Oktober 1992*. Mainz am Rhein: 67–75.

Bruzzi, S. 1997. *Undressing Cinema: Clothing and Identity in the Movies*. London.

Buchner, E. 1982. *Die Sonnenuhr des Augustus, Nachdruck aus "RM" 1976 und 1980 und Nachtrag über die Ausgrabung 1980/81*. Mainz.

Burel, J. 1911. *Isis et les Isiaques sous l'Empire romain*. Paris.

Burkert, W. 1987. *Ancient Mystery Cults*. Cambridge, Mass. and London.

Burstein, S. M. 1996. "Images of Egypt in Greek Historiography," in A. Loprieno, ed., *Ancient Egyptian Literature: History and Forms*. Leiden: 591–604.

———. 2004. *The Reign of Cleopatra*. Westport, Conn.

Butt, J., ed. 1963. *The Poems of Alexander Pope: A One-Volume Edition of the Twickenham Text with Selected Annotations*. New Haven.

Calvat, R. 1995. "Cléopâtre de Virgile à Mankiewicz: Origine et évolution d'un mythe," *Bulletin de l'Arelam* 32: 43–57.

Calvesi, M. 1980. *Il sogno di Poliphilo prenestino*. Rome.

———. 1996. *La 'pugna d'amore in sogno' di Francesco Colonna Romano*. Rome.

Campbell, S. J. 2005. "Mantegna's Triumph: The Cultural Politics of Imitation 'all'antica' at the Court of Mantua, 1490–1530," in S. J. Campbell, ed., *Artists at Court: Image-Making and Identity 1300–1550*. Boston: 91–105, 216–19.

Canfora, L. 1989. *The Vanished Library*. Berkeley.

Capodiferro, E. M. (called "Fausto"). Before 1527a. Codex Vaticanus Latinus 3351. Biblioteca Apostolica Vaticana.

———. Before 1527b. Codex Vaticanus Latinus 10377. Biblioteca Apostolica Vaticana.

Carcopino, J. 1968. *Jules César*. Paris.

Carettoni, G. 1983. *Das Haus des Augustus auf dem Palatin*. Mainz.

Casson, L. 1971. *Ships and Seamanship in the Ancient World*. Princeton.

Casteras, S. P. 1987. *Images of Victorian Womanhood in English Art*. Rutherford, N.J.

Céard, J., and J.-C. Margolin. 1986. *Rébus de la Renaissance: des images que parlent*. 2 volumes. Paris.

Celenza, C. S. 1999. *Renaissance Humanism and the Papal Curia: Lapo da Castiglionchio the Younger's "De curiae commodes"* (Papers and Monographs of the American Academy in Rome 31). Ann Arbor.

Chaney, E. 1998. *The Evolution of the Grand Tour.* London and Portland.

Charlier, G. 1947. *Passages: Essais.* Brussels.

Chauveau, M. 2000. *Egypt in the Age of Cleopatra: History and Society under the Ptolemies.* Trans. D. Lorton. Ithaca and London.

———. 2002. *Cleopatra: Beyond the Myth.* Trans. D. Lorton. Ithaca and London.

Clarke, G. W., ed. 1989. *Rediscovering Hellenism: The Hellenic Inheritance and the English Imagination.* Cambridge.

Codell, J. F., and D. S. Macleod, eds. 1998. *Orientalism Transposed: The Impact of the Colonies on British Culture.* Brookfield, Vt. and Aldershot.

Collins, A. 1998. "The Etruscans in the Renaissance: The Sacred Destiny of Rome and the 'Historia Viginti Saeculorum' of Giles of Viterbo (c. 1469–1532)," *Studi e materiali di storia delle religione* 65: 337–65.

———. 2000. "Renaissance Epigraphy and Its Legitimating Potential: Annius of Viterbo, Etruscan Inscriptions, and the Origins of Civilization," in A. E. Cooley, ed., *The Afterlife of Inscriptions: Reusing, Rediscovering, Reinventing, and Revitalizing Ancient Inscriptions.* London: 57–76.

Collins, J. H. 1955. "Caesar and the Corruption of Power," *Historia* 4: 445–65.

———. 1959. "On the Date and Interpretation of the *Bellum Civile*," *American Journal of Philology* 80: 113–32.

Colonna, F. 1999. *Hypnerotomachia Poliphili: The Strife of Love in a Dream.* Trans. J. Godwin. London.

Commager, S. 1958. "Horace, *Carmina* 1.37," *Phoenix* 12: 47–57.

Conner, P. 1983. "The British in Egypt," in P. Conner, ed., *The Inspiration of Egypt: Its Influence on British Artists, Travellers, and Designers.* Brighton: 145–50.

———. 1983. "Egypt and the Romantic Imagination," in P. Conner, ed., *The Inspiration of Egypt: Its Influence on British Artists, Travellers, and Designers.* Brighton: 75–82.

———, ed. 1983. *The Inspiration of Egypt: Its Influence on British Artists, Travellers, and Designers.* Brighton.

Conte, G. B. 1994. *Latin Literature: A History.* Trans. J. B. Solodow. Baltimore.

Cooke, A., and F. Simpson, eds. 2005. *Current Research in Egyptology* 2 (*BAR* International Series 1380). Oxford.

Cooke, J. D. 1927. "Euhemerism: A Mediaeval Interpretation of Classical Paganism," *Speculum* 11: 396–410.

Copenhaver, B. P. 1992. *Hermetica: the Greek "Corpus Hermeticum" and the Latin "Asclepius" in a New English Translation with Notes and Introduction.* Cambridge.

Crawford, D. J., J. Quaegebeur, and W. Clarysse, eds. 1980. *Studies on Ptolemaic Memphis* (*Studia Hellenistica* 24). Louvain.

Crawford, M. H. 1974. *Roman Republican Coinage.* 2 volumes. Cambridge.

Crook, J. A., A. Lintott, and E. Rawson, eds. 1994. *Cambridge Ancient History.*[2] vol. 9. Cambridge.

Cumont, F. 1911. *Oriental Religions in Roman Paganism.* Chicago.

Curl, J. S. 1991. *The Art and Architecture of Freemasonry.* London.

————. 1994. *Egyptomania: The Egyptian Revival: A Recurring Theme in the History of Taste.* Manchester and New York.

Curran, B. A. 1996. Rev. of J.-M. Humbert, M. Pantazzi, and C. Zeigler, eds. *Egyptomania: Egypt in Western Art 1730–1930* (Ottawa 1994), *Art Bulletin* 78: 739–44.

————. 1998. "The 'Hypnerotomachia Poliphili' and Renaissance Egyptology," *Word and Image* 14: 156–85.

————. "*De sacrarum litterarum aegyptiorum interpretatione*: Reticence and Hubris in Hieroglyphic Studies of the Renaissance: Pierio Valeriano and Annius of Viterbo," *Memoirs of the American Academy in Rome* 43/44: 139–82.

————. 2004. "The Sphinx in the City: Egyptian Monuments and Urban Spaces in Renaissance Rome," in S.J. Milner and S.J. Campbell, eds., *Artistic Exchange and Cultural Translation in the Italian Renaissance City.* Cambridge: 294–326.

————. 2007. *The Egyptian Renaissance: The Afterlife of Ancient Egypt in Early Modern Italy.* Chicago.

————, et al. 2009. *Obelisk: A History.* Cambridge, Mass.

Curran, B. A., and A. Grafton. 1995. "A Fifteenth-Century Site Report on the Vatican Obelisk," *Journal of the Warburg and Courtauld Institutes* 58: 234–48.

D'Alton, M. 1993. *The New York Obelisk, or How Cleopatra's Needle Came to New York and What Happened When It Got Here.* New York.

D'Onofrio, C. 1992. *Gli obelischi di Roma: Storia e urbanistica di una città dall' età al XX secola.*[3] Rome.

————, ed. 1989. *Visitiamo Roma nel Quattrocento: La città degli Umanisti.* Rome.

Daltrop, G. 1985. "Nascita e significato della raccolta delle statue antiche in Vaticano," in M. Fagiolo, ed., *Roma e l'antico nell'arte e nella cultura del Cinquecento.* Rome: 111–29.

David, R. 2000. *The Experience of Ancient Egypt.* London and New York.

Davidson, C. 1980. "Antony and Cleopatra: Circe, Venus, and the Whore of Babylon," in H.R. Garvin, ed., *Shakespeare: Contemporary Critical Approaches.* London and Toronto: 31–55.

Davis, G. 1990. *Polyhymnia: The Rhetoric of Horatian Lyric Discourse.* Berkeley and Los Angeles.

de Cordova, R. 1990. *Picture Personalities: The Emergence of the Star System in America.* Champaign, Ill.

De Meulenaere, H. 1992. *Ancient Egypt in Nineteenth Century Painting.* Brussels.

De Vos, M. 1980. *L'egittomania in pitture e mosaici Romano-Campani della prima età imperiale (EPRO 84).* Leiden.

Della Corte, M. 1951. *Cleopatra, M. Antonio e Ottaviano nelle allegorie storico-umoristiche delle argenterie del tesoro di Boscoreale (Pompei: rivivi 1).* Pompeii.

Dempsey, C. 1988. "Renaissance Hieroglyphic Studies and Gentile Bellini's 'Saint Mark Preaching in Alexandria,'" in I. Merkel and A.G. Debus, eds., *Hermeticism and the Renaissance: Intellectual History and the Occult in Early Modern Europe.* Washington, D.C.: 342–65.

Denvir, B. 1986. *The Late Victorians: Art, Design and Society, 1852–1910.* London.

Description de l'Egypte. 1809–1829. Paris. Repr. Cologne 1984.

Dijkstra, B. 1986. *Idols of Perversity.* Oxford.

Dils, P. 1998. "La couronne d'Arsinoé II Philadelphe," in W. Clarysse et al., eds., *Egyptian Religion, The Last Thousand Years: Studies Dedicated to the Memory of Jan Quaegebeur* 2 (*OLA* 85). Leuven: 1309–30.

Doane, M. A. 1989. "The Economy of Desire: The Commodity Form in/of the Cinema," *Quarterly Review of Film and Video* 11: 23–33.

Dreyfus, R., and E. Schraudolph, eds. 1996, 1997. *Pergamon: The Telephos Frieze from the Great Altar.* 2 volumes. Austin, Texas.

Dumont, H. 1988. "Chronologie du film historique à l'antique," *CinémAction* 89: 153 ff.

Dunand, F. 1973. *Le culte d'Isis dans le basin oriental de la Méditerranée* (*EPRO* 26). Leiden.

Dundas, G. 1994. "Pharaoh, Basileus and Imperator: The Roman Imperial Cult in Egypt" (diss. Univ. of California, Los Angeles).

Dyer, R. 1986. *Heavenly Bodies: Film Stars and Society.* London.

———. 1998. *Stars.*[2] London.

Dykstra, D. 1998. "The French Occupation of Egypt, 1798–1801," in M. W. Daly, ed. *The Cambridge History of Egypt*, vol. 2. Cambridge: 113–38.

Eckert, C. 1978. "The Carole Lombard in Macy's Window," *Quarterly Review of Film Studies* 3.1: 1–21.

Elia, O. 1956. "La tradizione della morte di Cleopatra nella pittura pompeiana," *Rendiconti dell'Accademia di Archeologia, Lettere e Belle Arti di Napoli* 30: 3–7.

Elsner, J. 1994. "From the Pyramids to Pausanias and Piglet: Monuments, Travel, and Writing," in S. Goldhill and R. Osborne, eds., *Art and Text in Greek Culture.* Cambridge: 224–54.

Emiliozzi, A. 1986. *Il Museo Civico di Viterbo: Storia delle raccolte archeologiche.* Rome.

Empereur, J.-Y. 1998. *Alexandria Rediscovered.* New York.

Erasmus, Desiderius. 1969. *Opera omnia.* Ordinis primi, Tomus primus. Amsterdam.

Everson, W. K. 1976. *Claudette Colbert.* New York.

Falb, R. 1902. *Il taccuino senese di Giuliano da Sangallo.* Siena.

Finzi, C. 1991. "Leon Battista Alberti: Geroglifiche e gloria," in C. M. Govi, S. Curto, and S. Pernigotti, eds., *L'Egitto fuori dell'Egitto: Dalla riscoperta all'Egittologia.* Bologna: 205–8.

Firpo, L. 1993. *Il processo di Giordano Bruno.* Rome.

Flamarion, E. 1997. *Cleopatra, The Life and Death of a Pharaoh.* New York.

Franklin, D. 1994. *Rosso in Italy: The Italian Career of Rosso Fiorentino.* New Haven and London.

Franzero, C. M. 1963. *Cleopatra Queen of Egypt.* London.

Fraser, P. M. 1972. *Ptolemaic Alexandria.* 3 volumes. Oxford.

Frayling, C. 1992. *The Face of Tutankhamun.* London.

Fumagalli, E. 1980. "Aneddoti della vita di Annio da Viterbo, O. P.," *Archivium Fratrum Praedicatorum* 50: 167–99.

Gaines, J. 1989. "The Queen Christina Tie-ups: Convergence of Show Window and Screen," *Quarterly Review of Film and Video* 11: 35–60.

Galliano, G., and M. Gabolde, eds. 2000. *L'exposition Coptos. L'Egypte antique aux portes du désert.* Lyon.

Gauthier, H. 1916. *Le livre des rois d'Égypte: Recueil de titres et protocoles royaux, noms propres de rois, reines, princes, princesses et parents de rois, 4: De la XXVᵉ Dynastie à la fin des Ptolémées (MIFAO 20)*. Cairo.

Gelzer, M. 1968. *Caesar: Politician and Statesman*. Cambridge, Mass.

Genini, R. 1996. *Theda Bara: A Biography of the Silent Screen Vamp*. Jefferson, N.C.

Gesche, H. 1968. *Die Vergottung Caesars*. Kallmünz.

———. 1976. *Caesar*. Darmstadt.

Giehlow, K. 1915. "Die Hieroglyphenkunde des Humanismus in der Allegorie der Renaissance," *Jahrbuch der Kunsthistorisches Sammlungen des Allerhöchsten Kaiserhauses* 32: 1–229.

Gledhill, C., ed. 1991. *Stardom: Industry of Desire*. London.

Goddio, F. 1998. *Alexandria: The Submerged Royal Quarters*. London.

Goldast, Melchior, ed. 1610. *Ovidii Nasonis Pelignensis Erotica et amatoria opuscula: de amoribus, arte, et modis amandi, & qua ratione quis amoris compos fieri debeat . . . : cum altis quibusdam ejusdem argumenti libellu., qui per fucum in Ocidianas inscriptiones transierunt, quorum auctores versa pagina exhibet*. Francoforti: Richerus; Kopffius.

Golden, E. 1996. *Vamp: The Rise and Fall of Theda Bara*. Vestal, N.Y.

Goldsworthy, A. 2010. *Antony and Cleopatra*. New Haven and London.

Golzio, V., ed. 1936. *Raffaello nei documenti, nelle testimonianze dei contemporanei e nella letteratura del suo secolo*. Vatican City.

Gombrich, E. H. 1985. "Hypnerotomachiana," in E. H. Gombrich, *Symbolic Images*³. London: 102–8. Originally printed in the *Journal of the Warburg and Courtauld Institutes* 14 (1951): 119–25.

Gorringe, H. H. 1882. *Egyptian Obelisks*. New York.

Goscinny, R. 1968. *Astérix et Cléopâtre*. Paris.

Grafton, A. 1991. "Invention of Traditions and Traditions of Invention in Renaissance Europe: The Strange Case of Annius of Viterbo," in A. Grafton, *Defenders of the Text: The Traditions of Scholarship in an Age of Science, 1450–1800*. Cambridge, Mass.: 76–103.

———. 1992. "The Renaissance," in R. Jenkyns, ed., *The Legacy of Rome: A New Appraisal*. Oxford: 97–123.

———, ed. 1993. *Rome Reborn: The Vatican Library and Renaissance Culture*. Washington, D.C.

Graindor, P. 1931. *La Guerre d'Alexandrie*. Cairo.

Grant, M. 1972. *Cleopatra: A Biography*. London and New York. Repr. 1995.

Green, P. 1990. *From Alexander to Actium: The Historical Evolution of the Hellenistic Age*. Berkeley.

———. 1991. *Alexander of Macedon*. Berkeley.

———. 2006. "Cleopatra: The Sphinx Revisited," *Arion* 14 (2006): 29–34.

Grenier, J.-C. 1989. "Notes isiaques I," *Bollettino dei Musei e Gallerie Pontificie* 9: 10 ff.

———. 1989. "Traditions pharaoniques et realités impériales: Le nom de couronnement du Pharaon à l'époque romaine," in L. Criscuolo and G. Geraci, eds., *Egitto e storia antica dall'ellenismo all'età araba*. Bologna: 403–20.

Griffin, M. 1986. "Philosophy, Cato, and Roman Suicide: I," *Greece & Rome* 33: 64–77.

Griffiths, J. G. 1961. "The Death of Cleopatra VII," *Journal of Egyptian Archaeology* 47: 113–18.

———. 1965. "The Death of Cleopatra VII: A Rejoinder and a Postscript," *Journal of Egyptian Archaeology* 51: 209–11.

Gross, K. 1993. *The Dream of the Moving Statue.* Ithaca.

Gruen, E. S. 1984. *The Hellenistic World and the Coming of Rome.* Berkeley.

———. 1985. "Augustus and the Ideology of War and Peace," in R. Winkes, ed., *The Age of Augustus.* Providence: 51–72.

———. 2003. "Cleopatra in Rome: Facts and Fantasies," in D. Braund and C. Gill, eds., *Myth, History and Culture in Republican Rome: Studies in Honour of T. P. Wiseman.* Exeter: 257–74.

Guarducci, M. 1964–65. "La 'morte di Cleopatra' nella catacomba della Via Latina," *Atti della Pontificia Accademia Romana di Archeologia,* ser. 3, vol. 37 (1964–65): 259–81.

Guillaume, J. 1972. "Cleopatra nova Pandora," *Gazette des Beaux-Arts* 80: 185–94.

Gurval, R. 1995. *Actium and Augustus: The Politics and Emotions of Civil War.* Ann Arbor.

Gwynne, P. 1996. "'Tu alter Caesar eris': Maximilian I, Vladislav II, Johannes Michael Nagonius, and the 'Renovatio Imperii,'" *Renaissance Studies* 10: 56–71.

Hamer, M. 1993. *Signs of Cleopatra: History, Politics, Representation.* London and New York.

Hanson, A. E., and M. H. Green. 1994. "Soranus of Ephesus: Methodicorum princeps," in W. Haase, ed., *Aufstieg und Niedergang der Römischen Welt* II.37.2. Berlin: 968–1075.

Haselberger, L., ed. 2002. *Mapping Augustan Rome (JRA* Suppl. 50).

Haskell, F., and N. Penny. 1981. *Taste and the Antique: The Lure of Classical Sculpture 1500–1900.* New Haven and London.

Hausmann, F.-R. 1977. "Kaspar Schoppe, Joseph Justus Scaliger und die Carmina Priapeia oder wie man mit Büchern Rufmord betriebt," in K. Elm, E. Gönner, and E. Hillenbrand, eds., *Landesgeschichte und Geistesgeschichte: Festschrift für Otto Herdina zum 65. Geburtstag.* Stuttgart: 382–95.

Havelock, C. 1971. *Hellenistic Art.* London.

Heinen, H. 1966. *Rom und Ägypten von 51 bis 47 v. Chr.* Tübingen.

———. 1969. "Cäsar und Kaisarion," *Historia* 18: 181–203.

———. 2009. *Kleopatra-Studien. Gesammelte Schriften zur ausgehenden Ptolemäerzeit (Xenia* 49). Constance.

Helbig, W. 1963. *Führer durch die öffentlichen Sammlungen klassischer Altertümer in Rome.* 4 volumes. Tübingen.

Herold, J. C. 1962. *Bonaparte in Egypt.* New York.

Hersey, G. L. 1992. *High Renaissance Art in St. Peter's and the Vatican.* Chicago.

Herzog, C. C., and J. M. Gaines. 1991. "'Puffed Sleeves before Tea-Time': Joan Crawford, Adrian and Women Audiences," in C. Gledhill, ed., *Stardom: Industry of Desire.* London: 74–91.

Higashi, S. 1978. *Virgins, Vamps, and Flappers: The American Silent Movie Heroine.* Montreal.

———. 1994. *Cecil B. DeMille and American Culture: The Silent Era.* Berkeley.

Hirsch, F. 1973. *Elizabeth Taylor.* New York.

Hölbl, G. 2001. *A History of the Ptolemaic Empire*. London.

Hollander, J., ed. 1994. *The Gazer's Spirit: Poems Speaking to Silent Works of Art*. Chicago.

Hollingsworth, M. 1994. *Patronage in Renaissance Italy: From 1400 to the Early Sixteenth Century*. London.

Homans, M. 1998. *Royal Representations: Queen Victoria and British Culture, 1837–1876*. Chicago.

Horsfall, N. M. 1990. "Dido in the Light of History," in S. J. Harrison, ed., *Oxford Readings in Vergil's Aeneid*. Oxford: 127–44.

Hughes-Hallett, L. 1990. *Cleopatra: Histories, Dreams and Distortions*. New York and London.

Hülsen, C. 1910. *Il Libro di Giuliano da Sangallo. Codice Vaticano Barberiniano Latina 4424*. 2 volumes. Leipzig.

Humbert, J.-M. 1994. "333: An Egyptian Widow," in J.-M. Humbert, M. Pantazzi, and C. Zeigler, eds., *Egyptomania: Egypt in Western Art 1730–1930*. Ottawa: 488–90.

———. 994. "Alethe, Priestess of Isis," in J.-M. Humbert, M. Pantazzi, and C. Zeigler, eds., *Egyptomania: Egypt in Western Art 1730–1930*. Ottawa: 493.

Humbert, J.-M., M. Pantazzi, and C. Zeigler, eds. 1994. *Egyptomania: Egypt in Western Art 1730–1930*. Ottawa.

Hutton, J. 1935. *The Greek Anthology in Italy to the Year 1800*. Ithaca.

Iversen, E. 1961. *The Myth of Egypt and Its Hieroglyphs in European Tradition*. Copenhagen. Repr. Princeton 1993.

———. 1968. *Obelisks in Exile*, vol. 1: *The Obelisks of Rome*. Copenhagen.

Jacks, P. 1993. *The Antiquarian and the Myth of Antiquity: The Origins of Rome in Renaissance Thought*. Cambridge.

Jasanoff, M. 2005. *Edge of Empire: Lives, Culture, and Conquest in the East, 1750–1850*. New York.

Jenkins, I., and K. Sloan. 1996. *Vases and Volcanoes: Sir William Hamilton and His Collection*. London.

Jenkyns, R. 1989. "Hellenism in Victorian Painting," in G. W. Clarke, ed., *Rediscovering Hellenism: The Hellenic Inheritance and the English Imagination*. Cambridge: 83–119.

Jex-Blake, K. 1896. *The Elder Pliny's Chapters on Art*, Chicago. Repr. 1968.

Jones, P. J. 2010. "Cleopatra's Cocktail," *Classical World* 103: 207–20.

Junker, H. 1940. *Die Götterlehre von Memphis: Schabaka-Inschrift (Abhandlungen der Preussischen Akademie der Wissenschaften 1939, philosophisch-historische Klasse 23)*. Berlin.

Kampen, N. 1996. "Omphale and the Instability of Gender," in N. B. Kampen, ed., *Sexuality in Ancient Art*. Cambridge: 233–46.

———. 1996. *Sexuality in Ancient Art*. Cambridge.

Kater-Sibbes, G. J. F., and M. J. Vermaseren. 1975. *Apis (EPRO 48)*. Leiden.

Kienast, D. 1969. "Augustus und Alexander," *Gymnasium* 76: 430–56.

Kinman, B. 1999. "Parousia, Jesus' 'A-Triumphal' Entry, and the Fate of Jerusalem (Luke 19:28–44)," *Journal of Biblical Literature* 118: 279–94.

Klaczko, J. 1903. *Rome and the Renaissance*. New York.

Kleiner, D. E. E. 2005. *Cleopatra and Rome*. Cambridge, Mass.

Koenen, L. 1993. "The Ptolemaic King as a Religious Figure," in A. Bulloch et al., eds., *Images and Ideologies: Self-Definition in the Hellenistic World. Papers Presented at a Conference Held April 7–9, 1988, at the University of California at Berkeley.* Berkeley.

Kolve, V. A. 1981. "From Cleopatra to Alceste: An Iconographic Study of the *Legend of Good Women*," in J. P. Hermann and J. J. Burke, Jr., eds., *Signs and Symbols in Chaucer's Poetry.* University, Ala.: 130–78.

Koortbojian, M. 2000. "Pliny's Laocoön?" in A. Payne, A. Kuttner, and R. Smick, eds., *Antiquity and Its Interpreters.* Cambridge: 199–216.

Koos, M., W. Pichler, W. Rappl, and G. Swoboda. 1996. *Begleitmaterial zur Ausstellung "Aby M. Warburg. Mnemosyne."* Hamburg.

Koshikawa, M., and M. J. McClintock, eds. 1993. *High Renaissance in the Vatican: The Age of Julius II and Leo X.* 2 volumes. Tokyo.

Kurz, O. 1953. "Huius Nympha Loci," *Journal of the Warburg and Courtauld Institutes* 16: 171–77.

La Riche, W. 1996. *Alexandria: The Sunken City.* London.

Laelius Podager, Antonio [Lellio]. Laelius Podager, personal copy of Jacopo Mazzocchi, *Epigrammata antiquae urbis.* Rome, 1521. Codex Vaticanus Latinus 8492, Biblioteca Apostolica Vaticana.

Lanciani, R. 1984–2002. *Storia degli scavi di Roma e notizie intorno le collezione romane di antichità*². 6 volumes. Rome.

———. 1897. *The Ruins and Excavations of Ancient Rome.* Boston and New York.

Land, N. E. 1994. *The Viewer as Poet: The Renaissance Response to Art.* University Park, Penn.

Lant, A. 1992. "The Curse of the Pharaoh, or How Cinema Contracted Egyptomania," *October* 59: 109–10.

Lefkowitz, M. R. 1996. *Not Out of Africa: How Afrocentrism Became an Excuse to Teach Myth as History.* New York.

Lefkowitz, M. R., and M. Fant. 1992. *Women's Life in Greece and Rome.*² Baltimore.

Lefkowitz, M. R., and G. M. Rogers, eds. 1996. *Black Athena Revisited.* Chapel Hill and London.

Lembke, K. 1994. *Das Iseum Campense in Rom: Studie über den Isiskult unter Domitian.* Heidelberg.

Lepsius, C. R. (1949–59). *Denkmaeler aus Aegypten und Aethiopien nach den Zeichnungen der von seiner Majestät dem koenige von Preußen Friedrich Wilhelm IV nach diesen Ländern gesendeten und in den Jahren 1842–1845 ausgefuehrten wissenschaftlichen Expedition.* 5 volumes. Berlin.

Levi, M. A. 1954. "Cleopatra e l'aspide," *Parola del Passato* 37: 293–95.

Ligorio, Pirro. Before 1583. *Libro XIIII delle Antichità di Roma di Pyrro Ligorio Pittore, il qual tratta degli obellischi et varie cose degli Egitti,* Ms. Canonici italian 138, Bodleian Library, Oxford.

Lindsay, J. 1971. *Cleopatra.* New York.

Llewellyn, B. 1983. "The Victorian Vision of Egypt," in P. Conner, ed., *The Inspiration of Egypt: Its Influence on British Artists, Travellers, and Designers.* Brighton: 115–19.

Lowenthal, D. 1998. *The Heritage Crusade and the Spoils of History.* Cambridge.

Lowrie, M. 1997. *Horace's Narrative Odes*. Oxford.

Luzio, A. 1886. "Federico Gonzaga, ostaggio alla corte di Giulio II," *Archivio della Reale Società Romana di Storia Patria* 9: 510–82.

MacDonald, W., and J. Pinto. 1995. *Hadrian's Villa and Its Legacy*. New Haven.

MacDougall, E. 1975. "The Sleeping Nymph: Origins of a Humanist Fountain Type," *Art Bulletin* 57: 357–65.

MacKenzie, J. M. 1995. *Orientalism: History, Theory, and the Arts*. Manchester.

Maffei, S. 1999. "La fama di Laocoonte nei testi del Cinquecento," in S. Settis, ed., *Laocoonte, fama e stile, con un apparato documentario a cura di Sonia Maffei su La fama di Laocoonte nei testi del Cinquecento*. Rome: 85–230.

Magill, F. N., ed. 1982. *Magill's Survey of Cinema: Silent Films*. 3 volumes. New Jersey.

Maltby, R. 1993. "The Production Code and the Hays Office," in T. Balio, ed., *Grand Design: Hollywood as a Modern Business Enterprise 1930–1939* (*History of the American Cinema* 5). New York. Repr. Berkeley 1995: 37–72.

Mann, T. 1936. *Freud und die Zukunft*. Vienna.

———. 1999. *Nobiltà dello spirito e altri saggi Milano*. Trans. A. Landolfi. Milan.

Manning, J. G. 2010. *The Last Pharaohs: Egypt Under the Ptolemies, 305–30 B.C.* Princeton and Oxford.

Marasco, G. 1995. "Cleopatra e gli esperimenti su cavie umane," *Historia* 44: 317–25.

Martin, L. 1987. *Hellenistic Religions*. Oxford.

Martindale, A. 1979. *The Triumphs of Caesar by Andrea Mantegna in the Collection of Her Majesty the Queen at Hampton Court*. London.

Mattiangeli, P. 1981. "Annio de Viterbo inspiratore di cicli pittorici," in G. Baffioni and P. Mattiangeli, eds., *Annio da Viterbo: Documenti e ricerche* 1. Rome: 257–303.

Maystre, C. 1992. *Les grands prêtres de Ptah de Memphis*. Freiburg, Switzerland.

McCahill, E. 2005. "Humanism in the Theater of Lies: Classical Scholarship in the Early Quattrocento Curia" (diss. Princeton University).

McKenzie, J. 2007. *The Architecture of Alexandria and Egypt, c. 300 B.C. to A.D. 700*. New Haven.

McNally, S. 1985. "Ariadne and Others: Images of Sleep in Greek and Early Roman Art," *Classical Antiquity* 4: 152–92.

Meedendorp, T., and L. Pijl. 1997. "8: An Egyptian Game," in E. Becker et al., eds., *Sir Lawrence Alma-Tadema*. New York: 140.

———. 1997. "27: An Egyptian Widow in the Time of Diocletian," in E. Becker et al., eds., *Sir Lawrence Alma-Tadema*. New York: 170–72.

———. 1997. "28: The Death of the Firstborn," in E. Becker et al., eds., *Sir Lawrence Alma-Tadema*. New York: 172–73.

———. 1997. "Alma Tadema's Artistic Training: Critics on the Continent 1852–1870," in E. Becker et al., eds., *Sir Lawrence Alma-Tadema*. New York: 21–32.

Meier, C. 1982. *Caesar, A Biography*. Trans. D. McLintock. New York.

———. 1995. *Caesar*. London.

Meiggs, R., and D. M. Lewis, eds. 1989. *Greek Historical Inscriptions*[2]. Oxford.

Merrian, A. C. 1883. *The Greek and Latin Inscriptions on the Obelisk-Crab in the Metropolitan Museum, New York*. New York.

Meskell, L. 1998. "Consuming Bodies: Cultural Fantasies of Ancient Egypt," *Body and Society* 4.1: 64–67.

Meyboom, P. G. P. 1995. *The Nile Mosaic of Palestrina: Early Evidence of Egyptian Religion in Italy (EPRO 121)*. Leiden.

Meyer, E. 1922. *Caesars Monarchie und das Principat des Pompeius*. Stuttgart.

Michaelis, A. 1890. "Geschichte des Statuenhofes im Vaticanischen Belvedere," *Jahrbuch des Kaiserlich Deutschen archäologischen Instituts* 5: 5–72.

Milanesi, G. G., ed. 1906. *Le opere di Giorgio Vasari*. 9 volumes. Florence. Repr. 1981.

Mond, R., and O. H. Meyers. 1934. *The Bucheum*. 2 volumes. London.

Montserrat, D. 2000. *Akhenaten: History, Fantasy, and Ancient Egypt*. London.

Müntz, E. 1886. *Les antiquitès de la ville de Rome aux XIVe, Xve, et XVIe siècles*. Paris.

Murray, P. 1962. "'Bramante milanese': the Printings and Engravings," *Arte Lombarda* 7: 25–42.

Nagy, G. 1998. "The Library of Pergamon," in H. Koester, ed., *Pergamon: Citadel of the Gods (Harvard Theological Studies* 46): 185–232.

Nanni, G. (Annius of Viterbo). 1498. *Commentaria Fratris Ioannis Annii Viterbensis ordinis praedicator, theologiae professoris super opera diversorum auctorum de Antiquitatibus loquentorum*. Rome.

———. 1550. *I cinque libri de la antichità de Beroso . . . con lo commento di Giovanni Annio da Viterbo*. Trans. P. Lauro. Venice.

———. 1552. *Berosi sacerdotis chaldaici, antiquitatum Italiae ac totius orbis libri Commentariis Joannis Annii Viterbensis . . . .* 2 volumes. Antwerp.

Nesselrath, A. 1998. "Il Cortile delle Statue: luogo e storia," in M. Winner, B. Andreae, and C. Pietrangeli, eds., *Il cortile delle statue: der Statuenhof des Belvedere im Vatikan. Akten des Internationalen Kongresses zu Ehren von Richard Krautheimer, Rom, 21–23 Oktober 1992*. Mainz am Rhein: 1–16.

O'Malley, J. W. 1968. *Giles of Viterbo on Church and Reform*. Leiden.

———. 1969. "Fulfillment of the Golden Age under Pope Julius II: Text of a Discourse of Giles of Viterbo," *Traditio* 25: 265–338.

Olshausen, E. 1963. *Rom und Aegypten von 116 bis 51 v. Chr*. Erlangen.

Onians, J. 1979. *Art and Thought in the Hellenistic Age*. London.

Osborne, J. 2006. "St. Peter's Needle and the Ashes of Julius Caesar," in M. Wyke, ed., *Julius Caesar in Western Culture*. Oxford: 95–109.

Osburn, W. 1854. *The Monumental History of Egypt as Recorded on the Ruins of her Temples, Palaces and Tombs*. London.

Panofsky, D., and E. Panofsky. 1962. *Pandora's Box*.[2] New York.

Parish, J. R. 1971. *The Fox Girls*. New Rochelle.

———. 1976. *The Paramount Pretties*. New Rochelle.

Parker, H. N. 1997. "The Teratogenic Grid," in J. P. Hallett and M. B. Skinner, eds., *Roman Sexualities*. Princeton: 47–65.

———. 1997. "Women Doctors in Greece, Rome, and the Byzantine Empire," in L. R. Furst, ed., *Women Healers and Physicians: Climbing a Long Hill*. Lexington, Ky.: 131–50.

———. Forthcoming. *Metrodora: The Gynecology. The Earliest Surviving Work by a Woman Doctor and Other Works from the Florentine Manuscript*.

Parker, H. T. 1965. *The Cult of Antiquity and the French Revolutionaries: A Study in the Development of the Revolutionary Spirit*. New York.

Parks, N. R. 1979. "On the Meaning of Pinturicchio's Sala dei Santi," *Art History* 2: 291–317.

Parsons, E. A. 1952. *The Alexandrian Library*. Amsterdam.

Partridge, L. 1996. *The Art of Renaissance Rome, 1400–1600*. New York.

Partridge, L., and R. Starn. 1980. *A Renaissance Likeness: Art and Culture in Raphael's Julius II*. Berkeley and Los Angeles.

Pastor, Ludwig von. 1891–1928. *The History of the Popes from the Close of the Middle Ages* 1–16. Trans. F. I. Antrobus, R. F. Kerr, et al. London.

Peek, C. M. 2000. "She, Like a Good King: A Reconstruction of the Career of Kleopatra VII" (diss. Univ. of California, Berkeley).

———. 2008. "The Expulsion of Cleopatra VII: Context, Causes, and Chronology," *Ancient Society* 38: 103–35.

Pelling, C. B. R. 1988. *Plutarch, Life of Antony*. Cambridge.

Perkins, D., ed. 1967. *English Romantic Writers*. New York.

Perosa, A., and J. Sparrow, eds. 1979. *Renaissance Latin Verse: An Anthology*. Chapel Hill.

Pfister, F. 1909–12, 1974. *Der Reliquienkult im Altertum (RGVV 5)*. Repr. Berlin 1974.

Phillips, J., and P. Phillips. 1978. *Victorians at Home and Away*. London.

Picard-Schmitter, M.-Th. 1971. "Bétyles Hellenistiques," *Fondation Eugène Piot Monuments et Mémoires* 57: 43–88.

Pigler, A. 1974. *Barockthemen. Eine Auswahl von Verzeichnissen zur Ikonographie des 17. und 18. Jahrhunderts*. 2 volumes. Budapest.

Plass, P. 1995. *The Game of Death in Ancient Rome: Arena Sport and Political Suicide*. Madison, Wisc.

Poeschel, S. 1989. "Age Itaque Alexander: Das Appartamento Borgia und die Erwartungen an Alexander VI," *Römische Jahrbuch der Bibliotheca Hertziana* 25: 129–65.

———. 1999. *Alexander Maximus: Das Bildprogramm des Appartamento Borgia im Vatikan*. Weimar.

Pohlman, U. 1997. "Alma-Tadema and Photography," in E. Becker et al., eds., *Sir Lawrence Alma-Tadema*. New York: 111–27.

Pollitt, J. J. 1986. *Art in the Hellenistic Age*. Cambridge.

———. 1990. *The Art of Ancient Greece, Sources and Documents*. Cambridge.

———. 1990. *The Art of Rome, c. 753 B.C.–A.D. 337, Sources and Documents*.[2] Cambridge.

Pomeroy, J. 1998. "Forging a Career in the Sixteenth Century: Lavinia Fontana of Bologna," *Women in the Arts* 16: 4–8.

Pomeroy, S. 1990. *Women in Hellenistic Egypt*. Detroit.

———. 1997. *Families in Classical and Hellenistic Greece: Representations and Realities*. Oxford.

Pope, M. 1999. *The Story of Decipherment from Egyptian Hieroglyphs to Maya Script*.[2] London.

Porter, B., and R. L. B. Moss. 1927. *A Topographical Bibliography*. 7 volumes. Oxford.

Powell, A. 1992. *Roman Poetry and Propaganda in the Age of Augustus*. London.

Praz, M. 1948. *La carne, la morte e il diavolo nella letteratura romantica*. Florence.

Premble, J. 1987. *The Mediterranean Passion: Victorians and Edwardians in the South*. Oxford.

Prettejohn, E. 1997. "13: *Phidias Showing the Frieze of the Parthenon to His Friends*," in E. Becker et al., eds., *Sir Lawrence Alma-Tadema*. New York: 144–49.

Quaegebeur, J. 1988. "Cleopatra VII and the Cults of the Ptolemaic Queens," in R. S. Bianchi, A. Fazzini, and J. Quagebeur, eds., *Cleopatra's Egypt: Age of the Ptolemies*. Brooklyn: 41–54.

Quenemoen, C. K. 2006. "The Portico of the Danaids: A New Reconstruction," *AJA* 110: 229–50.

Rachewiltz, B. de, and A. M. Partini. 1999. *Roma Egizia. Culti, templi e divinità egizie nella Roma Imperiale*. Rome.

Rausch, M., ed. 1998. *La gloire d'Alexandrie (7 mai-26 juillet 1998)*. Paris.

Rawson, E. 1994 "Caesar: Civil War and Dictatorship," in J. A. Crook, A. Lintott, and E. Rawson, eds. *Cambridge Ancient History*,[2] vol. 9. Cambridge: 424–67.

Reeves, M. 1992. "Cardinal Egidio of Viterbo: A Prophetic Interpretation of History," in M. Reeves, ed., *Prophetic Rome in the High Renaissance Period*. Oxford: 91–109.

Reid, D. M. 2002. *Whose Pharaohs? Archaeology, Museums, and Egyptian National Identity from Napoleon to World War I*. Berkeley and Los Angeles.

Renfrew, C. 2000. *Loot, Legitimacy and Ownership: The Ethical Crisis in Archaeology*. London.

Reymond, E. A. E. 1983. "Demotic Literary Works of Graeco-Roman Date in the Rainer Collection of Papyri in Vienna," in *Papyrus Erzherzog Rainer (P. Rainer Cent.). Festschrift zum 100-jährigen Bestehen der Papyrussammlung der Österreichischen Nationalbibliothek*. Vienna: 42–60.

RGVV = Religionsgeschichtliche Versuche und Vorarbeiten

Richard, C. J. 1994. *The Founders and the Classics*. Cambridge, Mass.

Richardson, M. 1995. "Edmonia Lewis' *The Death of Cleopatra*: Myth and Identity," *The International Review of African American Art* 2: 36–52.

Richlin, A. 1983. *The Garden of Priapus: Sexuality and Aggression in Roman Humor*. New Haven and London.

Ridley, M. R., ed. 1991. *The Arden Edition of the Works of William Shakespeare: Antony and Cleopatra*. London.

Ritschard, C., A. Morehead, M. Bal, and B. Baumgärtel. 2004. *Cléopâtre dans le miroir de l'art occidental*. Milan.

Robins, G. 1996. *Women in Ancient Egypt*. London.

Roehrig, C. H., ed. 2005. *Hatshepsut: From Queen to Pharaoh*. New Haven and London.

Roller, D. W. 2010. *Cleopatra, A Biography*. Oxford.

Rotter, A. J., K. E Fleming, and K. Biddick. 2000. "Review Essays: Orientalism Twenty Years On," *American Historical Review* 105: 1204–49.

Roullet, A. 1972. *The Egyptian and Egyptianizing Monuments of Imperial Rome*. Leiden.

Rowland, I. D. 1998. *The Culture of the High Renaissance: Ancients and Moderns in Sixteenth-Century Rome*. Cambridge.

Rowlandson, J. 1998. *Women in Society in Greek and Roman Egypt: A Sourcebook*. Cambridge.

Russmann, E. R. 1974. *The Representation of the King in the XXVth Dynasty*. New York.

Said, E. W. 1978. *Orientalism: Western Concepts of the Orient*. New York.

———. 1994. *Culture and Imperialism*. New York.

Saladino, V. 1998. "Centauri *restrictis ad terga manibus*: un'ipotesi sul Torso Gaddi," in G. Capecchi, O. Paoletti, A.M. Esposito, and A. Romualdi, eds., *In memoria di Enrico Paribeni.* Rome: 379–95.

Sandys, J. E. 1908. *A History of Classical Scholarship.* Cambridge.

Saslow, J. M. 1991. *The Poetry of Michelangelo.* New Haven and London.

Saxl, F. 1957. "The Appartamento Borgia," in F. Saxl, *Lectures* 1. London: 174–88.

Sbordone, F. 1930. "La morte di Cleopatra nei medici greci," *Rivista Indo-Greco-Italica* 14:14ff.

Schiff, S. 2010. *Cleopatra, A Life.* New York.

Schom, A. 1997. *Napoleon Bonaparte.* New York.

Schoppe, G. 1606. *Priapeia Sive Diversorum Poetarum In Priapum Lusus / illustrati Commentariis Gasperis Schoppii Franci, L. Apuleii Madaurensis Anechomenos / ab eodem [Gaspere Schoppio] illustratus. Heraclii Imperatoris, Sophoclis Sophistae, C. Antonii, Q. Sorani, & Cleopatrae Reginae Epistolae, De propudiosa Cleopatrae Reginae libidine. Francoforti, In Officina Typographica Wolffgangi Richteri, Sumptibus Conradi Nebenii.*

———. 1607. *Gasp. Scioppii Scaliger Hypobolimaevs, hoc est: Elenchvs epistolae Iosephi Bvrdonis Psevdoscaligeri De vetustate et splendore gentis Scaligerae.* Mainz.

Schrapel, T. 1996. *Das Reich der Kleopatra.* Trier.

Schütz, M. 1990. "Zur Sonnenuhr des Augustus auf dem Marsfeld," *Gymnasium* 97: 432–57.

Seznec, J. 1953. *The Survival of the Pagan Gods: The Mythological Tradition and Its Place in Renaissance Humanism and Art.* New York.

Shaw, C. 1993. *Julius II: The Warrior Pope.* Oxford.

Shohat, E. 1991. "Gender and Culture of Empire: Toward a Feminist Ethnography of the Cinema," *Quarterly Review of Film & Video* 13: 45–84.

Skeat, T. C. 1953. "The Last Days of Cleopatra: A Chronological Problem," *Journal of Roman Studies* 43: 98–100.

Smelik, K. A. D., and E. A. Hemelrijk. 1987. "Who knows not what monsters demented Egypt worships? Opinions on Egyptian animal worship in Antiquity as part of the ancient conception of Egypt," *ANRW* II 17.4. Berlin and New York: 1852–2000.

Smith, R. R. R. 1988. *Hellenistic Royal Portraits.* Oxford.

Sobchack, V. 1990. "'Surge and Splendor': A Phenomenology of the Hollywood Historical Epic," *Representations* 29: 35–36.

Solmi, A. 1982. *Lady Hamilton.* Milan.

Solomon, J. 2001. *The Ancient World in the Cinema.*[2] New Haven and London.

Southern, P. 1999. *Cleopatra.* Stroud.

Spach, I., ed. 1597. *Gynaeciorum sive de mulierum tum communibus, tum gravidarum, parientium, et puerperarum Affectibus & Morbis, libri Graecorum, Arabum, Latinorum veterum et recentium quotquot extant, partim nunc primum editi, partim vero denuo recogniti, emendati, necessarijs Imaginibus exornati, & optimorum Scriptorum autoritatibus illustrati, Opera & studio Israelis Spachii . . . Autorum catalogum post praefationem inuenire licet. Additi sunt etiam Indices Capitum, Rerum ac Verborum in his memorabilium locupletissimi & fidelissimi.* Regensburg.

Spiegelberg, W. 1925. "Weshalb wählte Kleopatra den Tod durch Schlangenbiss?" *Ägyptologische Mitteilungen*. Munich: 1–6.

Stacey, J. 1994. *Star Gazing: Hollywood Cinema and Female Spectatorship*. London.

Staiger, J. 1995. *Bad Women: Regulating Sexuality in Early American Cinema*. Minneapolis.

Stark, G., and E. C. Rayne. 1998. *El Delirio: The Santa Fe World of Elizabeth White*. Santa Fe.

Starkey, P., and J. Starkey, eds. 2001. *Travellers in Egypt*. London and New York.

Stephens, W. 1979. "Berosus Chaldaeus: Counterfeit and Fictive Editors of the Early Sixteenth Century" (diss. Cornell University).

———. 1989. *Giants in Those Days: Folklore, Ancient History, and Nationalism*. Lincoln, Nebr.

Stewart, A. 1993. *Faces of Power: Alexander's Image and Hellenistic Politics*. Berkeley.

Stinger, C. L. 1998. *The Renaissance in Rome.*[2] Bloomington.

Strathern, P. 2007. *Napoleon in Egypt*. New York.

Studlar, G. 1997. "'Out-Salomeing Salome': Dance, the New Woman, and Fan Magazine Orientalism," in M. Bernstein and G. Studlar, eds., *Visions of the East: Orientalism in Film*. New Brunswick, N.J.: 99–129.

Swanson, V. G. 1977. *Alma-Tadema: The Painter of the Victorian Vision of the Ancient World*. New York.

———. 1990. *The Biography and Catalogue Raisonné of the Paintings of Sir Lawrence Alma-Tadema*. London.

Takács, S. 1995. *Isis and Sarapis in the Roman World* (*RGRW* 124). Leiden and New York.

Taylor, B. 1977. "The Medieval Cleopatra: The Classical and Medieval Tradition of Chaucer's Legend of Cleopatra," *Journal of Medieval and Renaissance Studies* 7: 249–69.

Taylor, L. R. 1931. *The Divinity of the Roman Emperor*. Middletown, Conn.

Temple, N. 2006. "Julius II as Second Caesar," in M. Wyke, ed., *Julius Caesar in Western Culture*. Oxford: 110–27.

Terraroli, V. 1998. "Pioggia di opale e di perle: itinerario iconografico fra temi e invenzioni degli orientalisti italiani," in R. Bossaglia, ed., *Gli orientalisti italiani, Cento anni di esotismo. 1830–1940*. Venice: 39 ff.

Thiersch, H. 1909. *Pharos, Antike Islam und Occident*. Leipzig and Berlin.

Thomas, R. 2000. *Herodotus in Context: Ethnography, Science and the Art of Persuasion*. Cambridge.

Thompson, D. 1988. *Memphis under the Ptolemies*. Princeton.

———. 1990. "The High Priests of Memphis under Ptolemaic Rule," in M. Beard and J. North, eds., *Pagan Priests*. Ithaca: 97–116.

Thornton, A. 1998. "Vergil, The Augustans, and the Invention of Cleopatra's Suicide—One Asp or Two?" *Vergilius* 44: 31–50.

Tigerstedt, E. N. 1964. "Ioannes Annius and Graecia Mendax," in C. Henderson, ed., *Classical, Mediaeval, and Renaissance Studies in Honor of Berthold Louis Ullman* 2. Rome: 293–310.

Tintner, A. R. 1978. "The Sleeping Woman: a Victorian Phantasy," *The Pre-Raphaelite Review* 2: 12–26.

Tommasini, O. 1893. "Evangelista Maddaleni de' Capodiferro accademico . . . e storico,"

Atti della Regia Accademia dei Lincei, serie IV: Scienze morali storiche e filologiche 10: 3–20.

Traunecker, C. 1992. *Coptos, Hommes et Dieux sur le Parvis de Geb* (OLA 43). Leuven.

Troy, L. 1988. *Patterns of Queenship in Ancient Egyptian Myth and History* (Uppsala Studies in Ancient Mediterranean and Near Eastern Civilisations 14). Uppsala.

Truman, C. 1982. *The Sèvres Egyptian Service, 1810–12*. Kent.

Tyldesley, J. 1995. *Daughters of Isis: Women in Ancient Egypt*. Harmondsworth.

Urbini, S. 1993. "Il mito di Cleopatra. Motivi ed esiti della sua rinnovata fortuna fra Rinascimento e Barocco," *Xenia Antiqua* 2: 181–222.

van Essen, C. C. 1955. "La decouverte du Laocoön," *Mededelingen der Koninklijke Nederlandse Akademie van Wetenschappen* 18, no. 12: 291–308.

van Minnen, P. 2000. "An Official Act of Cleopatra (with a Subscription in Her Own Hand)," *Ancient Society* 30: 29–34.

———. 2003. "A Royal Ordinance of Cleopatra and Related Documents," in S. Walker and S.-A. Ashton, eds., *Cleopatra Reassessed*. London: 35–44.

Vance, N. 1997. *The Victorians and Ancient Rome*. Oxford.

Vandier, J. 1958. *Manuel d'archéologie égyptienne 3: Les grandes époques, la statuaire.* Paris.

Vasunia, P. 2001. *The Gift of the Nile: Hellenizing Egypt from Aeschylus to Alexander.* Berkeley and Los Angeles.

Vercoutter, J. 1962. *Textes Biographiques du Sérapéum de Memphis*. Paris.

Versluys, M. J. 2002. *Aegyptiaca Romana: Nilotic Scenes and the Roman Views of Egypt.* Leiden.

Vidman, L. 1969. *Sylloge inscriptionum religionis Isiacae et Sarapiacae* (RGVV 28). Berlin.

Vincent, E. 2003. *Nelson, Love and Fame*. New Haven.

Volkmann, H. 1958. *Cleopatra: A Study in Politics and Propaganda*. Trans. T. J. Cadoux. London.

von Moos, S. 1978. "The Palace as a Fortress: Rome and Bologna under Julius II," in H. A. Millon and L. Nochlin, eds., *Art and Architecture in the Service of Politics*. Cambridge, Mass.: 46–79.

Walbank, W. 1981. *The Hellenistic World*. Sussex and Atlantic Highland, N.J.

Walker, A. 1966. *The Celluloid Sacrifice: Aspects of Sex in the Movies*. London.

———. 1990. *Elizabeth*. London.

Walker, S., and P. Higgs, eds. 2001. *Cleopatra of Egypt: From History to Myth*. Princeton.

Walker, S., and S.-A. Ashton, eds. 2003. *Cleopatra Reassessed* (BM Occasional Paper 103). London.

Walker, S., and S.-A. Ashton. 2006. *Cleopatra: Ancients in Action*. London.

Wanger, W. 1963. *My Life with Cleopatra*. London.

Webster, T. L. 1965. *Hellenistic Poetry and Art*. New York.

Weinstock, S. 1971. *Divus Iulius*. Oxford.

Weiss, R. 1962. "An Unknown Epigraphic Tract by Annius of Viterbo," in C. P. Brand et al., *Italian Studies Presented to E. R. Vincent*. Cambridge: 101–20.

———. 1962. "Traccia per una biografia di Annio da Viterbo," *Italia mediovale e umanistica* 5: 425–41.

———. 1964. "The Medals of Julius II (1503–1513)," *Journal of the Warburg and Courtauld Institutes* 28: 163–82.

———. 1988. *The Renaissance Discovery of Classical Antiquity.*[2] New York.

Whitehorne, J. 1994. *Cleopatras.* London and New York.

Whiteley, J. 1997. "Alma-Tadema and the néo-Grècs," in E. Becker et al., eds., *Sir Lawrence Alma-Tadema.* New York: 69–78.

Winner, M. 1974. "Zum Nachleben des Laokoon Der Renaissance," *Jahrbuch der Berliner Museen* 16: 83–121.

Winner, M., B. Andreae, and C. Pietrangeli, eds. 1998. *Il cortile delle statue: der Statuenhof des Belvedere im Vatikan. Akten des Internationalen Kongresses zu Ehren von Richard Krautheimer, Rom, 21–23 Oktober 1992.* Mainz am Rhein.

Wiseman, T. P. 1984. "Cybele, Virgil, and Augustus," in T. Woodman and D. West, eds., *Poetry and Politics in the Age of Augustus.* Cambridge and New York: 117–128.

———. 1987. "*Conspicui Postes Tectaque Digna Deo*: The Public Image of Aristocratic and Imperial Houses in the Late Republic and Early Empire," in *L'Urbs, Espace Urbain et Histoire* (*Collection de L'École Française de Rome* 98). Rome: 393–413.

———. 1994. "The Senate and the *Populares*, 69–60 B.C.," in J. A. Crook, A. Lintott, and E. Rawson, eds., *Cambridge Ancient History,* vol. 9. Cambridge: 327–67.

Witt, R. 1971. *Isis in the Ancient World.* London. Repr. Baltimore 1997.

Wittkower, R. 1977. "Hieroglyphic Studies in the Early Renaissance," in R. Wittkower, *Allegory and the Migration of Symbols.* London: 114–128.

Wolf, C., ed. 1566. *Gynaecorum, Hoc Est, De mulierum Tum Aliis, Tum gravidarum, Parientium & Puerperarum affectibus & morbis, Libri veterum ac recentiorum aliquot, partim nunc primum editi, partim multo quam antea.* Basel.

———. 1586. *Harmonia Gynaeciorum sive de Mulierum Affectibus Commentarii.* Basel.

Wolf, C. M. 2002. *Die schlafende Ariadne im Vatikan: Ein hellenistischer Statuentypus und seine Rezeption.* Hamburg.

Wollen, P. 1987. "Fashion/Orientalism/The Body," *New Formations* 1: 17.

Wyke, M. 1992. "Augustan Cleopatras: Female Power and Poetic Authority," in A. Powell, ed., *Roman Poetry and Propaganda in the Age of Augustus.* London: 98–140.

———. 1997. *Projecting the Past: Ancient Rome, Cinema and History.* New York.

———. 2002. *The Roman Mistress: Ancient and Modern Representations.* Oxford.

———, ed. 2006. *Julius Caesar in Western Culture.* Malden, Mass.

Yates, F. W. 1964. *Giordano Bruno and the Hermetic Tradition.* Chicago.

Yavetz, Z. 1979. *Caesar in der öffentlichen Meinung.* Düsseldorf.

Zanker, P. 1988. *The Power of Images in the Age of Augustus.* Ann Arbor.

Zannini Quirini, B. 1989. "Le astuzie di Cleopatra," *Civiltà classica e cristiana* 10: 71–94.

Zimmern, H. 1902. *Sir Lawrence Alma-Tadema, R.A.* London.

CONTRIBUTORS

SALLY-ANN ASHTON is Senior Assistant Keeper at the Fitzwilliam Museum in Cambridge and the author of books on Cleopatra, her imagery, and Egyptomania, including *Ptolemaic Royal Sculpture* (2001), *Cleopatra Reassessed* (with Susan Walker, 2003), *Roman Egyptomania* (2004), and *Cleopatra and Egypt* (2008).

BRIAN A. CURRAN teaches at Pennsylvania State University and writes on the reception of ancient Egypt in the Renaissance and on Renaissance art. He is the author of *The Egyptian Renaissance: The Afterlife of Ancient Egypt in Early Modern Italy* (2007) and co-author of *Obelisk: A History* (2009), and is editor of the *Memoirs of the American Academy at Rome*.

PETER GREEN is the James R. Dougherty, Jr. Centennial Professor of Classics Emeritus at the University of Texas, Austin, and adjunct professor of classics at the University of Iowa. He is the author of numerous works of fiction and poetry, translations, and histories of the Greek and Hellenistic periods, including *Xerxes at Salamis* (1970), *Alexander to Actium* (1990), *Alexander of Macedon, 356–323 B.C.* (1991), *From Ikaria to the Stars* (2004), a bilingual edition of *Catullus* (2005), a short history of the Hellenistic period (2007), and *Diodorus Siculus, Books 11–14* (2010).

ERICH S. GRUEN is the Gladys Rehard Wood Professor of History and Classics Emeritus at the University of California, Berkeley, and author of numerous books on Hellenistic and Roman history and cultural identities, including *The Last Generation of the Roman Republic* (1974), *The Hellenistic World and the Coming of Rome* (1984), *Culture and National Identity in Republican Rome* (1992), *Heritage and Hellenism: The Reinvention of Jewish Tradition* (1998), *Diaspora: Jews amidst Greeks and Romans* (2002), and *Rethinking the Other in Antiquity* (2010).

ROBERT A. GURVAL teaches at the University of California, Los Angeles, and writes on the literature and history of ancient Rome and the reception of classical antiquity. He regularly offers an undergraduate seminar in the College Honors program, "Representations of Cleopatra: From Antiquity to HBO *Rome*." He is the author of *Actium and Augustus: The Politics and Emotions of Civil War* (1995).

MARGARET M. MILES is the Andrew W. Mellon Professor at the American School of Classical Studies at Athens, Greece, and professor of art history and classics at the University of California, Irvine. She writes on Greek architecture and religion, and on cultural property in antiquity. Her publications include *Agora XXXI: The City Eleusinion* (1998), and *Art as Plunder: The Ancient Origins of Debate about Cultural Property* (2008).

DOMINIC MONTSERRAT was an Egyptologist at Warwick and Open Universities, and author of books on ancient Egypt and its reception, including *Sex and Society in Ancient Egypt* (1996) and *Akhenaten: History, Fantasy and Ancient Egypt* (2000). He also curated the touring exhibition *Ancient Egypt: Digging for Dreams* (2002).

GIUSEPPE PUCCI teaches at the University of Siena and writes on Classical Archaeology and its reception, anthropological and semiological interpretations of the past, aesthetics and economic issues in antiquity. He has written numerous books and articles, including *Il passato prossimo: la scienza dell'antichità alle origini della cultura moderna* (1993), and *Manifattura ceramica etrusco-romana a Chiusi: il complesso produttivo di Marcianella* (2003).

INGRID D. ROWLAND teaches in Rome for the University of Notre Dame's architectural program and writes on intellectual history and the Renaissance. She is the author of *The Culture of the High Renaissance: Ancients and Moderns in Sixteenth-Century Rome* (1998), *The Scarith of Scornello: A Tale of Renaissance Forgery* (2004), a translation of Vitruvius' *Ten Books of Architecture* (1999), and *Giordano Bruno: Philosopher/Heretic* (2008).

MARGARET MARY DEMARIA SMITH is an independent scholar. Her dissertation *Athena and Minerva: Rhetoric, Gender, and Durability* (University of California, Irvine, 2007) examines portrayals of Athena and Minerva in authors from antiquity to the nineteenth century. She writes on reception of classical antiquity in the late medieval period and nineteenth century, and the social and political writings of Christine de Pizan and Margaret Fuller.

SAROLTA A. TAKÁCS is Dean of Sage College in Albany and professor of history. She is the author of several books on Roman history, including *Isis and Sarapis in the Roman World* (1995), and most recently, *The Construction of Authority in Ancient Rome and Byzantium: the Rhetoric of Empire* (2009).

MARIA WYKE is professor and chair of Latin at University College, London, and writes on Roman poetry and the reception of ancient Rome in modern culture. Her books include *Projecting the Past: Ancient Rome, Cinema and History* (1997), *The Roman Mistress: Ancient and Modern Representations* (2002), and *Caesar: A Life in Western Culture* (2008). She is currently completing a study of the reception of Julius Caesar in the United States titled *Caesar in the USA: Classical Reception, Popular Culture, American Identity*.

INDEX

Abu Simbel, 3
Actium, battle of, 3, 28, 39; literary depictions
of, 64, 69–70, 88–89, 119; use of imagery
after, 87–88
Agrippa, M. Vipsanius, 87, 121
Alberti, Leon Battista, 100–101
Alexander VI (pope), 16, 97, 102, 104, 106
Alexander the Great, 4, 12, 16; cult of, 22, 23, 25;
mimesis of, 81, 121; tomb of, 80–81, 188
Alexander Helios, son of Cleopatra, 1
Alexandria, Alexandrians, 4, 8, 64; "Alexan-
drianism," 90–92; as audience, 21, 25, 32;
Augustus in, 80–82; as capital, 38; Cleopa-
tra and, 39–41, 42–43, 65; Cleopatra and
Marc Antony in, 65, 66, 161–163, 170n61;
discoveries in 12–13, 14; "Donations of," 29,
31–32; Julius Caesar in, 43–45, 51n16; tourists in, 143, 151–155; Treaty of, 154. *See also*
library, lighthouse
Alma-Tadema, Lawrence, 150–151, 153–155,
157–164; catalogue of Egyptian paintings,
167–168; paintings of Cleopatra, 159–164
Ammianus Marcellinus, 100
Ammonius, Egyptian official, 47, 52n52
Annius, of Viterbo (Giovanni Nanni), 104–106,
109, 111, 124nn26–27, 124n29
Antony, Marc (M. Antonius, triumvir), 1–2, 3,
40, 76–77n25, 83, 172, 205; and Actium, 3,
87–88; and Augustus, 5, 61; coinage of, 57;
death of, 61, 66–67, 70, 71; as Dionysos, 89;
literary depictions of, 74, 81, 176–177, 187,
196; as Heracles, 196; letters attributed to,
132, 133, 145n4, 170n61; in painting, 162–164;
shrine in Alexandria to, 8–9
Antony and Cleopatra (Shakespeare), 13, 21, 74,
132, 161, 163, 173, 196
Aphrodite, 25, 56, 57, 195, 212
Apis, bull, 42, 80, 81, 91, 92–93n7; later depictions of, 102, *103*, 104, 106; King Apis, 82–83
Apollo, Actius, 70; Helios, 11–12; on Palatine,
87–88, 89–90; statue of (Apollo Belvedere),
113, 119
Ariadne ("Sleeping"), statue of, 114–115, *115*,
116, 203
Arsinoe II, 15; portraiture of, 21–24, 26–27, 28,
29–30
Arsinoe IV, sister of Cleopatra, 44, 48
asp, 1, 16, 54–55, 56–62, 67, 68–69, 72, 73–75, 92,
116, 203
Augustus, Roman emperor, 5, 9, 16, 73, 79,
83, 86, 91–92, 93–94n18; in Egypt, 80–82;
emulated by popes, 121; house on Palatine,
87–90; and obelisks, 11, 13, 99, 112. *See also*
Octavian

Bara, Theda, 17, 173, 178–181, *179*, 204
Bernhardt, Sarah, 165, 174, 177, 200, 201
Bonaparte, Napoleon, 6–7; in Egypt, 6, 18–
19n16, 206n8, 206n17; emulates J. Caesar
and Augustus, 6–7